O'NEILL AND HIS PLAYS

O'NEILL

AND HIS PLAYS

FOUR DECADES OF CRITICISM

EDITED BY

Oscar Cargill

N. Bryllion Fagin

William J. Fisher

NEW YORK UNIVERSITY PRESS 1961

LIBRARY OF CONGRESS CATALOG CARD NUMBER: 61-17631

DESIGN AND TYPOGRAPHY BY ANDOR BRAUN

MANUFACTURED IN THE UNITED STATES OF AMERICA

ACKNOWLEDGMENTS

THE EDITORS wish to acknowledge the great kindness of Mrs. Eugene O'Neill (Carlotta Monterey O'Neill) in permitting them to use letters and articles by Eugene O'Neill and quoted passages from the correspondence of O'Neill in the work of others, all within her copyright control, a permission which enormously enhances the value of this volume. Also to Random House, Inc., for quotations from *Nine Plays* by Eugene O'Neill, Copyright, 1932, by Liveright, Inc.; Copyright, 1921, 1922, 1924, 1926, 1927, 1928, by Boni and Liveright, Inc.; *Mourning Becomes Electra*, Copyright, 1931, by Horace Liveright, Inc., used by the authors of various reviews, articles, and essays in this book, where quotation exceeds what is regarded as "fair practice." All rights reserved, for these passages, including that of translation into foreign languages. All acting rights, both professional and amateur, including motion picture rights, are reserved in the United States, Great Britain, and all countries of the Copyright Union by the author. In their present form these plays are dedicated to the reading public only and no performance may be given without special arrangement with the author's agent.

To authors, agents, editors, publishers, and organizations who have helped us in assembling the materials used in this anthology, we wish here to express our deep gratitude. The specific acknowledgments requested appear as the first footnote to the individual pieces in this book which may not be reproduced without the permission of the indicated holder of the copyright. We are indebted to the Arts and Science Research Fund of New York University for assistance in preparing copy. Mrs. Sunny Trefman was a helpful co-ordinator. To Lillian Fisher and Gladys L. Cargill we owe much for help with permissions, and proofreading and indexing, respectively.

CONTENTS

O'NEILL AND HIS PLAYS

Four Decades of Criticism

INTRODUCTION

THE DEATH OF EUGENE O'NEILL on November 27, 1953 served as an occasion for critical evaluations and revaluations of the work of America's most eminent dramatist. He had been sick for many years, and the last play he had offered to the theatre world was *The Iceman Cometh*, produced in 1946 but written in 1939. In our hectic age, when dramatic reputations flare up one night and sputter out at the end of a week, seven years of silence remove an author into prehistory. O'Neill, when he died, was a forgotten man, or remembered only by literary historians, academicians, and an older generation of drama critics as someone who had once started a revolution in the theatre—a revolution which proved only partially victorious—had been rewarded with three Pulitzer awards and a Nobel Prize, and then was heard from no more.

It is significant that almost all the articles—whether editorial, critical, or "scholarly"—which the daily press and the weekly, monthly, and quarterly periodicals throughout the world printed on the occasion of his death displayed a tone of partisanship. They were either aggressively laudatory or violently antagonistic; few were "balanced." It looked as if the fire and violence which characterized O'Neill's plays had carried over into the mood of his critics: the revolution was still on and O'Neill was not dead at all.

As, indeed, he was not. Three years after his corporeal death, a play of his, written in 1940 but never produced or published, was given to the world by his widow, and it exploded as most of his plays, beginning with his early one-acters of the sea, had exploded during his lifetime. *A Long Day's Journey Into Night* brought him the plaudits of a new generation of theatregoers and drama critics wherever it was presented, whether in Stockholm, where it was first unveiled on the stage of the Royal Dramatic Theatre on the evening of February 10, 1955, or in New York, where it induced the Pulitzer judges for 1956 to bestow a posthumous prize upon its author, or in London, where it impressed another Nobel Prize winner, T. S. Eliot, as "one of the most moving plays" he had ever seen.

Everywhere it led to the revival of other plays by O'Neill, and in New York it also led to the naming of a theatre in his honor.

But the battle of the critics over the importance of O'Neill's contribution to American drama or to drama in general is not, however, over, and is not likely to be for some decades to come, if ever. O'Neill remains a controversial writer, a subject guaranteed to raise the blood pressure of contestants, and it would seem that everyone who has an opinion on O'Neill—whether professional critic, college professor, college student, or merely theatre patron—is a contestant. After the television version of *The Iceman Cometh* was shown in Baltimore on April 8, 1961, a new type of theatre public expressed its judgment; dozens of viewers wrote to their local newspapers either to praise or to damn the play, its sponsors, and the channel that made it available to the public. The veteran critic on the *Baltimore Sun*, Donald Kirkley, who had seen the original production on the stage fourteen years before, thought that the drama had grown in stature and that it was "a somber, terrifying masterwork," but many of his readers differed with him violently, just as violently as those who agreed with him.

The plays of O'Neill, it seems, touch something fundamental in those who expose themselves to their effect. They reach down to frightening depths; they step on private, social, religious, philosophical, aesthetic toes; they either evoke immoderate enthusiasm or provoke immoderate anger. Almost every one of his plays has produced warring factions, whose representatives have often been led to express themselves in dogmatic or categorical terms. In the January 1960 issue of *Theatre Arts* Louis Kronenberger summarized the achievements of American playwriting in the preceding decade and came to the conclusion that *Long Day's Journey* was "the great event in the American theatre of the '50's." He characterized the play as "overwhelming drama, something with all the thrust of great theatre and all the convincingness of life." But, writing in the same year, William L. Sharp, a university theatre director, lamented that "The popularity of Eugene O'Neill who can't write at all" attests "to the insensitive ear not only of the playwright and his audience, but the dramatic critic as well" (*Tulane Drama Review*, Winter, 1960). And, to add a later entry—and, incidentally, to indicate that the battle is global—Günther Crack, reviewing a performance of *Strange Interlude* in Berlin, exclaims that "This play could only have been written by O'Neill, who combined great theatrical talent with an enormous knowledge of the human soul" (*Cultural News from Germany*, April 1961).

It will be noted that none of the critics whose comments have been quoted in the preceding two paragraphs has been included in the anthology of critical writings on Eugene O'Neill now before the reader. The editors were confronted by a body of material so vast that to reprint it all would have required a set of volumes—and, in spite of much verbal fireworks, dull volumes at that. Many sharp, perceptive critics have had to remain unrepresented. And yet the editors believe that, in general, the criticism here assembled does fairly represent what has been written on Eugene O'Neill during his entire career, which apparently is not closed yet.

Perhaps it is too early to assign O'Neill a definite place in the history of dramatic writing. Certainly it is too soon after his death to do so, for in the case of writers who achieve great popularity and critical acclaim during their lifetime there is usually a sudden rush to downgrade them the moment their death is announced. Examples are numerous: Galsworthy, Barrie, Shaw, Romain Rolland, Anatole France, Hauptmann, Ernst Toller, Rabindranath Tagore, Robert Sherwood, Maxwell Anderson. It is as if the critics had been waiting for the celebrity to leave the room before they could say all the things they have resented about him.

And there is generally much to resent. Fame itself, like prosperity in general, tends to arouse resentment, secret and uncrystallized at first, in time open and articulate. In addition, critics, being but human, are subject to the mutability which shadows love affairs. By the time a famous writer is ready to die, some of his admirers have fallen in love with a new face, figure, image, voice, gesture. The newcomer may not fulfill his promise, but only time can test the durability of a lover or a writer. There is also, especially for younger critics, the problem of a Cause to fight for. Writers whose work is nonconformist or contains a shock to, or challenge of, the conventions can easily become a Cause. In the Twenties O'Neill was a Cause, as were Ibsen, Hauptmann, Verhaeren, Shaw, Brieux, and Andreyev before him. Sometimes a writer, if his "message," style, or shock of recognition is strong enough, becomes a Cause for a generation not his own—Chekhov, Brecht, Strindberg, Ghelderode. Complex sociological and psychological factors are involved. But, generally, time winnows greatness; distance provides comparison; emotions cool and judgment becomes balanced. Perhaps it was this process that Friedrich Duerrenmatt had in mind when he remarked, in an interview, "We are too close to him [O'Neill] now to appreciate him fully, but he will continue to grow" (*The New York Times*, May 25, 1958). O'Neill is apparently one of those writers who is destined to have more than one life. After a period of denigration they are rediscovered and reinstated in esteem, or a new generation discovers them for the first time and finds them important. All signs indicate that he will not have to wait as long as, for example, Georg Büchner has had to wait.

While the subject of this chrestomathy of the writings on O'Neill is O'Neill and his plays—their meaning, value, strengths, and weaknesses—other subjects emerge. One is the old question of whether absolutely objective dramatic criticism, or any kind of criticism, is possible. It seems clear once again that criticism can be only relatively objective, especially when it is competent, for then it partakes of the creative act, and all creative expression involves a commitment to a point of view, an orientation, and a strategy which, in turn, involves selection, organization, suppression, and stress—in other words, subtle participation as man and writer. A play is not only what it is but what it does to and for the critic, and what it does depends upon who he is and in what intellectual and aesthetic ambiance he moves.

The battle of words which centers on O'Neill is as interesting for what it tells us about the state of modern dramatic criticism and its practitioners as it is for the enlightenment it gives us of the works of our only Nobel Prize dramatist. One could derive a fairly complete history of recent critical attitudes and doctrine from a study of the record of opinion and speculation assembled between the covers of this book. Beginning with the first reviews of his one-act sea plays by Clayton Hamilton and Barrett Clark, in which he was hailed for his courageous depiction of the seamy side of life and for his use of dialogue which had been taboo on the American stage, and on through Henry Hewes on "Hughie," in which O'Neill is given credit for dramatizing "the whole cycle of life" in a forty-minute piece, the critics have written not only about O'Neill and his work but about the values in life and drama that matter to them.

After *Anna Christie* O'Neill can be said to have done with rigid realism or naturalism—except for a play of recollection such as *Ah, Wilderness!*—yet to the critics, especially in America, his "truthful" depiction of life was still of prime importance. O'Neill himself, like his acknowledged master, Johan August Strindberg, came to feel quite early in his career that the naturalistic mode constricted his imagination, and he began to experiment with other modes of dramatic expression. His critics, however, for the most part remained loyal to naturalism and hardly noticed his attempts to bring new forms to the American stage. It is, for instance, significant that the words "expressionism" or "expressionistic" do not appear in the reviews of *The Emperor Jones* by Heywood Broun, *The Hairy Ape* by Alexander Woollcott, *All God's Chillun Got Wings* by T. S. Eliot, and *The Great God Brown* by Gilbert Gabriel. To be sure, the reviewers are aware of certain elements of technique that seem novel—such as the use of masks or of special sound effects, the "fantastic" nature of plot, and the resort to distortion in setting and gesture—but emphasis is still laid upon "true talk" (Woollcott), "exact portrayal of a possible negro" (Eliot), and "splendidly positive language" (Gabriel).

In Europe the critics received O'Neill with equal enthusiasm but greater understanding. By 1946, when George Jean Nathan published his "Critical Summation" of O'Neill's impact on world criticism in the *American Mercury*, he found that in France, Italy, Russia, the Scandinavian countries, Rumania, Greece, Australia, and China the attitude had been "extremely favorable"; in Germany, highly appreciative; and only in England "lukewarm or chilly." We know that now, since the London production of *Long Day's Journey*, the critical attitude toward O'Neill in England too has become favorable, and many of his earlier plays are being revived. Perhaps one reason for England's resistance to these earlier plays can be found in the fact that nineteenth-century realism and naturalism—Robertson, Pinero, Jones, Galsworthy—dominated the English stage much longer than it did the stages of other European countries. Today, when Beckett, Ionesco, the later O'Casey, Pinter, and Mortimer are accepted, at least in off-West End, the experimental O'Neill too can be accepted.

It is interesting to read Rudolf Kommer's article, reprinted from the *Greenwich Playbill* for the season of 1924–1925. It shows that in Germany *Anna Christie* was not accepted—at least not by all critics—as the great masterpiece it was deemed to be in this country, where even Bernard DeVoto, whose "Minority Report" was an angry protest against the award of the Nobel prize to O'Neill, considered *Anna* O'Neill's "most effective play." O'Neill himself knew better, of course; as early as 1923 he remarked to Malcolm Cowley that he never liked this play too well because it was full of Broadway tricks and that, if he wanted to, he could turn out dozens of such plays. (See "A Weekend with Eugene O'Neill.") In contrast, Herr Kommer in Germany found *Anna Christie* a belated piece of "bygone Naturalism"; the plays that interested him, as they had interested Alfred Kerr, were *The Emperor Jones*, *All God's Chillun* and especially *The Hairy Ape*, which he described as the work of a poet, "a truly gigantic dramatization of pessimism."

Many European critics hailed O'Neill as the voice of "America," the untired voice of a still young country, a sort of twentieth-century Walt Whitman shouting his dramatic yawp over the stages of the world. But there were a few critics, like Rudolf Kommer and Julius Bab, who perceived that O'Neill, while writing in terms of his age and his country, was actually expressing—himself. Certainly his dramatic tradition was not American; one could clearly detect in his plays the "traces" of Ibsen, Strindberg, Wedekind, Freud, and other Europeans. These more perceptive critics took little stock in O'Neill's sociological, economic, or political "message" or wisdom; what they applauded was, in the words of Julius Bab, "the tireless curiosity with which O'Neill explored all theatric and dramatic forms." Kommer, especially, praised O'Neill for *not* being the voice of America but for possessing a voice of his own, for not representing "any group, movement . . . current or tendency"; O'Neill, he insisted was "a personality, human and creative, sincere and isolated."

His being a creative, isolated personality did not, however, protect O'Neill from the winds of critical doctrine. His ambition, he had written to Professor George Pierce Baker at the beginning of his career, was "to be an artist or nothing," but in the socially-conscious Twenties he attracted most attention with those plays that could be, and largely were, interpreted as dramatizations of an intensifying class struggle or of a society undergoing a social upheaval. It is possible, of course, for a playwright to be an artist with plays of "social" content, as it is possible to be an artist with plays of "unsocial" or nonsocial content, but there are hazards. Marxist critics at first applauded O'Neill because they thought his plays supported the ideology to which they were committed; when after a while they discovered that his social message was "confused" and that his major interest lay elsewhere, they turned upon him in sorrow and anger.

The best balanced of Marxist studies of O'Neill's earlier plays —when he did show, like most young writers at the time, an interest in social problems—was Charmion von Wiegand's "The Quest of Eugene O'Neill" (*New Theatre*, September 1935). A more recent essay expressing a similar point of view appeared in *Masses & Mainstream* for March 1954. In it John Howard Lawson, himself a playwright who had achieved considerable vogue in the Twenties, again attempted to balance the pluses and minuses of O'Neill's total performance. The result, which was favorable to O'Neill, evidently proved unacceptable to more rigid Marxists. One protest appeared in the June issue of the same periodical; its author, Lester Cole, another playwright and screen writer, demanded to know why one should "sing songs for him who, surrounded by his trophies and rich rewards, suffered 'spiritual' discomfort while continuing, actively or passively, to defend the *status quo*, explaining little else than its inevitability in images of God, Freud, and 'dat ole davil sea'?" For Cole the yardstick by which one ought to judge an artist was this: "when the artist has had a consciousness of social reality, and for whatever reasons turns his back upon it, *are the pains* outweighed by the compensations he receives to endure them?" An even more telling passage, though not italicized this time, is his question, "Is it possible that an artist can remain 'incorruptible,' while his work is steeped in ideological corruption?"

So much for sociological criticism of dramatic literature, except perhaps for a passing glance at Lawson's rebuttal. Much of it centered around *The Iceman Cometh*, which Lawson in his first article had called a confused play but one which nonetheless contained a "tormented indictment of a society that robs man of dignity and purpose." The central theme of the drama, as Lawson saw it, was the "stoolpigeon's betrayal of the working class." (Note: Cf. Helen Muchnic's conception of the central theme in her essay in this volume on *The Iceman* and Gorky's *The Lower Depths.*) In a word, it was "obvious" to Lawson—as presumably it should have been to Cole—that *The Iceman Cometh*, in spite of its confusion, "grapples with real problems of life." Perhaps one other point in this characteristic yea-nay defense of O'Neill by a Marxist critic deserves a moment's attention. Cole had attacked O'Neill's preoccupation with "Mysticism, Freudianism, Godism"; Lawson was willing to concede that such a "destructive" element existed in the later plays, but insisted that there still remained "the lyric affirmation of life" at the end of *The Great God Brown* and *Lazarus Laughed.*

Whether mysticism, Freudianism, and "Godism" (descriptive terms which could so easily apply to such an indisputably great novel as *The Brothers Karamazov*) have been destructive elements either in life or art is debatable, of course, but it is not debatable that O'Neill's interest in the inscrutable forces that shape human destiny, in the dark layers of man's psyche, and in the problems of faith and doubt was persistent throughout his dramaturgic life. He quickly disavowed a preoccupation with surfaces, with mere "facts," and began to create theatric symbols and objective correlatives for forces, concepts, instincts, and motives that had neither name nor definite habitation. Much has been made by some critics of "dat ole davil sea" (a phrase first used by a befuddled, superstitious Scandinavian sailor lamenting his misspent life), the fog horns, the Iceman, and numerous other symbolic inventions and repetitions, but perhaps as many critics, as well as countless playgoers, found them effective in conveying ideas and emotions for which language is, at best, an imperfect instrument.

O'Neill's interest in depth psychology is important only insofar as it helped him to write effective dramas. Much Freudianism and Jungianism was attributed to him by critics who, in our Freudian age, have learned to look at people and literature from a psychoanalytic point of view. O'Neill himself disclaimed any "conscious use of psychoanalytical material," although he admitted having read two books by Freud and two by Jung, and we know that he underwent psychoanalysis in 1927. His disclaimer matters little, however, since neither Sophocles nor Shakespeare had ever read Freud, and yet their plays resulted, millenia and centuries later, in a whole library of psychoanalytical criticism, some of it very enlightening indeed. The chapter devoted to O'Neill's plays in W.

David Sievers' *Freud on Broadway* (1955) shows that most of them contain tensions and mechanisms for which depth psychologists have names and explanations. The plays serve as capital illustrations of father figures and mother figures, sexual frustrations, guilt feelings, repetition-compulsions, death wishes, the racial unconscious, regression, the ambivalence of love and hate, unconscious Oedipal and incestuous drives, etc., etc. The conclusion to which Dr. Sievers comes is that psychoanalysis provided O'Neill with "illumination, suggestion, direction," but that the flesh and blood of his characters, their emotional agony, was "O'Neill's own." O'Neill enriched the drama with "new and renewed techniques," and he was led to do this because he had a "compulsion to express deeper-than-surface reality."

One aspect of this compulsion is O'Neill's search for a Faith in a world which showed all the signs of intellectual and spiritual bankruptcy. His "Godism" took various forms—socialism, syndicalism, anarchism, and, always, Roman Catholicism. In the world of the theatre he may have been an isolated figure, but in the world at large he was one of millions of searchers for gods that failed them, for ideals, beliefs, Causes that kept on changing, shifting, vanishing. A large group of intellectuals rediscovered the values of tradition and the orthodoxies of religion; the brash, mocking voice of H. L. Mencken was silenced by the cultivated, modulated voice of T. S. Eliot. (One could almost believe that O'Neill dramatized these two voices when he split John Loving into two characters in *Days Without End;* most certainly, these characters could easily serve as symbolic representations of the two forces at war within O'Neill himself.)

It was inevitable that drama critics should pay attention to a playwright who, according to his own avowal, was "interested only in the relation between man and God." Croswell Bowen in his biographical sketch in *PM* in 1946 told us that O'Neill had lost his faith when he was thirteen years old, but he also told us that he "struggled to regain it ever since." Did he succeed? That is where critics have differed. Certainly *Dynamo* gave no indication of it; it only showed the failure of science to serve as a satisfactory surrogate for God. *Days Without End*, however, was different; it set off speculation, hosannas, and imprecations. The review by John Anderson, reprinted in this book, condemns the play as undramatic or as bad drama—a judgment which it is the right and duty of a critic to make, if that is his judgment. But Anderson also congratulated himself on having predicted some years before that O'Neill, who was then "singing an ecstatic paganism," would ultimately return to the Church. Apparently, in Anderson's view, *Days Without End* was the fulfillment of his prophecy.

The Roman Catholic critics generally concurred in the opinion that *Days Without End* marked O'Neill's return, if not to the Church, at least to faith. What is more important, they held that *Days Without End* was a great play. Perhaps Arthur Hobson Quinn, who in the '30's was not only an eminent academician but also a drama critic for a quality magazine, may be permitted to represent the generality of the Catholic voices. "*Days Without End*," he wrote, "was a profound study of the conflict in a man's nature between his finer spiritual qualities and a cynical superstructure based upon 'Atheism wedded to Socialism . . . living in free love with Anarchism, with a curse by Nietzsche to bless the union.' . . . It is significant that *Days Without End* closes with the words 'Life laughs with God's love again.' " Perhaps it is also significant, as Professor Quinn dutifully noted, that while the play "received only mild acclaim in New York . . . its reception at the Abbey Theatre in Dublin . . . was enthusiastic" (*A History of the American Drama: From the Civil War to the Present Day*, 1936). And it is not surprising that in Soviet Russia, in spite of the honored position O'Neill had always occupied in its theatres, *Days Without End* was banned.

O'Neill himself answered the question as to whether he had returned to Catholicism with the blunt statement, "Unfortunately, no." How much value should we attach to his answer? Modern criticism—or a highly vocal and influential segment of it—is but little impressed by a writer's avowals. Since the birth of the Unconscious, the Intentional Fallacy, and the Biographical Fallacy, it has become accepted doctrine that a writer cannot possibly know what his plays say or do not say about himself; nor does it matter. In 1922 O'Neill told Oliver M. Sayler that he had come to feel "indifferent toward political and social movements of all kinds." Was this true? If so, how can one explain the unmistakably "social" implications of *All God's Chillun*, produced two years later? Wasn't that play part of a social movement?

The main reason, however, for ignoring O'Neill's avowals is

that they are irrelevant. A play, like any work of art—Messrs. René Wellek and Austin Warren and the other critics of the school to which they belong would maintain—has an independent existence of its own and the function of the critic is to explore, reveal, assess, and explicate it—the play—and not the author, his sociology, religion, or personal life. The late Professor Leo Spitzer, a literary scholar who was an ardent adherent of this theory of criticism, once propounded the thesis that one need not know that Milton was blind when he wrote his sonnet beginning "When I consider how my light is spent." Nor, apparently, does one need to know that *Long Day's Journey* is the personal story of O'Neill's own family. Mr. Eliot's "moving" response while seeing it was to the play as a dramatic structure, an artistic arrangement of a fiction, a fable, a myth, and not to the tribulations of O'Neill and his family.

Precisely what has been meant by the term "New Criticism" and who the New Critics are has never emerged clearly. Ransom, Tate, Cleanth Brooks, Robert Penn Warren, Blackmur, Heilman, and a few others have at one time or another accepted or acquiesced to the label. Several critics whose names have usually been associated with this movement have repudiated it. There can, however, be no doubt that the theories and methodology of the several kinds of New Critics have profoundly influenced dramatic criticism, even though the effect has been most pronounced in the study of poetry and fiction rather than drama.

The one indisputable contribution the movement has made is its emphasis on a careful, close study of the text—its structure, language, symbols, appropriateness, integration, inner logic, tone, temper, color, rhythm. But what is the text of a play? Is it the published version which gathers dust on library shelves or is it the live, palpitating something that comes into being as a result of the collaborative efforts of a number of creative artists? In the case of O'Neill especially, performance becomes a necessity before the "text" can be established. Critic after critic has noted that O'Neill wrote for the "theatre"; lines that in reading seem flat and lifeless acquire force and color in performance. Certainly most critics would agree with Harold Clurman's rather cautious statement: "It is indisputable that O'Neill's plays are nearly always more impressive on the stage than on the printed page" (*The Nation*, March 3, 1956).

If O'Neill has fared badly with the critics of the newer schools—

and he has—the reasons are not far to seek. Most of these critics are but inadequately trained to deal with drama; they are academicians, literary scholars, "classical" minded; moreover, if they are American, they are likely to have retained some of the suspicion of the theatre the "best" people in America have always had. If the theatre is no longer "the synagogue of Satan," as Cotton Mather called it, it is certainly no more than ephemeral entertainment—and, unfortunately, Broadway has done its best to confirm them in their suspicion. The few critics who have had training in the theatre as well as in the world of books, such as Eric Bentley and Francis Fergusson, have approached O'Neill with a set of standards derived from Aristotle, from overweening respect for European dramatists (as is, probably unconsciously, the case with Bentley), from a study of classical tragedy, of myth, ritual, decorum, manners, systematic philosophy, and stylistic analyses. To Bentley, O'Neill's thinking is shallow, primitive, inconsequential (*The Playwright as Thinker*). John Gassner may have sounded unkind when he charged that Bentley and his like-minded colleagues, in examining O'Neill's reputation, had merely tried to determine "in how many ways and with what thoroughness O'Neill's reputation could be undermined." ("Eugene O'Neill: The Course of a Modern Dramatist," *Critique*, February, 1958). Bentley, at least, has sincerely tried to "like" O'Neill, but it is possible that he has not succeeded for reasons that have as much to do with Bentley and his approach as with O'Neill.

But perhaps Fergusson's diatribe sums up even better the defects of O'Neill, as several contemporary critics see them. Like Bentley—and Mary McCarthy, and even Gassner and Krutch—he finds O'Neill's language inflated, bombastic, flat, and unprofitable. Unlike Gassner and Krutch, who find in O'Neill merits that place him in the category of great dramatists, despite his inadequate language, Fergusson discovers only melodramatic plots, characters without universal import, "cheap" symbolism, and "immature" ideas. It is significant that he singles out George Kelly and E. E. Cummings as two dramatists with whom to compare O'Neill unfavorably. He admits that Kelly's plays are, for the most part, Broadway trivia and that Cummings' *him* never commanded or could command an audience. The important thing, for Fergusson, is that both thought their plays through; they labored with the skill of disciplined craftsmen. Apparently O'Neill was neither disciplined nor a craftsman.

In this connection it is interesting to observe the frequency with which such words as "discipline," "craftsmanship," "skill," and "technique" appear in modern criticism. No doubt the emphasis on technique and manner of writing is related to the emphasis we place on technique and know-how in our technological civilization. The how—sometimes equivalent to neatness and tidiness—has become more important than the what. And methodology, often without sensibility, has come to dominate criticism. O'Neill's plays are particularly vulnerable to the newer critical methodology. Their meaning yields too easily; they lack the numerous levels upon which the New Critic can operate; while they contain many ambiguities, they are not ambiguities that can be classified into acceptable categories or types; they contain little myth and ritual; their symbolism is often, as in the case of *Dynamo*, gross rather than insubstantial and problematical (unlike Henry Adams' dynamo, which exists only in the imagination, O'Neill's must be presented on the stage, a huge, clumsy, weird, mechanical contraption); their ironies are too open to require unveiling; and their allusions—except in a few plays, such as *The Great God Brown* and *Mourning Becomes Electra*—require neither dictionary nor a great store of erudition.

There is an implication in Fergusson's discussion of Cummings's *him* that its inability to command an audience is somehow to its credit, and that, by contrast, O'Neill's ability to attract audiences to his plays is to his discredit. Fergusson is not alone in this feeling that the accolade of a good-sized audience stamps a playwright as a producer of inferior "art." It is part of the tendency among a certain alignment of modern critics, sociological as well as literary, to avoid contamination by participation in what Dwight MacDonald has called Masscult and Midcult. Mary McCarthy, in the introduction to her collection of dramatic reviews (*Sights and Spectacles*, 1956), admits that when she was a much younger critic she was haunted by the fear that she might like something that the public liked. And in fact, when she first saw *Our Town* she found herself *liking* it, but then she saw that the public liked it too and she began to wonder: "Could this mean that there was something the matter with me? Was I starting to sell out? Such haunting fears," an older Miss McCarthy remarks, "were common in the avant-garde in those days." A reading of critical essays in some contemporary avant-garde journals discloses that "such haunting fears" are not uncommon today. The irony of the situation, as it applies to O'Neill, is that during the first years of his career it was the avant-garde that fought his battle for public recognition and acceptance.

It will be noted that a whole section of this book is devoted to criticism of O'Neill's language. No playwright in modern times has created so much discussion and speculation about the language of drama as O'Neill. As early as 1922 Isaac Goldberg characterized O'Neill's dialogue as "a string of clichés." Yet at about the same time a critic in Ireland, Andrew Malone, thought that "His language may . . . prove . . . his greatest asset." O'Neill himself regretted that he was not gifted with "great language," but Krutch, who agreed with him, offered the consolation that he had the gift of "communication"—by means of situation, the characters, "and above all, the depth of his concern with them." And Diana Trilling, reviewing *Long Day's Journey*, supported Krutch's view: O'Neill's "rather tuneless language . . . is the instrument for communicating his knowledge of his characters" (*New Leader*, December 16, 1957). Perhaps it is worthwhile adding another voice to the chorus of nay-buts, this time that of a fellow-dramatist, S. N. Behrman. "Eugene O'Neill," he wrote in *The New York Times* (September 20, 1959), "had a tin ear for the sonorities of the English language, and it did him no harm whatever in the theatre."

Is it then quite certain that O'Neill had "no language"? Obviously not. We have noted Gilbert Gabriel's reference to O'Neill's "brightness of words" and "Imagery flares up . . . in ruddy beauty" and Andrew Malone's praise of O'Neill's language as an "asset," and we could add many, many more similar comments. But the most extended and most favorable discussion of O'Neill's language was written by Lionel Abel, an avant-garde playwright and contributor to the very same *Partisan Review* in which Mary McCarthy has published most of her play reviews and essays on the drama. In his article entitled "O'Neill and His Critics" (*New Leader*, January 6, 1958), Abel replies to Krutch, Bentley, and Mary McCarthy. "I think," he says, "O'Neill was a master of rhetoric, but not the kind of master that Mary McCarthy—or

Krutch, while under her tutelage—can recognize as such. O'Neill was a master of speech insofar as the words spoken by his characters convince us as coming from them. What matters on the stage is not that a speech should be elegant—unless the character is—but that the words spoken should be discovered by the character in himself in the act of saying them. O'Neill was certainly able to make characters speak authentically at the critical points of their life experience; to do this, one must have a superior command of language, even if not of the sort which could have imposed itself outside the theatre."

The critics of O'Neill have spoken. They have praised and blamed and buried and resurrected him; they have analyzed and explicated and sometimes forgotten him in their eagerness to prove a sociological, Marxist, Freudian, Jungian, religious, anti-religious, ontological, "New," avant-garde, or "aesthetic" point; but they have all helped—as good dramatic criticism should—to keep his plays on the boards and their printed versions read. They could not have done it, however, if the plays themselves had not had that certain quality which provides auditors and readers with a grateful experience.

For the influence of the critics on public opinion is highly problematical. No amount of thundering denunciation could deprive *Abie's Irish Rose* or *Tobacco Road* of a public; and no amount of trumpeting the virtues of *Billy Budd* could provide it with a public. It is too easy to account for the recalcitrance of the theatre public by the shoddy taste of Masscult and the slightly less shoddy taste of Midcult. Shakespeare did not hesitate to cast his poetry and his tragic vision before the groundlings of his day—and he did not fare badly at all. It would seem that the play's the thing after all. O'Neill, in his productive years, was a very prolific writer; time will no doubt winnow the chaff from the grain. And time seems to be on the side of O'Neill.

That's why the critics are still engaged in battle. They, with the aid of the public—Highcult and Lowcult—are the wind that does the blowing. No mediocre writer has ever inspired literary wars that last for almost half a century. It is obviously not enough for O'Neill to have seen life—as Sinclair Lewis described it in his Nobel Prize address—"as terrifying, magnificent and often quite horrible, a thing akin to a tornado, an earthquake or a devastating fire"; more important is the fact that he was able to transmit something of his vision to people watching his plays in a theatre. Whether these plays are always or wholly things of beauty is a problem for the critics; O'Neill himself thought they were not. Yet even those that are not are often—as Lee Simonson said of *Dynamo*—"brilliant" failures. They are examples of creative fire burning erratically or too impatiently.

Here then is the record—part of it anyway—of the criticism O'Neill's plays have inspired. The editors believe it is worth reading, both for the light it sheds on our first dramatist of sufficient stature to inspire a critical literature and for the light it sheds on dramatic criticism in our time.

I

THE MAN

Eugene O'Neill

"I WANT TO BE AN ARTIST OR NOTHING"

A Letter to George Pierce Baker

July 16, 1914
325 Pequot Ave.
New London, Conn.

Dear Sir:—

Mr. Clayton Hamilton, the dramatic critic, to whom I have frequently mentioned my ambition of becoming a playwright, has given me permission to use his name, and advised me to write to you personally regarding the possibility of my entrance, as a special student, into your several dramatic courses at Harvard University.

Let me explain my exact position. I am twenty-five years old. My university training consists of one year (Freshman) at Princeton University, Class of 1910, where I started to take a Litt. B. course. All my life I have been closely connected with the dramatic profession. My father is James O'Neill, the actor, of whom you may perhaps have heard; so, although I have never been on the stage myself, and my direct connection with the theatre is confined to a half-season as assistant manager with Viola Allen in *The White Sister*, nevertheless I can claim whatever knowledge there may be gained from a close connection with members of the profession.

Less than a year ago I seriously determined to become a dramatist and since that time I have written one long play—four acts—and seven one-act plays. Five of the latter are shortly to be published in book form by The Gorham Press of Boston. None of my plays have as yet been submitted to any manager for production but, of course, I intend to try and obtain a hearing for them the latter part of this summer.

From George Pierce Baker and the American Theatre *by Wisner Payne Kinne. Published by Harvard University Press,* 1954.

Although I have read all the modern plays I could lay my hands on, and many books on the subject of the Drama, I realize how inadequate such a hap-hazard, undirected mode of study must necessarily be. With my present training I might hope to become a mediocre journey-man playwright. It is just because I do not wish to be one, because I want to be an artist or nothing, that I am writing to you.

Will the Harvard regulations regarding special students permit my taking your courses—and whatever supplementary ones you would be kind enough to suggest as likely to help me? And if so, may I have your permission to enter your course?

One word more about myself: If varied experience be a help to the prospective dramatist I may justly claim that asset for I have worked my way around the world as a seaman on merchant vessels and held various positions in different foreign countries.

Hoping you may look favorably upon this earnest desire of mine to become your student, I remain

Sincerely your's [*sic*]

Eugene G. O'Neill

Gladys Hamilton

O'NEILL'S DEBT TO CLAYTON HAMILTON

My recollection of Eugene O'Neill goes back to the summer days of 1915 or 1916 when he visited our little cottage in New London, Connecticut. His penetrating eyes, seeing things invisible to the average citizen, were far more articulate than his tongue. I thought of him at the time as an unobtrusive young man who did not wish his silences interrupted. We respected his wish to be alone as we watched him across the cove in front of our house, and knew that soon he would be at ease in the sea.

My husband, Clayton Hamilton (dramatic critic for several New York magazines), and I first met Eugene O'Neill in January, 1914, at the breakfast table of Mrs. Rippin's boardinghouse where we were spending a week end. In accordance with his doctor's orders after his release from a tuberculosis sanitarium, Eugene already had taken a frigid winter swim. He was staying at Mrs. Rippin's, the most hospitable and economical place he could choose with the $8 weekly allowance granted him by his father, James O'Neill, the famous actor. His father considered even that much money badly spent, for he saw no future whatsoever for a son he then considered a wayward, worthless wanderer, unable to settle down to anything.

Mr. Hamilton's acquaintance with the elder O'Neill had begun a few years earlier, when Richard Mansfield, the actor, had summoned Clayton to New London to assist in the preparation of Ibsen's *Peer Gynt*. But Mansfield in all his glory did not consider the Irish O'Neill of sufficient stature to be invited to his formal parties at "The Grange" where, not having inherited a coat of arms, he had placed above the mantelpiece one of his own choosing—a pair of

---

Originally entitled "Untold Tales of Eugene O'Neill," Theatre Arts, *August, 1956. Reprinted by permission of the author and* Theatre Arts *Magazine.*

clasped hands bearing the French word *maintenant*, with its double meaning of "now" and "main tenant." Mr. O'Neill owned a much less pretentious home, and it was there that my husband would spend comfortable hours with the actor who had played the Count of Monte Cristo in countless cities.

Mrs. Rippin was a "homely" soul in the English sense of the word. She never found the aitches she had dropped in her native cockney environment, and I remember her remarking in later years to my husband, who answered to the name of Ham: "Mr. 'Am, you write about such nice people; Eugene's are all so 'orrible that I don't like his plays." But her daughters took turns in typing Eugene's first efforts, and in supplying the stamps to send them to potential producers.

With these manuscripts Eugene came to our cottage one day and approached my husband with the utmost trepidation, halting and hesitant in his speech, his eyes alone supplying the eloquence his tongue denied. He wondered if Clayton would read them and give him advice on the construction of the one-act play. A few days later, having discovered embryonic talent, my husband suggested to Eugene that he study with George Baker, conductor of the noted 47 Workshop at Harvard. The chief difficulty was persuading James O'Neill to pay the tuition. Clayton used all his eloquence in dealing with the old man who, after all, respected the judgment of a dramatic critic combined with that of family friend. Finally he was able to change the attitude of despair which the father long had held toward his wild, searoving, ineffectual son, into one of hope, and Clayton was given permission to write to Baker, endorsing his future pupil.

I often heard Clayton tell with amusement of a later encounter with the father at the Players' bar: "Mr. James O'Neill lived long enough," he would say, "to see *Beyond the Horizon* on the stage, and when that play was awarded the Pulitzer Prize, he came to see me, all aglow with pride. 'My boy,' he said, 'my boy Eugene. I always knew he had it in him! Remember how I always used to say that he would do something big someday? People told me he was wild and good for nothing, but I always knew he had it in him, didn't I?' "

Clayton never told Mr. O'Neill of his own quite different recollection. Eugene's memory was better, and in a letter from Provincetown, Massachusetts, dated April 6, 1920, he wrote to my husband:

"Ever since I read your fine tribute to *Beyond the Horizon* in *Vogue*—forwarded to me by the family—I have wanted to try to express my deep gratitude to you; but now that I'm 'all set,' pen in hand, I find I can't—without slopping over. I would like to tell the truth and say that what you have written makes me feel very humble, very much *non sum dignus;* but these statements are so connected in one's mind with the usual blather of unblushing insincerity that I despair of making them sound to you like truth.

"Well, darn it, they *are* true in this case; for although, respecting your critical judgment as I do and always have done, your high verdict on my work might be humanly calculated to change the size of my hat—well, it hasn't so far. Rather it makes me say to myself: 'Now, by God, you've got to work! You don't deserve this but you've got to do work which shall deserve it!' So the nearest I can come to defining the reaction your article produced in me is to say that I feel you have given me a star to shoot at—and I'll promise to keep on shooting."

Five years before, in April, 1915, my husband had reviewed Eugene's first book of one-act plays entitled *Thirst*, which his father had had published at his own expense. The review follows: "This writer's favorite mood is one of horror. He deals with grim and ghastly situations that would become intolerable if they were protracted beyond the limits of a single sudden act. He seems to be familiar with the sea; for three of these five plays deal with terrors that attend the tragedy of shipwreck. He shows a keen sense of the reactions of character under stress of violent emotion; and his dialogue is almost brutal in its power. More than one of these plays should be available for such an institution as the Princess Theatre in New York."

Apropos of this review, in the letter previously quoted, Eugene goes on to say: "I want to tell you of two things you did in those first days of my self-finding which, as I look back, had an extraordinarily far-reaching effect in keeping me going. Probably you have forgotten them. The first was when you reviewed my *Thirst* book of one-act plays—for *The Bookman*, I think. Do you know that your review was the only one that poor volume ever received? And, if brief, it was favorable! You can't imagine what it meant, coming from you. It held out a hope at a very hopeless time. It *did* send me to the hatters. It made me believe I was arriving with a bang; and at that period I very much needed someone whose authority I respected to admit I was getting somewhere.

"The second boon you would never guess in a million years. It was one day I met you down at the R.R. station in New London. I had just sent off the script of what was really my first long play to some manager or other. I innocently expected an immediate personal reading and a reply within a week—possibly an acceptance. I asked you for information regarding the reading habits of managers, the chances of scripts from unknowns, etc. You handed me the desired data—with both feet! You slipped me the unvarnished truth and then sandpapered it! You wound up in words to this general effect: 'When you send off a play remember there is not one chance in a thousand it will ever be read; not one chance in a million of its ever being accepted—(and if accepted it will probably never be produced); but if it is accepted and produced, say to yourself it's a miracle which can never happen again.' I wandered off feeling a bit sick and thinking that you were hardly a fit associate for budding aspirations. But finally I reflected that you knew whereof you spoke, that I was up against a hard game and might as well realize it and hew to the line without thought of commercial stage production. Your advice gradually bred in me a gloomy and soothing fatalism which kismeted many a rebuff and helped me to take my disappointments as all an inevitable part of the game."

In a subsequent letter from Sea Island, Georgia, bearing the postmark of April 5, 1935, Eugene again refers to the meeting at the railroad station with these words:

"But your advice stuck in my mind, and kept sticking there for many years, years in which managers kept proving to me how right you were. For example, the two plays I sent at the station that day (to be sure they got off in the very first mail!) were never read by [George] Tyler or anyone else. I finally got them back two years later, from the receiver after Liebler and Company went into bankruptcy—and they were still sealed in my original envelopes! But, thanks to your warning, I was forearmed and forewarned against disappointment and I was able to accept it with a fatalistic grin—and many, many other rebuffs of a similar nature in the years before 1920 when a long play, *Beyond the Horizon*, finally was produced at special matinées—my first uptown break.

"Yes, of all the help you were in those years, I think that bit ranks brightest in memory. It was a bitter dose to swallow that day but it sure proved a vital shock-absorbing tonic in the long run. It taught me to 'take it'—and God knows that's the first thing most apprentice playwrights need to learn if they are not to turn into chronic whiners against fate or quitters before their good break comes."

That same year, my husband's book *So You're Writing a Play!* was published with the following dedication: "To Eugene O'Neill, who began his career as one of my apprentices and is now fulfilling it as one of my masters." Eugene replied with: "Just a line to thank you for the book and its flattering dedication—above all, for the inscription. It was damned kind of you to add that and it moved me deeply. I'm going to put the book aside for the time being and not read it until I come to a breathing space in my present arduous job. My mind is so harassed right now by the thousand and one technical and psychological problems involved in rounding out the detailed outline of the interrelationships between the seven plays of this cycle that by the time I finish the daily stint I loathe the very mention of the word play! No time in which to read a book on playwriting, you'll agree! So I will save *So You're Writing a Play!* for the rest period between the finish of my outline and the starting of actual dialogue on the first play. Then I can be a bit more objective about this torturing trade—and really appreciate your creative comment on it."

In reply to the letter I sent Eugene upon the death of my husband in 1946, his wife, Carlotta Monterey, sent me this answer: "After your letter came, he sat silently thinking for a long time. Then he told me of days long past—you and your husband's great kindness to him—and how your husband had persuaded Gene's father that it would be worth while to send him to Harvard to Professor Baker's class. Years have passed but there was always a warm place for Clayton Hamilton in Gene's heart and great pleasure when a letter would arrive. I am writing to you because it is so terribly difficult for him to write. You no doubt know he has *paralysis agitans*, which is heartbreaking to us who love him."

John V. A. Weaver

I KNEW HIM WHEN

Of Baker's dozen for 1914–15 at the Harvard 47 Workshop, I remember only three members by name. There was somebody called Massey, who afterwards turned out a splendid little satire called "Plots and Playwrights," I think; there was a scion of the Elkins-Widener family, who matters in this narrative, since he was one of our own trio. And then there was Eugene O'Neill. He stuck out of that class like an oyster in a lunchroom stew.

The rest of us were decidedly awed by the grandeur of our ambitions. Learning to be playwrights! The name of Sheldon gleamed brightly always before us; Frederick Ballard seemed on the make; Cleves Kincaid was even then moulding his "Common Clay" into a meretricious but paying pattern; and a certain Lewis Beach was present for a "super-year," already impressing us with the inviolability of scripts. What an atmosphere! What a tradition!

We others listened with scared respect to the professorial admonitions, urgings and objurgations. Not so the fierce-browed, sardonic young man at whose left I sat. These theoretical vaporings were to him simply so much asafetida. While we sat open-mouthed and earnest, he would writhe and squirm in his chair, scowling and muttering in a mezzo-voce fearful imprecations and protests. This was, to me, delightful, fascinating anarchy. To have such a nerve as to pooh-pooh (that is a euphemism) this new gospel—and to get away with it—this O'Neill was a man indeed!

Of him, too, we were frightened. He kept so much to himself. He did not invite approach. For some weeks we let him alone. Then one day Dr. Baker read aloud a scenario by an aspirant. It was lugubrious, it was flamboyant, it was very, very earnest. Several of us gave timid suggestions. It came O'Neill's turn. He waited some

---

From the New York World, *February 21, 1926. Reprinted with permission.*

moments. Finally he said, without a smile, "Cut it to twenty minutes, give it a couple of tunes and it's sure-fire burly-cue."

Looking at it now, this remark does not seem to have been startlingly witty or amusing. Falling into the academic stuffiness of our "little group" it broke, once and for all, the ice. We howled with laughter. Dr. Baker smiled. From that time until we parted in June there was a new ease, a refreshing relaxation in the meetings.

Going out of the class-room Elkins (the society man) and myself moved on O'Neill. His diffidence seemed to have gone. We repaired to one of the Shamrock bars which in the past made Boston a thing of joy. We drank ale. We continued drinking ale until four in the morning, feet on the rail, one hand in the free lunch. It was just one of those nights. Ribald tales, anecdotes of experience, theorizing about the drama—what the collegians used to call a "bull session." A bull session de luxe.

We piled finally into a decrepit hack. We fell into O'Neill's room some time about five. I had just purchased that day a copy of *Spoon River Anthology*. When the dawn broke I was sitting on a trunk, Elkins sprawled across the bed, O'Neill reading in his powerful, melancholy bass, poem after poem from that disturbing collection.

I was told of life on and about the stage, from infancy onward; how 'Gene's earliest delight was to make the canvas waves into which his father, the unforgettable Count of Monte Cristo, dived, emerging a moment after to announce that "The world is mine!" nightly and matinees during some thirty years; of tours with *The White Sister*, of pitcher-and-bowl-circuit caravansaries as Joseph, who withstood the charms of Potiphar's insistent spouse; of the exodus from Princeton, caused by the shying of a beer bottle through Prexy Wilson's dormer window; of vagabondages, "wobbly" camps, long voyages as a stoker (vide *The Hairy Ape*), riots, street fights and mad escapades in foreign ports; of hospitals and the will to live. And I read and listened to many a scenario, many a half-formed plot.

Elkins contributed vitally to these halcyon episodes. He was an amusing conversationalist and he was a generous host. There were numberless dinners at the Beacon Street mansion, where I, very callow and greatly impressed, and 'Gene, jocularly insolent, in a dirty brown flannel shirt, feasted amidst quiet elegance and flunkies. An incongruous sight, surely. Always, afterwards, we would go to some new show. Elkins would buy up a whole box, and once we were seated, tear up the rest of the tickets. He was a good scout. He knew what he wanted, and he could afford it. Why not?

Women were forever calling for 'Gene. There was something apparently irresistible in his strange combination of cruelty (around the mouth), intelligence (in his eyes) and sympathy (in his voice). I would not say that he was "good-looking." But one girl told me she could not get his face out of her thoughts. He was hard-boiled and whimsical. He was brutal and tender, so I was told. From shop girl to "sassiety" queen, they all seemed to develop certain tendencies in his presence. What may have resulted, deponent sayeth not. About some things 'Gene was Sphinx-like. All I can report is the phenomena.

Meanwhile the course was proceeding. Over boiled beef and beer in Durgin and Parks, or salami and red ink at the Roma, we three discussed our efforts. Suffice it to tell about Elkins and myself that he is still hopeful of presenting some day a deft but tenuous high comedy of the Four Hundred, composed then, while I seemed to become more confused and less capable of creation as the days passed. But O'Neill, where he ever found the time for his output I can't imagine, but here is an incomplete list of his activities, as I remember them, for 1914–15:

Two of the one-acters in the Caribbean series, first drafts. A one-act play about a spy in the war then occurring—gruesome, devastating and wonderfully striking. A hasty draft of a full length play called at that time *The Second Engineer*, which formed, later, some of the basis for *Anna Christie*. A lovely little fantasy named "Abortion," all about a doctor who took his Hippocratic oath seriously and refused to perform an illegal operation upon his own fiancée—something to make one's blood chill. And conversationally, a play about a man who was always hoping to get away from his environment, to go "beyond the horizon." This took four years to crystallize. There was also much discussion of a contemplated farce in which some Mexican General was to hire a movie company to stage a fake revolution for the films, the fake eventually turning into reality. This last has evidently been abandoned.

All of us in the class were a little appalled at the savage radicalism of O'Neill. But we were all agreed that here was the One Best Bet. Even the most disapproving of our companions would say,

"Well, I wonder how long it will be before he is the country's greatest playwright." We said it seriously, almost perfunctorily. Baker himself recognized the smouldering genius which was five years later to flame. He begged 'Gene to return for a second year. 'Gene wouldn't. No more academic stuff for him.

On a stifling May morning the three of us shook hands and scattered, Elkins to the Pacific Coast, I to a job selling canned fish in Chicago, O'Neill to wanderings, Provincetown, and fame. He hit 'em between the eyes, and he deserved it. *Beyond the Horizon*, *Anna Christie*, *The Emperor Jones*, *The Hairy Ape* and *Diff'rent*—yes, and that poignant, ill-fated *The Straw.* These will live.

Something has happened to O'Neill. I have seen him only twice since, and he is a stranger. Gone is the old swaggering zest, vanished is the charming swashbuckling. He looks tired and tortured. Probably it is my fault, but he finds little beyond monosyllables to say to me. Even his infuriated sense of humor seems to have lost all its edge.

I guess it is the fault of his sycophants, his village yes-men. No human could withstand, I suppose, the frightful adulation which has been his lot. His work looks bad, too, these days. I haven't seen *The Great God Brown*, but from what I hear, there is too much in it of this artificial, manufactured "Great God O'Neill." As for *Welded*, *All God's Chillun*, *Desire Under the Elms* and *The Fountain*—well, they have all the appearance, to me, of rungs down a ladder into sterility.

I'm sorry. One cannot help a little sadness over the spectacle of a high, exuberant spirit, becoming lacquered. I would like to hear, some day, that 'Gene had suddenly turned on some of his flatterers and socked a couple of jaws. I'd like to hear that he had vanished, full of hooch and hellishness, for parts unknown, beyond some new horizon, to touch the earth again and return plain 'Gene and not the deity of Washington Square.

I wish he'd go to see our *Love 'Em and Leave 'Em*, and sit with me over a flock of beers, and tear hell out of it.

But I guess he will not. We aren't high-brow enough, I'm sure, for this strange, literary O'Neill. We wouldn't be worth bothering about.

Things change.

Susan Glaspell

O'NEILL'S FIRST READING

"One man cannot produce drama. True drama is born only of one feeling animating all the members of a clan—a spirit shared by all and expressed by the few for the all. If there is nothing to take the place of the common religious purpose and passion of the primitive group, out of which the Dionysian dance was born, no new vital drama can arise in any people."

He [Jig Cook] and Neith Boyce said it together. He came home and wrote it down as an affirmation of faith.

The people who came back that next summer had little chance of escaping. Purpose had grown in him, he was going to take whom he wanted and use them for the creation of his Beloved Community.

We hauled out the old boat, took oars and nets and anchors to various owners, bought lumber at the second wharf "up along," and Jig, Nordfeldt, Ballantine, Joe O'Brien, others helping, converted the fish-house into the Wharf Theatre, a place where ninety people could see a play, if they didn't mind sitting close together on wooden benches with no backs. The stage, ten feet by twelve, was in four sections, so we could have different levels, could run it through the big sliding-door at the back, a variety of set surprising in quarters so small.

We gave a first bill, then met at our house to read plays for a second. Two Irishmen, one old and one young, had arrived and taken a shack just up the street. "Terry," I said to the one not young, "haven't you a play to read to us?"

"No," said Terry Carlin, "I don't write, I just think, and sometimes talk. But Mr. O'Neill has got a whole trunk full of plays," he smiled.

From The Road to The Temple. *Copyright 1927 by Frederick A. Stokes Company. Reprinted by permission of the author's estate. Editor's title.*

That didn't sound too promising, but I said: "Well, tell Mr. O'Neill to come to our house at eight o'clock tonight, and bring some of his plays."

So Gene took "Bound East for Cardiff" from his trunk, and Freddie Burt read it to us, Gene staying out in the dining-room while the reading went on.

He was not left alone in the dining-room when the reading had finished.

Then we knew what we were for. We began in faith, and perhaps it is true when you do that "all these things shall be added unto you."

I may see it through memories too emotional, but it seems to me I have never sat before a more moving production than our "Bound East for Cardiff," when Eugene O'Neill was produced for the first time on any stage. Jig was Yank. As he lay in his bunk dying, he talked of life as one who knew he must leave it.

The sea has been good to Eugene O'Neill. It was there for his opening. There was a fog, just as the script demanded, fog bell in the harbor. The tide was in, and it washed under us and around, spraying through the holes in the floor, giving us the rhythm and the flavor of the sea while the big dying sailor talked to his friend Drisc of the life he had always wanted deep in the land, where you'd never see a ship or smell the sea.

It is not merely figurative language to say the old wharf shook with applause.

The people who had seen the plays and the people who gave them, were adventurers together. The spectators were part of the Players, for how could it have been done without the feeling that came from them, without that sense of them there, waiting, ready to share, giving—finding the deep level where audience and writer and player are one. . . .

Edna Kenton

PROVINCETOWN AND MACDOUGAL STREET

We were standing together, George Cram Cook and I, in the little Wharf Theatre at Provincetown. It was midsummer, 1916. I had just stepped off the Boston boat, and there was, it seemed, but one first thing to do, to go with him to the old remodelled fish house on the wharf and inspect "the theatre"—circus-seated, sand-strewn, and sea-weed hung. I see him now, leaping onto the tiny stage to give me the back drop for Eugene O'Neill's "Thirst." It was a simple shift—a mere throwing back of the two great doors at the rear; and, behold, the living sea dancing with light, its sound and space and all but its waters pouring in through the height and breadth of the stage. I see him standing there against the sea, smiling, vivid, his arms crossed in their habitual fashion, looking out across the waters quite as if they had been created for him and the Players and O'Neill's sea plays.

"You don't know Gene yet," he told me. "You don't know his plays. But you will. All the world will know Gene's plays some day. Last summer this thing began. This year, on the night he first came to Provincetown and read us "Bound East for Cardiff," we knew we had something to go on with. Some day this little theatre will be famous; some day the little theatre in New York will be famous—this fall The Provincetown Players go into New York, with "Cardiff" on their first bill. We've got our group of playwrights, and they have to have their stage. Gene's plays aren't the plays of Broadway; he's got to have the sort of stage we're going to found in New York. He's writing. Susan's writing; Jack Reed and Floyd Dell and the Hapgoods are writing; I'm writing—you're going to write us a play."

I never wrote a play for The Provincetown Players. But I was a member of the group from that day, and of its executive committee from its first New York season in 1916 to its last—the season of Eugene O'Neill's *The Hairy Ape*—in 1922. My place in the group was always a rather oddly detached one as to obvious interests, for I neither wrote, produced, designed sets for plays or acted in them. The interest was an inner interest, and just because there were no conflicts between that inner quest of curiosity and outer satisfactions in the particular special personal case, I could be and was fairly impersonally interested in the experiment itself and all of the material used in it—that of founding and sustaining an *experimental* theatre. Could it be done, or couldn't it—go on, that is, for a series of seasons; selecting, cooking and serving its own food without casting an anxious culinary eye towards the public "taste"; without seeking—or disdaining—the "critics"; without, as we so highly said, being afraid to go down to death if ever experiment for experiment's sake took on the false color of experiment for "success." "We will let this theatre die," we said, "before we let it become another voice of mediocrity." From the beginning to the end I was continuously interested in the whole adventure and in the adventure as a whole; interested in the "experimental" plays and productions—the latter so necessitously impoverished; in the ragged acting and direction when they agonizingly happened, quite as much as in the rarer, finer achievements when they bloomed. For what was experiment if not just the simple act of looking on and noting the steps of a process all duly set in motion, with the result no more than a step of the process, whether the result was failure or success. That was the way we looked at it in the beginning, and, a few of us, at the end. When we reached the end, in 1922, and George Cook sailed away, it was to Greece—always, for him, the source of the idea which is the seed of experiment.

Always—and it helped, I think, to keep the lamp of unendowed experiment burning through our six years of "results" (let us call them that instead of failures or successes)—we had before us a living example of what an experimental stage, an actual playwrights' laboratory, could do and was continuously doing for and to an experimental playwright. Let it be granted that, without The Provincetown Players, Eugene O'Neill would have reached eventually Broadway and high success. But there is no doubt at all that, had he not had our Playwrights' Theatre, and our experimental stage to use always precisely as he wished to use them, he would have reached Broadway by quite another road and with quite other plays. What it has meant and will mean to all of his future that he had, in those quite likely elsewhere unproducible years, so free a space in which to wield so free a hand, can hardly be estimated except by a few who watched him with the closest and most interested attention, as he tried form after form, struggled valiantly with this bit of "modern" psychology, played easily with that rag of old "theatricalism" deliberately resuscitated for testing out before a sophisticated audience. For he had not only our stage; he had our "subscription list," and he used its members, bill after bill, season after season, in ways they could never dream of; played with them and on them, with never need for a thought of them except as stark laboratory reactions to his own experimentations. No other American playwright has ever had such prolonged preliminary freedom with stage and audience alike. Perhaps no other audience has ever been, through six seasons of unconscious reactions to a playwright's experiments, so coldly disregarded before the act, and so carefully considered after it.

Of us all, George Cook saw this part of our experiment most clearly. In this particular case, his own basic idea for our group was working ideally; and, when the lamp of faith burned low, a new O'Neill play fed oil to the charred wick. I have seen this happen, time and time over, through to the end.

[For] we had fallen, with *The Emperor Jones*, into the flowery trap that lies in wait for the "unendowed." Face to face with the lure of "expansion," and without a treasury to aid us, we had taken the hand of the subtle enemy to experiment as if it were the hand of a friend. We had sent *The Emperor* uptown, had depleted our own actor-group, had enlarged the group, were for the first time paying "salaries," and were, for the first time, paying in spirit. Values had shifted overnight, astonishingly. To go uptown with our first success was higher honor than to stay downtown with our experiments. It was human, it was natural; we had worked and waited a long time—was the work and the waiting again and all humanly for "success?"—we were a little drunk with the wine of applause, and we lost our balance and fell. It was the hidden beginning of the end. . . .

Maxwell Bodenheim

ROUGHNECK AND ROMANCER

. . . When I first met O'Neill, ten years ago, he was seated in the backroom of a Greenwich Village saloon known as "Hell's Hole"—a place which has since deteriorated into a meanly greasy lunchroom. He was talking to a couple of gangsters—Hudson Dusters—on the subject of a friend of his, "Scotty," who had defrauded the gangsters in a furniture deal, and he managed to smother their rage and induce them to forego their intended vengeance. He did this with a curious mixture of restrained profanity, mild contempt, and blunt camaraderie which showed that he shared the spirit of these roughnecks and yet failed to share it. His spirit was made up of almost equal parts of deeply articulate proletarian and surface poet, with both blended to an undistinguishable whole. In using the noun "proletarian," I do not mean to indicate that he was in any way a social-radical. The underdog in one of his plays is a trapped, snarling, futile being, with recalcitrant feelings that lead only to fears, and profanities, and heavy toil, and the swishing of fists against his companions, and with barely enough mind to realize—in his most depressed moments—his own insignificant and enslaved condition. In his first plays, O'Neill wrenched human beings from the heaving mud of life but did not give them sermons, and voluble "aspirations" toward "freedom." Their dialogues were more restrained and cogent under his direction than they would have been in actual saloons, dives, ships, and jungles, but they were usually, in faithful and innate detail, expressions of the characters themselves, as far as any creator could make them so and still retain the unobtrusive aversions and dislikes that formed his individuality.

From The New Yorker, *February 6, 1926. Reprinted by permission.*

In the rear room of "Hell's Hole," with its cheap prints of race horses and chromos of unadorned women, its round, spotty tables, and the instrument of brazen agonies that played tunes of the day when you dropped a nickel into it, O'Neill would often utter his opinions on life. His sallowly brown face, with its small, black moustache, long nose, and black eyes crammed with humorous contempt, would seem to grow metallic beneath his words, in spite of the endless drinks that he consumed (in those days he could imbibe from twilight to dawn without showing any effects save those of an occasional irascibility). One of his favorite assertions then was that the under-world and the creative upper-world would have to unite before the earth could become a safe and unhampered place for intelligent people—an aristocracy of swift brawn and equally quick mind ruling over the more sluggish, hypocritical, and unimaginative men and women in all walks of life. Again, he would often vent the conviction that poetry lurks in all of the objects of life, from the most common to the most ethereal, except that in the most common ones it is buried with a desperate skill and is much more difficult to unearth—a broad and delicate curiosity that often glistens out between the more roughly realistic lines in his one-act plays, and in *Anna Christie* and *The Hairy Ape.*

Of course, ten years can turn topsy-turvy the surfaces and even the purposes of a man, and the present Eugene O'Neill has become the hero of a more polished and restricted environment—parlors and upper-studios, and suave clubs—although he is for the most part a hard-working hermit in his Provincetown and Connecticut retreats. His face has become soberly abstracted, and his tall, lean body has a just perceptible droop, and a flicking of grey mixes with his black hair, and his thick lips are more tightly glued, as though in an effort at conscious restraint. Much of his old spontaneous humor, and swaggering and cheery "What-Ho's!" have departed, and the former boisterous renegade-creator has altered to a reserved and polite-mannered gentleman, with a distant look in his eyes. Practically the same alterations can be observed in his latter plays, *All God's Chillun Got Wings*, *Desire Under the Elms*, and *The Fountain*, where the old O'Neill is abdicating to a more "aesthetic," refined, and redundant creator, who does not seem to care for his former oaths, and gasping cries from the darker bottoms of life, and sledge hammer dénouements, and probings of vicious realities. Yet, in spite of these changes, I do not believe that his basic spirit has died but merely that he has been surfacely hypnotized. I think that he will eventually return to the deeper "fountains" of his genius and that now, at thirty-eight, he has been only temporarily led astray from his fundamental purposes and attainments.

Eugene O'Neill

"A YOWL AT FATE":

A Letter to George Pierce Baker

West Point Pleasant, N. J.
May 9, 1919

My dear Professor Baker:

Not once but a dozen times since our chance meeting in Provincetown two years ago have I determined to write to you, but each time I hesitated, reflecting: Better wait until you have something real to relate. Not that the possession of any grand achievement emboldens me at present writing; but at least the burden of a yowl at Fate gives me ballast.

I have been hoping all during the past theatrical season to be able to give you the date and all other data of a forthcoming production of my long play, *Beyond the Horizon*, which has been under contract to John D. Williams since last spring. It is a play of two brothers, and Williams was sure he would produce it with the Barrymores in the cast—a fair hope, that!—as soon as *Redemption* petered out, as the consensus of wide opinion decreed it must. *Redemption*, however, refused to peter. And now comes *The Jest* —a very mocking irony of a title, it seems to me—which promises to beat all records for endurance.

That, in brief, is my plaint; and who can gainsay its justice when he sees this native-son steam-rollered by that foreign invasion? True, Williams has renewed the contract and promises a production before next December, and is still full of hope that in the end his devout wish will be consummated. Ah, yes—in the end! But my system has absorbed so much hope in the past six months that I am now immune. I turn a callous, cauliflower ear to all managerial fair promises. I have ceded my winter home in Spain for a permanent residence in Missouri.

From George Pierce Baker and the American Theatre *by Wisner Payne Kinne. Published by Harvard University Press, 1954.*

Since you last saw me I have completed three long plays. The first, finished a year ago, was immediately taken by Williams—with the resultant blighted dreams recorded above. The second, *Chris Christopherson*, is now awaiting the verdicts of both Hopkins and Belasco. I really have every confidence that, in spite of the fact that it is far removed in nature and treatment from the usual run of acceptable plays, it will eventually find a producer. The third play, [*The Straw*] the last act of which I have just finished rewriting, is still untyped. It is the best of them in my opinion, but on account of its subject matter, I anticipate a long period of waiting—unless the Theatre Guild like it enough to face the music.

I wish you could read these three plays. They would interest you I feel sure, because they are sincere and because they demand a freshness of treatment and a widened scope for the playwright's subject material. Will you let me send one or more of them to you sometime this summer? I know you are at your busiest just now. In truth, it has been the conviction that you have no season that isn't busy that has prevented my sending them to you as they were finished.

I hope you escaped seeing the production of my one-act plays by the Washington Square Players and Greenwich Village Theatre a year ago this season. You would have acquired a false opinion from these productions of the worth of the plays as written, I am sure. And as for "In the Zone" as mutilated by the vaudeville folk—it ran for over thirty weeks until peace and the Flu intervened—I had better turn the page. Well, a vaudeville audience never reads an author's name, anyway.

Under separate cover I am sending you a copy of the book of my one-act plays just published. All of the seven have been produced in New York, most of them originally by the Provincetown Players. I wish very much for you to have this book as a small token of my remembrance of all I owe to my year under your guidance. Let me only hope that these plays will justify that year in your eyes. I realize I must have seemed woefully lacking in gratitude because, seemingly, I have never had the decency to write—and I know the interest you take in the work of your former students. But I'm really not as bad as that. In all honesty, I have waited more out of small-boy ambition than anything else. I was confident that the night would come when I could approach you with that digesting-canary grin, and, pointing to the fiery writing on the wall of some New York theatre, chortle triumphantly: "Look, Teacher! See what I done!"

Very sincerely yours,
Eugene G. O'Neill

P. S. I hope you will pardon the typewriting; but I realized that this letter is long, and my handwriting is small, and your time is short.

Malcolm Cowley

A WEEKEND WITH EUGENE O'NEILL

Back in the early 1920's, Eugene O'Neill was the animating spirit of a group that surrounded the Provincetown Players. His success as a dramatist had enabled the Players to move to New York and had kept their venture alive in bad seasons. It had kept me alive, too, during a hard year when I was paid ten dollars a week to be a black ghost in *The Emperor Jones* and a white ghost in a revival of "Where the Cross Is Made"; I never aspired to play the part of any living person. Although I hadn't been eating much that year, I made a rather substantial wraith, even with streaks of aluminum paint over my ribs to make them look as if the flesh had rotted away. Then Gene stopped writing plays with ghosts in them and my stage career came to an end. It was a minor example of how his decisions affected all of us.

If the Provincetown Players drank at the Hell Hole—officially known as the Golden Swan—which stood at the southeast corner of Fourth Street and Sixth Avenue in Greenwich Village, that was also because of Gene. Before it became a speakeasy, the Hell Hole was a Raines Law hotel, which means that there were furnished rooms upstairs and that, in theory, it furnished meals to travelers. As legal proof of the theory, the same mummified sandwiches appeared Sunday after Sunday on the round tables in the back room. Not even the unfed stumblebums who slept there on winter nights would dust off the sandwiches and eat them. The Hell Hole before the First World War, when it stayed open all night, was one of the principal models that Gene copied for Harry Hope's saloon in *The Iceman Cometh*. It was the grubbiest drinking parlor west of the Bowery—the No Chance Saloon, Bedrock Bar, the End of the Line Café, the Bottom of the Sea Rathskeller, as Larry Slade calls it in

---

the play. "Don't you notice the beautiful calm in the atmosphere?" he continues. "That's because it's the last harbor. No one here has to worry about where they're going next, because there is no farther they can go."

Larry Slade in life was Terry Carlin, a gaunt, benign Irishman who had retired from gainful occupation after a working career that lasted one day. It was a Saturday, Terry explained, and the gainful occupation was that of helping behind the bar, where he had slaved from noon to midnight in order to empty the till after the saloon was closed. But the proprietor emptied it first, and Terry, disillusioned, had sworn never to do another day's work in his life. He kept the oath and lived to be nearly eighty, on a chiefly liquid diet. During Prohibition he used to drink canned heat, strained through a not very clean blue bandanna—that is, till the afternoon when I heard him say dreamily, "I'll have to stop drinking wood alcohol. It's beginning to affect my eyesight." Terry was a mystic of sorts who had been a radical syndicalist in his early days and then a philosophical anarchist. He had also been a patron of the Hell Hole when anyone would buy him a drink, as Gene often did. At Provincetown in the summer of 1916, Terry had repaid the debt by introducing his desperately shy friend to the Players as a young man with a trunkful of unperformed plays.

Outside of a few drunken radicals or ex-radicals like Terry and Hippolyte Havel (Hugo Kalmar in *The Iceman Cometh*), the denizens of the Hell Hole were more practical than the characters in Gene's play. Some of the latter were invented and others were carried over from Jimmy the Priest's, a waterfront dive that had been one of Gene's earlier haunts. At the Hell Hole the regular patrons included sneak thieves and shoplifters, touts, a square-shooting Negro gambler down on his luck, and a few bedraggled prostitutes—until 1917, that is, when "us girls" were driven off the streets and saloonkeepers were told not to serve them. There was a famous West Side gang known as the Hudson Dusters. Not many of the anti-social characters at the Hell Hole had spunk enough to be gangsters, but Hudson Dusters—or simply Dusters—was what we always called them. Gene had been drinking with them since 1915, when he first lived in the Village. The Dusters pitied him, sometimes fed him when he was starving, and one of them offered to steal him an overcoat when he was shivering with cold. "Tell you what, Gene," said an amiable shoplifter. "You make a trip up Sixth Avenue right away. Go to any store, pick out any coat you like, and tell me where it hangs on the rack. I bring you the coat tomorrow."

Gene hadn't accepted the offer, but he liked to tell about it, and anyone could see that he was proud to be accepted by the Dusters as one of the crowd. He had earned a place there by his apprenticeship in raggedness and drunkenness and near starvation, as well as by his unfailing good manners. He felt—and perhaps the Dusters felt—that he was leagued with them in a sullen rebellion against property and propriety. To a lesser extent he was also leagued with the Greenwich Villagers, particularly if they were poor and eccentric and a little outside the law. I think that for him the world was divided into downtowners and uptowners, as for a later generation of rebels it would be divided into hipsters and squares. For some time after becoming a successful playwright, he entered the uptown world with trepidation and in disguise, almost like a scout in enemy country, fearful of being caught and condemned to death or forced to abandon his loyalties. He wouldn't even go to see his own plays when they were produced on Broadway. In the plays he depicted uptowners as hypocritical and sex-obsessed, and also as representatives of the paternal authority that he defied. He wanted to fling the truth about them into their smug faces. He wanted to show the uptowners, including his father, what he could do to enforce his dreams, but he didn't want to win them over; he wanted to impress and overawe, not persuade. In the back room of the Hell Hole, which was lighted by two flickering gas jets, with the corners of the room in darkness so that it looked like an expressionistic setting for *The Lower Depths*, among the honest sneak thieves and panhandlers at the very end of the line, he was safe from his father's reproaches; he could take off his mask and be understood.

That was what I felt about O'Neill, but what did I really know about him? Today how much do I really remember? I had seen him perhaps a dozen times, in the street, in the back room of the Hell Hole, at the Provincetown Playhouse, and once in the cold-water flat of Spanish Willie Fernandez, a bootlegger and small-time politician who worshiped him. I had heard some of his stories about life on shipboard and in a tuberculosis sanitarium, but it seems to me now that I heard them from others, his good friends and mine. I know that he liked to sing chanteys, omitting the obscene stanzas, and that his favorites were "Whiskey for My Johnny" and "Blow the Man Down." When ordering another round of drinks, he might sing in a low voice:

"Whiskey is the life of man,
(Whiskey—Johnny),
Oh, I drink whiskey when I ca-a-an
(Whiskey for my Johnny)."

In humming the other chantey, he would pause to say that the slow rise and fall of the refrain, "Way-O, blow the man down," was like the movement of a ship on an ocean swell, and he would illustrate his meaning with a wavelike gesture of his right hand. But did I really see him make the gesture or was it someone else who made it in telling me about an evening spent with Gene? Often we fall into the illusion that the good friends of our friends are our good friends too.

Searching through my mind, discarding the questionable pictures and the stories told by others, I find that most of what I truly remember about Gene is connected with a visit to the O'Neills' country house at the beginning of November, 1923, when the other guests were the poet Hart Crane, whom we had met that summer, and my first wife, Peggy Baird. And what remains is not a continuous memory but a series of pictures, as if one's mind were a theatre, and a spotlight moved to illuminate one corner of the stage and then another while leaving the intervening spaces in blackness.

Hart Crane and I are climbing out of a nearly empty Harlem Division local at Purdy's Station on a Friday evening just after dark. Nobody else gets off the train. Gene's second wife, Agnes Boulton, had taken Peggy to the country earlier in the week, and now they are waiting for us on the dimly lighted platform. There are hugs, twitters, and Hart's boom of greeting. Shivering a little in the country air, I look up at the shadowy presence of big trees to the south of the station. Just north of it a sinister-looking bridge crosses the railway. A very bright electric bulb is burning at the top of the embankment, against a starless sky. A long flight of steps rises through shadows toward the single light. It is a stage setting by

Robert Edmond Jones and makes me feel like a ghost again in one of Gene's early plays.

Carrying our bags, we struggle up the steps to where the O'Neills' new touring car is waiting under the light. The chauffeur, whose name is Vincent Bedini, drives us eastward by narrow roads lined with stone walls. From time to time, far back from the road, we catch glimpses of big houses among the trees, sailing past us like brilliantly lighted wooden ships. At some point we cross the Connecticut state line. . . .

The O'Neills have recently bought one of the big houses in Ridgefield, I think with part of a legacy from Gene's brother Jim, or Jamie, though there have also been big royalties from *Anna Christie* and smaller ones from *The Hairy Ape*. The house is an 1890-ish affair called Brook Farm by its former owners, with a wide tree-dotted lawn and more than forty acres of land. Gene meets us in the hallway and so does his new dog—an Irish wolfhound, we are informed, the color and texture of a coarse sandpaper and the size of a three-month-old calf. "He's extinct," I say, patting his head. "The *Encyclopaedia Britannica* tells us that Irish wolfhounds are an extinct breed." Offstage the telephone rings. With his hind paws slipping a little on the pale yellow hardwood floor, the dog rises to his full height, which is greater than mine, puts his forepaws on my shoulders, and looks down into my eyes. Enter Mrs. Fifine Clark, the housekeeper, known as "Gaga" by the family; she says there is another call from New York, from the Theatre Guild. "I'll take it," Gene murmurs. He comes back with a brief report, "I said no." There aren't any other guests and we sit down to an excellent dinner without being offered a drink. The door to the hallway is closed against Finn, the dog, who hasn't learned table manners.

After luncheon on Saturday, Gene and I are alone in a window nook at the left rear of the enormous living room. Hart has disappeared, I don't know where, and the girls are in Agnes's bedroom exchanging confidences over glasses of whiskey and water, I suspect, but there is no liquor downstairs. Gene picks up a heavy green medical-looking book from the table beside us; it is one of Wilhelm Stekel's treatises on sexual aberrations—perhaps *The Disguises of Love*, which has recently been translated from the German. There are enough case histories in the book, Gene says, to furnish plots to all the playwrights who ever lived. He turns the pages and shows me the clinical record of a mother who seduced her only son and drove him insane. Then he talks about the German Expressionists, Toller and Kaiser and Hasenclever, whose plays he has read because they are said to resemble his own. Gene thinks their work is bold and interesting, but much too easy. The word "easy," which seems to be his strongest expression of disapproval, reminds him of *Anna Christie*. "I never liked it so well," he says, "as some of my other plays. In telling the story I deliberately employed all the Broadway tricks I had learned in my stage training. Using the same technique, and with my early experience as a background, I could turn out dozens of plays like *Anna Christie*, but I won't ever try. It would be too easy."

Nodding politely, I look down at the polished beech floor, with tiny eyes here and there in the wood. I think it is the handsomest floor I have ever seen.

Gene has taken me upstairs to the room where he works, a big bedroom so meagerly furnished that it looks like an abbot's cell. (Croswell Bowen, who is writing one of the books about O'Neill, tells me there was a crucifix over the bed, but I don't remember seeing it.) There are no books or pictures in the room. Between the two north windows is a dark mahogany secretary with drawers at the bottom, a cabinet at the top, and a drop-leaf table for writing. There are no papers on the writing surface. Gene opens the doors of the cabinet and takes out two or three medium-sized bound ledgers; "I write in these," he says. Each ledger contains several plays. Opening one of them, he shows me the text of *The Emperor Jones*, written with a very fine pen, in characters so small that they are illegible without a reading glass. There are no blank lines, and the text of the whole play fills only three pages of the ledger—or is it five? I think of the Lord's Prayer engraved on the head of a pin.

Gene tells me he is writing a play about New England, but he doesn't want to discuss it until it is finished. He is being extraordinarily kind to a shabby young man without a reputation. Partly that is because I am a friend of his friends, definitely not an uptowner, but there is something else involved—perhaps a need to explain himself to a new generation of writers, to a representative of the future by which he will be judged. I listen but do not respond as I might well have done if he were French or English. In this country, as a result of the First World War, there has come to be a gulf between literary generations, besides that older gulf between fame and obscurity. Although Gene is only ten years older than I, he had come of age in a different world, and I feel we have very few admirations or even interests in common. Gene is trying to cross the two gulfs, but, in my defensive pride and foolish reticence, I do nothing to help him.

Rather late in a dry evening, Gene takes Hart and me down to the cellar, the only part of the house that seems to arouse his pride of ownership. He shows us the big coal furnace, with pipes radiating in all directions like the arms of an octopus. Standing under a bare electric light, he points to the cement floor and says that Vincent keeps it as clean as the living room. Vincent is a European who can't stand the way Americans let things go to waste. Last month he had gathered apples from the old orchard and made three barrels of cider. There they are—Gene points a finger into the shadows, where three fifty-gallon casks stand on a rack.

As a country boy I offer a disquisition on the virtues of hard cider, the wine of the Puritans, the interior sunlight of New England. "Let's broach a cask," Hart says. Gene demurs, but hesitantly; Vincent mightn't like it, he says, the cider is only three weeks old, and besides he doesn't know how a barrel should be tapped. Here I interrupt with my country knowledge. There is a spigot lying on the rack, I say, with a maul beside it. Cider doesn't have to ferment all winter; sometimes it tastes even better when the sugar hasn't quite worked out.

Gene goes upstairs to Gaga's kitchen and comes back with a white china pitcher and three glasses. By that time I have tapped a barrel, spilling more than a little cider on Vincent's clean floor. We stand with our full glasses under the bare electric light. "I can see the beaded bubbles winking at the brim," Hart says. Gene takes a sip of cider, holds it in his mouth apprehensively, gives his glass a gloomy look, then empties the glass in two deep nervous swallows. After a while we fill the pitcher again. When I go upstairs to bed, long after midnight, Gene is on his knees drawing another pitcher of cider, and Hart stands over him gesturing with a dead cigar as he declaims some lines composed that afternoon.

Soliloquy. I am lying awake while the clear gray morning light pours in through the bedroom windows. I am saying to myself that the O'Neills rattle around in this big country house like the last dried peas in a box—or better, like castaway sailors who have blundered into a deserted palace on the shore. But the sailors would laugh if they found wine in the cellar, where Gene hardly even smiles.

Peggy and I are running over the immense lawn in pursuit of the wolfhound. He musn't be allowed to cross the road because, in spite of his amiable temper, the mere size of him terrifies the neighbors; he has developed a bad habit of killing chickens, and there have been threats that he would be shot. Finally he lets us catch him and lead him, or be dragged by him, back to the house. "The O'Neills—were kings in Ireland," I pant as we go. "It's like Gene—to buy—a dog of an extinct breed—the royal hunting dog of Irish kings—that kills the neighbors' chickens."

The big round table has been set for luncheon, with a plateful of hors d'oeuvres at each plate. I look through the glass doors of the dining room and see the extinct dog walking gravely round the table, lowering, not raising, his head to empty each plate in turn. At luncheon Mrs. Clark gives soup to us instead. We are told at the last moment that Gene won't be down because he's working.

That evening we are in Woodstock, New York, sixty miles from Ridgefield as the crow flies. I know from one of Hart's published letters that we had been taken there in the O'Neills' touring car, which means that Vincent was at the wheel, but I don't remember by what roads, or how we crossed the Hudson, or anything that was said. A sort of curtain had fallen, to rise on another scene. My one intervening impression, a faint one, is that Agnes came along for the ride, then left rather hurriedly before dinner.

Now we are in a sort of eviscerated farmhouse, where ceilings and partitions have been ripped out to make an immensely high living room, with a balcony at one side and bedrooms opening out of it. There are six of us, all of an age except Niles Spencer's kid sister, who is pretty and sixteen. We have organized a game of hide-and-seek and go storming in and out of doors, up and down the balcony stairs, in alternate troughs and crests of laughter—first laughter pushed down, as into the hollow of a wave, then laughter splashing over us in breakers, with Hart's voice booming above them. For the Ridgefield pilgrims, it is as if a thin but perceptible mist of constraint, of jokes not made and differences of opinion that mustn't be aired, had suddenly been laughed away.

Hart stayed at the Woodstock farmhouse until after Christmas. Peggy and I went back to New York, where on Thursday of that week I wrote a letter to one of my literary friends. I told him briefly about the trip and said, "Eugene O'Neill, Mr. O'Neill the playwright, Gene . . . speaks a language so different from ours that we seemed to converse from different worlds." So the trip had ended for me in a failure of communication that was largely my fault.

There was, however, a sequel. All that Sunday, instead of working Gene had kept on drawing pitchers of cider from the tapped barrel. While Agnes was away from Brook Farm he had called a taxi that took him to Purdy's, where he vanished. Agnes went to New York and spent a frantic week in search of him. Afraid of what the newspapers might say, she avoided the Bureau of Missing Persons; instead she made telephone calls to his friends and kept visiting his old haunts, including the Hell Hole.

On the last of her visits there, the proprietor confessed to her that Gene had sat in the back room and drunk himself into a coma. To avoid trouble with thc police, he had been stashed away in the mysterious upstairs that none of us had seen, where Gene said that a crazy old woman wandered through the hallways, opening and closing doors. Agnes had him driven to Ridgefield, where in a few days he went back to work on *Desire Under the Elms*. That was not the last of his alcoholic misadventures, but his need to write plays proved stronger than his impulse toward self-destruction. A few years later, faced with the choice between writing and drinking, he stopped drinking for the rest of his life.

George Jean Nathan

PORTRAIT OF O'NEILL

In all the many years of our friendship, I have heard Eugene O'Neill laugh aloud once and only once. We were walking, after dinner one evening in July, up the long, lonely road just beyond the château he was then living and working in at Saint Antoine du Rocher in Touraine. In the country, men who live in cities generally find themselves talking out of character. If they are sober, sedate fellows in the city, they become orally frisky in the country; if they are flippant in the city, they become more or less solemn and even wistful at the smell of flowers and manure. Their discourse alters with the scene. O'Neill, who in the city—for he is essentially a man of cities despite his inability to write save a cow is mooning or a sea is swishing beneath his window—has the mien and the conversational élan of an embalmer, presently proceeded thus: "When Princeton, after kicking my tail out of place as an undergraduate because I was too accurate a shot with an Anheuser-Busch beer-bottle and hit a window in Woodrow Wilson's house right where it lived,[1] some years later suddenly got proud of its old beer-bottle heaver but magnanimously allowed Yale to claim the

1. Editors' note: This is one of the standard episodes in the O'Neill legend and one which he may have enjoyed perpetuating. On December 11th, 1953, a letter appeared in *The New York Times* from Professor Edward Hubler of Princeton, who said he wanted to set the record straight once and for all, in the name of O'Neill's "kindliness and the gentleness of his nature," and of Princeton's characteristic tendency "to take a tolerant view of the manly follies." The fact of the matter, wrote Professor Hubler, is that O'Neill received a suspension of no more than two weeks for throwing at and breaking some glass insulators on trolley wires, as one of a gang of boys walking back to Princeton from Trenton. (At any rate, O'Neill apparently never returned to college until he started receiving honorary degrees—Eds.)

---

hoodlum for its own with an honorary degree, I found myself in New Haven late one night viewing a number of old boys of the class of 1880 or thereabouts having a hot reunion with themselves. Three of them in particular, that I ran across on one of the street-corners, were so grandly stewed that I had to stand still and watch them. One of them, it appeared, was president of a big bank in New York; another was vice-president of one of the big railroads; and the third was a United States Senator. After playing leap-frog for about ten minutes, during which one of them fell down and rolled half-way into a sewer, the three, singing barber-shop at the top of their lungs, wobbled across the street to the opposite corner where there was a mail-box. With a lot of grunts and after much steaming and puffing, the bank president and the vice-president of the big railroad got down on their knees and hoisted their old classmate, the Senator, up on their shoulders in a line with the slit in the mail-box. Whereupon the Senator proceeded to use the mail-box for a purpose generally reserved for telegraph poles and the sides of barns."

The boisterous roar that followed his recollection of the scene marked, as I have said, the only time within my knowledge of O'Neill that he has laughed outright at anything. In all the years I have known him, the most that has ever issued from him has been a quiet little chuckle and I have only, in all that time, heard him chuckle twice, once in New York when he indulged in a reminiscence of the wonderful free-lunch that he and his brother Jim used to get with a five-cent glass of beer (and live on) in a saloon opposite the old Madison Square Garden, and once at Le Plessis, in France, when he handed me a newspaper article in Spanish, treating of the time he once spent in Buenos Aires during his sailor days, asked me to translate it for him, and I inserted several imaginary paragraphs describing in rich detail his great proficiency as a tango dancer. He is constitutionally the antithesis of *l'homme qui rit.* Nothing even faintly amuses him, unless it be the remembrance of his dead brother's gift for Rabelaisian monkeyshines, the singing (in a voice capable of just three notes, all sour) of old barroom ballads, or remembered tales of his father, the late James O'Neill who, during the years when he was a matinée idol, used to parade Fourteenth Street at high noon daily—after at least three hours spent in dolling himself up—by way of giving the girls a treat, and who always made it a practice on Sundays to get to church half an hour late by way of staging an effective entrance for himself.

Contrary to finding amusement in the world, O'Neill finds endlessly the materials for indignation. The body of his dramatic writing reflects him more closely, I venture to say, than that of any other playwright in the present-day American theatre. Let the dramatic critic of some yokel newspaper in some yokel town that he has never even heard of write that he isn't all he should be as a dramatist, and he lets out a vituperative blast of such volume that, once done, he finds himself completely exhausted. Several times I myself have been denounced, if somewhat more politely, for expressed opinions on his work. Once, he let me read the manuscript of his play, *Welded*, in which he had great faith. When I reported to him that all I could discern in it was some very third-rate Strindberg, he sharply observed that I couldn't conceivably understand any such play as I had never been married, put on his hat, walked out and didn't let me hear from him for two months afterward. When, several years later, he sent me the manuscript of *Lazarus Laughed* and I wrote to him that I didn't care for it, he replied in the next mail that my judgment of it couldn't be taken seriously by him because I was lacking in all religious feeling and was therefore prejudiced against any such play, and that it was really a masterpiece whatever I thought about it. On this occasion, he was so disgusted with my critical gifts that he didn't write to me again for three months. The same thing happened in the case of *Dynamo*, which in a preliminary manuscript reading struck me as being close to caricature. Even after the play was produced and almost unanimously condemned, he stuck to his loyalty toward it and to his conviction that all the critics were dolts. "It maybe wasn't all it should have been," he subsequently admitted to me, "because I was going through a lot of trouble in family matters when I was writing it, but just the same you're dead wrong about it." And—I happened to be visiting him at the time—he sulked for the rest of the day and condescended only to exchange a curt good night with me at bed-time. If a newspaper or any other kind of photographer snaps him without his formal permission, he seethes. If he gets a letter with something in it that displeases him, he mutters sourly over it for twenty-four hours. The petty nuisances and annoyances that every man suffers and quickly dismisses from mind and attention cause him something bordering on acute agony.

After many years of being very hard up, his plays gradually began to make him money. But real money came only with the tremendous success, both as a performed play and published book, of *Strange Interlude*, which netted him close to a half-million dollars. Since boyhood, he had had just two wishes: one, to have some shirts tailored by a first-class London shirtmaker and, two, to own a carriage dog such as he had seen loping after the rigs of the rich in his youngster days. His greatest satisfaction in *Strange Interlude* was that it had made the gratification of the two wishes possible.

He has a dislike of meeting people that amounts almost to a terror. Even with his few close friends he is generally so taciturn that it is sometimes necessary to go over and poke him to make certain that he is neither asleep nor dead. He sits glumly for hours at a time without opening his mouth, brooding deeply over some undecipherable concern which, upon ultimate revelation, turns out to be a worried speculation as to whether his wife has ordered spaghetti, his favorite dish, for dinner for him that night. Having sat at different tables with him countless times, I have, with rare exception, heard him during the course of a meal say more than two words and they have invariably been—in reply to an inquiry as to whether he would care for any more of this or that—"Why sure." The way to lose O'Neill's friendship is to ask him for oral expressions of opinion on anything (if he feels like expressing an opinion, he will write a letter, and a satisfactorily long one), or to introduce him to any man other than one who knows a great deal about professional sports and who will confine his conversation to that subject. The one great admiration that he has temporarily achieved for any man in the last four years was for Sparrow Robertson, the chief sporting writer of the Paris *Herald*, whom he met just once and found to be "a grand bird." He has a great respect for Sean O'Casey, but beyond that an aversion to most men of his own profession, asserting that the majority of them are not worth the powder to blow them up, and of all those whom he has met in later years only W. S. Maugham and H. R. Lenormand have any interest for him. He goes to a theatre about once in every five years and then only in Europe because he has heard that some play of his is being done there in a language that he cannot understand. I have known him on only one occasion really to admit that he had been in a theatre. That was when the Russian Tairoff did *All God's Chillun* in Russian in Paris several years ago. He professed to have found it the best production of any of his plays that he had ever seen. "But," I protested, "you don't know a word of Russian. How could *you* tell?" He looked at me pityingly. "You should have seen the way Tairoff's wife, in the rôle of the girl, brushed those books off the table in that scene in the last act!" he replied with grave seriousness.

Displaying outwardly all the glow and effervescence of a magnum of ice water, he is internally given to huge enthusiasms of all sorts and varieties. Whatever piece of work he happens currently to be working on arouses him to such a pitch of incandescence over its virtues that he will go around all day wreathed in broad, mysterious smiles. And when O'Neill thus smiles, it is as if any other man stood gleefully on his head, waved his arms and legs and let out a bellow that shook the heavens. Familiar with all his longer, as well as with a number of his shorter plays, since their manuscript infancy, I recall only one time when doubt over a script that he was writing assailed him. In all the other cases he was as excited over their merits as a child of the wealthy anticipating on Christmas Eve the gifts he was certain to get. The one exception was a trilogy which he had undertaken. "Would to God," he wrote me, "that this damned trilogy of mine were off of my neck! I'm beginning to hate it and curse the day I ever conceived such an idea. The notion haunts me that I've bitten off a good deal more than I can chew. On my return, the first two acts of the first play struck me as not right, so I've started to rewrite them. And so it goes on! It looks as if the rest of my life was doomed to be spent rewriting the damned thing. I honestly feel very low about it and am anxious to get done with it and free my mind from the obsession of it and get on to something else. When these two acts are done, for better or worse, I'm going to call quits. I don't think I can go through the ordeal of typing it myself now. I'm too fed up. Think it wiser to get it typed. It would bore me so that before the end I would probably burn it."

But not so usually. Confidence generally permeates his being, warming him to the very toes. He says nothing, or at best very little, but the mysterious smiles embroider his features. Of *The Straw*, he informed me, "I have complete confidence in my own valuation of it." "Where the Cross Is Made," was "great fun to write, theatrically very thrilling, an amusing experiment in treating the audience as insane." "I would like to stand or fall"—in each instance—"by 'Bound East for Cardiff,' 'The Long Voyage Home,' 'The Moon of the Caribbees,' *Beyond the Horizon*, *The Straw* and *Gold*," he wrote me. Each of these plays, he duly announced, was "my sincerest effort and was written purely for its own sake." Of *All God's Chillun Got Wings*—"Well, I've got it done and I'm immensely pleased with it!" Of *Desire Under the Elms*—"Its poetical vision illuminating even the most sordid and mean blind alleys of life—that is my justification as a dramatist!" Of *Marco Millions*—"there's a whole lot of poetical beauty in it and fine writing." *The Great God Brown* was "a devastating, crucifying new one." *Lazarus Laughed* was "*far* the best play I've ever written." Of *Dynamo*—"I thoroughly disagree with you about the play. It is *not* far, far below me. I'm sure of that! Wait and see! It will come into its own some day when it isn't judged as a symbolical trilogy with a message to good Americans about what's wrong with them and what to do about it. I think you're wrong this time—as wrong as about *Lazarus Laughed*. Not that you're not right about the excessiveness of the stage directions, but then I thought you knew that my scripts get drastically weeded out in that respect when I read proof and that I always let them slide as they first occur to me until then. A slovenly method, perhaps, but the way I've always worked. Then again, I don't think it's fair to take the speeches of a lot of admittedly inarticulate characters in a particular play as expressions of the general underlying theme of a trilogy—which I obviously never intended them to be." Indeed, even in the case of the later trilogy, *Mourning Becomes Electra*, about which there were the preliminary doubts already recorded, I received, when the play at length was finished, this comment: "It has been one hell of a job! Let's hope the result in some measure justifies the labor I've put in. To get enough of Clytemnestra in Christine, of Electra in Lavinia, of Orestes in Orin, etc., and yet keep them American primarily; to conjure a Greek fate out of the Mannons themselves (without calling in the aid of even a Puritan

Old Testament God) that would convince a modern audience without religion or moral ethics; to prevent the surface melodrama of the plot from overwhelming the real drama; to contrive murders that escape cops and courtroom scenes; and finally to keep myself out of it and shun the many opportunities for effusions of personal writing anent life and fate—all this has made the going tough and the way long! And even now it's done I don't know quite what I've got. All I *do* know is that after reading it all through, in spite of my familiarity with every page, it leaves me moved and disturbed spiritually, and I have a feeling of there being real size in it, quite apart from its length; a sense of having had a valid dramatic experience with intense tortured passions beyond the ambition or scope of other modern plays. As for the separate parts, each play, each act, seem better than I hoped. And that's that."

Wherever he happens to be at the moment happens enthusiastically also to be the place of all places for him to be and forever live in. Provincetown was "ideal, quiet, and the only place where I could ever work." When in Bermuda, he wrote me, "I didn't start this letter with any view of boring you by an expounding of inner principles. It was rather to recommend Bermuda to you as a place to 'take the waters' in case you're planning a Spring vacation. The climate is grand. The German bottled beer and English bottled ale are both excellent. And the swimming is wonderful, if you like such, which I do above everything. It has proved a profitable Winter resort for me. I've gotten more work done than in the corresponding season up North in many years." When at Belgrade Lakes, in Maine, he sent me a postcard: "There's tranquillity here. A place to think and work if ever there was one! Ideal for me." "Well, after a week in London," he wrote, "I am strong for it! It seems to me that if it were possible for me to live contented in any city this would be the one. There is something so self-assuredly nerveless about it. Of course, the weather has been unexpectedly fine—warm and sunny every day—and that helps. In short, I've been happier here since I left New York than ever in my life before." While he was living in Guéthary in the Basque country, I received the following: "The Basque country and the Basques hit me right where I belong! According to present plans and inclinations it is here that I shall settle down to make a home for the rest of my days. Europe has meant a tremendous lot to me, more than I ever hoped it could. I've felt a deep sense of peace here, a real enjoyment in just living from day to day, that I've never known before. For more than the obvious financial reasons, I've come to the conclusion that anyone doing creative work is a frightful sap to waste the amount of energy required to beat life in the U. S. A. when over here one can have just that more strength to put into one's job." When he was in Indo-China, this arrived: "This is the place! There is nothing more beautiful and interesting in the world. It is grand!" Settled for several years in Touraine, he wrote: "This is the place for me! The most beautiful part of France. Here is the ideal place to live and work!" During a motor trip through Spain, I received three postcards from him at different times. One, from Madrid, conveyed this message: "I've never seen a more beautiful spot. It would be a great place to work in." One, from Granada, this: "Spain is most interesting and I'm darn glad we picked it out for a vacation. Granada is quiet, peaceful and immensely attractive. What a place to live and work in!" One, from Malaga, this: "This is the best place I have ever struck in Europe—Really good stuff! It'd be a swell place to live and work in." Returned to New York again, he said to me, "Why I ever left here, damned if I know. There's life and vitality here. It's the place for ideas! This is the spot for me and my work!" His present passion is for a small island off the Georgia coast. "The best place to live and work I've ever found!"

O'Neill and Sinclair Lewis are alike in one respect. Both have naturally a boyish quality, an innocent artlessness in a number of directions, that will doubtless remain with them to their last years. In it lies much of their charm. Lewis is as excited over a party as any débutante, and a trip to Hoboken on the ferry works him up to a degree of delight comparable only to Robert Fulton's first sensation when he saw his steamboat actually working. O'Neill, for all his solemn exterior, gets an unparalleled pleasure from splashing around in a swimming pool and making funny gurgling noises, from putting on the fancily colored dressing gowns he bought several years ago in China, from singing raucous duets with a crony—"Rosie, You Are My Posy" and "'Twas Christmas in the Harem" are two of his favorites, from lying on the ground and letting Blemie, his pet dog, crawl over him, the meanwhile tickling him on the bottom, from watches with bells in them, from the idea that one day he may master the accordian and be as proficient a performer as the vaudeville headliner, Phil Baker, and from drinking enormous glasses of Coca-Cola and making everyone believe it is straight whiskey. When his very lovely wife, Carlotta, comes down to dinner in some particularly striking gown, his face lights up like a county fair. She knows well the effect it has on him and quietly lays in a constantly replenished wardrobe for his relish. "Do you like it?" she will delicately ask on each occasion. And, though his infinite satisfaction is clearly to be perceived, like a little boy who doesn't want to give in and admit anything too quickly, he will invariably mumble, "Well, it's pretty, but I like blue better."

Years ago, he was a drinker of parts. In fact, there were times when he went on benders that lasted a whole month and times when he slept next to the bung-hole of a whiskey barrel at Jimmy the Priest's and when Jimmy, the proprietor, coming to work the next morning, found the barrel one-eighth gone. About four or five years ago, however, he hoisted himself onto the water-wagon and has since sat thereon with an almost puritanical splendor and tenacity. Like many another reformed bibber, he now views the wine-cup with a superior dudgeon and is on occasion not averse to delivering himself of eloquent harangues against it and its evils. It is not easy to forget his pious indignation when Barrett Clark once ventured to mention his old drinking bouts to him. "Altogether too much damned nonsense has been written since the beginning of time about the dissipation of artists!" he exploded. "Why, there are fifty times more real drunkards among the Bohemians who play at art, and probably more than that among the people who never think about art at all. The artist drinks, when he drinks at all (note the whimsy of that *at all*), for relaxation, forgetfulness, excitement, for any purpose except his art!" So today, it is Coca-Cola, followed by Kalak, with vengeance.

O'Neill is very slow in making friends. He tests a potential friendship much after the technique of a fisherman, trying out various personal and metaphysical lines, flies, and worms to determine what kind of fish the stranger is and to what degree, personally or philosophically, he resembles a sucker. Once he has made a friend for himself, that man remains a friend, in his eyes, until Hell freezes. In all the world I suppose that there are not more than five men at the very most whom O'Neill really regards as friends, and at least three of these are relics of his early more or less disreputable days in Greenwich Village and the adjacent gin-mills. I had known him for exactly ten years until we got to the point where we called each other by our first names.

He has done much of his more recent writing in an enormous chair that he had manufactured for himself in England. It is a cross between a dentist's and a barber's chair, with all sorts of pull-in and pull-out contrivances attached to it and with a couple of small shelves for reference books. A board is so arranged that it can be manoeuvred in front of him and on it he rests his pad. Stripped to the waist—he never works, if he can help it, with anything on above his navel—and with his legs stretched out to their full length, he writes everything in long hand and his chirography is so minute that it takes a magnifying glass for average eyes comfortably to read it.

I have never known him to tell a smoking-car story and, if someone happens to venture one while he is around, he sits silent and wide-eyed at its conclusion, as if he couldn't possibly understand it and wonders just what the point is. As for himself, he has just one story and will repeat it, to his apparent own infinite amusement, on the slightest provocation. It is the venerable one known as "The Old Bean," and concerns the braggadocio of an old souse who, despite all the dire catastrophes that befall him, imagines that the tremendous shrewdness of his intellect allows him on all occasions to get the best of everyone else. It is a long story, lasting at least an hour if related at top speed, and I have heard it from him regularly twice a year. Once, telling it to me again and embroidering its details, it occupied the entire time it took us to walk the seven miles from Le Plessis to Tours. The sole other occasion for unwonted loquacity on his part is the reminiscence of his vagrant New York days at the dive known as the Hell Hole and at Jimmy the Priest's where, with a pot-companion named Joe Smith, he shared a room—which they always referred to as "the garbage flat"—for the fine sum of three dollars a month. His particular comrades at Jimmy's, in addition to Joe, included a number of odoriferous colored gentlemen, a press-agent for Paine's Fireworks named Jimmy Beith, and one Major Adams, a red-nosed inebriate of sixty-odd who had been cashiered years before from the British army. This fraternity, hardly ever with more than fifty cents at a time in its combined treasury, subsisted on raw whiskey for breakfast and on what free lunch it could cabbage off the end of the bar during the rest of the day. From time to time, other habitués of the place were accepted into the fold, including an old sea captain named Chris Christopherson, whom O'Neill in later years incorporated name and all into his play, *Anna Christie*, a sailor named Driscoll, whose name suggested to him the Driscoll of "Bound East for Cardiff," "The Moon of the Caribbees" and "In the Zone," and a septuagenarian miser who had lived in a small, bare room above the saloon for twenty-two years, who never could persuade himself to throw away a newspaper and who could hardly find room enough to sleep on the floor for the enormous stacks of accumulated copies of *The New York Times*. The favorite tipple of the brotherhood, when one or another of the members—usually O'Neill, who at intervals would contrive to cozen a dollar out of his father—managed in some way to get hold of the price, was, aside from the breakfast rye, Benedictine drunk by the tumblerful. But such treats were rare and makeshifts were necessary. Alcohol mixed with camphor was found—after one got used to the taste—to have a pretty effect. Varnish diluted with water was also discovered to have its points. And there were days when even wood alcohol mixed in small doses with sarsaparilla, with just a soupçon of benzine to give it a certain bouquet, was good enough, in the brothers' view, for any man who wasn't a sissy.

For weeks on end, the brotherhood would sit, or lie, in Jimmy's without stirring out for even a moment's breath of air. That is, all save the Major, who had a hobby for collecting old and wholly useless books of all descriptions, which he never read, and for attending funerals. If he came home any evening without at least three frowzy books garnered from God knows where or without having attended at least two funerals of persons entirely unknown to him, he would mope for the rest of the night and would regain his cheer only after he had drunk a half dozen or so toasts to His Majesty, the King, in beakers of varnish. It was apparently not the royal toasts, however, that caused the Major's demise, but something ponderously diagnosed by a hastily summoned neighborhood medico as "malicious liver complaint." The Major's funeral was a gala affair, with the remaining brotherhood so melancholiously but none the less richly in its cups that no fewer than three of the mourners lost their balance and tumbled into the grave on top of their late brother's coffin.

Nor was it the nature of the brotherhood's refreshments that unwound the mortal coil of Brother Beith. Learning one night, while full of Pond's Extract mixed with one-eighth whiskey and three-eighths gasoline, that his dear wife, whom he had forgotten all about in the fifteen years he hadn't laid eyes on her, had run off with a fellow in South Africa, he committed suicide by jumping out of one of Jimmy's upper windows. Beith's suicide, together with certain personal emotional misfortunes in an encounter with Cupid, weighed upon O'Neill's mind and—now it may be told—a month or so after Beith took his life the man who was to become the first of American dramatists attempted, with an overdose of veronal, to follow suit. When, one afternoon at two o'clock—the conventional hour for rising and having whiskey breakfast—O'Neill failed to stir, failed even to respond to the brothers' nudges, pokes and peremptory kicks, an ambulance was quickly summoned and our friend was carted off at a gallop to Bellevue. With the brothers grouped solicitously about his cot, two internes worked over him for an hour before he again gave signs of life. Three hours later, the dose of veronal not having been so large as he believed, O'Neill was back in the world once more and, with a whoop of joy, the brothers put on their hats and moved mysteriously toward the door. "We'll be back soon," they observed significantly—and were gone. Four hours later, they reappeared, all beautifully and magnificently drunk. It developed that they had rushed to O'Neill's father and had got fifty dollars from him to pay the hospital fee for his son's resuscitation. "You dirty bums!" groaned O'Neill, with what vocal strength he could muster. "How much you got left?" Thirty-two dollars, they reluctantly informed him. "All right, divide!" he insisted. And with his sixteen dollars safe in hand, he rolled over, grinned satisfiedly, and went happily and peacefully to sleep.

We were sitting one late Summer afternoon about two years ago in my rooms in the Avenue Maréchal Foch, in Paris, looking out at the merry-go-round of motor cars in the Étoile and at the Arc de

Triomphe in the sinking sun. I asked him—his reflective mood seemed to inspire the question—what he would like more than anything else out of life.

"The Nobel Prize?" I hinted out of the side of my apéritif glass.

"On careful consideration—and no sour grapes about it because I have had no hopes—I think the Nobel Prize, until you become very old and childlike, costs more than it's worth. It's an anchor around one's neck that one would never be able to shake off," he answered, gulping his tea.

"A more intelligent critical appraisal of your work?" I smiled.

His ears, as is their wont when critics and criticism are mentioned, stood setter-like and challenging on end. "I expect denunciation! It's generally sure to come. But I'm getting awfully callous to the braying, for or against. When they knock me, what the devil!, they're really boosting me with their wholesale condemnations, for the reaction against such nonsense will come soon enough. These tea-pot turmoils at least keep me shaken up and convinced I'm on my way to something. I know enough history to realize that no one worth a damn ever escaped them—so it gives me hope. When I'm generally approved of, I begin to look in the mirror very skeptically and contemplate taking up some other career I might succeed at. So it's all tonic."

He finished his tea.

"I'll tell you what I want and it's the God's truth. I want just what I've now at last and for the first time in my life got! Life has certainly changed for me in the last year or so and for the first time in God knows how long I feel as if it had something to give me as a living being quite outside of the life in my work. The last time I saw you I told you I was happy. A rash statement, but I now make it again with a tenfold emphasis. And, believe me, it has stood tests that would have wrecked it if it wasn't the genuine article. I feel younger and more pepped up with the old zest for living and working than I've ever felt since I started working. I may seem to slop over a bit, but you don't know into what a bog of tedium and life-sickness I was sinking. I was living on my work as a fellow does on his nerves sometimes, and sooner or later my work would certainly have been sapped of its life because you can't keep on that way forever, even if you put up the strongest of bluffs to yourself and the world in general. Now I feel as if I'd tapped a new life and could rush up all the reserves of energy in the world to back up my work. Honestly, it's a sort of miracle to me I'd become so resigned to the worst. So be a little indulgent and don't mind my unloading a little of the pop-eyed wonder of it at you!"

At this point Carlotta, his wife, came in, put her arm around him and kissed him.

"Where've you been?" he asked, his face suddenly lapsing again into that perverse little-boy expression.

Carlotta gave him another little kiss.

"I've been shopping for dresses, Genie dear," she said. "Blue ones."

Croswell Bowen

THE BLACK IRISHMAN

That just and merciful God in Whom Eugene O'Neill has struggled to believe ever since he was 13 and lost his Faith, certainly endowed him with a family, an environment and a temperament extraordinarily favorable to the making of a playwright.

The theatre was in his bones: His father was the celebrated James O'Neill, an actor of the old uninhibited school who played the lead in *The Count of Monte Cristo* some 6,000 times, and a substantial part of Eugene's childhood was spent in theatre wings.

Dramatic conflict was part of his earliest life: His mother, born Ella Quinlan, was a devout Catholic who, Eugene remembers, never approved of her husband's profession but, because she was an old-fashioned wife, followed him wherever he went. In addition that part of Eugene's boyhood that was spent away from the theatre centered around the waterfront in New London, Conn., where he could absorb the romance of the sea, and sense the dry rot of provincial New England.

But most important of all was the disposition through which Eugene has always viewed the world. Recently in New London, "Captain" Thomas Francis Dorsey, an intimate friend of James O'Neill and something of a fabulous Irishman himself, was discussing Eugene whom he had known well as a boy.

"Always the gloomy one," the Captain said, "always the tragedian, always thinkin'. My God, when he looked at you he seemed to be lookin' right through you, right into your soul. He never said much and then spoke softly when he did speak. Brilliant he was too, always readin' books. We're all Irish around here and knew the type. He was a real Black Irishman."

A Black Irishman, the Captain went on to explain, is an Irish-

From PM, *November 3, 1946. Reprinted by permission of the author and the Executors of the Estate of Marshall Field.*

man who has lost his Faith and who spends his life searching for the meaning of life, for a philosophy in which he can believe again as fervently as he once believed in the simple answers of the Catholic Catechism. A Black Irishman is a brooding, solitary man—and often a drinking man too—with wild words on the tip of his tongue. American letters are the richer for Black Irishmen. And of the lot of them, and the list includes F. Scott Fitzgerald, James T. Farrell, and John O'Hara among others, O'Neill is the blackest one of all.

O'Neill himself gives full weight to his Irish heritage. Talking to his son, Eugene, Jr., a bearded professor of Greek, he said not long ago, "One thing that explains more than anything about me is the fact that I'm Irish. And, strangely enough, it is something that all the writers who have attempted to explain me and my work have overlooked."

It is no accident that O'Neill's newest play, *The Iceman Cometh*, certainly the biggest event of this season, is about "pipe dreams"—which may be a Black Irishman's name for Faith. It is no accident that its characters are lost men to whom the world and its ways are an eternally insoluble enigma. It is no accident that Larry Slade, the one character who at the end is left utterly without illusions, is a tired Anarchist and an Irishman.

It has been said by a number of reviewers that, when the curtain falls, nothing is left for Larry but to die. One observer has thought of an alternative. "Larry," he said, "could write plays."

James O'Neill and Ella Quinlan O'Neill, his wife, both came from substantial lace-curtain Irish Catholic families. James was born in the town of Thomastown, County Kilkenny, Ireland, Nov. 15, 1846, and was brought to America at the age of eight. His family settled in Cincinnati, Ohio. His wife was a Cincinnati girl, and they were married in 1875, after James O'Neill had established himself as an actor.

James and Ella O'Neill had three children. The first, Edmond Dantes, named after the hero in James's most successful play, *The Count of Monte Cristo*, died soon after birth. A year later a second son was born and was named James, Jr. The third son, Eugene Gladstone, was born 10 years after James, Jr., on Oct. 16, 1888.

Two years after James, Jr., had been born, the O'Neills had

moved from Cincinnati to a small cottage in New London which was a pleasant place to spend the Summer and not too far from New York. The cottage was the closest the road-touring O'Neills ever came to a real home.

James O'Neill was a very worldly man according to the standards of his wife who is still remembered by New Londoners as an "unworldly, saintly woman." His friend Tom Dorsey, however, remembers him as "a soft-hearted man, always good for a touch. He was a great Irishman, a great Democrat and good Catholic." He was one of the leading figures in town. There was only one man to rival him: Richard Mansfield. The two were not boon companions.

When the time came for Gene to go to school, he was sent to a Catholic Convent run by the Ursuline Sisters. There he learned his Catechism thoroughly:

> Who made the world?
> God made the world.
> Who is God?
> God is the Creator of heaven and earth,
> and of all things.
> What is man?
> Man is a creature composed of body and soul,
> and made to the image and likeness of God.

When Eugene was 13 and ready for high school, his parents sent him to a non-Catholic military school in New York City. It was there that he lost his Faith. He does not know exactly at what moment or why.

When he was 14, Gene entered Betts Academy at Stamford, Conn., to prepare for college. In the Fall of 1906, when he was 17, he enrolled at Princeton. He spent as much time as he could with his older brother, James, Jr., in New York. It was about that time that the great drinking legend about O'Neill began. From reports of what went on, it would seem that O'Neill and his fellow hellers did not surpass the later exploits of another Princetonian, F. Scott Fitzgerald. Certainly such drinking today is run of the ginmill.

Gene had scarcely put on long pants before Jimmie, 10 years

his senior, took him out on the town. Jimmie, in his middle 20s, was aspiring to be a New York newspaperman. Somehow, he never got around to doing much about his career because his drinking was more important to him. He thought it amusing to teach Gene to drink and be a heller with women. He even told his friends: "Gene learned sin more easily than other people. I made it easy for him."

But Jimmie did not make it easy for Gene to live with the feeling of guilt from which he never fully recovered. A Catholic who has lost his Faith travels a road on which there is no turning back and no destination. His conscience stays in his mind to plague him, but there is, for him, no Confession and no Absolution.

O'Neill pointed out recently that at an age when most young men were romantically in love with a "pure girl," he was "a Broadway wise-guy."

"At the time *Ah, Wilderness!* was on Broadway," he said, "many people said that I had written about my adolescence. The truth is that I had no youth. *Ah, Wilderness!* was a nostalgia for a youth I never had."

In the Spring of 1907, O'Neill was suspended from college. He and his undergraduate drinking companions had missed the milk train from New York to Princeton one Sunday night. This meant they had to get off a Trenton train at Princeton Junction. The drawbridge across Carnegie Lake was up and they had to swim across and walk several miles to college. En route, O'Neill threw a bottle through the window of the home of the division superintendent of the Pennsylvania Railroad. It was not, as the legend goes, President Wilson's house. Later that Spring O'Neill flunked all his final examinations and was dropped from the class.

His family were bitterly disappointed. Jimmie's drinking deeply had grieved both his mother and father, and now it looked as if Gene was going the way of Jimmie. O'Neill remembers his next four years as a period of "just drifting."

In the Summer of 1909, he drifted into a marriage with Kathleen Jenkins, a young girl he had met in New York. Both the O'Neill and Jenkins families objected to the marriage because Eugene was not making a living. A month or so after the wedding he sailed with a mining engineer for Spanish Honduras on a gold-mining expedition financed by his father. "At the end of six months I was invalided home, tropical malarial fever, no gold."

During his absence, his wife had borne a child who was named Eugene, Jr. When Gene came home, his wife continued to live with her family. Their marriage was terminated by divorce in 1912. O'Neill was not to see his firstborn until 1921 when the boy was 12.

Some months after his return, O'Neill went on a drinking spree in New York. One night he found himself with Jimmie on a train for New Orleans. When they arrived there, they found their father was in town acting in *The White Sister*. He refused to give the boys any money, but offered them work. Gene was made assistant manager. He toured with the show for three months before deciding he didn't like theatrical life. Finally, his father, disgusted with his son's drinking and apparent unwillingness to work, acted in his New London home one of the greatest scenes in his dramatic life, charging Eugene with filial ingratitude, and the wasting of precious opportunities.

"Go before the mast!" he told his son.

Eugene's first voyage was on a Norwegian freighter, 65 days to Buenos Aires. There he got a job with Westinghouse, then with Swift and Co., and later with the Singer Co. His father had cut him off from any family funds, and the jobs only served to keep him alive. His real interest was in bumming around the waterfronts and drinking with the men and women he met there.

At one point, he says, he was in complete destitution in Buenos Aires, and signed as a seaman on a British tramp steamer bound for New York. There, he lived at a lower West Side hotel and bar called Jimmy the Priest's "where you could sleep with your head on the table if you bought a schooner of beer." He was later to make Jimmie the Priest's the scene of *The Iceman Cometh*. From New York, he occasionally shipped out as a seaman, going to South Africa and England.

O'Neill expressed his revolt from his well-to-do, almost Victorian upbringing by this period of almost two years when he was completely at sea.

The return of the prodigal son, however, was not quite the

joyous reunion the elder O'Neill might have hoped for. Eugene ended his wanderings by turning up at the stage door of a theatre in New Orleans where his father, as usual, was playing *Monte Cristo*. His father once again dreamed of Gene's accepting the heritage of his family and becoming a great actor. He was given the part of the jailor in *Monte Cristo*. He wasn't very good, he didn't like acting and he didn't like the play. As the tour wore on, his father complained about the quality of his son's performances.

"It is a wonder," his son said gravely, "that in a play like *Monte Cristo* I can do *anything* at all."

When the tour ended in the Spring, the O'Neills went home to New London. The publisher of the New London *Telegraph*, Frederick P. Latimer, a friend of the O'Neills, had a special fondness for Gene and a sympathy with his love of reading books and his intellectual and spiritual probings. He knew Gene liked to write sea poems, and he gave him a job as a reporter on the *Telegraph*. Part of the job was to write a piece of verse twice a week for a column on the editorial page called *Laconics*.

Latimer gave Gene a feeling of confidence he had never gotten from his family. "He's the first one," O'Neill wrote to Barrett H. Clark, one of his biographers, "who really thought I had something to say, and believed I could say it." Latimer later told Clark that when he and O'Neill "used to talk together and argue our different philosophies, I thought he was the most stubborn and irreconcilable social rebel that I had ever met."

All summer and fall, Gene worked as a reporter and rewrite man. He covered the waterfront, attended meetings, interviewed town leaders. In *Laconics* he wrote verse about "The sullen vessel straining at its chain" and "The bright green lawns that lean down to the bay" and he kidded his job:

When my dreams come true all my comments wise and sage
Will be featured double column on the editor's own page.
Personals will be no object, I won't have to go and hunt
The history of the tugboats that infest the waterfront.
Fire alarms may go to blazes, suicides and murders too,
I'll be editing Laconics *when my dreams come true.*

That Summer he also fell in love.

"That was a long time ago," he said recently, when he was

asked if the love poems he wrote for *Laconics* were autobiographical. "She's married, I understand, to a highly placed person."

Her name was Beatrice and the legend of Gene O'Neill's great love for the tall beautiful choir singer with the voice of an angel still persists in New London.

In October, 1912, he wrote:

Is all off twixt I and you?
Will you go and wed some other gent?
The things I done, I'd fain undo,
Since thou hast went.

At the end of November, he composed a long poem for *Laconics* called "The Lay of the Singer's Fall." He expressed his general disillusionment with life and with love:

And the singer was sad and he turned to Love
And the arms of his ladye faire,
He sang of her eyes as the stars above
He sang of—and kissed—her hair;
Till the Devil whispered, "I fondly trust
This is folly and nought beside,
For the greatest of loves is merely lust!"
—And the soul of the singer died.

Three years later, O'Neill contributed to *The Conning Tower* in the New York *Tribune* some verses entitled "Speaking, to the Shade of Dante, of Beatrices."

"She doesn't class with mine at all," he wrote of Dante's Beatrice. That ends the story of O'Neill and Beatrice. But we may learn more some day. One of O'Neill's unproduced plays, *The Long Day's Journey into Night*, is locked up in a safe with instructions that it is not to be produced until 25 years after his death. O'Neill, however, has revealed a few details. It concerns the period of his life when he knew Beatrice. One of the characters in the play is still living.

On Dec. 9, 1912, O'Neill wrote his last poem for the *Telegraph*, "To Winter":

My eyes are red, my lips are blue
My ears frost bitt'n;

Thy numbing kiss doth e'en extend
Thro' my mitten.
. . . O Winter, greater bards have sung I loathe thee!

A few days later a doctor told him he had a touch of tuberculosis. On Christmas Eve he entered Gaylord Farm Sanatorium on the top of a windswept hill overlooking the Housatonic River at Wallingford, Conn.

What happened to him there, he was to describe later, in 1923, in the *Journal of Outdoor Life:*

> It was at Gaylord that my mind got the chance to establish itself, to digest and evaluate the impressions of many past years [he was just 24] in which one experience had crowded on another with never a second's reflections. At Gaylord I really thought about my life for the first time, about past and future. Undoubtedly the inactivity forced upon me by life at a san [patient's slang for sanitorium] forced me to mental activity, especially as I had always been high-strung and nervous temperamentally.

It was in the sanatorium that O'Neill, who liked composing poetry and had considered writing fiction, decided to be a playwright.

At the end of May, 1913, O'Neill was told that his TB was arrested and he was discharged from the san.

Recently, O'Neill was asked what he thought had suddenly happened to him at this time to cause him to begin a period of sustained creative effort from which he has never since wavered:

> I kept writing, he said, because I had such a love of it. I was highly introspective, intensely nervous and self-conscious. I was very tense, I drank to overcome my shyness.
>
> When I was writing I was alive.
>
> I could scarcely write, if at all, and live in the city. I would pick a place out of the ordinary run of places to do my writing.

One of the places he picked was a hut on the coast at Provincetown, Mass.

The discovery of what writing did for him was perhaps a substitute for the Faith he'd lost at 13, O'Neill said recently. His life at the san, he thinks, was almost a religious experience in which he faced the possibility of death, looked for a new faith and found it in creative writing.

The elder James O'Neill, then 59, was glad that his younger son had finally found some reasonably respectable work. It wasn't acting, but writing plays was connected with the theater.

"He did believe in me—in a way," O'Neill wrote later, explaining that his feeling of guilt because he had not become a great man in the eyes of his father was lessened. "But as I've said, he just thought I was crazy. He didn't see why I should write the kind of plays I did because there was no market for them, but he must have thought there was something to them. He believed I might some day amount to something—if I lived."

O'Neill destroyed the first 11 plays he wrote. Until a few years ago he thought they were gone forever. However, when Archibald MacLeish became head of the Library of Congress, he found that O'Neill had filed the plays with the copyright office, and they had therefore come into the archives of the library. For most of O'Neill's early plays he drew on his experience at sea.

The Gorham Press in Boston offered to print *Thirst* and four other early Eugene O'Neill plays in their American Dramatists Series. Richard G. Badger, head of the publishing house, wanted costs of printing guaranteed by the author. James O'Neill provided the money and 1,000 copies of *Thirst* were printed. Very few were sold, and the actor didn't recover his investment. Today a copy of *Thirst* is worth about $75.

In the Fall of 1914, James O'Neill also paid his son's tuition at Harvard to take English 47, George P. Baker's famous playwriting course which was later moved to Yale and expanded to the 47 Workshop, the drama department of the School of Fine Arts.

O'Neill wrote two sea plays while at Harvard and both were undistinguished. Baker also read a third, "Bound East for Cardiff," written before O'Neill entered the class. Baker's comment on it was that it was not a play at all, but it was the first O'Neill work to be produced. It was presented at the Wharf Theatre by the Provincetown Players in the Summer of 1916.

Two fellow students have written their impressions of him at Harvard:

". . . he was good-looking, very nervous, extremely impatient with 47, and anxious to get down to live in Greenwich Village. . . . He was friendly, though rather uneasy and inarticulate at times. . . . But when he delivered himself of a remark, it was impressive. . . ."

John V. A. Weaver, the poet wrote: "Women were forever calling for Gene. There was something apparently irresistible in his strong combination of cruelty (around the mouth) and boyish charm. One girl told me she could not get his face out of her thoughts. He was hard boiled and whimsical. He was brutal and tender. From shopgirl to society queen they all seemed to develop certain tendencies in his presence."

After his Harvard course, O'Neill did go down to live in Greenwich Village. In the Summer he went to his hut in Provincetown. The drinking periods continued, followed by terrible remorse, and then by the days of seclusion.

"The legend that I wrote my plays when I was drunk," O'Neill has said, "is absurd. It was when I was not writing that I drank. I'd drink for a month and then go out and snap out of it by myself. It was during these periods that I wrote."

For more than a year after leaving Harvard, O'Neill wrote comparatively little, according to a date table of his plays which he later drew up for the late Richard Dana Skinner, drama critic of the Catholic *Commonweal*. Then, in the Winter of 1917, at his Provincetown hut, he wrote four sea plays: "In the Zone," "Ile," "The Long Voyage Home" and "Moon of the Caribbees."

O'Neill's poor health prevented his being drafted in the First World War. How he felt about it he told his eldest son recently. Eugene, Jr., was rejected by the Army on physical grounds during the Second World War. He remarked to his playwright father that although he had escaped, he was sorry not to have taken part in so important an experience.

"You have escaped now, but it will catch up with you in the end," the playwright said.

In 1918, O'Neill married a slender ash-blonde girl from New York named Agnes Boulton. Author of a novel, *The Road Before Us*, and very friendly and sociable, she attempted to make less of a recluse of her husband.

Barrett Clark, who wrote an authorized biography of O'Neill, noted as of 1926 that "the marriage has been happy and successful. . . . To Mrs. O'Neill the dramatist owes a great deal more than can be properly set down in these pages." Certainly during this marriage, he produced some of his best work: *Beyond the Horizon* (Pulitzer Prize winner), *Anna Christie* (Pulitzer Prize winner), *Emperor Jones*, *Desire Under the Elms*, *The Great God Brown*, and *Strange Interlude* (Pulitzer Prize winner).

Two children were born of this (his second) marriage, and to both he gave traditional Irish names suggested by James Stephens: Shane, born a year and a half after his marriage, and Oona, born five years later.

Oona, in 1943, when she was 18, married Charlie Chaplin, then 54. Although Mrs. Agnes O'Neill said she was "very happy" about the marriage, Eugene O'Neill told friends he did not approve. He refuses now to discuss the matter.

Recently, O'Neill confirmed an apparently apochryphal story about his first Broadway play. He had been sitting one day on the beach at Provincetown looking out across the sea. A little boy sat beside him asking questions. O'Neill was gentle and patient:

"What's beyond the ocean?"
"Europe."
"What's beyond Europe?"
"The horizon."
"What's beyond the horizon?" the little boy persisted.

Beyond the Horizon opened at the Morosco Theatre in New York on Feb. 2, 1920. With his first Broadway production O'Neill won the Pulitzer Prize.

It was the story of two brothers, a materialist and a dreamer, in love with the same girl. The materialist, who was about to embark on a sea voyage, loses out. In the end, the rich materialist returns to find his brother dying. The girl falls in love with him, but it is too late. People live, O'Neill concluded, by dreaming about something beyond the horizon, something they can never attain.

Sixty-three-year-old James O'Neill attended the play's opening night. Although he couldn't figure out why, he knew the audience was receiving it favorably. Afterward, congratulating his son, he said: "Are you trying to send the audience home to commit suicide?" But there were tears of gladness in his eyes; his boy had made good in the theatre.

In the Winter of 1921–22, O'Neill began rehearsals for *The Hairy Ape*. For the part of Mildred Douglas, the girl in white who calls out "Oh, the filthy beast" and faints when she sees the hairy ape stoking the furnace in the ship's hold, he cast Carlotta Monterey. She was beautiful and an experienced actress. Her performance in *The Hairy Ape* was good.

A year later, Carlotta Monterey married Ralph Barton, caricaturist on *The New Yorker*. Seven years later she was to marry Eugene O'Neill.

In 1922, Eugene O'Neill, Jr., the playwright's son by his first wife, met his father for the first time. The first Mrs. O'Neill had remarried and was living in New York. O'Neill and his ex-wife discussed the boy's future, and O'Neill agreed to take on the responsibility for his son's education.

Father and son liked each other immediately. Eugene, Jr., had been brought up to feel very friendly toward the father he had never met. The more he heard about his father, the better he liked him.

In the Winter of 1920 the elder James O'Neill, then living in New York, had been struck by an automobile and knocked to the pavement. He had been taken to a hospital and, when he had recovered sufficiently, had had himself moved to New London to the Lawrence and Memorial Hospital. He had died there on Aug. 10, 1920.

"He came back to New London to die," Captain Dorsey said. There was a real Irish wake for the old actor. Gene and Jim came home for the funeral, and New Londoners remember that they mourned their father in the true Irish fashion—by drowning their sorrow.

By 1923, O'Neill had lost his mother and his brother. From then on his plays tended to become more and more preoccupied with death. In 1925, he wrote *The Great God Brown*. In one of the play's most moving passages, Dion speaks of his dead mother and father:

"What aliens we were to each other! When he lay dead, his face looked so familiar that I wondered where I had met that man before. Only at the second of my conception. After that, we grew hostile with concealed shame. And my mother? I remember a sweet strange girl, with affectionate, bewildered eyes as if God had locked her in a dark closet without any explanation. I was the sole doll, our ogre, her husband, allowed her and she played mother and child with me for many years in that house until at last through two years I watched her die with the shy pride of one who has lengthened her dress and put up her hair."

While he was married to Agnes Boulton, his second wife, Eugene O'Neill bought and sold two large homes, one in Ridgefield, Conn., and one in Bermuda. "He never could stay in any one place very long," a friend said. "Each time he'd buy a place, he'd be sure that that was where he wanted to spend the rest of his life."

During the '20s, O'Neill was turning out, in some years, as much as two complete plays.

In the Summer of 1926 O'Neill met Carlotta Monterey again. Miss Monterey, who came from a wealthy California family and had been divorced from Ralph Barton the year before, was visiting at the Belgrade Lakes in Maine where O'Neill and his family were spending the Summer.

O'Neill and Carlotta Monterey fell violently in love, their friends said. That Fall, O'Neill and his family returned to Bermuda, but two years later, on June 21, 1928, Agnes O'Neill announced that she would seek a divorce. On June 2, 1929, she obtained a decree in Reno.

Carlotta Monterey and O'Neill were seen together in 1928 and 1929 in various parts of the world—Shanghai, Manila, France. On July 23, 1929, they were married in Paris "at a quiet ceremony."

Today, Carlotta Monterey, said to be 56 but still beautiful and vivacious, has taken a capable and strong hold on the job of keeping O'Neill sufficiently isolated for the pursuit of his work.

After their wedding in 1929, the O'Neills went to live at the Chateau de Plessis at St. Antoine de Rocher, near Tours, France. *The New York Times* reported that O'Neill had signed a 13-year lease for the chateau, where he at once set to work on *Mourning Becomes Electra.*

O'Neill dedicated the manuscript of *Mourning Becomes Electra* to his wife. Mrs. O'Neill sent 50 copies of the inscription to friends with the following printed note:

Fifty copies of Eugene O'Neill's inscription to the final longhand manuscript of *Mourning Becomes Electra* have been reproduced in facsimile. This copy is No. ——.

CARLOTTA MONTEREY O'NEILL

To Carlotta,

In memory of the impenetrable days of pain in which you privately suffered in silence that this trilogy might be born. Days when I had my work and you had nothing but household tasks and a glimpse through the salon windows of a gray land of Le Plessis; with the black trees dripping and the Winter wraths outside; days when you had only selfforgetting love to sustain you—when lunchtime was spent discussing such pre-occupations with a courageous, cleaving banter; days which for you were entirely lonely when I seemed far away and lost to you by a grim, savage, gloomy country of my own making; days which for you were like hateful living with unspeakable nagging at your nerves and spirit until an intolerable [ennui] in life silences and soothes the spirit. In short, days in which you collaborated as only a deep love can in the writing of this trilogy of the damned!

These scripts are like us and my presenting them is a gift which, already, is half yours. So, in hopes that what this trilogy may have in it may repay the travail we have gone through for its sake—I say I want them to remind you that I have known your love with my love even when I have seemed not to know; that I have seen it even when I have appeared most blind; that I have felt it warmly around me always (even in my study in the closing pages of my heart) sustaining and comforting, a warm, serene sanctuary for the man after the author's despairing solitude and inevitable deceits—a victory of love over life. Oh, mother and wife and mistress and friend! —And collaborator! I love you.

Since his marriage to Carlotta Monterey, O'Neill's life had taken on a new pattern. He had kept apart from the world. She had helped provide the seclusion necessary for his creative work. In 1931 they returned to the U. S. A. for the first time since their wedding because of the forthcoming production by the Theatre Guild of *Mourning Becomes Electra*.

They arrived in New York City on Sunday morning [May 17,] 1931, on the *Statendam* and secretly checked in at an uptown East Side hotel. The following Wednesday morning Ralph Barton was found dead in bed in his penthouse at 419 East 57th St. with a bullet in his brain and a .32-caliber pistol in his hand. On the bed with him were found a copy of Gray's *Anatomy* opened to the section on the heart, a copy of Carl Bateman's cartoon book, *Suburbia*, and a photograph of Carlotta Monterey. In the flyleaf of the book of cartoons was an inscription written to Barton by Carlotta while they were still married. It read: "To Ralph sometime on a certain Friday or was it Saturday?"

After some delays Homer Barton, brother of the dead man, released the suicide note. "I have always had excellent health," Ralph Barton had written, "but since my early youth I have suffered from a melancholia which in the last five years had begun to show definite symptoms of manic-depressive insanity.

". . . I have run from wife to wife, from house to house and from country to country in a ridiculous effort to escape from myself. . . .

"In particular, my remorse is bitter over my failure to appreciate my beautiful lost angel, Carlotta, the only woman I ever loved and whom I respect and admire above all the rest of the human race. . . . I do hope that she will understand what my malady was and forgive me a little. . . . I kiss my dear children —and Carlotta."

All the papers carried the suicide note, and the morning after the suicide, the New York *Journal* printed a story stating that Barton had had 92 girls in his life, but "not one came to mourn him today. . . . Of these, he loved one. She was not there [at the Campbell Funeral Home] for a final look at the man she once held tightly in her arms. . . ."

Homer Barton was quoted: "If Carlotta won't see him, nobody shall see him. It is the O'Neill influence that has kept Carlotta from this final farewell to Ralph."

O'Neill refused to discuss the suicide with reporters. His attorney, Harry Weinberger, later issued this statement:

> Mr. and Mrs. O'Neill have asked me to state that contrary to newspaper reports of statements by Homer Barton,

brother of Ralph Barton, they have not seen Mr. Ralph Barton since their return to the United States and Mrs. O'Neill, the former Carlotta Monterey, desires to state that she never saw or heard from Mr. Barton since her divorce more than five years ago.

After *Mourning Becomes Electra* was produced, O'Neill's restlessness was again asserting itself. Instead of returning to their French chateau, the O'Neills built a house at Sea Island Beach, Ga.

With O'Neill settled again in his own country, his old friends expected to see something of him. They looked forward to night-long discussions in the old bars, to visiting the six-day bicycle races and ball games he liked so much.

They were disappointed. Gene O'Neill of the Greenwich Village days, the barroom days, the Broadway days, was gone.

At the O'Neill Sea Island retreat Mrs. O'Neill dressed for dinner every night in a long, flowing and gorgeous evening gown, but O'Neill, one visitor reported with satisfaction, wore dungarees and tennis shoes. His workroom there was built like a shipboard captain's cabin and faced the sea.

For the first year after the O'Neill's return to the U. S. A., the playwright accomplished little. In the Spring of 1932 he wrote the first draft of *Days Without End*. He was not satisfied with it and kept rewriting it for the next year and a half.

During September, 1932, he took two weeks out to write *Ah, Wilderness!* It was his first really conventional play, something everybody, even the drama critics, could understand, and it was a commercial success.

Richard Dana Skinner, author of a book on O'Neill called *A Poet's Quest*, said of *Ah, Wilderness!*:

> This appealing and innocent and tender little comedy of adolescence is really much more important than it seems in the poet's unconscious scheme of things. It marked an end to that terrible fear which had made every symbol of youth appear like some hideous monster. It was unquestionably the beginning of a third and entirely new period in O'Neill's creative life, the period of full manhood of the soul.

Or perhaps Carlotta Monterey had become a mother to him, the "mother" he had hailed in the inscription to *Mourning Be-*

comes Electra. Perhaps she had shown him that things would be all right. Perhaps she brought a new youth to him, who was just 44.

His next play, *Days Without End*, about adultery, he found very difficult to write. Skinner, whose book O'Neill recently strongly recommended to an admirer who wanted a key to an understanding of his work, thinks it was because the playwright needed "to clear the path . . . to complete the play of deeper spiritual conflict."

Just how deeply the affair of the Barton suicide had affected O'Neill, one cannot say. He does not want to discuss it. Of the original *New Yorker* group, however, Harold Ross, the editor, Neysa McMein, the artist, and the others remember that Carlotta's marriage to Barton was violent and tempestuous. She bitterly resented Barton's interest in other women.

The heroine of *Days Without End* is a woman married to her second husband to whom fidelity is of the utmost importance. She considers marriage "a true sacrament." The hero had been unfaithful to her, and the conflict of the play is concerned with the hero's attempts to resolve the problem of telling her and thus perhaps destroying their love but achieving some kind of spiritual peace.

O'Neill solved the problem by introducing a Catholic priest who shows the hero the way. At the end of the play, the hero prostrates himself before the Cross to ask the help of the Son of Man—the One Whom, in all these years, he could never forgive for taking the love of his parents from him.

A light from the Crucifix illuminates the hero, and he cries: "I am forgiven! I can forgive, myself through Thee! O Lord of Love, forgive Thy poor blind fool!"

"Thou hast conquered, Lord," the hero's bad self calls out, "the damned soul—of John Loving!"

The play threw the critics into a tailspin and was not a success.

Then came a blow that hurt him very much. The Catholic Church refused to put the play on the White List. Only a few plays are placed on the White List. They must be plays that a committee of Catholic laymen decides it is safe to take young people to, plays that follow the principles of Catholic morality.

The committee said they would put *Days Without End* on the White List if O'Neill would insert a line in the play making it clear that the heroine's husband, whose infidelity had so upset her, was dead. The idea was abhorrent to O'Neill for two reasons. In the first place, such a change involved his artistic integrity, something he had never compromised with. In the second place, it struck at his own life. Both he and his wife had been divorced.

Shortly after *Days Without End*, O'Neill started work on his most ambitious undertaking, a nine-play cycle of American Life from 1775 to 1932 to be called *A Tale of Possessors Self-dispossessed*.

In the '30s O'Neill's old restlessness reasserted itself, and in 1937 he and his wife sold their Georgia home and moved to California where they designed a country house which they had built near San Francisco. They called it Tao House after the liberal Chinese philosophy of The Right Way of Life.

While working on his American Life cycle, O'Neill completed three other plays, *A Moon for the Misbegotten*, which is to be produced in December. *A Touch of the Poet*, to be produced next year and *Long Day's Journey Into Night*, the manuscript which is not to be published until 25 years after his death.

In 1938 O'Neill felt he had gone stale on his nine-play series, and the next year he turned back to his past for relief as he had when he had written *Ah, Wilderness!* This time he wrote *The Iceman Cometh* about a waterfront saloon in 1912.

O'Neill's life was upset by the war which forced him to close his house and move to a San Francisco apartment. The invasion of France so distressed him that he stopped writing. "The Germans invaded that part of France where I had lived," he said. "I felt as badly as if they had moved into Brooklyn when I was living in New York."

During the war he accomplished almost nothing. He had a stroke, from which he recovered except for a palsy, but from the shock of the world conflict he did not recover. A year before *The Iceman Cometh* opened he moved back to New York City.

John Mason Brown in *The Saturday Review of Literature* advanced an interesting theory about the play. He was discussing Hickey, the leading character, the hardware salesman who is shown reforming all the bums, until they discover the source of his newly found faith—he's murdered his wife. ". . . Whether he (and the whole story)," wrote Brown, "represents Mr. O'Neill's subconscious protest against those who have chaperoned and tidied-up his own recent living—is a matter for individual conjecture."

Whether Carlotta O'Neill influences O'Neill's views is also a matter of conjecture. This Fall she upbraided a reporter who, she thought, had been talking to her husband about politics. "A writer who talks about politics," she said, "is a fool. He should never talk about politics because politics change, art doesn't."

During the rehearsals of *The Iceman*, O'Neill sat most of the time next to Eddie Dowling, the director. Dowling tended to have the actors overplay some parts. O'Neill was for more subtle touches.

At one rehearsal a puzzled actress asked, "Was Hickey, the salesman, a good man?"

"Raw emotion," O'Neill said, "produces the best and worst in people. Remember, goodness can surmount anything. The people in that saloon were the best friends I've ever known. Their weakness was not an evil. It is a weakness found in all men.

"Revenge is the subconscious motive for the individual's behavior with the rest of society. Revulsion drives man to tell others of his sins. . . . It is the furies within us that seek to destroy us. In all my plays sin is punished and redemption takes place.

"Vice and virtue cannot live side by side. It's the humiliation of a loving kiss that destroys evil."

An eager, aggressive young actor stood up and asked O'Neill where he stood on "the movement." Two of the characters in the play are disillusioned radicals.

"I am a philosophical anarchist," O'Neill said, smiling faintly, "which means, 'Go to it, but leave me out of it.' "

O'Neill gives people the impression sometimes when he is talking to them that he is a cross between a Bowery bum and a Victorian gentleman. During a large press interview in September, a girl reporter came in late. "I've heard," the girl said, "that the cast of *The Iceman* consists of 14 men and four tarts."

"Fourteen men and four—ladies." O'Neill replied.

A reporter asked him what he was going to do on the opening night. "If I weren't in temperance," O'Neill said with a twinkle in his eye, "I'd get stinko."

My longest talk with Eugene O'Neill took place on the darkened stage of the Martin Beck Theatre where *The Iceman* was about to open. Around us were the sets by Robert Edmond Jones, O'Neill's old friend from the Provincetown days. We sat on a bench backstage, for a while, talking about his early life. He seemed old and sick, but I did not agree with *Time* that "his paralysis agitans involved his whole emaciated body in one miserable stammer."

He looked sharply at me as he talked and his face was still a face difficult to put out of your mind. He was well-groomed and expensively and quietly dressed in a double-breasted blue suit, but he gave the impression of a down-and-out man who had been completely outfitted the day before by some well-meaning friend.

He was still handsome. His hair was only slightly graying, a distinguished iron gray. He was thin and slightly bent over. His eyes were deep-set and sad and occasionally he cocked his head as he eyed me. His jaw was lean and forceful.

After talking a while, O'Neill got up and walked over to one end of a stage bar. He pulled up a stool, sat at the bar, and motioned for me to join him. He seemed to straighten up and come alive.

"Of course," he said, "America is due for a retribution. There ought to be a page in the history books of the United States of America of all the unprovoked, criminal, unjust crimes committed and sanctioned by our government since the beginning of our history—and before that, too. There is hardly one thing that our government has done that isn't some treachery—against the Indians, against the people of the Northwest, against the small farmers."

As he talked, he seemed in the tradition of all the great half-drunken Irishmen who sound off in bars all over the world. Their talk is always the same, extravagant, rambling, full of madness and violence, but studded with enough essential truth and insight to force you to listen with troubled fascination.

"This American Dream stuff gives me a pain," he went on. "Telling the world about our American Dream! I don't know what they mean. If it exists, as we tell the whole world, why don't we make it work in one small hamlet in the United States?

"If it's the constitution that they mean, ugh, then it's a lot of words. If we taught history and told the truth, we'd teach school children that the United States has followed the same greedy rut as every other country. We would tell who's guilty. The list of the guilty ones responsible would include some of our great national heroes. Their portraits should be taken out and burned." He fondled a prop whiskey glass and a prop bottle with water and caramel syrup in it.

As his words took on more and more vigor, I got the feeling that O'Neill was, in a sense, the conscience of America asserting itself. I realized that one could say of him even today what his boss on the New London *Telegraph* had said of him in 1912: "He was the most stubborn and irreconcilable social rebel that I had ever met." He wrote about oppressed workers (*The Hairy Ape*) and about the tragedy of color discrimination (*All God's Chillun Got Wings*) long before they were fashionable subjects. I got the feeling that O'Neill's social views spring from the very pit of his soul, from a deep abiding love of humanity, from a deeply cherished dream of what the world could be.

"The great battle in American history," he went on, "was the Battle of Little Big Horn. The Indians wiped out the white men, scalped them. That was a victory in American history. It should be featured in all our school books as the greatest victory in American history."

O'Neill brought his fist down on the top of the bar. "The big business leaders in this country! Why do we produce such stupendous, colossal egomaniacs? They go on doing the most monstrous things, always using the excuse that if we don't the other person will. It's impossible to satirize them, if you wanted to."

The actors and stagehands began drifting back onto the stage. Two grips came to move the bar. We moved to the side. The conversation shifted to religion. Had he, I asked, returned to Catholicism, as one biography had implied he might?

A great look of sadness came into O'Neill's eyes. "Unfortunately, no," he said.

"*The Iceman* is a denial of any other experience of faith in my plays. In writing it, I felt I had locked myself in with my memories."

When he said that I thought of another remark he'd made: "Those people in the saloon were the best friends I ever had."

Mary Welch

SOFTER TONES FOR MR. O'NEILL'S PORTRAIT

Since Eugene O'Neill's death on November 27, 1953, there have been many tributes which mourned "our greatest American playwright." Most of these spoke of the tremendous talent and challenge he brought to the theatre, and then went on to discuss his many plays. Few words were written about O'Neill's daily life or his contact with people, however. If anything was said about his private life, for the most part we received the legendary picture we had while he was alive—that of a lonely, passionate, tormented genius, living in isolated spots as far from Broadway as possible, and remaining completely aloof from any contact with the needs and problems of other people. Having had direct, personal contact with him, I would like to add some warmer, softer tones to what I feel is an overly stark and limited portrait of O'Neill. I want to recall his sensitivity and generosity toward me during the preparations for the tryout of the last of his plays to be staged in his lifetime.

It was in May, 1946, that I first read an item in a New York newspaper which began: "The Theatre Guild is desperately searching in America and Ireland for a tall, Irish girl to play Josie, the lead in Eugene O'Neill's new play, *A Moon for the Misbegotten.*" The next morning I walked into the imposing building which housed the Guild. I had just returned from a tour of Philip Barry's *The Joyous Season*, starring Ethel Barrymore, and was full of youthful arrogance. I announced that I was ready to play the part for them.

The several casting officials looked me over and concluded. "You are of the right age, temperament, and origin, but you have

From Theatre Arts, *May 1957. Reprinted by permission of* Theatre Arts *Magazine.*

little or no chance. You are too normal! We are looking for a huge girl with some of your qualifications—but in addition, at least another fifty pounds and preferably many more years' acting experience. Josie is the lead and only woman in Mr. O'Neill's play. She is a great mother-earth symbol, and the actress who plays her should have a range from farce to Greek tragedy."

This protest only made me more interested. I answered them with a long list of plays I had done in college and stock, which more than covered this small range. I don't remember when I have been so tenacious. Back of my boldness was this line of thought: "What do you have to lose? At least you might get a peek at your hero, Eugene O'Neill. How many other actresses can say the same?"

Completely snowed under by my self-praise, the weary Guild officials said, "It seems ridiculous but we'll give you a quick interview with Mr. O'Neill next week when he will be screening many actors."

Despite the Guild's doubts, my daydreams during the following week had their own range, from how I would impress the great O'Neill to how I would take my curtain calls. I arrived for my appointment at least eight pounds heavier (also padded) and dressed in green. I waited more than a full hour, sitting among girls whose proportions made me feel tiny. Finally Armina Marshall, one of the Guild producers, said, "You're next for Mr. O'Neill!"

I was shown into a small den furnished with only a big desk and two chairs. Behind the desk, four feet from me, sat Eugene O'Neill.

No wonder the many legends exist. He did look exactly as I had always seen him in all the photographs and drawings. He *was* "gaunt," "intense," "tragic." I didn't have to take time to adjust the reality of his appearance to my expectation, as one frequently does on meeting a distinguished person for the first time. While Miss Marshall talked to him about me, I had a chance to study him more. He was impeccably dressed in an expensive dark suit but he seemed more bone than flesh. I liked him immediately; I like the look of men who carry no excess baggage.

O'Neill nodded pleasantly but remained silent as he was told my qualifications. He seemed embarrassed by this kind of talk. It wasn't until we were left alone that he seemed to relax and then tried to put me at ease. His searching eyes focused constantly right on my face, but instead of arousing a self-conscious behavior in me, they seemed to put me on my absolute honor to express myself as clearly and as simply as I could. In those days, like many young actors, I smiled too much in my desperate anxiety to please. He must have sensed this when I first entered the room, but instead of being irritated, he just kept staring, as though he were burning me down to a purer core. I always felt the same way with him—as though I were purified. I had to be completely myself because I knew he would detect the slightest tendency to impress or charm him.

His first questions were, "Are you Irish with that pug nose? What per cent? From what part of Ireland are your people? I want as many people as possible connected with my play to be Irish. Although the setting is New England, the dry wit, the mercurial changes of mood, and the mystic quality of the three main characters are so definitely Irish."

I answered, "Of course, Irish, 100 per cent, County Cork."

His first smile appeared on "County Cork." It made me bold enough to slip into a brogue and tell him about my grandmother who used to say, "I'll never eat a plate of stew—those dishes of mystery!" This and a joke about a friend of hers getting caught in the wrong field of "taters" made him laugh. We were both off on Ireland and didn't mention the play. Relaxed, I could have gone on talking with him for hours, forgetting my first mission, but the next actress was growing insistent and I realized I should leave.

As I got up to go, O'Neill said, "Here now, take the play with you and come back and read for me in two weeks." As he handed the script to me I noticed for the first time the severe tremble in his hands, caused by Parkinson's disease, which made him suffer so greatly during his last years.

I started reading the play on the subway on my way home, but it took me many hours to finish it. I had to keep stopping constantly to recover from the emotional impact of each act; I had never felt so identified with a part. In those days I kept a diary and I wrote, "Every bluff and hurt and discovery of Josie's seems to have occurred to me. This is what every actor looks his whole lifetime for—*his* role. This is *my* role. For once I feel moved by fate. I know I have to play this part and will."

The next time I saw O'Neill was two weeks later, at the first official reading in a luxurious room on the third floor of the Theatre Guild building. He was there with his wife and the Guild producers to weed out the final candidates for the role of Josie. O'Neill's previous warmth and my own overwhelming love and desire for the part had given me courage to memorize large sections of the play, and boldly to use Josie's main prop, an old broom—thereby giving myself over to the part instead of delivering the customary stumbling first reading. The Guild seemed impressed by the long preparations I had made, but there was still an element of worry.

"The reading was good."

"The accent is perfect."

"But she still seems too normal for Josie's problem of feeling misbegotten."

Mr. O'Neill, who had written the dimensions for his leading lady, then proceeded to overlook his own measurements. "That doesn't matter to me," he retorted. "She can gain some more weight, but the important thing is that Miss Welch understands how Josie feels. These other girls, who are closer physically to Josie, somehow don't know how tortured she is, or can't project it. The inner state of Josie is what I want. We'll work the other problem out in clothes and sets. I think the emotional quality is just right."

The Theatre Guild and the director, however, still had to be convinced, so in the next few months I gave at least three more auditions in costume and in make-up, and with each new appearance I had added five more pounds on a diet of potatoes, bananas, and pies. Finally came the day of decision when I would meet and read with James Dunn, the leading man.

The day before this final audition I received a phone call from a Guild secretary, who said that O'Neill wanted me to meet him and his wife in their apartment an hour before my appointment at the theatre. I had no idea what to expect and was afraid that this meeting might mean an easy letdown. When I arrived at the door of the O'Neill penthouse apartment in the East Seventies, the very patrician and beautiful Mrs. O'Neill greeted me warmly and took me across a large living room into her husband's den.

"Hello, Miss Welch—Mary. I thought we'd just have a chat and a cup of tea before the final inquisition."

He had simply wanted to put me at ease and build my confidence. His eyes twinkled as if he were ready for a minor skirmish and was sure he would win.

"Now don't worry, I don't care what anyone says. You are my choice and you are going to play Josie."

It seemed unbelievable to me that I was sitting in the O'Neills' lovely living room, filled with books and plants and one of the first television sets ("given to me by a friend so I can watch the fights"), and that I was listening to Eugene O'Neill bolstering my shaky actor's ego. We spoke of other things, too. O'Neill brought up his earlier plays, particularly the ones he had written about the Negro people. He had felt deeply about them, and his face grew bitter and forceful as he recalled how some of the New York professional theatre crowd had accepted these works. His words were, "They didn't really understand what I was writing. They merely said to themselves, 'Oh look, the ape can talk!' " These words shocked me; but besides ringing with true bitterness, I am sure they were spoken to furnish the pride and arrogance I lacked.

I remember Mrs. O'Neill getting all of his winter wraps ready for him, and insisting that he put on his overshoes. In the taxi on our way to the theatre he was still telling me not to be afraid of any doubts I might have about myself. That day I signed a contract to play Josie, and it had this very unusual clause: "The artist agrees to gain the necessary weight required for the role."

I next saw O'Neill at our first rehearsal, when the whole cast was gathered to read *A Moon for the Misbegotten* for the first time. James Dunn and I both had to stop several times because we were weeping. And when we raised our eyes from our scripts and looked at the playwright and all three Guild producers, we realized that we were not alone in this. O'Neill came over to us at the end of rehearsal and said humorously, "Oh, here we go again. I wept a great deal over Josie Hogan and Jim Tyrone as I wrote the play. I loved them." The day ended with Mrs. O'Neill adding a homey touch, passing around a box of chocolates.

Mr. O'Neill was ill during most of the three weeks of rehearsals, but he was able to come three times to give us notes which proved a definite help. His first major note was that we were playing the tragedy of the work too early. *A Moon for the Misbegotten* is almost farcical in places in the first act, though it becomes almost Greek in its tragic stature in the fourth and final one. The playwright often told us jokes about his early days. He seemed to look for humor everywhere. And always I felt he understood my terrible worry over the responsibilities of such a large part. He made me feel he really believed in me. On the three occasions when he was at rehearsals, I dared to be as free as I always should have been.

Illness prevented O'Neill from attending the première in Columbus, Ohio, but he came to bid us good-by in New York. Once more he said, "I know you will play Josie the way I want it." We embraced and I told him some of the personal reasons why the part meant so much to me—things that I have told no other person. I recall that when he left a rehearsal one afternoon in New York, I said to myself, "This man compels me to behave at my best level, to express the absolute core of whatever is my soul. I can only be me—honest, sincere, no matter how revealing." I felt an unaccustomed relief on shedding all the layers of convention I had felt it necessary to assume for contact with other people.

I want to mention another incident at that rehearsal, and this will surprise many people. O'Neill cut several sentences from his finished script, upsetting the legend that he steadfastly refused to cut a single line, once a script was handed over to the producer. He performed this operation at the bidding of James Dunn and myself, and it came about when he realized that we were obviously upset at having just too much to say. After this I always felt that he might have made some appropriate cuts in his other plays, if people had had the courage to approach him—provided, of course, that they had had his respect.

Several weeks later when the play was on the verge of being closed by the police in Detroit on the false claim that it is "a slander on American motherhood," other cuts had to be made to satisfy the local politicians. I shall never forget a meeting with the local police officials, who actually set themselves up as editors of O'Neill. And we were forced to listen to them in order that we might open again that evening, the second night of the engagement; we couldn't even wait for the cuts the playwright had agreed to make so that the tryout tour might continue. One of their more brilliant contributions was: "Well, you can't say tart, but you *can* say tramp."

The tour began February 20, 1947, and closed the following March 29. We played Columbus, Cleveland, Detroit, Pittsburgh and St. Louis. Some of the critics were profoundly moved by the work; others missed it entirely, calling it another *Tobacco Road*. We closed after the St. Louis engagement due to a combination of circumstances, foremost among which were O'Neill's illness (which prevented him from working on the play) and casting problems relating to certain of the male roles.

My last communication with Eugene O'Neill (other than the note he wrote after we had closed, thanking me for my work) was in the form of a gift of a dozen red roses on opening night in Columbus, together with a card which read, "Again my absolute confidence, Eugene O'Neill." I can think of nothing finer to say to an actress on opening night.

Seymour Peck

A TALK WITH MRS. O'NEILL

"June 21, 1939. A hot, sleepless night. Gene talks to me for hours—about a play (in his mind) of his mother, father, his brother and himself."

This note, written in a diary seventeen years ago by Mrs. Eugene O'Neill, was her first awareness of the play that was to be known as *Long Day's Journey Into Night*, which may, when it opens here Wednesday, lift O'Neill's name out of the comparative limbo into which it has fallen in the last decade.

Emerging briefly from the hermit-like seclusion in which she has lived for almost thirty years, both as O'Neill's wife and as his widow, Mrs. O'Neill talked the other day of her husband, his life, his death, and *Long Day's Journey Into Night's* long journey to Broadway.

A short, slightly plump but darkly handsome woman who appears about 55, Mrs. O'Neill wore no makeup and was sternly dressed all in black—suit, sweater, hat, hose, low-heeled shoes. Even black glasses covered her eyes. Her speech has the rich, deep tones and grandeur of the actress; Mrs. O'Neill was on the stage and screen as Carlotta Monterey before she became the playwright's third wife in 1929.

She spoke nervously but volubly, frequently clasping and unclasping her hands. She said she and O'Neill were living at Tao House, a Chinese-styled residence they built on a mountainside thirty-five miles from San Francisco, when O'Neill began to plan the autobiographical *Long Day's Journey Into Night* in 1939.

"He wasn't well even then," Mrs. O'Neill said. "He didn't sleep well, and when he was very worried and nervous, he would call me

---

From The New York Times, *November 4, 1956. Reprinted by permission of the author and* The New York Times.

to come to his room or he would come to mine and he would talk, frequently all night, about his work or about this terrible thing of whether we were going to have a World War again. He was terribly disturbed that mankind was so stupid; to go through war only meant destruction for everybody. It really did something awful to him. Then he explained to me that he had to write this play about his youth and his family. It was a thing that haunted him. He was bedevilled into writing it, it was something that came from his very guts, he had to get it out of his system, he had to forgive whatever it was that caused this tragedy between himself and his mother and father.

"When he started *Long Day's Journey*, it was a most strange experience to watch that man being tortured every day by his own writing. He would come out of his study at the end of a day gaunt and sometimes weeping. His eyes would be all red and he looked ten years older than when he went in in the morning. I think he felt freer when he got it out of his system. It was his way of making peace with his family—and himself."

Long Day's Journey was completed in 1941. It was written just after *The Iceman Cometh* and just before *A Moon for the Misbegotten*, which was O'Neill's last work. O'Neill always wrote in longhand; he could never type or dictate. In 1943 his physical condition became so poor, and his hands shook so badly, that he could do no work for the ten years before his death, at 65, in 1953. "He died," said Mrs. O'Neill, "when he could no longer work. He died spiritually. And it was just a matter of dragging a poor, diseased body along for a few more years until it too died."

The O'Neills first met when she was in his play, *The Hairy Ape*. "He asked me if he could come to tea. I hardly knew the man. He came up on three afternoons. And he never said to me, 'I love you, I think you are wonderful.' He kept saying, 'I need you. I need you. I need you.' And he did need me, I discovered. He was never in good health. He talked about his early life—that he had had no real home, no mother in the real sense, or father, no one to treat him as a child should be treated—and his face became sadder and sadder."

After their marriage, the O'Neills went to live in Europe. "Gene had never lived in a chateau and the idea of a chateau he thought chichi, putting on airs. But we rented one for three years outside of Tours, in France. And though he was a rather tough Irishman, he finally saw that you could be polite and live in a charming place without being ridiculous. That is where he wrote *Mourning Becomes Electra.* And he got a racing car, a Bugatti, and when he was very nervous and tired, he would go out in it and drive 95, 98 miles an hour and come back looking 19 years old, not a wrinkle and perfectly relaxed."

But O'Neill still talked most fondly of his youthful, impoverished years when he was a seaman "and drank too much and inferior liquor, and wore his body and soul out, without proper food or even a bed at night."

"The strange part of it is," Mrs. O'Neill said, "that Gene's pride seemed to be in *those* years. I said to him once, half-jokingly, 'I have dragged you about Europe, I have worked like anything to show you all the beautiful spots and I have never heard you once say you liked this or that or the other.' 'Well,' he said, 'I liked them but they weren't very exciting.' So that was that."

The O'Neills led a lonely existence, for O'Neill "didn't care anything for being with people. He had this terrible nervous disease. In a public dining room his hands would begin to shake and his face would sink and he would get circles under his eyes and begin to sweat. We could never go to the theatre here. We never saw one of his plays open. We saw the dress rehearsal and when the dress rehearsal was over, the car would be outside, we would hop in and go. He always used to say to me, 'If only I could just write and never bother to go to New York.'"

O'Neill was always working on three or four plays at a time, Mrs. O'Neill said. Even while he was doing *Long Day's Journey*, he was also occupied with a cycle of nine plays covering an American family from the Eighteen Twenties to modern times. *A Touch of the Poet*, the first play in the cycle, was completed, but six others, which needed revision and cutting, were destroyed by the O'Neills in the Boston hotel where they were living before his death.

"He didn't want to leave any unfinished plays and he said, 'It isn't that I don't trust you, Carlotta, but you might drop dead or get run over or something and I don't want anybody else finishing up a play of mine.' We tore them up, bit by bit, together. I helped him because his hands—he had this terrific tremor, he could tear just a few pages at a time. It was awful, it was like tearing up children."

With what an essayist has called "his infatuation with oblivion," O'Neill specified that at his death no newspaper or person was to be informed what funeral parlor he was in or where he was to be buried. "He wished nobody to be at his funeral but me and his nurse. He wished no religious representative of any kind. He had been born Catholic but he was not a religious man. No, he never thought of returning to religion, never at any time, at any moment."

O'Neill expressed the wish that *Long Day's Journey* be given its world première by the Royal Dramatic Theatre of Stockholm, Sweden—the same group that had produced his *A Moon for the Misbegotten* very successfully. This play had to be closed out of town, before coming to Broadway, when the Theatre Guild tried to do it in America in 1947. The Royal Dramatic Theatre staged *Long Day's Journey Into Night* to wild praise last February.

Its production has been largely responsible, Mrs. O'Neill feels, for the current revival of interest in her husband's work. "Sweden did this for O'Neill," she said, "not America. America was not a damn bit interested, excuse my language." And it was the fine job director José Quintero did with the off-Broadway revival of *The Iceman Cometh* that made Mrs. O'Neill decide to let him direct *Long Day's Journey* in its American première. "Oddly enough, José was the only director or producer in New York who did not ask me could he do the play," Mrs. O'Neill said. "I finally said to him one day, 'José, would you like to put on *Long Day's Journey?* I ask you because you deserve it for what you did for *The Iceman Cometh.* You took a play that had been badly produced on Broadway and revived it—though in New York revivals are poison—and you made a success of it. Now I trust you. I know you, your subtlety, the way you know what O'Neill says, and nobody else I know of in this business does.' I thought the man was going to faint. He stumbled out and said, 'I'm a wreck.' "

But Quintero is staging *Long Day's Journey* and both he and Mrs. O'Neill are looking forward to the opening. "In Europe they think it's the greatest play they've had in years," Mrs. O'Neill said. "Count it with the Greeks and God knows what." She smiled. "That makes me feel nice and warm for Gene," she said.

Sean O'Casey

TRIBUTE TO O'NEILL

You do well to honor a theatre-building with the great name of Eugene O'Neill; for what finer memorial could a great Dramatist have than that of a temple dedicated to the Art he loved, and to which he added many a wide and deep honor, and, more than once, a glory.

The soul of O'Neill was a restless one, always seeking out the storm, crying out from the midst of tumbling waves, loudly enough to be above the tumult of the strongest winds, till the dark lull of death brought silence and a well-earned peace.

Yet this man could be gay. Yes, indeed, for I saw him so; I was with him a number of times in the company of his dear friend, George Jean Nathan, and then we talked and talked merrily in the surge of a gay time together; and then often I saw the somber face of the Dramatist break into the sunniness of deep and generous laughter. It was good to have met this remarkable man; to have looked into his deep wine-dark eyes; to have pressed his hand as the hand of a friend in joyful and lasting affection; and to have heard his laughter.

I am glad that in his American soul there was, not only the touch of a poet, but also the touch of an Irishman, for the O'Neills had their origin in Ireland. This great Dramatist of America and the world tells me again that our Shamrock twines a leaf or two around every flower symbolizing each State of O'Neill's great and urgent Country. The Shamrock is an unassuming and humble plant, but it is always there.

May this Theatre in New York, dedicated to Eugene O'Neill, be ever worthy of the Name's greatness and the Name's pride.

A letter to Lester Osterman, owner of the Eugene O'Neill Theatre in New York City. Published in The New York Times, *November 9, 1959. Reprinted by permission of Sean O'Casey.*

2

CREDO

SOME OFF-STAGE OBSERVATIONS
BY EUGENE O'NEILL

Eugene O'Neill

"INSCRUTABLE FORCES"

A Letter to Barrett Clark

[1919]

. . . I by no means agree with you in your high estimate of "In the Zone." To me it seems the least significant of all the plays. It is too facile in its conventional technique, too full of clever theatrical tricks, and its long run as a successful headliner in vaudeville proves conclusively to my mind that there must be "something rotten in Denmark." At any rate, this play in no way represents the true me or what I desire to express. It is a situation drama lacking in all spiritual import—there is no big feeling for life inspiring it. Given the plot and a moderate ability to characterize, any industrious playwright could have reeled it off. Whereas, "The Moon of the Caribbees," for example—(my favorite)—is distinctively my own. The spirit of the sea—a big thing—is in the latter play the hero. While "In the Zone" might have happened just as well, if less picturesquely, in a boarding house of munition workers. Let me illustrate by a concrete example what I am trying to get at. Smitty in the stuffy, greasepaint atmosphere of "In the Zone" is magnified into a hero who attracts our sentimental sympathy. In "The Moon," posed against a background of that beauty, sad because it is eternal, which is one of the revealing moods of the sea's truth, his silhouetted gestures of self-pity are reduced to their proper insignificance, his thin whine of weakness is lost in the silence which it was mean enough to disturb, we get the perspective to judge him—and the others—and we find his sentimental posing much more out of harmony with truth, much less in tune with beauty, than the honest vulgarity of his mates. To me "The Moon" works with truth, and *Beyond the Horizon* also, while "In

---

From a letter to Barrett Clark published in Eugene O'Neill; The Man and His Plays *by Barrett H. Clark ($1.25) Dover Publications, Inc., New York 14, New York.*

the Zone" substitutes theatrical sentimentalism. I will say nothing of the worth of the method used in the two short plays save that I consider "In the Zone" a conventional construction of the theatre as it is, and "The Moon" an attempt to achieve a higher plane of bigger, finer values. But I hope to have all this out with you when we meet. Perhaps I can explain the nature of my feeling for the impelling, inscrutable forces behind life which it is my ambition to at least faintly shadow at their work in my plays.

Eugene O'Neill

PLAYWRIGHT AND CRITIC

A Letter to George Jean Nathan

Provincetown, Mass.
June 20, 1920

Dear Mr. Nathan:

I mailed a letter to you on a trip to the village yesterday—after which I bought the July *Smart Set* and read your article on American playwrights. *After*, s'help me! I underline that word because my letter of yesterday might well appear to you in its too-aptness to have been inspired by what you wrote; and I do not want you to suspect, even for a second, that I would mask my rebuttal that cunningly.

Your criticism of me and mine in the magazine is sure invigorating—grateful as keen salt breeze after much hot air puffing from all sides. If my sublime head were bumping the stars askew, your acid test would sure put a blister of truth on my heinie that would disturb any squatting at ease on the softest complacency. However, I honestly don't need blistering—on that account. My head retains its proper proximity to sea level, I think. But your weighing in the balance is a tremendous lift to me in other ways. For one thing, it gives me the added urge of attempting to make you out a false prophet—in ten years or so. For I refuse to accept your serious doubt, but rather snatch at your "But it may be . . . that I am wrong," and will try to prove it to you, given the time.

In this connection, I would like to make you my confession of faith where my work is concerned. Honest confession. I am familiar enough with the best modern drama of all countries to realize that, viewed from a true standard, my work is as yet a mere groping. I rate myself as a beginner—with prospects. I acknowledge

From the Boston Evening Postscript, *October 31, 1925. Reprinted in* The Theatre of George Jean Nathan, *by Isaac Goldberg, Simon and Schuster, 1926.*

that when you write: "He sees life too often as drama. The great dramatist is the dramatist who sees drama as life," you are smiting the nail on the head. But I venture to promise that this will be less true with each succeeding play—that I will not "stay put" in any comfortable niche and play the leave-well-enough-alone game. God stiffen it, I am young yet and I mean to grow! And in this faith I live: That if I have the "guts" to ignore the megaphone men and what goes with them, to follow the dream and live for that alone, then my real significant bit of truth, and the ability to express it, will be conquered in time—not tomorrow nor the next day nor any near, easily-attained period, but after the struggle has been long enough and hard enough to merit victory.

"In the Zone"—your "vaudeville grand guignolism" is my own verdict—but I am out of that zone now, never to return. As for "The Rope," I do believe that is sound enough, although it's a year or more since I looked at it and perhaps I'd agree with you now. But where did you get the idea that I really valued "Where the Cross Is Made"? It was great fun to write, theatrically very thrilling, an amusing experiment in treating the audience as insane—that is all it means or ever meant to me. You will see by my last letter how I came to write it, that it was a distorted version of a long play idea and never intended for a one-act play in my mind. And, by the way, it was not "Where the Cross Is Made" that you advised me to tear up for reputation's sake. You must have confused it with another I submitted to you—"Honor Among the Bradleys"—a very false and feeble piece of work which you "bawled me out" for writing—now in limbo.

To make sure of my accuracy in this matter of "Where the Cross Is Made." I have been looking up your old letters and I find this in one written in October, 1918: "I have read 'Where the Cross Is Made' and like it very much indeed. It would please me to print it in the *Smart Set*. But I fear that the performance of the play by the Provincetown Players around the first of December would interfere with such publication. It would be impossible for us to use the play before our January issue," etc. So you see you have confused "The Cross" with that other play. I am at pains to state all this merely to show you that it was not "The Cross" you advised me to destroy.

Your scheme of measurement to the contrary, I would like to

stand or fall by "Bound East for Cardiff" (with due consideration that it was written in 1914); "The Long Voyage Home," "The Moon of the Caribbees," *Beyond the Horizon*, *The Straw*, *Gold*—because these plays are my sincerest at different stages. They were written purely for their own sake. The others had their contributing causes. There are so many intermediate reasons that enter into the writing of a play between the two serious extremes of art and money. Such intermediate dramas are but an instructive form of recreation when one cannot remain inactive—and it takes time to get over the itch to put everything on paper, regardless.

In the light of what you say in your article that you hope I may top my writings from year to year, your later opinion that *Gold* is a better piece of work than *Beyond the Horizon*, is more than ever welcome to me.

Let me again urge you to try and make the trip up here with John Williams. I'd sure love to have you.

And again let me thank you for your estimate in the *Smart Set*. Those are the things that count. A prod in the rear and a pointing to a distant goal, not without hope—that is what it means to me.

Sincerely,
Eugene O'Neill

Eugene O'Neill

"DAMN THE OPTIMISTS!"

Diff'rent, as I see it, is merely a tale of the eternal, romantic idealist who is in all of us—the eternally defeated one. In our innermost hearts we all wish ourselves and others to be "Diff'rent." We are all more or less "Emmas"—the more or less depending on our talent for compromise. Either we try in desperation to clutch our dream at the last by deluding ourselves with some tawdry substitute; or, having waited the best part of our lives, we find the substitute time mocks us with too shabby to accept. In either case we are tragic figures, and also fit subjects for the highest comedy, were one sufficiently detached to write it.

I have been accused of unmitigated gloom. Is this a pessimistic view of life? I do not think so. There is a skin deep optimism and another higher optimism, not skin deep, which is usually confounded with pessimism. To me, the tragic alone has that significant beauty which is truth. It is the meaning of life—and the hope. The noblest is eternally the most tragic. The people who succeed and do not push on to a greater failure are the spiritual middle classers. Their stopping at success is the proof of their compromising insignificance. How pretty their dreams must have been! The man who pursues the mere attainable should be sentenced to get it —and keep it. Let him rest on his laurels and enthrone him in a Morris chair, in which laurels and hero may wither away together. Only through the unattainable does man achieve a hope worth living and dying for—and so attain himself. He with the spiritual guerdon of a hope in hopelessness, is nearest to the stars and the rainbow's foot.

This may seem to be soaring grandiloquently—and somewhat

From the New York Tribune, *February 13, 1921. Reprinted by permission of Mrs. Carlotta Monterey O'Neill and the* New York Herald Tribune. *Title supplied by editors.*

platitudinously—far above "a poor thing but mine own" like *Diff'rent*; but one must state one's religion first in order not to be misunderstood, even if one makes no rash boast of always having the strength to live up to it.

Diff'rent, whatever its faults may be, has the virtue of sincerity. It is the truth, the inevitable truth, of the lives of the people in it as I see and know them. Whether it is psychoanalytically exact or not I will leave more dogmatic students of Freud and Jung than myself (or than Freud and Jung) to decide. It is life, nevertheless. I stick out for that—life that swallows all formulas. Some critics have said that Emma would not do this thing, would undoubtedly do that other. By Emma they must mean "a woman." But Emma is Emma. She is a whaling captain's daughter in a small New England seacoast town—surely no feminist. She is universal only in the sense that she reacts definitely to a definite sex-suppression, as every woman might. The form her reaction takes is absolutely governed by her environment and her own character. Let the captious be sure they know their Emmas as well as I do before they tell me how she would act.

There are objections to my end; but given Caleb and Emma the end to me is clearly inevitable. The youthful Emma refuses to accept the compromise of a human being for her dream Caleb. As the years go by she lives alone with her dream lover, the real Caleb fading into a friend. But suddenly she realizes youth is gone and the possibility of her dream lover forevermore. She snatches after him in a panic—and gets a Benny. She must re-create her god in this lump of mud. When it finally is brought home to her that mud is mud, she cries after the real Caleb, seeing him now for the first time. But he is gone. There is nothing for her to do but follow him. As for Caleb, he dies because it is not in him to compromise. He belongs to the old iron school of Nantucket-New Bedford whalemen whose slogan was "A dead whale or a stove boat." The whale in this case is transformed suddenly into a malignant Moby Dick who has sounded to depths forever out of reach. Caleb's boat is stove, his quest is ended. He goes with his ship.

There are objections to the play as pathological, but I protest that is putting the accent where none was intended, where only contributing circumstance was meant. And someone has said to me that all the people in the play were either degenerates or roughs

—at which I was properly stunned, because I consider all of the characters, with the exception of Benny, to be perfectly regular human beings even as you and I. Dividing folks into moral castes has never been one of my favorite occupations.

And then there was someone, I have heard, who attributed to the author Caleb's remark that "folks be all crazy and rotten to the core." Upon which I grab the shoelace (but did they have them, though?) of the author of Hamlet, and going aloft to the dizzy height of his instep, inquire pipingly whether it was he or Macbeth who said "It is a tale told by an idiot, full of sound and fury, signifying nothing."

Damn the optimists anyway! They make life so darned hopeless!

Eugene O'Neill

WHAT THE THEATRE MEANS TO ME

The theatre to me *is* life—the substance and interpretation of life. . . . [And] life is struggle, often, if not usually, unsuccessful struggle; for most of us have something within us which prevents us from accomplishing what we dream and desire. And then, as we progress, we are always seeing further than we can reach. I suppose that is one reason why I have come to feel so indifferent toward political and social movements of all kinds. Time was when I was an active socialist, and, after that, a philosophical anarchist. But today I can't feel that anything like that really matters. It is rather amusing to me to see how seriously some people take politics and social questions and how much they expect of them. Life as a whole is changed very little, if at all, as a result of their course. It seems to me that, as far as we can judge, man is much the same creature, with the same primal emotions and ambitions and motives, the same powers and the same weaknesses, as in the time when the Aryan race started toward Europe from the slopes of the Himalayas. He has become better acquainted with those powers and those weaknesses, and he is learning ever so slowly how to control them. The birth-cry of the higher men is almost audible, but they will not come by tinkering with externals or by legislative or social fiat. They will come at the command of the imagination and the will.

From an interview with Oliver M. Sayler published in Century Magazine, *January 1922. This material was incorporated into Sayler's book* Our American Theatre *(Brentano, 1923). Title supplied by the editors.*

Eugene O'Neill

STRINDBERG AND OUR THEATRE

In creating a modern theatre which we hope will liberate for significant expression a fresh elation and joy in experimental production, it is the most apt symbol of our good intentions that we start with a play by August Strindberg; for Strindberg was the precursor of all modernity in our present theatre, just as Ibsen, a lesser man as himself surmised, was the father of the modernity of twenty years or so ago when it was believed that *A Doll's House* wasn't—just that.

Strindberg still remains among the most modern of moderns, the greatest interpreter in the theatre of the characteristic spiritual conflicts which constitute the drama—the blood—of our lives today. He carried Naturalism to a logical attainment of such poignant intensity that, if the work of any other playwright is to be called "naturalism," we must classify a play like *The Dance of Death* as "super-naturalism," and place it in a class by itself, exclusively Strindberg's since no one before or after him has had the genius to qualify.

Yet it is only by means of some form of "super-naturalism" that we may express in the theatre what we comprehend intuitively of that self-defeating, self-obsession which is the discount we moderns have to pay for the loan of life. The old "naturalism"—or "realism" if you prefer (would to God some genius were gigantic enough to define clearly the separateness of these terms once and for all!) no longer applies. It represents our Fathers' daring aspirations toward self-recognition by holding the family kodak up to ill-nature. But to us their old audacity is blague; we have taken too many snap-shots of each other in every graceless position; we have

---

From The Provincetown. *Copyright by Helen Deutsch and Stella Hanau, 1931, 1959. Used by permission of MCA Artists, Ltd. Used on a playbill for* The Spook Sonata, *Jan. 3, 1924.*

endured too much from the banality of surfaces. We are ashamed of having peeked through so many keyholes, squinting always at heavy, uninspired bodies—the fat facts—with not a nude spirit among them; we have been sick with appearances and are convalescing; we "wipe out and pass on" to some as yet unrealized region where our souls, maddened by loneliness and the ignoble inarticulateness of flesh, are slowly evolving their new language of kinship.

Strindberg knew and suffered with our struggle years before many of us were born. He expressed it by intensifying the method of his time and by foreshadowing both in content and form the methods to come. All that is enduring in what we loosely call "Expressionism"—all that is artistically valid and sound theatre—can be clearly traced back through Wedekind to Strindberg's *The Dream Play*, *There Are Crimes and Crimes*, *The Spook Sonata*, etc.

Hence, *The Spook Sonata* at our Playhouse. One of the most difficult of Strindberg's "behind-life" (if I may coin the term) plays to interpret with insight and distinction—but the difficult is properly our special task, or we have no good reason for existing. Truth, in the theatre as in life, is eternally difficult, just as the easy is the everlasting lie.

So pray with us—and (although we don't need it, of course, but it may do some good) for us.

Eugene O'Neill

O'NEILL TALKS ABOUT HIS PLAYS

I am no longer interested in the one-act play. It is an unsatisfactory form—cannot go far enough. The one-act play, however, is a fine vehicle for something poetical, for something spiritual in feeling that cannot be carried through a long play. In the case of my cycle at the Provincetown Theatre the individual plays are complete in themselves, yet the identity of the crew goes through the series and welds the four one-acts into a long play. I do not claim any originality though for this idea, as Schnitzler has already done the same thing in *Anatol.* And doubtless others.

Many of the characters in my plays were suggested to me by people in real life, especially the sea characters. In special pleading I do not believe. Gorky's *A Night's Lodging*, the great proletarian revolutionary play, is really more wonderful propaganda for the submerged than any other play ever written, simply because it contains no propaganda, but sinply shows humanity as it is—truth in terms of human life. As soon as an author slips propaganda into a play everyone feels it and the play becomes simply an argument.

The Hairy Ape was propaganda in the sense that it was a symbol of man, who has lost his old harmony with nature, the harmony which he used to have as an animal and has not yet acquired in a spiritual way. Thus, not being able to find it on earth nor in heaven, he's in the middle, trying to make peace, taking the "woist punches from bot' of 'em." This idea was expressed in Yank's speech. The public saw just the stoker, not the symbol, and the symbol makes the play either important or just another play. Yank can't go forward, and so he tries to go back. This is what his shaking hands

---

From an interview with a staff member of the New York Herald Tribune, *March 16, 1924. Reprinted by permission of the* New York Herald Tribune.

with the gorilla meant. But he can't go back to "belonging" either. The gorilla kills him. The subject here is the same ancient one that always was and always will be the one subject for drama, and that is man and his struggle with his own fate. The struggle used to be with the gods, but is now with himself, his own past, his attempt "to belong."

The most perfect plotless plays are those of Chekhov. But the newest thing now in playwriting is the opposite of the character play. It is the expressionistic play. For expressionism denies the value of characterization. As I understand it, expressionism tries to minimize everything on the stage that stands between the author and the audience. It strives to get the author talking directly to the audience. Their theory, as far as I can make it out, is that the character gets interested in the kind of man he is and what he does instead of the idea. But plenty of people will probably damn me for saying this, because everyone has a different idea of expressionism and mine is just what I have acquired through reading about it.

I personally do not believe that an idea can be readily put over to an audience except through characters. When it sees "A Man" and "A Woman"—just abstractions, it loses the human contact by which it identifies itself with the protagonist of the play. An example of this sort of expressionism is *Morn Till Midnight*, with character abstractions like "A Bank Clerk." This is the point at which I disagree with the theory. I do not believe that the character gets between the author's idea and the audience. The real contribution of the expressionist has been in the dynamic qualities of his plays. They express something in modern life better than did the old plays. I have something of this method in *The Hairy Ape*. But the character Yank remains a man and everyone recognizes him as such.

I believe that *What Price Glory?* is one of the most significant events in the history of our theatre. It is a splendid thing that the first fine, true war play should come from the most reactionary country in the world. It is still more wonderful and encouraging to all who love the theatre that there should be such a great public for it, because even two years ago it would have been possible only at special matinees or for invited audiences.

I hardly ever go to the theatre, although I read all the plays I can get. I don't go to the theatre because I can always do a better production in my mind than the one on the stage. I have a better time and I am not bothered by the audience. No one sneezes during the scenes that interest me. Nor do I ever go to see one of my own plays—have seen only three of them since they started coming out. My real reason for this is that I was practically brought up in the theatre—in the wings—and I know all the technique of acting. I know everything that everyone is doing from the electrician to the stage hands. So I see the machinery going around all the time unless the play is wonderfully acted and produced. Then, too, in my own plays all the time I watch them I am acting all the parts and living them so intensely that by the time the performance is over I am exhausted—as if I had gone through a clothes wringer.

Eugene O'Neill

ARE THE ACTORS TO BLAME?

I believe that there is no possibility of real progress in the creative interpretation of plays of arresting imagination and insight until we develop a new quality of depth of feeling and comprehensive scope of technique in actors and actresses. For only when a play is self-expressed through sensitive, truthful, trickless acting is "the play the thing."

In the acting lies the acted play. Great acting has frequently made bad plays seem good, but a good play cannot penetrate bad acting without emerging distorted—an uneven, bumpy, ugly duckling of an offspring at whom any playwright father must gaze with a shudder. And this in spite of the finest and most intelligent and inspiring direction. Directors can only direct. They cannot give the actors the right developing experience unless they can plan over a long period of years with the same people. This plainly isn't possible under any present system. For actors are conceived by and born of the parts they have been permitted to play.

Are the actors to blame for the present conditions in *all* theatres which urge them toward the easy goals of type casting, rather than the long, painstaking self-training in the acquiring of an art? Well, if actors are partly to blame, then we others of the theatre, including the audience who accept them are equally at fault. Do we give them parts other than the apparent one God cast them in as persons? Do we take a chance on them? Not often. We cannot afford to in an era when the theatre is primarily a realtor's medium for expression. One mistake and then comes the landlord with notice of eviction. He is usually not an artist in the theatre, this landlord! He could see Shakespeare boiled alive in Socony gasoline and have

From The Provincetown. *Copyright by Helen Deutsch and Stella Hanau, 1931, 1959. Used by permission of MCA Artists, Ltd. Originally a playbill for "Adam Solitaire," Nov. 6, 1925.*

qualms only as to our diminishing national Standard Oil reserves. The answer? Repertoire. Genuine repertoire. We all know it—it's as simple as truth—and perhaps that is why we make no attempt to live and work accordingly.

What is the Provincetown going to do about acting? Does it plan to lay emphasis on building up a medium for achievement in acting that will make young actors want to grow up with it as part of a whole, giving their acting a new clear fakeless group excellence and group eloquence that will be our unique acting, our own thing, born in our American theatre as not so long ago Irish acting was born in the Irish Players, modern Russian acting in the Moscow Art Theatre, or modern German acting in the Reinhardt group? All these had humble beginnings as we have had. If we do intend to work with the future of our acting at least equally in view with the artistic production of good plays and great plays, then I am high with hope.

The immediate future of the theatre is in the actor. Until he gets his real opportunity we others—I speak as a playwright—this applies equally to all artists in the theatre—but wait for ours, or try to be contented with what we know must be an unrealizable dream.

Eugene O'Neill

ON MAN AND GOD

Most modern plays are concerned with the relation between man and man, but that does not interest me at all. I am interested only in the relation between man and God.[1]

The playwright today must dig at the roots of the sickness of today as he feels it—the death of the Old God and the failure of science and materialism to give any satisfying new One for the surviving primitive religious instinct to find a meaning for life in, and to comfort its fears of death with. It seems to me that anyone trying to do big work nowadays must have this big subject behind all the little subjects of his plays or novels, or he is simply scribbling around on the surface of things and has no more real status than a parlor entertainer.[2]

Title supplied by the editors.

1. A conversational remark quoted by J. W. Krutch in "Introduction" to *Nine Plays* by Eugene O'Neill. Used by permission of Random House.

2. From a letter to George Jean Nathan published in Nathan's *Intimate Notebooks* (Knopf, 1932). Used by permission of Mrs. Carlotta Monterey O'Neill.

Eugene O'Neill

MEMORANDA ON MASKS

Not masks for all plays, naturally. Obviously not for plays conceived in purely realistic terms. But masks for certain types of plays, especially for the new modern play, as yet only dimly foreshadowed in a few groping specimens, but which must inevitably be written in the future. For I hold more and more surely to the conviction that the use of masks will be discovered eventually to be the freest solution of the modern dramatist's problem as to how—with the greatest possible dramatic clarity and economy of means—he can express those profound hidden conflicts of the mind which the probings of psychology continue to disclose to us. He must find some method to present this inner drama in his work, or confess himself incapable of portraying one of the most characteristic preoccupations and uniquely significant, spiritual impulses of his time. With his old—and more than a bit senile!—standby of realistic technique, he can do no more than, at best, obscurely hint at it through a realistically disguised surface symbolism, superficial and misleading. But that, while sufficiently beguiling to the sentimentally mystical, is hardly enough. A comprehensive expression is demanded here, a chance for eloquent presentation, a new form of drama projected from a fresh insight into the inner forces motivating the actions and reactions of men and women (a new and truer characterization, in other words), a drama of souls, and the adventures of "Free wills," with the masks that govern them and constitute their fates.

For what, at bottom, is the new psychological insight into human cause and effect but a study in masks, an exercise in unmasking? Whether we think the attempted unmasking has been success-

From The American Spectator, *November 1932 ("Memoranda on Masks"); December 1932 ("Second Thoughts"); January 1933 ("A Dramatist's Notebook").*

ful, or has only created for itself new masks, is of no importance here. What is valid, what is unquestionable, is that this insight has uncovered the mask, has impressed the idea of mask as a symbol of inner reality upon all intelligent people of today; and I know they would welcome the use of masks in the theatre as a necessary, dramatically revealing new convention, and not regard them as any "stunty" resurrection of archaic props.

This was strikingly demonstrated for me in practical experience by *The Great God Brown*, which ran in New York for eight months, nearly all of that time in Broadway theatres—a play in which the use of masks was an integral part of the theme. There was some misunderstanding, of course. But so is there always misunderstanding in the thing beyond what is contained in a human-interest newspaper story. In the main, however, *The Great God Brown* was accepted and appreciated by both critics and public—a fairly extensive public, as its run gives evidence.

I emphasize this play's success because the fact that a mask drama, the main values of which are psychological, mystical, and abstract, could be played in New York for eight months, has always seemed to me a more significant proof of the deeply responsive possibilities in our public than anything that has happened in our modern theatre before or since.

2

Looked at from even the most practical standpoint of the practicing playwright, the mask *is* dramatic in itself, *has always* been dramatic in itself, *is* a proven weapon of attack. At its best, it is more subtly, imaginatively, suggestively dramatic than any actor's face can ever be. Let anyone who doubts this study the Japanese Noh masks, or Chinese theatre masks, or African primitive masks—or right here in America the faces of the big marionettes Robert Edmond Jones made for the production of Stravinsky's *Oedipus*, or Benda's famous masks, or even photographs of them.

3

Dogma for the new masked drama. One's outer life passes in a solitude haunted by the masks of others; one's inner life passes in a solitude hounded by the masks of oneself.

4

With masked mob a new type of play may be written in which the Mob as King, Hero, Villain, or Fool will be the main character—The Great Democratic Play!

5

Why not give all future Classical revivals entirely in masks? *Hamlet*, for example. Masks would liberate this play from its present confining status as exclusively a "star vehicle." We would be able to see the great drama we are now only privileged to read, to identify ourselves with the figure of Hamlet as a symbolic projection of a fate that is in each of us, instead of merely watching a star giving us his version of a great acting role. We would even be able to hear the sublime poetry as the innate expression of the spirit of the drama itself, instead of listening to it as realistic recitation—or ranting—by familiar actors.

6

Consider Goethe's *Faust*, which, psychologically speaking, should be the closest to us of all the Classics. In producing this play, I would have Mephistopheles wearing the Mephistophelean mask of the face of Faust. For is not the whole of Goethe's truth *for our time* just that Mephistopheles and Faust are one and the same—*are* Faust?

Second Thoughts

What would I change in past productions of my plays if I could live through them again? Many things. In some plays, considerable revision of the writing of some of the scenes would strike me as imperative. Other plays—*The First Man*, *Gold*, *Welded*, *The Fountain*—I would dismiss as being too painfully bungled in their present form to be worth producing at all.

But one thing I most certainly would not change: the use of masks in *The Hairy Ape*, in my arrangement of Coleridge's "Ancient Mariner," in *All God's Chillun Got Wings* (the symbol of the African primitive mask in the last part of the play, which, in the production in Russian by the Moscow Kamerny Theatre I saw in Paris, is dramatically intensified and emphasized), in *The Great*

God Brown and, finally, in *Lazarus Laughed*, in which all the characters except Lazarus remain masked throughout the play. I regard this use of masks as having been uniformly successful.

The change I would make would be to call for more masks in some of these productions and to use them in other productions where they were not used before. In *The Emperor Jones*, for example. All the figures in Jones's flight through the forest should be masked. Masks would dramatically stress their phantasmal quality, as contrasted with the unmasked Jones, intensify the supernatural menace of the tom tom, give the play a more complete and vivid expression. In *The Hairy Ape* a much more extensive use of masks would be of the greatest value in emphasizing the theme of the play. From the opening of the fourth scene, where Yank begins to think he enters into a masked world; even the familiar faces of his mates in the forecastle have become strange and alien. They should be masked, and the faces of everyone he encounters thereafter, including the symbolic gorilla's.

In *All God's Chillun Got Wings*, all save the seven leading characters should be masked; for all the secondary figures are part and parcel of the Expressionistic background of the play, a world at first indifferent, then cruelly hostile, against which the tragedy of Jim Harris is outlined. In *The Great God Brown* I would now make the masks symbolize more definitely the abstract theme of the play instead of, as in the old production, stressing the more superficial meaning that people wear masks before other people and are mistaken by them for their masks.

In *Marco Millions* all the people of the East should be masked —Kublai, the Princess Kukachin, all of them! For anyone who has been in the East, or who has read Eastern philosophy, the reason for this is obvious. It is an exact dramatic expression of West confronted by East. Morever, it is the only possible way to project this contrast truthfully in the theatre, for Western actors cannot convey Eastern character realistically, and their only chance to suggest it convincingly is with the help of masks.

As for *Strange Interlude*, that is an attempt at the new masked psychological drama which I have discussed before, without masks —a successful attempt, perhaps, in so far as it concerns only surfaces and their immediate subsurfaces, but not where, occasionally, it tries to probe deeper.

With *Mourning Becomes Electra*, masks were called for in one draft of the three plays. But the Classical connotation was too insistent. Masks in that connection demand great language to speak —which let me out of it with a sickening bump! So it evolved ultimately into the "masklike faces," which expressed my intention tempered by the circumstances. However, I should like to see *Mourning Becomes Electra* done entirely with masks, now that I can view it solely as a psychological play, quite removed from the confusing preoccupations the Classical derivation of its plot once caused me. Masks would emphasize the drama of the life and death impulses that drive the characters on to their fates and put more in its proper secondary place, as a frame, the story of the New England family.

A Dramatist's Notebook

I advocate masks for stage crowds, mobs—wherever a sense of impersonal, collective mob psychology is wanted. This was one reason for such an extensive use of them in *Lazarus Laughed*. In masking the crowds in that play, I was visualizing an effect that, intensified by dramatic lighting, would give an audience visually the sense of the Crowd, not as a random collection of individuals, but as a collective whole, an entity. When the Crowd speaks, I wanted an audience to hear the voice of Crowd mind, Crowd emotion, as one voice of a body composed of, but quite distinct from, its parts.

And, for more practical reasons, I wanted to preserve the different crowds of another time and country from the blighting illusion-shattering recognitions by an audience of the supers on the stage. Have you ever seen a production of *Julius Caesar?* Did the Roman mob ever suggest to you anything more Roman than a gum-chewing Coney Island Mardi Gras or, in the case of a special all-star revival, a gathering of familiar-faced modern actors masquerading uncomfortably in togas? But with masks—and the proper intensive lighting—you would have been freed from these recognitions; you would have been able to imagine a Roman mob; you would not even have recognized the Third Avenue and Brooklyn accents among the supers, so effectively does a mask change the quality of a voice.

It was interesting to watch, in the final rehearsals of *The*

Great God Brown, how after using their masks for a time the actors and actresses reacted to the demand made by the masks that their bodies become alive and expressive and participate in the drama. Usually it is only the actors' faces that participate. Their bodies remain bored spectators that have been dragged off to the theatre when they would have much preferred a quiet evening in the upholstered chair at home.

Meaning no carping disrespect to our actors. I have been exceedingly lucky in having had some exceptionally fine acting in the principal roles in my plays, for which I am exceedingly grateful. Also some damned poor acting. But let that pass. Most of the poor acting occurred in the poor plays, and there I hold only myself responsible. In the main, wherever a part challenged the actors' or actresses' greatest possibilities, they have reacted to the challenge with a splendid creative energy and skill. Especially, and this is the point I want to make now, where the play took them away from the strictly realistic parts they were accustomed to playing. They always welcomed any opportunity that gave them new scope for their talents. So when I argue here for a non-realistic imaginative theatre I am hoping, not only for added scope for playwright and director and scenic designer, but also for a chance for the actor to develop his art beyond the narrow range to which our present theatre condemns it. Most important of all, from the standpoint of future American culture, I am hoping for added imaginative scope for the audience, a chance for a public I know is growing yearly more numerous and more hungry in its spiritual need to participate in imaginative interpretations of life rather than merely identify itself with faithful surface resemblances of living.

I harp on the word "imaginative"—and with intention! But what do I mean by an "imaginative" theatre—(where I hope for it, for example, in the subtitle of *Lazarus Laughed:* A Play for an Imaginative Theatre)? I mean the one true theatre, the age-old theatre, the theatre of the Greeks and Elizabethans, a theatre that could dare to boast—without committing a farcical sacrilege—that it is a legitimate descendant of the first theatre that sprang, by virtue of man's imaginative interpretation of life, out of his worship of Dionysus. I mean a theatre returned to its highest and sole significant function as a Temple where the religion of a poetical interpretation and symbolical celebration of life is communicated to human beings, starved in spirit by their soul-stifling daily struggle to exist as masks among the masks of living!

But I anticipate the actors' objection to masks: that they would extinguish their personalities and deprive them of their greatest asset in conveying emotion by facial expression. I claim, however, that masks would give them the opportunity for a totally new kind of acting, that they would learn many undeveloped possibilities of their art if they appeared, even if only for a season or two, in masked roles. After all, masks did not extinguish the Greek actor, nor have they kept the acting of the East from being an art.

Eugene O'Neill

O'NEILL'S IDEAL OF A THEATRE

A Letter to the Kamerny Theatre

Having witnessed your productions of *Desire Under the Elms* and *All God's Chillun Got Wings*, my feeling is one of amazement—and most profound gratitude! Let me humbly confess I came to the theatre with secret misgivings. Not that I doubted your presentation would be a splendid thing in itself, artistically conceived and executed. I know the reputation of the Kamerny as one of the finest theatres in Europe too well for that. But I did have an author's fear that in the difficult process of transition and transformation into another language and milieu the inner spirit—that indefinable essential quality so dear to the creator as being for him the soul of his work!—might be excusably, considering the obstacles, distorted or lost.

Hence my amazement and gratitude when I saw your productions, which in every way delighted me because they rang so true to the spirit of my work! And they were not only that! They were also productions conceived by your director, Alexander Tairov, with that rarest of all gifts in a director—creative imagination! They were interpreted by Mme. Koonen and the other extraordinary artists of your company with that rarest of all gifts in actors and actresses—creative imagination!

A theatre of creative imagination has always been my ideal! To see my plays given by such a theatre has always been my dream! The Kamerny Theatre has realized this dream for me. I will never forget that experience nor cease to be grateful for it and for the privilege of meeting all of you and the warm friendliness of your reception. Most gratifying of all was my feeling that, despite the

---

From the New York Herald Tribune, *June 19, 1932. A letter from O'Neill to the manager of the Kamerny Theatre (June 2, 1930) after O'Neill had attended Kamerny Theatre productions in Paris.*

barrier of language, you all felt the kinship with me as I immediately did with you—that we had known one another a long time and were united in old and tried friendship—comradeship!—by the love of the true theatre.

To the Kamerny Theatre, my gratitude, my admiration and my friendship! May all your dreams be realized!

Your friend,
Eugene O'Neill
June 2, 1930

Eugene O'Neill

NEGLECTED POET

A Letter to Arthur Hobson Quinn

It's not in me to pose much as a "misunderstood one," but it does seem discouragingly (that is, if one lacked a sense of ironic humor!) evident to me that most of my critics don't want to see what I'm trying to do or how I'm trying to do it, although I flatter myself that end and means are characteristic, individual and positive enough not to be mistaken for anyone's else, or for those of any "modern" or "pre-modern" school. To be called a "sordid realist" one day, a "grim, pessimistic Naturalist" the next, a "lying Moral Romanticist" the next, etc. is quite perplexing—not to add the *Times* editorial that settled *Desire* once and for all by calling it a "Neo-Primitive," a Matisse of the drama, as it were! So I'm really longing to explain and try and convince some sympathetic ear that I've tried to make myself a melting pot for all these methods, seeing some virtues for my ends in each of them, and thereby, if there is enough real fire in me, boil down to my own technique. But where I feel myself most neglected is just where I set most store by myself—as a bit of a poet, who has labored with the spoken word to evolve original rhythms of beauty, where beauty apparently isn't—*Jones*, *Ape*, *God's Chillun*, *Desire*, etc.—and to see the transfiguring nobility of tragedy, in as near the Greek sense as one can grasp it, in seemingly the most ignoble, debased lives. And just here is where I am a most confirmed mystic, too, for I'm always, always trying to interpret Life in terms of lives, never just lives in terms of character. I'm always acutely conscious of the Force behind—Fate, God, our biological past creating our present, whatever one calls it—Mystery certainly—and of the one eternal tragedy of Man in his glorious, self-destructive struggle to make the Force express him instead of being, as an animal is, an

From a letter to Arthur Hobson Quinn published in Quinn's A History of the American Drama, *vol. II, F. S. Crofts & Co., 1945.*

infinitesimal incident in its expression. And my profound conviction is that this is the only subject worth writing about and that it is possible—or can be—to develop a tragic expression in terms of transfigured modern values and symbols in the theatre which may to some degree bring home to members of a modern audience their ennobling identity with the tragic figures on the stage. Of course, this is very much of a dream, but where the theatre is concerned, one must have a dream, and the Greek dream in tragedy is the noblest ever!

3

REVIEWS

THE INDIVIDUAL PLAYS

Heywood Broun

"BOUND EAST FOR CARDIFF"

Here is a play which owes more to the creation of mood and atmosphere than to any fundamentally interesting idea or sudden twist of plot. "Bound East for Cardiff" merely shows the death of a sailor in the forecastle of a British tramp on a foggy night. The appeal lies in the successful approximation of true talk in such a speech as the one where the dying sailor fretfully complains: "Why should it be a rotten night like this, with that damn whistle blowin' and people snorin' all around? I wish the stars was out, and the moon, too; I c'd lie out on deck and look at them, and it'd make it easier to go—somehow."

Approximation, rather than faithful reproduction, must be the aim of the dramatist who deals with the looser talking sort of folk. Obviously, it is impossible to set down the conversation of sailors word for word. And yet it is possible to make their talk sound real, as in the speech we have quoted, or unreal, as in the scene where Driscoll, "a red-haired giant, with the battered features of a prize-fighter," refers to one of his boon companions as a "divil-may-care rake av a man." This is false, not so much because the phrase is obviously one which would not be heard from the mouth of a sailor, but because the spirit is false.

Such slips are few in the play. Eugene O'Neill has written several short plays about the sea, and is probably familiar with that subject. At any rate, he strikes a rich vein, the old Kipling vein, in the bit where the dying man and his pal mull over the times they used to have. "The moving pictures in Barracas? Some class to them, d'yuh remember?" And they talk of sounds in Paseo Colon, and smells in La Plata, rows in Singapore and sprees in Port Said,

---

From the New York Tribune, *January 30, 1917. Reprinted by permission of the* New York Herald Tribune.

to say nothing of the fight on a dock in Cape Town, when knives were drawn.

Appropriately enough, there is a touch of sentiment about the pleasant-spoken barmaid at the Red Stork, in Cardiff. Perhaps it is of her that Yank is thinking just before he dies, when he gulps at the dipper of water and gasps: "I wish this was a pint of beer."

Helen Deutsch

"BEFORE BREAKFAST"

"Before Breakfast" is a one-character play, essentially a stunt of the playwright, who was at this time intrigued by stage tricks and melodramatic situations. Lovely Mary Pyne drew back her red hair into a sloppy knot and gave a fine performance as the ugly, nagging wife. O'Neill played the off-stage husband, who reaches through the open door for a bowl of shaving water and, just before the closing curtain, utters an agonized gurgle as he commits suicide with a razor. This invisible character was the shy playwright's favorite role, and his "last appearance on any stage." His father, James O'Neill, the veteran actor of *The Count of Monte Cristo*, was invited to Macdougal Street to direct "Before Breakfast." Father and son, in a perfect Freudian pattern, disagreed on every point. O'Neill Senior tried to instill in Mary Pyne some of the histrionic technique of an era which the Players had no wish to revive, while O'Neill Junior stalked up and down, muttering his displeasure.

From The Provincetown, *copyright by Helen Deutsch and Stella Hanau, 1931, 1959. Not a review, but the only record of this production.*

Louis Sherwin

"ILE"

The best that can be said for the latest program at the Greenwich Village Theatre is that it is much more interesting than the two that came before it. In fact, if it were not for the amateurish, slovenly performance of Schnitzler's *The Big Scene* one might even say that it was on the whole excellent. As it was, however, only one of the three divisions of the program was in every way worthy of praise. And that was Eugene O'Neill's "Ile." Not only did it prove to be a playlet of a very high order, but the acting, the staging, and the atmosphere were quite admirable.

The man O'Neill arouses the keenest interest in me. I don't know of any young man writing for the stage today, either in Europe or America, who shows more promise. His sailors live as Joseph Conrad's Marlow and Lord Jim and the unforgettable crew of the *Narcissus* live. He knows life, at any rate the life of the sea. He knows the people of the sea and their women. He has a feeling for irony, for the sardonic humor with which the gods plot the drama of human affairs. He knows not only how his people talk, but what they feel and what they hope and how destiny mocks their pathetic ambitions. Take, for instance, the captain of the whaler in this little play, driving his crew to despair and his wife to madness with his determination to go on and on and on until he has a shipload of "Ile." It is not for the money—he has plenty for his needs. It is not for fear of being jeered at by the folks at home—they would not dare jeer to his face. It is because he has always returned with a full shipload before and his vanity won't let him sail home with less. Very simple and obvious psychology, isn't it? But it is true, it is real, and it is the sort of truth

---

From the New York Globe, *April 19, 1918. Reprinted with permission.*

you seldom find in plays. And, above all, it is so well done, so powerfully, tersely, vividly written.

Mr. O'Neill's talent so far has been displayed only in one-act pieces. I am really eager to see what he will do with a full three-act play. He has a rare gift—a gift to be envied. It is to be hoped that he is making the utmost of it.

Alexander Woollcott

"THE DREAMY KID"

It is a provocative and almost continuously interesting evening that is provided in Macdougal Street, where another week remains for the first bill of short plays staged this season by the Provincetown Players. In the cramped and dismal little theatre off Washington Square, where the dramatic pauses are sometimes rudely interrupted by the boisterous hubbub of nearby plumbing, the kind of fare is served which used to be looked for at the Bandbox in the palmy days of the Washington Square Players.

"The Dreamy Kid" is another good play from Eugene O'Neill, many of whose shorter pieces for the stage had already seen the somewhat dim light of this same theatre. He is the son of James O'Neill of *Monte Cristo* fame, and a long play of his called *Chris* is to be produced after the holidays by the same George Tyler who ran through the lamp-lit streets of Chicago that night thirty years ago when this playwright came into the world. *Chris* is a play of the sea, on which O'Neill has served before the mast.

"The Dreamy Kid" is a sketch which has as its central figure a young, crap-shooting, gang-leading, gun-toting darky who has just killed a white man in a scrap and who, with the police hot on his trail, has nevertheless crept to the deathbed of his grandmother, because he knows in his heart he will have no luck all the days of his life if he does not obey her final summons. It is interesting to see how, just as Dreiser does in *The Hand of the Potter*, so here the author of "The Dreamy Kid" induces your complete sympathy and pity for a conventionally abhorrent character.

From The New York Times, *November 9, 1919. Reprinted by permission of* The New York Times, *and the Executor for the author's estate. Copyright 1919 by the New York Times Company.*

Alexander Woollcott

BEYOND THE HORIZON

There came to town last Tuesday afternoon, as a tentative and hesitant candidate for whatever hospitality this capricious and somewhat harassed city might be moved to offer, a play which, for all its looseness and a certain high-and-mighty impracticability, is possessed of elements of greatness. This was *Beyond the Horizon*, a vital and valid tragedy by Eugene G. O'Neill—a play that is as native as *Lightnin'* and which has the mood, the austerity and, all in all, the stature of a novel by Thomas Hardy. Seldom has an American playwright written for our theatre a piece half so good and true.

It is O'Neill's first long play to reach the stage—the first of three scheduled for production in this country before the strawberries come again. It has been preceded by six or seven one-act pieces, produced at different times by one or another of the experimental theatres in the byways of New York, those oft-derided, semi-amateur companies which are serving one of their chief purposes in life when they thus aid and encourage the short, trial flights of men like Eugene O'Neill.

Beyond the Horizon unfolds the tragedy of a young, farm-born dreamer, whose romantic mind and frail body yearn for the open sea, the swarming ports of the mysterious East, the beckoning world beyond the line of hills which shut in the acres of his home. By all that is in him, he is destined for a wanderer's life, but Fate, in a wanton mood, tethers him to this little hill-cupped farm and watches coolly the misery and decay this means for all his house. You meet him first at this cross-roads of his life and see him take

---

From The New York Times, *February 8, 1920. Reprinted by permission of* The New York Times, *and the Executor for the author's estate. Copyright 1920 by the New York Times Company. The essay also appeared in the author's book* Shouts and Murmurs.

the wrong turning. To him, on the night before he is to set sail for a three years' cruise around the world, comes love in the form of a neighbor's daughter whom he and all his people had thought marked rather for his brother. Blinded by the flame kindled in that moment of her confession, he lightly forgoes all thought of the world beyond the horizon, plans to settle at once on the farm with his jubilant bride, and watches serenely enough while his heart-wrenched brother sets forth on the cruise that was to have been his—the bluff, unromantic brother who, irony of ironies, is a true son of the soil, born to do nothing but work its fields and sure to wither if uprooted.

Then you follow through the years the decay of that household, the tragedy of the misfit. You see the waning of love, the birth of disappointment, the corrosion of poverty and spite and disease. You watch the romance burn itself out to an ugly cinder. You see the woman grow drab and dull and sullen, and you see the man, wasted by the consumption that in another life might have been avoided, crawl at last out of the hated house to die on the road he should have traveled, straining his eyes toward the hills he never crossed.

All this is told with sure dramatic instinct, clear understanding, and a certain quite unsentimental compassion. To an extent unfamiliar in our theatre, this play seems alive. This is not merely because truth works within it nor because of the realness of its people. It is rather because of the visible growth and change that take place as the play unfolds.

The aging of the people is evidenced by more than the mere graying at the temples and the change of clothes, those easy symbols by which the theatre is wont to recognize, if at all, the flight of the years. In a hundred and one ways, it is evidenced as well by the slow changing of character and the steady deterioration of the souls—a progression of the spirit which, by the way, asks great things of the actors, and, for the most part, asks not in vain. O'Neill paints his canvas with what Henley called "the exquisite chromatics of decay." You might almost say, then, that the play is alive because it follows the inexorable processes of death. Not since Arnold Bennett's *Old Wives' Tale* has any book or play given us quite so persuasively a sense of the passage of time.

We have in O'Neill evidence a-plenty of a predisposition for the dramatic that is as pronounced as the Barrymore inheritance. But we have one who has lived so remote from the theatre that he has been uncorrupted by the merely theatrical and has carried over into his own workshop not one of the worn stencils and battered properties which are the dust-covered accumulations of years.

This same remoteness, which so freshens the air of his play, is probably responsible, also, for its considerable impracticability. He was an impractical playwright, for instance, who wrote into his play the character of a two-year-old girl and gave her two long scenes with business to do and lines to speak. He might have known that the part would have to be given to a child disturbingly, almost comically older than the baby called for by the context.

Certainly it was a quite impractical playwright who split each of his three acts into two scenes, one outside and one inside the Mayo farmhouse. It was natural enough for him to want to show the high-road of Robert Mayo's dreams, inevitable that he should itch to place one scene on the hilltop, with its almost protagonistic vista of the distant sea. But no essential purpose is served by these exteriors which could not have been served had they been unfolded within the farmhouse, without a break of any kind.

Some of a novelist's luxuries must be forgone by a writer when he goes into the theatre, and one of the lessons he must learn is that the ever illusion-dispelling process of dropping a curtain, releasing an audience and shifting a scene is accepted twice and sometimes three times by a modern audience without even an unconscious resistance. But any further interruption works havoc with the spell. It may be reported here that, at the second performance, the third act was telescoped into a single scene, and it may be guessed that the play would not only be a better knit but a much more popular piece if the same violence were done the other acts as soon as possible.

In the theatre, what you want and what you get are very different. A more shop-wise playwright would have known that for his exteriors, each of them but a portion of an act and therefore certain to be of a hasty and makeshift nature, he could scarcely count on so illusive and charming a vista, so persuasive a creation of the outdoors as glorifies the final act of the Lee Simonson investiture for *The Power of Darkness*. The conspicuously dinky expanses of nature provided for *Beyond the Horizon* must have been a good deal of a shock to O'Neill. The wrinkled skies, the portière-like trees, the clouds so close you are in momentary expectation that a scrub-lady will waddle on and wash them—these made doubly futile the dashes in and out of the Mayo farmhouse.

It is one thing for O'Neill to sit at his faraway seacoast study and dream a scene—another thing to find it provided for his play when the first curtain rises in New York. It is instructive to compare the unillusive setting for his first scene with the stage picture as he had imagined it and set it forth in his script:

> A section of a country highway. The road runs diagonally from the left forward to the right, rear, and can be seen winding toward the horizon like a pale ribbon between the low, rolling hills with their freshly plowed fields clearly divided from each other, checkerboard fashion, by the lines of stone walls and rough snake-fences.
>
> The forward triangle, cut off by the road, is a section of a field, from the dark earth of which myriad bright-green blades of Fall-sown rye are sprouting. A straggling line of piled rocks, too low to be called a wall, separates this field from the road.
>
> To the rear of the road is a ditch with a sloping grassy bank on the far side. From the center of this an old, gnarled apple tree, just budding into leaf, strains its twisted branches heavenward with despairing gestures, black against the pallor of distance. A snakefence sidles grotesquely from left to right along the top of the bank, passing beneath the apple tree.
>
> The dreamy twilight of a day in May is just beginning. The horizon hills are still rimmed by a faint line of flame, and the sky above them is radiant with the dying flush of the sunset. This disappears gradually, and stars awake in the infinite, drowsily, one by one.
>
> At the rise of the curtain, Robert Mayo is discovered sitting on the fence.

What O'Neill actually found on the Morosco stage was what people usually get who cry for the moon—instead of sixpence.

There is scarcely room left to expatiate on the details of the deeply satisfying performance given by the composite company assembled for these special matinées. Except in one secondary role—that of Mrs. Mayo—the cast is admirable. Richard Bennett gives an eloquent and finely imagined performance as the dreamer—a part John Barrymore would revel in. Indeed, *Beyond the Horizon* is such a play as belongs in his repertoire. Edward Arnold and the gifted Helen MacKellar are completely convincing. There must be special mention of the gorgeous performance given by Louise Closser Hale as the semiparalyzed mother-in-law who carps away at life from her wheel chair and regards Robert's yearnings with about as much sympathy as that intensely local old lady who bought David Copperfield's cowl, she whose motto in life was: "Let there be no meandering." It is worth going miles to see the way Miss Hale makes that wheel chair take a part in the play. She uses it as Mrs. Fiske uses a fan or a lorgnette, something to brandish, something wherewith to bridle and emphasize a thought or point a bit of wit.

The cast for *Beyond the Horizon* was assembled from the two companies which in the evening devote themselves to *For the Defense* and *The Storm*. The success of the amalgam which gave the producer almost as much freedom of choice as he needed, suggests that the double theatre is probably the best solution of the problem confronting the producer who is minded to create a repertory theatre. While New York awaits the somewhat doubtful benefit of a repertory theatre, it may be noted that much of the work expected of such an institution is being done by the modest institution known as the special matinée, which brought *The Yellow Jacket* to life again, and which, in *Beyond the Horizon*, has given us one of the real plays of our time.

Anonymous

CHRIS

At the Broad Street Theatre, Philadelphia, Eugene O'Neill's new play *Chris* was given its first presentation. It is a rough sea-story divided into six scenes, yet with a surprisingly slim plot and very little action. Most of the credit goes to Emmett Corrigan, Lynn Fontanne, and Arthur Ashley for their excellent acting, and to Frederick Stanhope for his well directed staging.

Chris is an old sea-dog from Sweden, who had sunk from "bo'sun" to being captain on a dirty coal-barge. He has hated the sea for years—ever since it separated him from his wife, who died while he was away. His child, Anna, has been carefully brought up in England and is now coming to America to seek out her father. Anna arrives, is shocked at the ugliness of the old barge which is "home" for her father. However, she is so happy to be with her father again, Chris easily persuades her to take a trip on the barge —which she does "for the fun of it." Gradually, she feels the call of the sea within her, and grows to love it.

They are run down in a fog by a tramp steamer, taken aboard, and carried to Buenos Aires, a four weeks trip. Anna falls in love with the handsome second mate and in spite of her father's warning, decides to marry her hero. At first Chris attempts to forbid it, and even tries to kill the second mate (in the one dramatic-action scene of the play) but eventually relents, and accepts the job of "bo'sun" on the tramp steamer.

The material is very slim, but the play carries itself along from sheer excellence of presentation. Emmett Corrigan, in a blond wig, enacts Chris with considerable skill, and his Swedish accent is well assumed. Lynn Fontanne, as Anna, was pleasing, and her refinement did much to off-set the common coarseness of the coal-

---

From The Stage, *March 27, 1920. Reprinted by permission of* Theatre Arts *Magazine.*

bargers. Arthur Ashley was the good-looking mate, and played with ease and quiet manliness the rather brief part. Mary Hampton as the drab old Marthy made much of the one scene in which she appeared. There were numerous other "bits," all well done, mostly the rough types of men with whom Chris associated. John Rogers as "Jonsey" was particularly good.

Alexander Woollcott

"EXORCISM"

The current bill of the Provincetown Players is interesting all the way through, with its climax provided in "Exorcism"—an uncommonly good one-act play by Eugene O'Neill. Absence of any comment here on their two preceding programs was due neither to indolence, the remoteness of Macdougal Street, nor hardening of the artistic curiosity as to what could and might be done in the side-streets of New York. These earlier bills were merely too dank and dull for the details to survive in the memory of your correspondent. There lingers there now only a confused impression of dark cellars, fitful candle-light, and voices lifted in the gloom—usually wailing something like "O Moishe, Moishe!" or words to that effect. . . .

This new O'Neill play exhibits a young man of a substantial and correct family who is so full of contempt for it that he has walked out, head high, and fallen into the gutter. He is down in the dregs of existence when the play begins, equally revolted by the character of his life and by the prospect of a surrendering, prodigal-son return. He is so plagued by the questioning devils within him that even a fresh start on a farm out West has no appeal to him. So he swallows poison, placidly says, "That's over," and curls up on his miserable bed.

Twenty-four hours elapse and you find him stretched out under the delighted ministrations of two drunken friends, who are bibulously pleased with themselves for having yanked him back from the brink of the grave. You see him slowly reviving, only to find the ugly, inescapable world still closing in around him, with its intolerable tedium represented by the two souses, each still telling, over and over again, his favorite story. The suicide comes

---

From The New York Times, *April 4, 1920. Reprinted by permission of* The New York Times *and the Executor for the author's estate.*

back to find everything wearisomely the same—everything except himself. Slowly he realizes that he is different—that the devils have gone out of him. Slowly it dawns on him that, when a fellow tries hard to kill himself and seems to fail, the effect is quite as though he had succeeded. The person revived is a new person, the life ahead is life in a new world. With a real appetite for that world you leave him all worked up about that beckoning farm out West.

One of the most important factors in O'Neill's force as a playwright is visible in "Exorcism," and that is the surplus creative energy which enables him, after the essential structure of the play has been attended to, to people it with original and distinctive characters, brought into the theatre with the breath of life in them and backgrounds that ask no aid from the man with the brush.

It is common enough in our theatre to find a single vivid character stalking amid puppets—witness *Erstwhile Susan*, or *Grumpy*, or *Lightnin'*. But it is decidedly uncommon to find the secondary roles alive and real and individual. The average playwright is quite exhausted when he has worked out his plot and done a bit of portraiture in the leading role. When other figures are needed, he feels it quite all right to take the mannequins from the property room, dust them off, paint them different colors, and then set them to work. He feels he has fairly outdone himself if he provides one with red hair, another with an English accent and a third, say, with a rheumatic walk. Of course, the favorite outburst of characterization consists in giving one of the puppets cocaine, a dramatic drug, which furnishes the maximum of emotion, facial expression and gesture with the minimum of thought behind it. But with O'Neill, the smallest roles have a certain sovereignty. In an O'Neill play, no one can play "straight," as the actors have it. All the parts are clearly what theatre folk call character parts, as if, poor dears, there were really any other kind.

O'Neill's aptitude for sketching in a figure in a few telling speeches has been apparent from the first of his plays. Witness, for example, the Captain in "Bound East for Cardiff." As more and more of his plays have come to life, the mere abundance of this extra energy grows interesting. Consider both *Beyond the Horizon* and "Exorcism," which in this respect are unmatched by any other plays of the season save the two which have established St. John Ervine—*John Ferguson* and *Jane Clegg*.

Heywood Broun

THE EMPEROR JONES

Subject to later reservations and revisions, when all the missing districts are in, Eugene O'Neill's *The Emperor Jones* seems to us just about the most interesting play which has yet come from the most promising playwright in America. Perhaps we ought to be a little more courageous and say right out the best of American playwrights, but somehow or other a superlative carries the implication of a certain static quality. We never see a play by O'Neill without feeling that something of the sort will be done better within a season or so, and that O'Neill will do it.

As gorgeous a piece as *The Emperor Jones* has loose ends fluttering here and there as they trail along with the clouds of glory. This is a play of high trajectory and up above the country stores and the lobby of the Palace Hotel, Wuppinger Falls, ten months later and Yvette's boudoir there is a rarer atmosphere which makes it difficult to avoid an occasional slip this way and that.

The Emperor Jones tells of an American negro, a Pullman porter, who, by some chance or other, comes to an island in the West Indies, "not yet self-determined by white marines." In two years Jones has made himself emperor. Luck has played a part, but he has been quick to take advantage of it. Once a native tried to shoot him at point-blank range, but the gun missed fire, whereupon Jones announced that he was protected by a charm and that only silver bullets could harm him. When the play begins he has been emperor long enough to amass a fortune by imposing heavy taxes on the islanders and carrying on all sorts of large-scale graft. Rebellion is brewing. When Emperor Jones rings the bell which should summon his servants no one appears. The palace is deserted, but from deep in the jungle there comes the sound of the steady beat

---

From the New York Tribune, *November 4, 1920. Reprinted by permission of the* New York Herald Tribune.

of a big drum. The islanders are whipping up their courage to the fighting point by calling on the local gods and demons of the forest.

Jones, realizing that his reign is over, starts to make his escape to the coast where a French gunboat is anchored. First it is necessary for him to travel through the jungle and as time presses he must go through at night. Back in the States he was a good Baptist and he begins the journey through the dark places unafraid. But under the dim moonlight he cannot recognize any familiar landmarks and, hard as he runs, the continuous drumbeat never grows any less in his ears. Then demons and apparitions begin to torment him. First it is the figure of a negro he killed back in the States. He fires and the dim thing vanishes, but immediately he reproaches himself, for in his revolver now he has only five shots left. Four are lead bullets and the fifth is a silver one which he has reserved for himself, if by any chance capture seems imminent.

Other little "formless fears" creep in upon him. As his panic increases the fears become not things in his own life, but old race fears. He sees himself being sold in a slave market and then, most horrible of all, a Congo witch doctor tries to lure him to death in a river where a crocodile god is waiting. It is at this point that he fires his last bullet, the silver one.

During the night he has discarded his big patent leather boots and most of his clothes in order to run faster from the drumbeat. But it is louder now than ever and in the last scene we find the natives sitting about in a circle weaving spells and molding bullets. And it is to this spot that the defenseless and exhausted emperor crawls, having made a complete circle in the jungle as his panic whipped him on.

The play is of eight scenes and it is largely a monologue by one character, the Emperor Jones. Unfortunately, production in the tiny Provincetown Theatre is difficult and the waits between these scenes are often several minutes in length. Each wait is a vulture which preys upon the attention. With the beginning of each new scene, contact must again be established and all this unquestionably hurts. Still we have no disposition to say, "If only the play had been done in 'the commercial theatre'!" This is a not infrequent comment whenever a little theatre does a fine piece of work and it seems to us to have in it something of the spirit of a man standing on the deck of a great liner who should remark, "Wasn't Columbus a bally ass to come over in such a little tub!"

The Emperor Jones is so unusual in its technique that it might wait in vain for a production anywhere except in so adventurous a playhouse as the Provincetown Theatre. As a matter of fact, the setting of the play on the little stage is fine and imaginative and the lighting effects uncommonly beautiful. There is nothing for complaint but the delays. Also, if *The Emperor Jones* were taken elsewhere we have little doubt that the manager would engage a white man with a piece of burnt cork to play Brutus Jones. They have done better in Macdougal Street. The Emperor is played by a negro actor named Charles S. Gilpin, who gives the most thrilling performance we have seen any place this season. He sustains the succession of scenes in monologue not only because his voice is one of gorgeous natural quality, but because he knows just what to do with it. All the notes are there and he has also the extraordinary facility for being in the right place at the right time. Generally he seems fairly painted into the scenic design. One performance is not enough to entitle a player to the word great even from a not too careful critic, but there can be no question whatever that in *The Emperor Jones* Gilpin is great. It is a performance of heroic stature. It is so good that the fact that it is enormously skillful seems only incidental.

Aside from difficulties of production there are some faults in O'Neill's play. He has almost completely missed the opportunities of his last scene, which should blaze with a vast tinder spark of irony. Instead, he rounds it off with a snap of the fingers, a little O. Henry dido. We cannot understand just why he has allowed the Emperor to die to the sound of off-stage shots. It is our idea that he should come crawling to the very spot where he meets his death and that the natives should be molding silver bullets there and waiting without so much as stretching out a finger for him. Of course all this goes to show that *The Emperor Jones* is truly a fine play. It is only such which tempt the spectator to leap in himself as a collaborator.

Kenneth Macgowan

DIFF'RENT

This is a year of triumphs for the Provincetown Players. For six seasons, they have plodded along in their little improvised playhouse off Washington Square, mounting much that was bad, along with some excellent plays by Susan Glaspell and other strangers to the Broadway theatres, which have found their way to almost all the "little theatres" and amateur groups of the country. The chief distinction of the Provincetown Players, however, besides a rare determination to stick to their job of giving the American author a chance, has been the discovery and development of the most powerful and adept playwright that America has ever produced, Eugene O'Neill. Perhaps he has not yet written the finest of American plays, though his tragedy of tuberculosis, *The Straw*, not yet produced, seems in manuscript a piece of fine power. But in everything O'Neill has done, there is a type of true, clear, and exciting dialogue such as no other American writes or has written in the theatre. This year his powers have come closer than before to fruition and have carried the Provincetown Players through half of what promises to be a vastly successful season. *The Emperor Jones* proved so popular that it was continued at their little playhouse for over a month, then carried uptown for special matinées, and finally pushed into the evening bill of a theatre where commercial successes have proved very rare. Now comes another O'Neill play which has won almost as much renown and which also has been carried up to Broadway for the delectation of its matinée-goers.

I am loathe to confess that I cannot feel quite the enthusiasm for *Diff'rent* that it has aroused in even the most critical who have

---

seen it. It is written with all O'Neill's command of dialogue. Its construction is excellent, and its story moving. Yet because of its material and because of *The Emperor Jones*, it is disappointing.

Diff'rent is the story of a woman who refused love and marriage because of a very tiny and excusable irregularity in a sailor's life. In the first of the two acts of the play, we come upon the girl and her lover in the sitting-room of her parents' home. We sense the fine fiber that runs through her; we learn of her illusions, which make her, as she says, "diff'rent" from the other girls of the sea-port town. Presently comes a rumor of a joke played upon her lover while he was in command of a sailing vessel in the South Seas, a joke which involved one of those strong, handsome women of the tropics, so much celebrated today in the fact and fiction of the Gauguin revival. It is an episode which leaves the so-called virtue of the man in doubt, but which certainly places his human qualities and his fundamental decency and devotion in a most favorable light. But the girl is "diff'rent." She sends him off. In the second act, thirty years later, we find the couple still unmarried, the man still devoted to her, but the woman seeking elsewhere some part of the pleasures of youth that are slipping from her. She paints, she dresses in absurdly youthful fashion, she pouts and snickers, and she makes love openly and shamelessly to an unmitigated young rotter, who promises to marry her in order to get money from her. The outcome is a double tragedy. The old lover hangs himself when he learns of her degrading match, and when the woman learns this and finds that the boy has been tricking her, she makes the same end of herself.

Only the close of the play, the double hanging, seems at all inept, and even for this there is defense. Certainly the characters are drawn with the greatest skill, and the language of every-day is made powerful and pregnant with drama. The development of the principals and of certain subsidiary characters over the thirty years is well managed. The talk of the rotter is usually real and convincing; ordinarily such young villains are the merest sticks. Yet the unescapable impression of anyone who remembers *The Emperor Jones* and its fine imaginative quality, its color, and its spiritual power, and compares it with *Diff'rent*, must be that the newer play is a step backward for its author. It is no more than a powerful document on the pathology of a woman in her forties. For those who care for "messages," there is, of course, a vigorous and healthful attack upon the puritanism that eats away so much of the creative happiness of life; but, in the end, *Diff'rent* remains a "thriller" upon a sex topic uncommonly well handled.

There is one passage in the first act of *Diff'rent* which gives one a sense of what fine possibilities there are in O'Neill for a continuance of the remarkable strain which gives *The Emperor Jones* its distinction. The descriptions of the tropical islands, the naked women in the sun, and the heat and beauty of those Southern seas, are full of the strong and uplifting lyricism which in *The Emperor Jones* takes the shape of a dark and beautiful and terrifying dirge. In such stuff there is the future of the theatre. There lie imagination and vision based upon reality, but springing upward into the strange and mysterious reaches of the soul which modern psychology has opened for us.

The playing, as well as the plays of the Provincetown Players, shows a considerable improvement this year. There is no such performance in *Diff'rent* as Charles Gilpin gives in *The Emperor Jones*, yet the cast is pretty evenly effective, and there is, at least, one exceedingly good piece of acting. It is not, unfortunately, in the part of the woman. This role is far more difficult than Juliet, for it calls not alone for an actress who can look sixteen and have the knowledge and emotions of maturity, but for an actress who can also simulate forty-six, and forty-six trying to be young. Mary Blair plays the first act with real skill and charm. In the second act, she does surprisingly well with what is to her almost impossible material, but still falls far short of the necessary illusion. James Light plays the momentarily inconstant lover with a good deal of success. The honors, however, go to Charles Ellis as the degenerate youth of the last act. His work is thoroughly professional in finish and detail. It goes beyond all impersonations of young wastrels that have appeared on Broadway by keeping an aspect of more or less normal and good-looking manhood, while indicating spiritual degradation, cruelty, and lasciviousness by tone and glance. In this one part, Ellis comes forward as the best actor that the Provincetown Players have ever numbered among their permanent company.

Heywood Broun

GOLD

Eugene O'Neill leaps high in *Gold*, which was produced at the Frazee Theatre last night, but it is a leap which requires a running start of three acts. The fourth act—the one in which O'Neill comes into his own—was seen several years ago as a one-act play called "Where the Cross Is Made." *Gold* is not an expansion of that, strictly speaking, for the short piece was made by snatching it from a full-length play.

Nevertheless, there seems to be a good deal of circumstantial evidence that *Gold* is a play written for the sake of one or two brief moments close to the final curtain. Much of the rest appears to be mere maneuvering in preparation for these moments.

The scene which we found striking is one in which an old sea captain, crazed by hope of treasure, is able in the enthusiasm of his frenzy to make his son share his delusion for a moment. So potent is the old man's madness that the son, too, sees the dead and gone ship sail home to port and hears upon the stairs the tread of the sailors carrying the chest of gold and jewels. This is audacious and magnificent. In the one-act form it was still more audacious, from the fact that the audience was enlisted as a party to the old man's imaginings, and actually saw the men from the sea come across the stage. In the longer form the author has suffered a little from a lack of courage. He has been over-conscientious in explaining again and again that the sea captain is mad. And now he is not willing that the phantoms shall take actual form.

Madness, to be sure, is a stage convention, much abused. Ophelia can hardly have died in any such untimely manner as Shakespeare pretends. She has left too many grandchildren to the dramatists of all succeeding centuries. But when a playwright

From the New York Tribune, *June 2, 1921. Reprinted by permission of the* New York Herald Tribune.

adopts a dramatic device like the convenient fluid madness of the theatre which may be turned on and off at will, he might as well do it boldly and without excuses. The apology implied by the long three-act preparation which precedes the big scene in *Gold* merely suggests timidity on the part of the playwright and distrust of his own material.

The long expository scenes are often distressingly conventional and in a vein not in the least characteristic of O'Neill. This is not altogether true of the first act in which we see the manner in which the shipwrecked captain and his crew become so crazed by heat and thirst that they mistake a chest of brass trinkets for treasure. Here, after a slow start, there are some thrilling scenes. But after that exposition sets in most malignantly.

The exigencies of the plot require that the captain shall tell of the finding of the treasure and of the murder of two members of the crew again and again. Nor is there the usual excuse that such long discursive interludes are put in as a favor to the audience. This time the audience knows and does not need to be told.

Some of the blight of an injudicious technical scheme is removed by the exceedingly able performance of Willard Mack. His New England whaling captain is too proficient in brogue and a number of conventional stage tricks which have availed Mr. Mack as a member of the Canadian mounted and in other roles are dragged in by the heels now and again. But beyond all this there is unflagging vitality in the performance and much imagination. It is the best performance which Mr. Mack has shown New York.

The rest of the cast, with the exception of Ashley Buck as the boy, is not adequate, and John D. Williams has provided the play with a cheap and tasteless setting. The play is not up to O'Neill at his best, but even all the wrinkles in the first act sky cannot conceal the fact that something of sun fire has come into the play through the mists of writing and production.

Francis Hackett

ANNA CHRISTIE

Some people, including Lord Dunsany, seem to think that you cannot introduce fantasy into the theatre unless you have gods and demons. After seeing Mr. Eugene O'Neill's *Anna Christie* at the Vanderbilt Theatre, (presented by Arthur Hopkins), I am so drunk with fantasy extracted from hard-boiled human beings that I don't know how to become sober.

Mr. O'Neill is full of capable trickiness. He knows how to lard his tears with laughter, his fog with lamplight, his violence with love. He helps himself with a heaping spoon to all the big elemental things of the theatre: booze, prostitutes, father-love, life on the ocean wave, knives, revolvers, and the clenched fist. But what is more than a trick, what makes him both fascinating and amusing, is his audacious use of all this material to produce what he wants, pathos and romance inside the theatre. A prostitute to him has great romantic values, the right kind of prostitute, but no more than a rawboned Irish stoker who "carries on his hairy chest" the cross his mother wore. An old Swedish bo'sun who keeps talking of Old Devil Sea—that seems a useful pigment to Mr. O'Neill in the scene he is trying to concoct. So does the very title of Act Two: "the barge, *Simeon Winthrop*, at anchor in the harbor of Provincetown, Mass.," or the title of Act One: "Johnny-the-Priest's saloon near the Waterfront, New York City." But to use such sweetened symbols without something harsh and strong is never likely to betray Mr. O'Neill. He makes his saloon with the romantic name a gray-lighted, somber barrel-house. He hangs it like a drab backdrop behind Anna Christie, the tough kid from Minnesota who was seduced by her own cousin on the drudging farm and who lived in a "house" in St. Paul and who hates every son of a gun of a man and who talks piquant, comic, filliping slang. Her old father, Chris Christopherson, has her meet him in this saloon after their years of

From The New Republic, *November 30, 1921. Used by permission of the author.*

separation. She braces herself with whisky before he arrives, pouring out her story to an old prostitute, Marthy Owen. Anna has been in prison-hospital. She is weak, disillusioned, suspicious, but young and naive. The old man is hungry for her. He meets her shyly and kindly. She stands off, comes to him tentatively, begins to thaw. But both of them have the roughness that is so desirable in simple people, in terriers and in automobile overcoats. Both of them say "yust" yust at the right moment. The melting mood is adroitly tempered with quaintness, a drop of lemon. And Mr. O'Neill can make his melting audience gasp and run to laughter time and time again.

Anna Christie, still an innocent young girl to her kindly father, goes with him to gladden his heart on the coal-barge. There she finds, in the clean peace of the wide sky and water, that the sea is in her blood as in the blood of all Scandinavians. She finds that a coal-barge is not black with coal-dust and that even a barge goes away from shore. But her "rest-cure" in the Provincetown fog does not go on forever. A boat from the open sea full of wrecked sailors comes alongside and out of the fog limp and stagger the survivors of the Old Devil Sea. One of them is an Irish stoker, the broth of a boy, boastful, chivalrous, romantic, blasphemous, superstitious. He is just as useful for pathos as any prostitute, and just as resourcefully managed. In the first ten minutes of his rescue, alone with Anna Christie on that part of a barge which is set back like an alcove with a long bench in it, and with one solitary lamp glimmering around them through the fog, the big Irishman falls roaring in love with her, especially after she knocks him down. He does everything that he ought to do as a romantic Irishman. "A fine lady the like of yourself," "the great strenth in me" "I'll bate any ten scuts, I'm tellin' ye." In a voice that would have made his fortune as a shouting parish priest, Mr. Frank Shannon rivals Miss Pauline Lord in creating exactly the kind of pathos that Mr. O'Neill intended. And Mr. George Marion as the old father madly jealous of the Irish swine comes right into the picture.

The show-down is obvious. Mat Burke, the noisy and eloquent stoker, comes to Boston with the barge and defies the father to keep him from marrying Anna. In the midst of their primitive fight, when the father tries to pull a knife, Anna arrives and sees the situation. She loves Mat Burke but she doesn't think she's good enough to marry him. Being "on the level," enraged at her false position, and maddened by the obstinate conflicting passions of lover and father, she shoves both wrangling men from her in the little cabin and screams out her own story of what she really is.

The primitive males recoil, as primitive males do. Each goes his own way, to get drunk, to beat up the innocent bystander, to forget his black shame and broken heart. But there has to be a fourth act. With a certain amount of cheerful impudence Mr. O'Neill reassembles everybody and establishes the reunion between Mat and Anna. This is not on the same romantic or pathetic level as the rest of the drama. But what can a poor dramatist do? He has gone the limit in hanging the female kitten over the abyss from which she's been rescued. He has exploited to the last the extravagant glories of the Irish coal-passer. He has laid bare the throbbing paternal heart. If Anna goes back to prostitution, or the old man kills Mat Burke, or Mat Burke really quits and ships to Capetown, the delicious fantasy of Gael and Gall goes all to pieces, and ugly common-sense emerges. It is therefore necessary to cheat. The least loss is involved in a somewhat inglorious happy ending.

After so many thrills as *Anna Christie* affords, and after such admirably sustained acting as that of the principals, it seems a pity not to rush out with a full heart believing that Mr. O'Neill is a genius. He seems to me in this play to prove that he can, when he wants to, catch the idiom of chorus girls. Anna talks like a pert chorus girl. He seems also to have a really lavish capacity for fantasy, with any number of pleasant and original inflections that only go with a quick imagination. He seems also to have inside the bolus of his Irishman and his Swede a certain amount of reality. But he does not appear, on the whole, to be keenly interested in reality. He thinks that it is enough to tip people's emotions up and down, especially to give them pathos and excitement, with an appearance of what the Irishman calls "strenth." The development of his genius certainly cannot be along these theatrical lines. Anna Christie is, essentially, a hoax. Sailor men, girls who've "gone wrong," stokers, don't pictorialize themselves in these familiar ways. To make a real composition, corresponding not only to the theatre but to life, Mr. O'Neill must undoubtedly handle people for something besides their effectiveness. The American theatre cannot be modelled on American advertising, which is so obsessed with effectiveness. It must, to become adult, see people for themselves.

Alexander Woollcott

THE STRAW

Heralded for two years by rumors of its coming and foreshadowed months ago by its appearance on the book shelves, *The Straw* was finally produced last evening at the Greenwich Village Theatre, where a keen and overexpectant audience found it an interesting and moving play. It is the work of Eugene O'Neill, and though it lies considerably below the level of the best work he has done for the theatre, it still has enough of his force and his quality to make it worth seeing.

Only part of his dream for it was realized in the spotty performance that was its fate last evening in Sheridan Square. Otto Kruger, summoned into the cast at the last moment, is its most satisfying and sustaining member, but the lovely and gifted Margalo Gillmore is beyond her depth in the more critical role of Eileen Carmody. It is not a role which asks more than she has to give, but it is a role which seems to ask more than she yet knows how to give.

The Straw is O'Neill's study of hope—hope in its most extraordinary and ironic manifestation. It is the hope that grows and grows in the heart of anyone who lies sick with tuberculosis—the hope which is strongest and brightest on the very eve of death. The masters of the merry-merry theatre who have been so tremendously jocose at the somberness of all this newcomer's writings for the stage will fairly split their sides laughing at the very thought of this play in Greenwich Village, for it builds and destroys the romance of two young consumptives and four of its five scenes have as their background a crowded sanitarium for tuberculosis. However, the squeamish and the delicate may feel reassured. The piece is not unduly clinical and of the coughing

From The New York Times, *November 11, 1921. Reprinted by permission of* The New York Times *and the Executor for the author's estate.*

heard last evening at the first performance of *The Straw*, not more than one per cent came from the stage.

The final scene of *The Straw* has a pathos and a tragic irony seldom paralleled in the theatre. After a difficult and clumsy assembling of its forces, that scene leaves the two young people together on Eileen's sleeping-porch at the sanitarium. Outside, the New England hills are ablaze with the reds and russets of Autumn.

The two, hugging each other close, are jubilant in their plans for their marriage, for their flight to a little mountain lake they know of, for the idyllic regime which is to lead them back to a life of happiness and work together. They have the embrace and the smile that has given the cue to the curtain-man in nearly every play since the theatre began. But this time the onlooking doctors and nurses and you, watching from the other side of the footlights, know that theirs is the delusion, the hectic hope around which the play is wrought. You know she has just a little time left to live. It was this scene which the publishers of the play in book form quaintly described as a happy ending.

Last evening was clearly Mr. Kruger's. The knowledge, widespread enough among the wiseacres who make up a first-night audience, that the part was first shoved into his hands last Saturday, may have added something to their evident appreciation—but it was appreciation of a performance good in itself, an actor's work full of truth and vitality and simplicity. There were times, too, when Miss Gillmore met the occasions of the text, and much of her playing in the two final scenes was admirable. She seems brimful of talent, a born actress—but one not born long enough ago.

In scene after scene, her inexperience betrayed her—betrayed her into grimaces of fearful portent, sudden and explosive assaults on the emotion of the role, grotesquely abrupt transitions. She did things which bred the dark suspicion that her performance had been ignorantly and helplessly directed—suspicions which deepen when you saw how archaicly the horde of supers was managed in the third scene of the play. Miss Gillmore, who blazed into evidence in the company of *The Famous Mrs. Fair* two years ago, has much to give the theatre and much to learn in it. She has to learn some of the things which Kruger knows backward—Kruger and Katherine Grey and Harry Harwood, who, by the way, is capital as the elder and drunken Carmody.

Maida Castellun

THE FIRST MAN

Whether he writes a good or a bad play Eugene O'Neill never sinks into pleasant mediocrity. *The First Man*, now being produced at the Neighborhood Playhouse by Augustin Duncan is without the creative originality, the artistic inevitability, the vivid characterization, and the life-like dialogue of his best work; but it is not feeble. Its defects are positive. Following sardonic classification, one may call it an "unpleasant play," but it has a vital idea, however its mechanism, characters, and language may fail.

The play is badly constructed, so that one of its ideas interferes with the other. It is overwritten, so that one wearies of the superfluous repetitions. It should have been severely blue-pencilled but it has a humanely significant theme.

It deals with the conflict of creative impulses in the modern, highly developed woman who can write books and go on exploring expeditions, but who herself feels that her supreme work is to create children. Because Martha Jayson is the wife of an explorer to whom she gives unending assistance, she is forced to choose between having a child or losing her husband's sympathy.

This is perhaps the first time that any dramatist has shown that the sermons preached in the pulpit and on the stage against women for "race suicide" are one-sided, that it is the man quite as much as the woman who may object to children. In Curtis Jayson this complex is distorted into a mania, so that his antagonism toward his child leads to the family gossips assuming that there is a scandalous relation between Martha and Jayson's best friend, Richard Bigelow.

The death of the wife in childbirth and Jayson's discovery of the mean suspicions of his family lead to a complete revulsion in

---

From the New York Call, *March 9, 1922. Used with permission of* The Call Association, Inc.

his attitude, too late. His departure on the exploring expedition through Asia, leaving his young son to an old great-aunt, passionately devoted to children, may seem a happy ending, unless one faces candidly the fate of an unfortunate child brought up by an emotionally unbalanced, morbid old woman. Possibly Mr. O'Neill wishes to indicate the queer strain in Jayson's stock to make his egotistic, self-centered personality more tolerable.

While there is no "old devil sea," the small town is the villain. As an atrabilious study of meanness, pettiness, jealousy and backbiting, the Jaysons rival some of Ibsen's Norwegian Main Streeters. If Mr. O'Neill, by writing *The First Man*, has rid himself of any bitterness and hostility that he plainly has felt toward some such pillars of society, this psychoanalytic drama may be a milestone in his development. One may even forgive him for introducing the whole tribe—father, aunt, brothers, sisters, brothers-in-law and sister-in-law—not only to talk obstetrics, but to hear them in the tortured cries of the mother in childbirth. In 18th-century royal circles, such a custom existed; but it surely does not prevail in Connecticut today? The end of this scene, however, is dramatically striking in the management of suspense before the death of the young wife.

The play is not greatly improved by a production that tends to caricature some of the characters. Mr. Duncan himself plays the explorer and anthropologist, who suffers from egocentric mania, with understanding but complete inability to realize the part. In the first two acts his difficulty with his lines was a stumbling block; and while he conveyed the feeling of the thwarted husband in the last two acts finely, the tempo dragged where there should have been variety of movement.

Miss Margaret Mower is a beautiful and charming creature, but never did she suggest a girl from the free West who had traveled and explored, lived and loved until she reached the age of 34. Hers is a superficial portrait, graceful and decorative, but without the vital spark. Incidentally, we wish actresses would not wear coiffures that keep the audience on edge lest their hair come tumbling down at the most tragic moment. Miss Mower and Miss Christine Norman in *The Nest* quite spoil their emotional scenes by this distracting detail.

Of the smaller parts, Miss Eva Condon as the cattish sister-in-law, Miss Marjorie Vonnegut as the outspoken sister, and Eugene Powers as a smug brother-in-law are the best, though Miss Vonnegut is inclined to make her effects with a bludgeon.

With its unsympathetic characters and its gray atmosphere, *The First Man* could scarcely hope for popularity, but this would matter little if it were a great play. In this case one may change Kipling and say, "It's ugly, but is it Art?"

Alexander Woollcott

THE HAIRY APE

The little theatre of Provincetownsmen in Macdougal Street was packed to the doors with astonishment last evening as scene after scene unfolded in the new play by Eugene O'Neill. This was *The Hairy Ape*, a bitter, brutal, wildly fantastic play of nightmare hue and nightmare distortion. It is a monstrously uneven piece, now flamingly eloquent, now choked and thwarted and inarticulate. Like most of his writing for the theatre, it is the worse here and there for the lack of a fierce, unintimidated blue pencil, but it has a little greatness in it, and it seems rather absurd to fret overmuch about the undisciplined imagination of the young playwright towering so conspicuously above the milling, mumbling crowd of playwrights who have no imagination at all.

The Hairy Ape has been superbly produced. There is a rumor abroad that Arthur Hopkins, with a proprietary interest in the piece, has been lurking around its rehearsals and the program confesses that Robert Edmond Jones went down to Macdougal Street and took a hand with Cleon Throckmorton in designing the eight pictures which the play calls for. That preposterous little theatre has one of the most cramped stages New York has ever known, and yet on it the artists have created the illusion of vast spaces and endless perspectives. They drive one to the conclusion that when a stage seems pinched and little, it is the mind of the producer that is pinched and little. This time O'Neill, unbridled, set them a merry pace in the eccentric gait of his imaginings. They kept up with him.

O'Neill begins his fable by posing before you the greatest visible contrast in social and physical circumstance. He leads you

---

From The New York Times, *March 10, 1922. Reprinted by permission of* The New York Times *and the Executor of the author's estate.*

up the gangplank of a luxurious liner bound for Europe. He plunges you first into the stokers' pit, thrusting you down among the men as they stumble in from the furnaces, hot, sweaty, choked with coal dust, brutish. Squirm as you may, he holds you while you listen to the rumble of their discontent, and while you listen, also, to speech more squalid than an American audience heard before in an American theatre, it is true talk, all of it, and only those who have been so softly bred that they have never really heard the vulgate spoken in all its richness would venture to suggest that he has exaggerated it by so much as a syllable in order to agitate the refined. On the contrary.

Then, in a twinkling, he drags you (as the ghosts drag Scrooge) up out of all this murk and thudding avengeance and brawling of speech to a cool, sweet, sunlit stretch of the hurricane deck, where, at lazy ease, lies the daughter of the President of the line's board of directors, a nonchalant dilettante who has found settlement work frightfully interesting and is simply crazy to go down among the stokers and see how the other half lives aboard ship.

Then follows the confrontation—the fool fop of a girl and the huge animal of a stoker who had taken sort of a dizzy romantic pride in himself and his work as something that was real in an unreal world, as something that actually counted, as something that was and had force. Her horrified recoil from him as from some loathsome, hairy ape is the first notice served on him by the world that he doesn't belong. The remaining five scenes are the successive blows by which this is driven in on him, each scene, as written, as acted and as intensified by the artists, taking on more and more of the nightmare quality with which O'Neill seemed possessed to endow his fable.

The scene on Fifth Avenue when the hairy ape comes face to face with a little parade of wooden-faced church-goers who walk like automata and prattle of giving a "Hundred Percent American Bazaar" as a contribution to the solution of discontent among the lower classes: the scene on Blackwell's Island with the endless rows of cells and the argot of the prisoners floating out of the darkness: the care with which each scene ends in a retributive and terrifying closing in upon the bewildered fellow—all these preparations induce you at last, to accept as natural and inevitable and right that the hairy ape should, by the final curtain, be found dead inside the cage of the gorilla in the Bronx Zoo.

Except for the role of the girl, which is pretty badly played by Mary Blair, the cast captured for *The Hairy Ape* is an exceptionally good one. Louis Wolheim, though now and then rather painfully off the beat in his co-operation with the others, gives a capital impersonation of the stoker, and lesser parts are well managed by Harry O'Neill as an Irish fireman dreaming of the old days of sailing vessels, and Harold West as a cockney agitator who is fearfully annoyed because of the hairy ape's concentrating his anger against this one little plutocrat instead of maintaining an abstract animosity against plutocrats in general.

In Macdougal Street now and doubtlessly headed for Broadway, we have a turbulent and tremendous play, so full of blemishes that the merest fledgling among the critics could point out a dozen, yet so vital and interesting and teeming with life that those playgoers who let it escape them will be missing one of the real events of the year.

Ludwig Lewisohn

WELDED

From time to time Mr. Eugene O'Neill starts his career all over again. He gives the impression not so much of developing as of making a series of excursions into various provinces of the drama's domain and of returning from each of these excursions a little dissatisfied, a little disillusioned, a little hopeful that his next experiment will result in something not quite so fragmentary and unfinished from within. I repeat, from within. His works leave me with the sense of never having been permitted to ripen, of having been written when another mood, another method, another philosophy had already shadowed the field of the creative vision. One need but reflect upon a few of his plays in more or less chronological order to see quite clearly the wavering, tentative, unequal character of his productivity: *Beyond the Horizon*, *The Emperor Jones*, *Gold*, *The Last Man*, *Anna Christie*, *The Hairy Ape*.

Welded, at the Thirty-ninth Street Theatre, is a new departure still. Mr. O'Neill enters the province of Strindberg, the Strindberg of *Comrades*, *Creditors*, *The Link*. He wants to exhaust the problem of the intricate relations between two people. His difficulty is that he has not thought out the question of these relations to their last depth, to a last clarity. That is what Strindberg always did. In that fact lies the endless fascination of those earlier plays of his. They are complete. They are, like all things utterly complete, crystalline. Only what has not been thought out and thought through is murky. And *Welded*, though I strained my powers of attention to the utmost, remains murky.

The fable is, as it should be, simple. He is a playwright; she an actress. He is jealous of her past; she is resentful of the fact that her successes have been chiefly in his plays, a fact that seems to

From The Nation, *April 2, 1924. Reprinted with permission of the editors and Mrs. Ludwig Lewisohn.*

make her wholly his creature. It is a fine touch—the finest in the play—that he, conscious of creative power, wanting to emphasize his possession of her, his superiority, hurls at her but one word: "Actress!" But the artistic rivalry in which, from the nature of things, she must always, in her character of a mere interpreter, be defeated, is obscured by other motives far less clarified. She does not grow cold at ultimate moments through this fruitless assertion of her ego, but through some other inhibition which is never clearly defined. At the end of a scene which is supposed to be terrible but which leaves one rather cold, each tries to kill love by throwing away body and soul. Each finds it impossible. They are reunited not in hope but in hopelessness, in acceptance of unhappiness by which they hope to be exalted.

So many things are untouched, so many gaps unbridged. Love, to begin with, is less esoteric than this; it is also more fragile. These two, furthermore, were never married. That has nothing to do with a ceremony or an official stamp. They had no tenderness for each other; one is quite sure that they had no compassion for each other's human needs, weaknesses, failures. Their union was, from the start, the contact of two voracious vanities. It was long ago described in *Comrades*. It is not thoroughly grasped here at any point. Strindberg shows that his two people were not married. Mr. O'Neill wants us to believe that these two were and that their acceptance of their unhappiness constitutes union. We do not believe him. Union must have rapture; it must also have peace.

The dialogue is distressing. For once I could not blame the well-fed bourgeois all around who tittered and giggled. There is not a living word in the play, none that is torn from the depths of passionate experience. The speech is the speech that superior Greenwich Villagers would, some years ago, have imagined themselves as using on such occasions, in such a situation. The prostitute who appears in one scene is the only character who talks like a human being. Michael and Eleanor do not talk as people talk in either life or Strindberg or Porto-Riche or Schnitzler. They talk like people in a Greenwich Village novel by . . . Well, that is perhaps not Mr. O'Neill's fault. Perhaps we have no society in America of this particular kind homogeneous enough, cultivated enough, usual enough, to furnish him with an idiom. Whatever the causes, the fact remains.

The result is that both Mr. Ben-Ami and Miss Doris Keane seemed to be attitudinizing at every moment. It was at this that the audience laughed; it was this laughter that I could not but forgive. Mr. Stark Young, who directed *Failures* so admirably, failed here. For even this gritty dialogue with its constant flights into false and untimely eloquence might have been softened and made human by the simplest delivery, by subduing its artificial emphasis. Nothing of the kind is done. In the scene with the prostitute Mr. Ben-Ami's lines are preposterous enough in form, however good in substance. Had he used a visionary simplicity of delivery one might have suspended disbelief. He preaches. The direction is rhetorical. Mr. Ben-Ami and Miss Keane act. They never do anything at any moment but act in the crass and obvious sense. The audience laughed. For on this one point the uninstructed are at one with sound critical doctrine; they want the illusion of reality. You may produce that illusion by any means you like, from stark naturalism to ultra-expressionism. The artistic and spiritual result must be ultimately and in effect the same—to show truth, to show life, to come a little closer to nature.

George Jean Nathan

THE RIME OF THE ANCIENT MARINER

Under the recent delusion that he made a dramatization of Coleridge's *The Rime of the Ancient Mariner*, what Eugene O'Neill actually made was a moving picture. What drama lies in the poem, he extracted, and in its place put a series of cut-backs and fade-outs that needed only a few additional scenes showing the Bride running through a daisy field, the Third Wedding Guest standing in meditation beside a high waterfall, and the Ancient Mariner silhouetted at the close against the evening sky to convert the whole thing into a film of the popular order. O'Neill's theory of dramatizing the Coleridge ululation reposed in the typical cinema notion of leaving nothing to the imagination. While an actor with a voice full of cramps and a face full of whiskers, thus depicting the Ancient Mariner, stood at stage right and declaimed the lines, the electrician periodically turned on and off a green light which illuminated the center of the stage and revealed a group of sailors engaged in retailing a pantomimic accompaniment. Thus, when the interlocutor recited that portion of the poem which has to do with the blight that fell upon the ship, the green light came on and showed the sailors lying flat on the floor, and when the recitation recalled the passing of the blight, the light came on again and showed them getting slowly to their feet. It was all as literal as the late Charlie Bigelow's Weber and Fields recitation of "The Midnight Ride of Paul Revere," with its off-stage accompaniment of hollow cocoanut shells and its shaking of a cowbell to indicate the heroic messenger's frantic ringing of the countryside's front door bells.

The weakness of the Provincetown Theatre group, as with the majority of semi-amateur organizations, lies in its preoccupation with lighting and scenery at the expense of drama. Thus, as a

---

From The American Mercury, *June 1924. Reprinted with permission.*

forepiece to the O'Neill contribution, a production was made of Molière's *George Dandon, or the Husband Confounded*, apparently for no other reason save that it offered the Messrs. Macgowan and Jones an opportunity to frame it in the kind of Redoutensaal setting so enthusiastically set forth by them in their last year's eminently readable volume on Continental stagecraft. The O'Neill offering, too, was doubtless welcomed chiefly as an occasion to experiment with masks and shadow lighting. All such experiments, of course, are valuable in their way, and many of them turn out to be possessed of much beauty and theatrical effectiveness, but the cornerstone of every theatre in the world is a typewritten manuscript, not a new kind of bunchlight or a new way of draping curtains. A barn with a burlap backdrop and a row of oil lamps is a great theatre if a Rostand writes its plays. A palace with scenes by Michelangelo and lighting by the German government itself is something less than a theatre if it fails to realize that the play is ever and alone the thing.

T. S. Eliot

ALL GOD'S CHILLUN GOT WINGS

NOTE: In granting permission to reprint this review, Mr. Eliot has asked the editors to add the following note:

> This note on *All God's Chillun Got Wings* first appeared in *The Criterion* of April 1926. I should like to make it clear to the present readers that at that time I had never seen any of Eugene O'Neill's plays on the stage. Since then I have gained experience of the theatre myself and I realize that a play must be judged from seeing it on the stage as well as from reading the text. This is particularly true, I think, of the plays of Eugene O'Neill. It is only within the last two or three years that I have seen plays by him performed: *A Long Day's Journey Into Night* in the London production and *A Touch of the Poet* in New York. I should like to say that I place his work very high indeed, and *A Long Day's Journey Into Night* seems to me one of the most moving plays I have ever seen.

One is diffident of passing judgment upon a play which one has not seen upon the stage, but Mr. O'Neill's plays—especially the first of these three—are so readable, and so impressive when read, that their publication in a book must be noticed.[1] I believe that in America, where Mr. O'Neill's plays have had a prodigious success, their author is placed with Pirandello, or even above Pirandello, as the author of a renascence of the drama. This enthusiasm, for either Mr. O'Neill or Signor Pirandello, I cannot share. I know that Pirandello is a master of the technique of the theatre, as I have seen one or two of his plays; I believe O'Neill to be the same, because of the esteem which he enjoys. In reading *All God's Chillun Got Wings*, we stick at the representation of the two principal actors, in successive scenes, in childhood, in adolescence, and in

1. The volume under review was *All God's Chillun Got Wings* (with *Desire Under the Elms* and *Welded*). London, Jonathan Cape.

maturity; we wonder whether the play must not somewhat drag, from the lack of unity due to the attempt to cover such a span of time. But Mr. O'Neill has got hold of a "strong plot"; he not only understands one aspect of the "negro problem," but he succeeds in giving this problem universality, in implying a wider application. In *this* respect, he is more successful than the author of *Othello*, in implying something more universal than the problem of race—in implying, in fact, the universal problem of differences which create a mixture of admiration, love, and contempt, with the consequent tension. At the same time, he has never deviated from exact portrayal of a possible negro, and the close is magnificent. The other plays show the same ability at work, but are intrinsically less interesting.

Percy Hammond

DESIRE UNDER THE ELMS

In *Desire Under the Elms* Mr. O'Neill again eats his heart out in the bitter torments of despair. The three hours of his new play in Greenwich Village is three hours of eloquent agony in which hell is emptied and all the devils let loose upon a New England farm. Its distresses range from unholy lust to infanticide, and they include drinking, cursing, vengeance, and something approaching incest. So alarming an interpretation of Nature is it that even the most hardened of Mr. O'Neill's disciples last night shuddered at its honest terrors and were subdued.

Let it not be suspected from the foregoing catalogue that *Desire Under the Elms* is not an enjoyable entertainment. On the contrary, it provides inspiration for unhappy playgoers to forget such woes as may pester them. Mr. O'Neill's dramas always make me glad that I am not one of the characters involved. My tire trouble; my battles with Kronos and the composing room after the play; my loss of appetite and other discomforts, vanish as I observe Mr. O'Neill's people writhing and wailing in difficulties much more incorrigible. I leave his theatres with a song on my lips, congratulating myself that my glooms are insignificant.

It is 1850 on a New England farm and old Ephraim Cabot, as stony as his hostile acres, is bringing "hum" a bride, his third. Two sons by his "fust" wife, foreseeing their disinheritance, start for the gold fields of California, leaving Eben, their handsome step-brother, to face his new "ma." She is an odd New Englander, a combination of hot blood and cold heart. Casting her inscrutable eyes on Eben's pleasing person, she devises a means to be happy though married.

Aided by her step-son's hatred for his grim father, she seduces

---

From the New York Herald Tribune, *November 12, 1924. Reprinted with permission.*

the boy, and as a consequence of that misbehavior has a child by him. Later in the play, when life as Mr. O'Neill sees it comes to grips with life, she murders the babe, thinking to please the irresolute Eben. That action at first horrifies him, and he gives her up to the constables. All the time this is going on, Mr. O'Neill's black and fascinating wings hover above the drama. But at the end [Eben] returns to the kisses of her thin, red lips and goes, so far as I know, to the gallows with her.

There is one picture in *Desire Under the Elms* which I shall not forget, as the saying goes, for quite some time. That is when old Ephraim in his bedroom tells Abbie the story of his life. Of course, he had told her that story previously, but the exigencies of the drama, even of the Eugene O'Neill drama, demand that it be told again. While he is drooling about his past, his young wife is looking through the wall into the chamber of Eben. I have seen few pictures in the theatre so stark as that.

The principal players are very good. I think that the impersonations of Miss [Mary] Morris, Mr. [Charles] Ellis, and Mr. [Walter] Huston are perfect.

Stark Young

THE FOUNTAIN

The Fountain represents a beautiful mood on Eugene O'Neill's part and a departure from his familiar paths. It is set down as a romance; its general tone is poetic; and it is more or less historical subject matter. The entertainment that we get at the Greenwich Village Theatre is pretty dull on the whole; from the vision scene, the death, the quarrel with the bishop, and somewhat from the torture scene with Nano the Indian, we get a certain amount of thrill and beauty; most of the rest leaves us half bored. The way to take *The Fountain* is to see that it has a moving and high theme, and that it expresses a significant phase in the dramatist's development. It tries after a field that cannot but enlarge his scope in both material and style. From this effort Eugene O'Neill may, if he will, profit for his future. It was worth his while to try it. And a genuine interest in his accomplishment now and after could not overlook *The Fountain* or fail to see it.

The defects of *The Fountain* are largely those of style, of words almost. Its outline is fairly well established. Ponce de Leon in a courtyard of Granada is visited by a lady with whom he has had an affair. They are to part forever. He is young, hard, full of ambition. A Moor is killed. The lady's husband, after she has gone, appears. There is a quarrel, a wound. Ponce de Leon leaves Spain with Christopher Columbus, to escape retribution, to seek new fortunes. In the New World he becomes governor. Beatriz comes to him, sent by her mother, who loved Ponce de Leon till her death. He falls in love with Beatriz. The dream of youth seizes him. He tortures the Indian captive for the secret of the fountain whose rumor has spread abroad; from it he will drink and renew his youth. In the jungles of the newly discovered Florida he is

From The New Republic, *December 30, 1925. Reprinted by permission of the author.*

betrayed and set on by the Indians. In the monastery where he lies dying Beatriz comes to him, bringing his nephew. In him she has found again the young Ponce de Leon of old whom her mother had taught her to adore. The dying man finds his youth in the eternal fountain of the soul.

If the pattern of this narrative is not so strong as that of *The Emperor Jones* or *The Hairy Ape*, it is at least clear. The single scenes have also a fair security of design. But in a play like *The Hairy Ape* the story form itself is the play. The myth pattern expresses almost all there is to be expressed. Such a play has also the advantage of an easier and more accessible diction. Its language is of the God-damn, get-to-hell-out-of-here type, which can more or less shoulder and explode its own way as it goes. But in *The Fountain* we must have an engaging and powerful diction, words that are beautiful, biting, inevitable, that delight and compel, that move and carry us along with the high design, that persuade and create, that grow radiant and unforgettable with the needed darkness and light. For such writing we listen far too often in vain; the written style of *The Fountain* is almost embarrassingly unequal. I cannot quote exactly but, for one of many instances, Beatriz said something once about Ponce de Leon's being to her mother the supreme example of the highest chivalry; if she did not say that she was quite capable of saying worse. And even that is nothing to the words that the Indian braves speak beside the spring. On the other hand, the last scene and many of Ponce de Leon's lines are beautiful and exalted, though not enough so to carry off the whole effect that the writing produces on us.

The case of *The Fountain* brings up the issue that we have all got to begin talking about in our theatre: words, the value of written dialogue, which, it cannot be forgotten, is of all the elements that go to make up the art of the theatre, the most engaging, the most permanent, immediate and binding.

The excellence of *The Fountain* lies in its superb reach after a certain poignant, tragic beauty and variety of idea. The lure of new-springing life and of the secret in the strange, far eyes of the savage captive, the single soul as the drop from the eternal fountain and returning into it, such motives make a fine and gallant theme to try.

The production of *The Fountain* is the most difficult problem of this season in the theatre. The direction was by Mr. Robert Edmond Jones. Taken all in all it is an interesting accomplishment, sometimes a dull one, sometimes important. The eleven scenes are expertly managed in their time intervals. The settings are always at least adequate. The scene on Columbus' flagship is admirable. The setting for the spring to which Ponce de Leon comes for the enchanted drink is an out-of-doors design that is most distinguished and splendid. In color it is all black and somber green. In form it is harsh and severe, clawing, hard edges, simple, strict forms. It is easily the pinnacle of the whole occasion. . . .

The rôle of Ponce de Leon fell to Mr. Walter Huston, and over his performance there will be many diverse opinions. The part fitted obviously the obvious romantic actor, and, to tell the truth, its theatrical fortunes might have gained in other hands than Mr. Huston's. But to me he seemed a piece of good casting, taken all in all. He fell too often into the tone and ways of old Cabot in *Desire Under the Elms*. His diction was unequal, sometimes rustic and blunt. He might have been warmer in places, more suave and elaborate as a Spanish nobleman. But this part of Ponce de Leon as Eugene O'Neill has written it is not easy. It is not the obvious, romantical, swaggering and spouting historical cavalier, but a figure in whose soul there is passion with some degree of hardness and drouth, there is a dream full both of obsession and austerity. And not a little of the portrait remains somewhat incomplete, left to the actor's imaginative invention and technical devices for getting along. If Mr. Huston lacked often distinct style and rhythm, he had something for such a part much more significant. I mean a certain authority of character. He knew intelligently what the rock-bottom of the rôle was about. He had no hint of the actor ass, almost inevitable in such a part. He has a fine natural voice and a direct virility of attack. His method is sometimes thin and dry, but it is pure. Even when he is bad he could always be bad in so much worse a way. Seeing his Ponce de Leon we may say that as an artist he has the youth and truthful vigor of this New World; what he needs now also is more of the Old World's rich investiture.

Gilbert W. Gabriel

THE GREAT GOD BROWN

Eugene O'Neill's long promised play, *The Great God Brown*, was presented at their theatre by the Greenwich Village triumvirate last Saturday night. It is a deep minded and compassionate fantasy, often thrilling in the brightness of its words, sometimes perplexing in the shadows of its meaning. It is a cycle of our naked souls and the masks in which we shield them.

How immediately likable *The Great God Brown* will prove is beside the point. If Mr. O'Neill writes for anything beyond the satisfaction of his own urge, it is for posterity, not for popularity. Here he experiments bravely and strangely. The poet and technician in him come to grips and fight it out along their own lines through more than a dozen unequal but always interesting scenes. Compelled or repelled by it, thinking it sublime or silly, you will go away carrying the memory of it as the tragic heroine herself does —"under your heart."

Perhaps the literary sire of *The Great God Brown* was *The Hairy Ape*. In that past play of O'Neill's you may remember a scene where creatures in masks walk up and down the Avenue out of all reach and understanding of the burly, bare-faced Yank. Terrific, that mechanism of the masks. Here, in his latest drama, O'Neill intends to put it to continuous and more subtle use. Here, each of his main characters will put on and take off for each other's benefit or delusion the crisp false faces behind which throb their tremulous innerselves. And where the fantasy flings furthest, one of them will even steal the mask of his friend's dead self, in order to possess his friend's widow.

This, as you see, is no pretty pastoral like that of Beerbohm's *Happy Hypocrite*, whose face grew to the loveliness of the mask he

From the New York Sun, *January 25, 1926. Reprinted with permission.*

wore. But, rather, it is the intricate, relentless discord of personalities behind symbols skin deep. These three personalities: Dion, the "dark spiritual, poetic, passionately supersensitive, helplessly unprotected" type, the "monkey in the moon"; Margaret, the young girl, lover, wife and mother; Billy Brown, the "great god Brown" of commonplaces, single-mindedness, with the virtues and perplexities of a Babbitt, the jealousies of an all too decent man. Over these three, over Dionysus especially, the big beefy arms of Cybel, common prostitute and yet mother of all things living, pronounces earth's cracked-lipped, pitying benediction.

Back to the secret springs of psychoanalysis, goes O'Neill. Further back, I think, than he has gone in any other of his plays. The parentages, boyhoods, lacks, and stifled yearnings of his two men he explains with a vivid, accurate stenography of science. Yet out of these notes he makes a story utterly macabre in mood. Poesque in its impossibilities, violent under the strait jacket of theatrical restrictions.

As it continues beyond the point where Brown clamps upon his hungry face the malign mask of the dead genius, the plot seems almost to torture itself to moral conclusions. Quite as torturesome would be the attempt to retell those conclusions here. Enough that, as in every recent O'Neill play, a refrain of phrases bends the action artificially back into a complete cycle and locks the epilogue to that same sense of aching inevitability, youth without wisdom and world without end, which the prologue had begun. Whereas I, for one, regret this epilogue as a sentimental and dissolving repetition, it only reminds me that O'Neill is a poet and wants a poet's neat satisfaction from his plays.

Certainly there is in *The Great God Brown* some of the author's most exquisite writing, some of his most burning. He does milk the Beatitudes dry with variations. He does whip his scenes with colloquials to keep them humble. But it is a strong, splendidly positive language he uses, ringing finely even when ringing overloud. Imagery flares up in it in bursts of ruddy beauty. Listen to the ironic Dion, selecting his Margaret of a spring night in their youth: "You are my evening star and all my Pleiades! Your eyes are blue pools in which gold dreams glide, your body is a young white birch leaning backward beneath the lips of spring."

And, again, this short remark of Cybel's (what gorgeous beings

O'Neill always makes of his prostitutes!) as she leans down, a full-blown, too-wise Candida, and strokes the damp hair of the poor, doomed artist: "You're not weak. You were born with ghosts in your eyes and you were brave enough to go looking into your own dark—and you got afraid."

It is the fate of O'Neill, in so many of his plays, to imprison himself in some technical scheme. *Desire Under the Elms* had to beat continually at the bars of its unusual scene-plot. The wild, soulful theme of *The Great God Brown* is ball-and-chained to this embarrassing trickery of masks. The actors are apt at using them. Once you are used to them, and to the muffled tones behind them, you accept them as implicitly as you can. But they are never wholly free from difficulty, always a thorn in your imagination.

The cast, the staging, the entire production, are the best the Greenwich Village has been able to assemble this season. The four principal parts are truly well taken. William Harrigan, in the title role, has the chance of his life to show what open sincerity and intensity are in him. So has Leona Hogarth the blessed opportunity to break away from routine stuff and put her personality to worthy use. Robert Keith and Anne Shoemaker are equally in and of their parts. A large parcel of large Jones boys are used as younger sons, assorted sizes.

Familia Jones is further represented, if not by the Emperor, then at least by the celebrated Robert Edmond of that ilk, who not only directed the performance but likewise provided it with suitably effective and symbolic sets. Of these, and of much else close to the heart of *The Great God Brown*, more will have to be written some other time. This review can be only a mask over the hot but troubled admiration I have for Mr. O'Neill's most poetic and penetrating play.

George C. Warren

LAZARUS LAUGHED

Eugene O'Neill's mystic drama, *Lazarus Laughed*, had its first performance on any stage tonight at the Pasadena Community Playhouse before an audience that filled the house to its utmost capacity, and was received with tremendous enthusiasm.

The play is simpler in content than anything O'Neill has written since he entered the realm of psychology with *The Great God Brown*, of which it might be called a continuation for it is based on the dying Dion's last speech.

In the new drama O'Neill makes confession of faith in a guiding omnipotence; affirms his belief in life beyond the grave, and makes a plea for men to love life and laughter and to forget sorrow and death.

The production of the play presents almost insuperable difficulties and an outlay of money that is prohibitive to commercial producers. It was because the Pasadena players are a community body with several thousand workers that it was possible to make the production here.

When it is stated that there are used in its presentation 400 costumes; 300 masks, which include the double size masks of Greek tragedy; the half face of the commedia dell' arte and the ordinary full-faced mask, and as many wigs, it will be seen the expense of production is extraordinary. The play is in four acts and eight scenes. But by the use of a geometric, architectural setting, which permitted the rearrangement of platforms, sets of stairs, and huge columns, this expense, while considerable, was lessened.

The production was a triumph for Gilmor Brown, director of the Playhouse, the crowning of fifteen years of work in Pasadena

From The San Francisco Chronicle, *April 10, 1928. Reprinted by permission of* The San Francisco Chronicle.

with the first performance anywhere of an important drama by America's most distinguished dramatist.

It is as a pageant, perhaps, more than as a play, interesting as the text is, that *Lazarus Laughed* succeeded tonight. The play is a mass play, and Brown had a body of 125 supernumeraries and choristers trained to the minute, to give effect to the mobs that are a continual procession before the audience.

In this respect nothing greater in mass acting has been seen in California with the exception of Reinhardt's *The Miracle*, which had greater space for maneuvers and numbers. The capacity of the Playhouse stage was taxed, but the crowds never became mere mobs.

The use of chorus and crowds that speak take the play to the period of Greek tragedy, but O'Neill has superimposed on this base a structure of melodrama, effective, tense, terrible.

Brown's problem was to harmonize these various elements, and to do this he stylized his action, unified the movements of his crowds, and produced highly colored tableaux. The most effective moments were those of the second and the final scene, where the action of the crowds made superb pictures. In the first of these episodes two levels were used, with Lazarus and his followers above, while below the warring factions among the Jews, the followers of Jesus, and the orthodox Hebrews, fought and killed, while the Lazarites danced and laughed.

In the final scene the crowd on a high platform watched the martyrdom of Lazarus at the stake, the flame lighting the faces of the Roman mob, which when Lazarus began to speak, swarmed down four flights of stairs and into the arena, bringing the play to an end on a magnificent piece of stage direction.

Lazarus Laughed begins just after the miracle of his resurrection and the departure of Jesus, who is not seen. The joy of parents and people at his return to life is soon overshadowed by their bigotry, and presently they battle over him, while the Roman legions come to take him to Rome, for Tiberius Caesar has heard the story of his return from the grave and hopes that the Jew may bring him renewed youth and failing to win a way of new life from Lazarus, he has him burned at the stake.

"There is no death!" the cry of Lazarus is made the theme for many of the choruses, the music for the play having been written by Arthur Alexander, formerly head of the Eastman orchestra at Rochester, N. Y. His score has dignity, much of beauty, and a great deal of dramatic intensity.

More than twenty of the characters in the play speak, but there are only five that stand out. Lazarus was played superbly by Irving Pichel, whose technical equipment is tremendous. The laughter, which at one time runs without cessation for four minutes; the necessity for absolute repose and poise, and Pichel's splendid and resonant voice carried him to a triumph.

Gilmor Brown chose one of the three human roles in the play, that of Tiberius, and scored by a fine impersonation. Victor Jory was the Caligula, making him half animal, with dangling arms and bended knees, and giving him a snarling speech. Dore Wilson, cast for Pompeia, played that cruel wanton with distinction and power, and Lenore Shanewise made much of the gentle Miriam, wife of Lazarus.

John Mason Brown

MARCO MILLIONS

The most elaborate of the new American plays, as well as by far the most glamorous, is Eugene O'Neill's *Marco Millions*, which has finally come to a generous and abundant production at the hands of the Theatre Guild. As everyone knows by now, *Marco* is the story of Babbitt retold in ancient dress, wherein the smoking-car wit and the Rotarian complacency of the Polos, and particularly of the younger Polo, are set against the splendor and the mystic wisdom of the court of Kublai, the Great Kaan. There is no gainsaying that Mr. O'Neill and the Guild have labored mightily for what may, at first, seem a simple, even an obvious, satiric idea, that was fresher four years ago when the play was written than it can appear today. But it is not fair to dismiss *Marco* as a one finger exercise rendered heroically by a symphony orchestra. It is far more than a "lady-comc-to-see" version of Sinclair Lewis, because in it Mr. O'Neill has not admitted satire as his final goal. Instead he has written with a haunting and savage beauty that lifts the play far above the mockery which is ordinarily aimed at Kiwanians. Although he has employed the usual Babbitt-scorner methods, they have, in his hands, taken a form that is peculiarly his own. His satire is colored by a wit that has no skill in parrying but that strikes out with heavy and downright blows. If it is far from agile, and permits no pauses for those verbal interchanges which are the delight of comedy, it is because its grim strength is nearer to a tragic virtue than a comic necessity. Mr. O'Neill shows up the full-fledged absurdity of this Marco, whose shrewdness is masked in all the "getting ahead" clichés of the "bigger and better" school of business beatitudes, shows him up again and again in the same ludicrous light, with scarcely a variation, in a way that, for

From Theatre Arts, *March 1928. Reprinted by permission of the author and* Theatre Arts *Magazine.*

all its broadness of attack, is never hilarious, though it is steadily diverting. If *Marco* depended solely on its satire, its gruff jokes would soon go stale. They are, however, so at odds with the opulence of their setting and so blended with a mellow tale of tragedy and romance, that they gain all the sharper values of antithesis. Nor are they, by any means, Mr. O'Neill's sole concern. His picaresque drama makes a more special comment on the disintegration of Marco, as success finally stifles the poet that was in him, just as it narrates, with a tenderness and beauty rarely found in his plays, the lyric infatuation of the young princess, Kukachin, for the leather-pated Marco. In it, too, Mr. O'Neill, who is ever intrepid in the face of experiment, differentiates the dialogic styles of each of the various elements which combine to make his story, with a sensitive ear for prose rhythms. If, at first, his play seems more obvious in production than in its printed form, it is partly due to Mr. O'Neill's failure to underline his meaning with that indelible red ink that the theatre invariably demands. More certainly, it is that incapacity of his to give his plays a final finish, which stands in his way now as it has so often in the past, and which permits him to let his last act, both in the acting and the printed versions, slough off into the grandiose phrases of a deeply felt but weakly thought mysticism, when a little sharpening in line and finality of thought would keep his intention clear throughout. He has not sinned alone, however, for the direction, as well as some of the acting, at the Guild is, at times, more than a little heedless of his literary values. Rouben Mamoulian, whose ensemble work in *Porgy* was remarkable, directs *Marco* with a fine, unerring eye for pictorial imagery. In his compositional effects he shows a virtuosity seldom rivalled in our theatre, but his hand is not equally strong in keeping the satire pointed for its most vital meaning, or in outlining the sad romance of the little princess and the even sadder decline of Marco against the swarming pageantry of the play. Of the actors, it is Alfred Lunt who blurs the script most, by making fatigue a characteristic of his Marco, and, more unforgivably, by showing the young Marco, who in the text is still unformed and capable of both imagination and emotion, as an infant Babbitt, shallow and false, and already afraid of both sincerity and beauty. Baliol Holloway, instead of shielding the weaknesses of the final scenes, exaggerates them by running away from the impressive simplicity he shows as the young Kaan to let loose a deep-throated and meaningless series of vocalizations. The full sweep of this opulent production is, however, as studded with compensations as it is dimmed by obscurities. Of the many acute characterizations, Dudley Digges' shrivelled Cathayan sage, Chu-Yin, stands out in the highest relief, cold with the imperturbability of the East and wise with the wisdom of the ages. Morris Carnovsky's Tedaldo is created with a majesty that allows this papal legate to be witty as well as clerical. Those crass elder Polos, who are played by Henry Travers and Ernest Cossart, contribute a zestful vulgarity, and Margalo Gillmore as the Princess Kukachin does the most moving work of her career in the scene on the Royal Junk when she speaks her love to Marco. The groupings of Mamoulian are heightened by the ever-colorful and often superb costumes of Lee Simonson, and backed by some of the most effective settings Mr. Simonson has ever designed. Seen without their color these sets would immediately confess that their lines are not distinguished; but lighted as they are at the Guild they present a steady sequence of richly contributive backgrounds. By his ingenious use of permanent set pieces, Mr. Simonson not only makes the production possible, by solving the difficulties presented by the globe-trotting of the script, but lends the play a unity which considerably strengthens its picaresque form.

Joseph Wood Krutch

STRANGE INTERLUDE

No play of recent years has aroused so much preliminary speculation as has Eugene O'Neill's *Strange Interlude* (John Golden Theatre). Rumors of its odd method and its extraordinary length contributed no less than the fame of its author to make "news" of the coming production, and there was not, I fancy, a single commentator on things theatrical who did not await the fatal afternoon (for the play begins at five-fifteen) more tensely than a hardened observer is permitted to confess. Each knew that he would be expected to have a decided opinion and each was balanced between two fears—the fear lest he be hynotized into believing himself more impressed than he really was and the opposite fear lest he lean over backward into mere insensibility. Between the devil and the deep sea. Which should he choose—the risk of going down to posterity as a soft-headed fool or the worse risk of being reminded some ten years later that he had greeted a masterpiece with wisecracks popping like thorns under a pot? He must, unaided, trust the adequacy of his perceptions and, taking his courage in his hands, pronounce an unequivocal opinion. *Strange Interlude* had unwound its five-hour length. What of it?

For a long time to come critics will be busy with their reconsiderations and their second thoughts. There will be a time for interpretations of the theme and analyses of the characters; but for the moment what those who have not yet gone to the John Golden want is a vigorous "aye" or an equally vigorous "nay"; and there can be no doubt, I think, that the "ayes" must ultimately have it. Nor is it to be forgot that this must mean infinitely more than it would mean in the case of any mere everyday dramatic production, for extraordinary things can receive only extraordinary justi-

---

From The Nation, *February 15, 1928. Reprinted by permission of the author and the publisher.*

fications. Not only must Mr. O'Neill justify his taking a very unusual amount of our time but he must also justify his very unusual disregard of the conventions of dramatic writing. No play has, so to speak, a right to consist of nine long acts in which the dialogue is continually interspersed with speeches representing the unspoken thoughts of the characters—to be written, that is to say, as no play was ever written before—unless it justifies the liberties which it takes by giving us in return something which no play ever gave before. Yet *Strange Interlude* survives even this very hard test. It does give something—some depth, some solidity—which no play has ever had, and its strange method does make possible a kind of virtue new to dramatic art.

The drama has always seemed the form of expression best suited to an heroic age and the novel the form best suited to a complex and baffled one, since a certain simplicity of presentation has been inseparable from playwriting. The production of a play has implied both a story elementary enough to be recounted almost in the form of an anecdote and a view of human life uncomplicated enough to be presented almost without shadings. While the modern mind has found itself unable to express its reactions without the infinite qualifications and the subtle half-thoughts which its most characteristic literary form makes possible and while, in the hands of its masters—the Dostoevskys and the Prousts—only the things not quite sayable have seemed any longer worth saying, the stage has seemed destined to remain, perforce, content with simple outlines. It has been, in short, a place where only major chords could be struck even though existing in an age which had lost the power to be moved by any but the subtlest and most difficult harmonies. It knew best the language which stirs the blood of confident and thoroughly integrated people, it could remember how it had swayed passions of unified societies like those of Periclean Athens or Elizabethan England; but it had remained, as even those of us who study it most closely must admit, far less capable than the novel of speaking to baffled and divided spirits.

What Mr. O'Neill has done, then, is to take a story which is not only longer than the ordinary story of a play but one which invites, or rather demands, that brooding subtlety of treatment impossible in the ordinary dramatic form, and he has made out of it something which not only holds every one of our faculties employed but remains, like one of the greatest modern novels, to tease the mind with the sense that there will be, for a long time to come, new discoveries to be made in the memory of its labyrinthine passages. Without the many innovations of his method this particular story could not be told, these particular effects could not be obtained upon the stage, and he has, therefore, conquered a new province for the theatre. He is, for example, the first to dare to make full use in the drama of that introspection without which it would be impossible to imagine the existence of a large part of modern literature, and he is the first to employ there our newly won knowledge of the unconscious, not in such a way as to make it the foundation of a highly simplified pattern like that of *The Silver Cord* or *Hidden*, but in such a way as to make it cast over all the events that uncertain, flickering light which it sheds in the life around us. Yet no enumeration of such specific or detailed originalities will serve adequately to indicate the originalities of the play, and it can only be said, as it was said before, that *Strange Interlude* conquers a new province for the theatre. In the past our dramatists have been lazily content to say that most of the things which gave modern literature its excuse for being were "not suited to the stage." Mr. O'Neill has succeeded in making them dramatic.

I hope to return again to this production and to say something both of the wholly admirable work of the chief performers—Lynn Fontanne, Glenn Anders, Earle Larimore, and Tom Powers—and more especially of the magnificent work of the director, Philip Moeller, who created a style to fit the drama. *Strange Interlude* is Mr. O'Neill's best play and it has received by far the best—the "rightest"—production which his plays have ever received.

Robert Benchley

DYNAMO

Those few of us who looked with something less than ecstasy on *Strange Interlude* when it appeared on that long afternoon over a year ago, may find a little justification for our scepticism in Mr. O'Neill's latest drama *Dynamo*. Nobody who could write *Dynamo* is above being kidded. And *Dynamo* gives the tip-off on *Strange Interlude* and *The Great God Brown*. They *were* just as bad as we thought they were. Now we know.

It takes a great deal of concentration on *The Emperor Jones* and *The Hairy Ape* to keep alive the thought that Mr. O'Neill is America's greatest dramatist. Of course, if he isn't, the question arises "Who is, then?" and we scurry right back to Mr. O'Neill, with apologies. But it does seem too bad that America's greatest dramatist should be a man entirely devoid of humor.

In wishing that Mr. O'Neill had a sense of humor we do not mean that we want him to write humorously or gag up his plays. Nine-tenths of the value of a sense of humor in writing is not in the things it makes one write but in the things it keeps one from writing. It is especially valuable in this respect in serious writing, and no one without a sense of humor should ever write seriously. For without knowing what is funny, one is constantly in danger of being funny without knowing it.

It has long been a characteristic of the O'Neill drama to burlesque itself as it draws toward its close. The first acts, as in *The Great God Brown* and *Desire Under the Elms*, fill you with the thrilling hope that here is something great. And then things begin piling up, and Pelion is not only put on Ossa but Mt. Monadnock and a couple of funny-looking hills are added, until the whole thing turns into a comedy. Of course, nobody could tell what the last part

From Life, *March 8, 1929. Reprinted with permission.*

of *The Great God Brown* was about, not even Mr. O'Neill, but *Desire Under the Elms* began to get comical when the old gentleman flounced out of the house to go down and sleep with the cows. A sense of humor on Mr. O'Neill's part would have kept him from writing that. (It would also have kept him from writing the last half-dozen "purty, ain't its.")

Strange Interlude, with its splendid fifth and sixth acts, goes burlesque on itself in that incomparable comedy scene at the boat races when people begin dropping dead, but the first act is no slouch as parody. And the famous "aside" method, which is quite all right if you think you need it to get your point across, in the hands of a man with no humor is always on the verge of being ridiculous and often much nearer than that. With a sense of humor Mr. O'Neill could have made *Strange Interlude* a two-and-a-half hour play and a great one.

It is doubtful if even a sense of humor could have made *Dynamo* a great play but it could have made it less dull and less obvious. Roaming through its maze of random soliloquies, asides, apostrophes, and dialogue are some fine things. And the royal blood of the *Count of Monte Cristo*, which is always with Mr. O'Neill and which, unlike the daisies, always tells, gives him the power to throw a dramatic spot-light on all his works so that the lurid glow of the theatre lies over even his dullest passages. It is a question if this inheritance from his trouper father is not his most valuable quality as a dramatist. Certainly without it, many of his works would be practically nothing to watch.

Dynamo, then, has this quality of latent excitement, even if it never comes to much, and Mr. Simonson's Erecto-houses and last-act power plant help to keep it alive. There is also a character (played by Catherine Calhoun Doucet) which always threatens to come to life—the vapid mother who is struggling with a big idea in a small way, but nothing much is done with her except to leave her petting a dynamo in the inevitable burlesque fashion of most of O'Neill's grand characters.

The rest of the cast performs with the efficiency of all Theatre Guild casts—Glenn Anders, George Gaul, Helen Westley, Dudley Digges and, as an excellent bit of casting, Claudette Colbert. But there are such handicaps imposed on actors by this O'Neill method that it is difficult for even the best to do much more than just recite. If this school of dramatic writing is coming into any vogue at all, we might as well teach our actors to project their voices properly and let it go at that. There is no sense in trying to act when the only person you have to feed you and talk to is yourself or a piece of scenery.

A while ago to treat a play of Eugene O'Neill's flippantly or, condescendingly, to pick out its good points would have been presumptuous. Another like *Dynamo* and it will be about all one can do. And we are promised two more!

John Hutchens

MOURNING BECOMES ELECTRA

Of *Mourning Becomes Electra* it is first to be said that Eugene O'Neill's sense of the theatre—of deep emotion evoked sharply and sustained by extraordinary narrative skill—has never fulfilled itself more completely than in this trilogy as the Theatre Guild has presented it. We have seen him fumble over his analysis of the spiritual ills of the time; brood in the terms of advanced psychology and the asides of the Victorian theatre, as he probed the thoughts and more often the nightmares at the heart of a complex humanity; and no matter what eloquence and persuasion he has sometimes achieved in the grim pursuit of various pseudo-philosophies, there had been of late this uneasy sensation: that he was too often sacrificing his greatest gift as an emotional writer, the power to tell a tale superbly. Here now, in the three plays of this trilogy—*Homecoming*, *The Hunted* and *The Haunted*—he has gone back to one of the world's greatest stories, the *Electra*, not reinterpreting it exactly in terms of the America of 1865-66, not reproducing consistently the Greek mood and imagery, but choosing from the various Greek versions such points of analogy and departure as serve best a horrific murder story. Mr. O'Neill was never more fully an artist than in filling out this pattern to the limit of its possibilities as melodrama. That it has neither the exaltation of poetic drama nor the "final radiantly sad contentment" of great tragedy will be of concern only to those who claim too much for him. They are absent qualities having little to do with the fact that the great story is for the most part finely rendered in this, its latest telling.

The skill with which he has adapted from the Greek pattern, redirecting its suspense to that of the inner movement of the trilogy,

---

From Theatre Arts, *January 1932. Reprinted by permission of the author and* Theatre Arts *Magazine.*

is apparent in a quick synopsis. The House of Atreus is the House of Mannon, the time is April, 1865, when Lee's surrender is as yet an unconfirmed rumor. The first scene of the first play is the exterior of the Mannon house, its Doric columns rising in reminiscent austerity. The family awaits the return from the war of Brigadier-General Ezra Mannon, the Agamemnon of the play, who had won fame in the Mexican War, become rich in the shipping trade, been the mayor of the small New England town in which he lived, and won further glory in the Civil War. The return of his son, Orin, (the Orestes), is also imminent. The first scene is compact in exposition. Christine Mannon (Clytemnestra), wife of Ezra, and their daughter Lavinia (Electra) are at swords' points of mutual hatred and suspicion. Lavinia is in love with a sea captain, Adam Brant (the Aegisthus), an illegitimate son of her great-uncle by a French servant girl. She discovers that her mother has been having an affair with Brant, has been seeing him at intervals in New York, whither she has been going on some pretext. She acquaints her mother with her knowledge of the affair, makes her promise to see no more of Brant, and together the two women await the return of Ezra. In a hurried interview with the captain, Christine has plotted the murder of Mannon, which takes place on the night of his homecoming a week later. By telling him of her affair with Brant she brings on one of the heart attacks to which he is subject, then gives him poison instead of medicine, a fact which Lavinia ascertains as she breaks into the room and hears her father accuse her mother.

With the return of Orin two days later, there begins a struggle between the two women to dominate him, ending in victory for Lavinia when she takes him to Brant's ship at a Boston wharf and, from the deck above, they look down into the cabin and see Christine with her lover. When she has left him, Orin murders Brant, the brother and sister return to their home and confront their mother with the fact of Brant's death, upon which she commits suicide and brings the trilogy to its climax at the end of the second play. Thereafter Mr. O'Neill's invention is more or less free of its Greek background. The furies that haunt Orin consist not only of an active madness of blood-guilt for the death of his mother, but also the transition of his fixation for her into an incestuous passion for Lavinia, of which his sudden awareness is provocation for his suicide. She, who had "tried to become the wife of her father and the mother of Orin," has grown recognizably into a likeness of her mother; Orin's and her own knowledge of this, their mutual guilt and twisted relationship are the culmination of the theme which has flared fitfully throughout the play: that the dead shall come back to haunt and pillory the living; that heredity and crime shall be expiated only as Lavinia expiates them when she forsakes her own future, bars the house and retires into it forever.

In spinning his selective way in and out among the sources of the story, Mr. O'Neill has evolved a structure whose five hours of playing time are not free from prolixity, particularly in the third play which is raised to the artistic level of the first two only by the final portrait, complete in picture, mood and feeling. In other words, it is in the first two-thirds of the trilogy, or in the crescendo of its action, that his skill for sustaining a narrative is at its exciting best, the third play and its interpretation of the action falling into old faults of wordiness and repetition. In perspective the great effective moments of *Mourning Becomes Electra* are those of melodramatic situation carefully prepared and caught at the crest of their suspense, suffering no anti-climax; the sinister plotting of Ezra Mannon's murder in the shadows of his study; the murder itself, and Mannon gasping out an accusation as his daughter breaks into the room; the scene in which Lavinia, in the presence of her brother, places the poison on the corpse of her father and admits their mother into the room of wavering candlelight to test her weakening nerves; the scene on the boat, with Brant and Christine in a cross-section of his cabin giving away their secret while Lavinia and Orin stand concealed on the deck above them; the wracking half minute while Brant is returning to his certain death at the hands of Orin; the suicide of Christine.

There is no implication here of inadmissible stage trickery or of insincerity. Mr. O'Neill's writing in this trilogy is admirably straightforward and full of fine splendor, particularly in the soliloquies, which are beautifully written and, by no accident, shrewdly expository. And to the vibrant needs of the play the Guild gives bountiful aid. Philip Moeller's direction is scarcely less distinguished than in *Strange Interlude*, a more difficult technical task, three years ago. He gives to the performance as a whole a background of slowly increasing force and deliberate quietude from which it draws an additional starkness of outline (the sluggishness of the last play could hardly be lessened without cutting the text severely). There are in the trilogy three individual performances of genuine stature, finely wrought in the face of different problems, and in particular of the one which stands between Mr. O'Neill's work and real tragedy—the fact that not a character in the trilogy is of heroic mold, that whatever happens to any of them is not conceivably a fall from greatness. They are small people. Alla Nazimova's Christine is a sinister and deeply realized creation, all her fine technical resourcefulness responding flawlessly to the role through which the themes of the trilogy run most fiercely during the first two plays. More stringent in the demands upon its continuity, the task of Alice Brady, the Lavinia, has been differently conceived. Through the entire action and its final interpretation she moves now as a participant, now as a passive figure in whom the doom is foreshadowed and finally symbolized, and always with a mask-like rigidity which in formalized style is set apart from the rest of the performance. The slow pace which the part has been given by Mr. Moeller is open to question, an unnecessary connection between slowness and impressiveness being suggested, but within its deliberate repression it is a performance almost perfectly sustained, never blurred and triumphant in its pictorial values. Earle Larimore reaches the highest point in his career in the acting of Orin, a constantly emotional role in which he is entirely free from the falsity of average theatrical neuroticism and alert in conveying the tortured relationships which swirl around him.

The settings of Robert Edmond Jones are never inadequate, and in two instances—the pillared front of the House of Mannon and the deck of the clipper ship by night—they are intensely dramatic. The former is entirely complementary to the action, entering into the changing moods of the play and closing it exactly on the note it has sought and gained by turns. In the moment when Lavinia, in black, stands framed between the white pillars of the House of Mannon, the sunset dying at her feet, the course of passion run—in that moment, playwright, performer and artist come together in a superb conclusion that belongs as completely and solely to the theatre as Mr. O'Neill himself.

Gilbert W. Gabriel

AH, WILDERNESS!

Last night the Theatre Guild began its sixteenth season by presenting Eugene O'Neill's new play, *Ah, Wilderness!* This morning all the dolts in creation and criticism will be remarking that O'Neill has turned Tarkington. But then, we shall have at once to add, as a matter of truth, news, and salutation, that *Ah, Wilderness!* gave us an evening of slyly superfine delight, and that it and its cast's chief visitor, George M. Cohan, met the première's crowd on terms of inexhaustible pleasantness and friendship.

O'Neill himself, so I hear, explains *Ah, Wilderness!* as "a comedy of recollection." Comedy is all it pretends to be—a very native American folk-comedy, with none of those cosmic rumbles to which folk plays are usually prone—and recollection certainly is in it, all around it, permeating it as happily as the smell of drench lilacs in the garden of any grown man's half-forgotten youth.

But so light a mood it has, so smiling and benevolent and utterly optimistic a meaning, I make bold to wonder whether it isn't also entitled to be called a comedy of recantation.

For here is the cavernous eye of O'Neill doing nothing except twinkle. And here are at least six or seven of the former O'Neill's pet tragic situations—of misunderstood boyhood, for instance, and of gentleman and prostitute, and of drunkard and spinster—all treated to the very opposite of their old-time terror and tears, all given the benefit of a quiet but unmistakable and contagious chuckle.

Or perhaps this new O'Neill is self-displayed chiefly to confound the few who still thought that the old O'Neill dealt only in overtones and no good humor. Little as they deserve the pleasure, let these go sit in the front rows now.

From the New York American, *October 3, 1933. Reprinted by permission of the* New York Journal-American.

Early in his dramatic career O'Neill was already recounting "the background of real life behind my work" as proof "that I have not written out of the top of my head." And in *Ah, Wilderness!* he is obviously again recalling one of the first chapters of that background, and writes it out of the bottom of his heart. There is a light of such paternal kindliness, an aureole of such genial nostalgia, hung around the young high school lad named Richard Miller in this new play, you are bound to know him as a creature of autobiography, and to recognize Richard as Eugene in search of his lost youth.

In "a large small-town in Connecticut" (could it be New London, where O'Neill himself was once a cub reporter and columnist, and where the famous James, his father, had long had a Summer home?) in the year of innocence of 1906, *Ah, Wilderness!* is set. It is all strictly domestic, in spite of one barroom spree scene, and all wistfully reminiscent of the days when family life was the life.

Editor Nat Miller of the town paper; Mrs. Miller, a couple of adult in-laws, and the four Miller children . . . these are the staple goods of the play. A few other youngsters and oldsters tread on the fringe of it, sloe-ginning, spooning, full of the prose and patter of perfectly sensible, ordinary people, in benevolent contrast to Richard, the Millers' second son, the Millers' problem-child, the Millers' poet-in-their-midst.

But there's no special coddling or unhumorous pity for this Junior O'Neill. He is just young Dick, not Young Woodley. He reads Ibsen and Shaw on the sly, he spouts Swinburne and Kipling at the wrong moment—and to the wrong people—and he is as gangly and ornery as he [can be].

Young Richard is the fond, fuzz-covered young histrion that all sadly middle-aged men have to admit that they, too, were in their prep-school Galahad days. He is you, I, all of us at the damnfool age of seventeen—provided we were seventeen somewhere around the jog-trot year of 1906, before youth was labelled flaming.

Young Richard has made the social error of sending some too fervid poetical quotations to his best girl. Called to account by two family heads, he celebrates this Independence Day by swanking off with a college chum to prove his manhood in the most sordid resort in town. But his evil intentions fail as fast as his good. Afraid of the cheap little female chippie, thrown out of the barroom for being under age, he comes home at awful midnight to give an exhibition of first souse before the entire outraged family, and to be swished off ingloriously to bed.

Next day brings rewards: clean romance and katzenjammers, and a gentle but abysmal lecture from Dad on the subject of 1906 morality and social hygiene. Maybe 1933 is wiser as well as worldlier, after all.

But, anyway, there's a tender spray of moonlit sentiment between good boy and good girl, and a benediction of moonlight over the parents, too. "I can only remember a few nights that were as beautiful as this," says Dad, "and they were long ago, when your mother and I were young and planning to get married." And only a little while thereafter, with a snatch of the Rubaiyat practically sung to "Silver Threads Among the Gold," the curtain comes down on the Familia Miller of Smalltown, Connecticut, one-score-and-seven years ago.

Outside the theatre, a hitherto unheard-of honor, the Guild throws George Cohan's name up in large electric letters. In fair exchange for which Mr. Cohan presents the Guild with the best performance most of us have ever seen him give, either in his own plays or anybody's. A performance heart-deep in fatherly wisdom and humanity, as honest as natural, and thoroughly understanding, masterly spoken throughout. He and the boy, played by Elisha Cook, Jr.,—and played beautifully, too—make their scenes together unforgettably touching.

The cast is good all up and down the line, however. It includes Gene Lockhart, welcomed back to straight roles, Marjorie Marquis, Eda Heinemann, and a shrewd little youngster's bit by Walter Vonnegut, Jr. And out of Robert Edmond Jones's memory book of the wallpaper and cherry-mahogany of his youth come some of his most authentic settings.

It is a comfort and a treat, this *Ah, Wilderness!* I for one found it paradise enow.

Lawrence Gilman

THE EMPEROR JONES *AS OPERA*

For an hour and ten minutes yesterday afternoon the stage of the Metropolitan was swept clear of the Lohengrins and Aidas and Fausts and Lucias and Rigolettos of the decorous operatic tradition, and was given over to the nightmare horrors of a tropical jungle and the menacing rites of voodoo worship and the swarming of frenzied native tribesmen and the epileptic prancings of a Congo Witch Doctor painted blue and red, with antelope horns and a charm-stick tipped with cockatoo's feathers. Through this unusual phantasmagoria moved the figure of an ex-Pullman porter who had made himself ruler of the native tribes. We saw him disintegrate before our eyes, falling from the pride of his strutting glory to the groveling desperation of his inevitable end—saw him turn from a swaggering despot in gold braid and medals to a haunted, half-naked, terror-stricken fugitive, reclaimed by the primitive ancestral savagery that had spawned and doomed him.

For this we were, primarily, indebted to *The Emperor Jones* of Mr. Eugene O'Neill, that classic of the American theatre which stirred us all so deeply when the beating of its incessant tom-tom was first heard at the Provincetown Playhouse a dozen years ago, and which Mr. Louis Gruenberg, Russian-born American composer, has made into an opera. We were indebted scarcely less at yesterday's première to the brilliant performance of Mr. Lawrence Tibbett as Brutus Jones, the Negro bad man and fugitive Emperor, who dominated the proceedings from the moment that he appeared, blustering, insolent, preposterous, in his blue military coat with the brass buttons and gold chevrons and his bright red breeches, until, an abject and ghost-ridden savage, praying, pleading, whimpering, and hysterical, shorn of his thin caking of sophistication,

From the New York Herald Tribune, *January 8, 1933. Reprinted by permission of the* New York Herald Tribune.

he shot himself with his cherished silver bullet, an atavistic sacrifice.

One hesitates to apply to the achievement of a gifted and serious artist the cheap word "triumph"—a word debased by facile and irresponsible employment. But one need not hesitate to use the word concerning Mr. Tibbett and his Emperor Jones as enacted at yesterday's performance.

It was, beyond question, his afternoon, his and O'Neill's—though that lonely and inimitable genius was nowhere to be seen, and was reputed to be far away. Mr. Tibbett's imaginative grasp and embodiment of a cruelly exacting role, his power of spacing and his control of climax, the long inexorable crescendo of his progressive panic and degradation, were accomplished with a great artist's economy and reserve and cumulative power.

The thunderous tribute which the young American received from the vast audience (which filled the house to the last square foot of standing room) was as unmistakably heartfelt and irresistible as the most fanatical of operatic patriots could have wished.

It is not possible to speak so unrestrainedly of Mr. Gruenberg's part in the affair. Some of us have doubted whether O'Neill's superb play is the sort of drama to which music can profitably be added. There are plays which invite adaptation as operas, which cry more or less plaintively for the heightening and intensification, the imaginative completion that music can give. O'Neill's brief masterpiece is not, I think, of that class. It has its own sufficing and self-contained element of musical intensification, that of the famous and incessant drum-beat which seems to project for us the pulse of the fugitive's heart, and, finally, the rhythmic frenzy of his atavistic terrors, as he stumbles through the jungle night back to the darkness of his ancestral savagery and his own end.

Mr. Gruenberg has, naturally, taken advantage of this celebrated feature of the original play, and it has, indisputably, its own effectiveness and power as he uses it—though it is less obsessing in the opera than in the play.

It is not easy to feel that Mr. Gruenberg's musical additions to the drama are truly contributive. His orchestral commentary is skillful, discreet, ingeniously adapted to the action and the discourse, sympathetically reflective of mood and of emotional growth. I do not think that it heightens or intensifies the play. On the contrary, there are many passages in which it seemed intrusive and superfluous; and I cannot believe that, in most instances, the words of Jones and of Smithers gain by being sung—though Mr. Gruenberg often contents himself with allowing the characters to speak their lines, or he gives them something roughly equivalent to the "Sprechgesang" of Schönberg or Alban Berg.

The most conspicuous of his musical embellishments are the choral interjections, which proceeded, at yesterday's performance, from singers half concealed behind stockades of decorative palm leaves and from others behind the scenes. These choral passages—which have less the effect of singing than of a kind of polyphonic yelling—supply a commentary upon the action, minatory and prophetic; and they provide a crude variety of excitement. Their value as musical enhancement, per se, is negligible.

The score as a whole, indeed, seems to me negligible from almost every point of view; though it is a pleasure to recognize the craft and earnestness with which Mr. Gruenberg has gone about his unproductive task.

The Metropolitan has given the opera an admirable production —surely one of the best in its recent history. On an antiquated stage, and hampered by notoriously inadequate facilities, the institution has accomplished a mounting of the difficult work that is richly and continuously illusive.

The effectiveness of the production owes much to the extraordinary power and beauty of the settings provided by the gifted Mr. Jo Mielziner. Indeed, the honors of this occasion go, first, to Mr. O'Neill and Mr. Tibbett, and secondly to Mr. Mielziner, whose settings really do supply that imaginative extension and that added spiritual dimension which the music fails to provide. If one wanted to pay a just tribute to the genuinely creative contribution of Mr. Mielziner, one might describe the work revealed to us yesterday as "*The Emperor Jones*, play by Eugene O'Neill, set to scenery by Jo Mielziner."

Mr. Mielziner should be permanently annexed by the Metropolitan in the interests of American operatic art.

John Anderson

DAYS WITHOUT END

Mr. O'Neill emerged from the *Ah, Wilderness!* mood of adolescent memories last night to resume his old soul-searching, the quest which has led him into such self-tortured dramas as *The Fountain*, *The Great God Brown*, and *Dynamo*. In *Days Without End*, which the Guild presents at Henry Miller's Theatre, he hits at last the road which has loomed beyond his horizon for many years, the road which in this hurried midnight examination, seems to be spiritually and emotionally, the sawdust trail. I take it to be the old-time religion at which Mr. O'Neill arrives after three acts of self-conscious, unmoving, and generally embarrassing discourse upon the nature of Faith. His hero is on his knees before a crucifix, his masked spirit of evil dead on the floor beside him, and the remnants of a pretty bad play strewn about in the wreckage of what sounds like an emotional binge. The Guild invests it with all solemnity, gives it benefit of Simonson's excellent settings, and illuminates it with an extraordinary performance by Earle Larimore. But to no avail; it remains Mr. O'Neill in his most difficult and trying aspect.

Some six or seven years ago when Mr. O'Neill was singing an ecstatic paganism in *The Fountain* I predicted that he would, dramatically anyway, ultimately return to the church. But no one could have predicted, except after seeing *Dynamo*, that he would return in such disorder. I mean no disrespect for his beliefs, if this new play is to be taken personally, for a man's beliefs are his own—until he writes a play about them. The gentlemen who sat on the rooftops at Patchogue some years ago, waiting for the end of the world in their nightgowns, had full privileges to do as they pleased. In fact, they may have been right.

Mr. O'Neill's fundamental error, dramatically, lies in the notion

---

From the New York Evening Journal, *January 9, 1934. Reprinted by permission of the* New York Journal-American.

that Faith is an intellectual process to be touched through words. Its very point, I take it, is that it lies beyond reason. His own hero prays for the "gift of Faith" as something which he cannot reach by his own mental processes.

Thus in the theatre the existence of Faith in a character, or the achievement of Faith on the stage is not dramatic in O'Neill's intellectual sense. It is not the climax of a rational dramatic process such as you might make of a man working three acts to understand the Einstein Theory and finally getting it, and so lifting the mortgage or crying "The world is mine." It is a thing you have or you haven't, and to that extent it is a personal miracle. Mr. O'Neill calls *Days Without End* a modern miracle play, and then writes not a simple, graceful miracle but a sort of Sunday school debate with Q. E. D. attached at the end. And to weaken the play further the debate is couched in the tritest sort of dramatic formulas.

His central character is John Loving, a successful man, who finds himself, after a life of questioning rebellion, peacefully married, and working on a novel which is obviously autobiographical. It is the story of a young man, brought up a devout Catholic, who spurned God when his parents died, took up atheism and such, and finally, in his beautiful wife, found a God of Love. But impelled by his Evil Spirit he dishonored even that deity, and when his wife finds out his sin he torments himself as she lies dying in the next room, unable to forgive him.

O'Neill returns to a mixture of the *Strange Interlude* technique and the mask business of *The Great God Brown*. This Evil Spirit or "Damned Soul" of John Loving is embodied on the stage by Stanley Ridges, hideously made up for grotesque effect, who never leaves Mr. Larimore's presence. He is the personification of the aside. He speaks the lines sometimes for John Loving; sometimes Mr. Larimore speaks them. When John Loving is in the throes of spiritual agony their dialogue monkeyshines become a joint debate between the Gold Dust Twins, or as some irreverent wag remarked in the intermission, a session between Mr. Loving and his spiritual stooge.

It is this devil that is finally cast out at the end, through the intercession of a priest, and Loving returns triumphantly to his old faith, Safe in Abraham's bosom. There is the intimation, at least, that Mrs. Loving will get well and that God is love.

My objections to all this have not, I repeat, anything whatever to do with the nature of O'Neill's faith, or of Loving's conversion. They are based on the suspicion that it is all dramatically phony; that O'Neill has substituted some florid emotion, and some muddy thinking for the dignity and simplicity of religious conviction. It is the place for poetry, not bombast; humility, not melodramatics.

The Guild has given this, under Philip Moeller's brilliant direction, one of its finest productions—even if it is wasted. The mechanical problem of two actors playing the double nature of one character is solved with unbelievable subtlety by Mr. Ridges and Mr. Larimore in superbly integrated performances. Mr. Larimore, in the more difficult rôle, does by far the finest work of his career, and one of the best jobs of this or any season. Robert Loraine, as the patient, kindly, sweetly reasoning priest, his uncle, gives a performance that is rich, balanced, and well sustained. Selena Royle, after getting past some bad spots of wifely banality, contributes an excellent scene before she takes to her deathbed, and Ilka Chase gives a sharp and vivid sketch of the talkative friend who happened to sin with Loving when dat ol' debbil in him was uppermost.

But *Days Without End* sounds like part of that religious trilogy which O'Neill started to write in *Dynamo* and which he had apparently abandoned. It seems a pity it wasn't, for while it is interesting as a phase of O'Neill's development, its values are more clinically personal than dramatic or stirring.

Rosamond Gilder

THE ICEMAN COMETH

Eugene O'Neill's return after twelve years of absence has done more than give the new season a fillip of interest: it has restored to the theatre something of its intrinsic stature. O'Neill's gift for puzzling, infuriating and delighting his audiences makes everything he writes important even to those whom it exasperates. *The Iceman Cometh* presented by the House of O'Neill, the Theatre Guild, in an admirable production directed by Eddie Dowling has stirred Broadway from its daydreaming even as his hero Hickey stirs the bums in the backroom of Harry Hope's dump from their alcohol-ridden fancies. Sardi's and Twenty-One, Walgreen's and El Morocco seethed with indignant argument after an opening "night" that began at 4:30 in the afternoon and continued until 10 —an opening for which the theatrically knowing and those who like to be seen at important events turned out in force. Though baseball and the movies may draw greater crowds, the theatre can console itself with the fact that in the end playwrights last longer in man's recollection. And certainly Eugene O'Neill will, because his plays, and this one in particular, exist on more than one plane. *The Iceman Cometh* is made of good theatre substance—meaty material for actors, racy dialogue, variety of character, suspense and passion—all within the strait-jacket of a rigid pattern. It is also primarily an allegory of man's pitiful estate, a parable of his search for redemption.

O'Neill has gone back to the saloons and gin-mills of his early days—and plays—for the setting of *The Iceman*, which he wrote

---

Originally entitled "Each in His Own Way," by Rosamond Gilder, from Theatre Arts, *December 1946, Copyright 1946 by Theatre Arts, Inc. and from* Theatre Arts Anthology, *edited by Rosamond Gilder, Hermine R. Isaacs, Edward Reed and Robert M. MacGregor.*

in 1939. Harry Hope's bar and the backroom behind it is a composite of the dives he himself used to frequent in his restless youth. Hope's place is, according to one of its "inmates," the No Chance Saloon, Bedrock Bar, the End of the Line Café where five-cent whiskey—"cyanide cut with carbolic acid to give it a mellow flavor" —is sold to a motley collection of down-and-outers by an amiably boozy proprietor. The whole action of the play, such as it is, swings between the bar itself with its half-door on the street and the dingy backroom where, as the curtain rises, a dozen assorted drunks sit at round tables drinking and dreaming of that golden tomorrow which will see them restored once more to a living world. They are waiting for Hickey, a traveling salesman, who comes to them from time to time to live out a "periodical," a fabulous bender in which they share his whiskey and listen to his jokes, particularly that one about his loving wife whom he has treated so badly but who is all right now because he left her safely at home in bed—"with the iceman." While waiting for Hickey, Larry, the philosophic ex-anarchist, tells the newly-arrived Parritt (who is the son of a famous woman anarchist now under arrest for participating in a bombing episode on the West Coast) all about the other members of this dead-end club. Each has a story of fraud or failure behind him; each lives in an alcoholic "pipe dream" of future hope—till Hickey arrives.

Then the trouble starts. Hickey has reformed. He is off the booze; he has found salvation and he intends to make all his friends follow his path to peace and happiness. They are to face their dream tomorrows in actual fact. But the results of his proselytizing are disastrous. Hate, fear, anguish and despair descend on the inhabitants of the erstwhile fools' paradise. Hickey finds to his horror that his gospel of disillusionment does not work. He is forced to explain the cause of his own reform in order to prove he is right. He pours out the story of his life, of his relations with his wife whom he loved and who loved him too well—and whom he killed to save her from the suffering he was forever inflicting. He had left her that very morning safe in bed—"with the iceman," Death. And then as Hickey tells the story of the woman he murdered for love he realizes with a sudden blinding flash that this too was illusion, that he had killed her because he hated her; he killed her and cursed her for her intolerable, overwhelming love. This last confession brings a final reversal. The murder and the cursing were madness. "I must have been crazy," Hickey cries out in despair. The bums who had been listening to his story in a sort of horrified stupor stir at the words. Hickey was crazy all the time! His reform was a pipe dream too. They can go back to their old illusions, their whiskey, their dreams; they reach thirstily for their bottles. Only the boy Parritt, Larry, and Hickey himself are changed. Hickey gives himself up to the police for murder, Parritt commits suicide realizing he is as guilty of mother-murder as Hickey of wife-murder and Larry the philosopher faces the fact that for him too death is the only answer. The cycle is complete. If this is life then indeed "The best of all were never to be born."

Like Peer Gynt's onion, the story of *The Iceman* has its layers and layers of meaning. It touches on a dozen different themes and relationships. While the subsidiary characters are separate microcosms of despair, the three chief figures, Hickey, Larry, and Parritt, are three aspects of man—each element loving and loathing the other. The play is in a very special sense a summary of much of O'Neill's past writing. Superficially it goes back as far as the vigorous sea plays with which he made his debut. Its frank barroom talk, its conventional tarts, its amiable drunks, its passion and violence are reminders of the impact of his first writing. Don Parritt, the boy rejected by his mother, haunted by the guilt of his betrayal of her, which is nothing less than matricide, recalls O'Neill's days of absorption in psychoanalysis while Larry the philosopher is the O'Neill who attempted a detachment and objectivity never native to him.

But it is through Hickey who has known the love that passeth understanding and has rejected it that we glimpse O'Neill's ultimate meaning. Blind, besotted, and misguided, man haunted by death lives by lies. "The lie of a pipe dream is what gives life to the whole misbegotten mad lot of us, drunk or sober," Larry says at the opening of the play. But there is a truth which is not the truth of alcohol or political shibboleths, or psychology or philosophy, or even the truth of "facing the truth" which Hickey preaches. The greatest illusion of all is to believe that disillusionment—the unaided processes of the intellect—can solve man's dilemma. There is a force that, like the love that Hickey's wife bore him, is made of understanding and forgiveness. Man finds such love intolerable.

"I couldn't forgive her for forgiving me," Hickey explains. "I caught myself hating her for making me hate myself so much. There is a limit to the guilt you can feel and the forgiveness and pity you can take." And so man denies, destroys and blasphemes such love, only in the end to find that this too will be forgiven. The denizens of Hickey's world and of the world at large find a simple answer to Hickey's final revelation. The man is mad! Hamlet to the contrary notwithstanding, there is nothing more in heaven and earth than can be compassed in any current philosophy. Pass the bottle. Drink up. What the hell! It's a good play, brother, why bother?

And it is a good play, excellently acted and directed, full of substance. It would seem that it could readily be compressed into a more reasonable running time, but O'Neill has a tendency to shirk the task of selection and condensation. He has so much to say that even this four-and-a-half-hour play must seem short to a man who thinks in terms of trilogies and nine-play cycles. For the onlooker, however, a shorter play would have brought into sharper focus the conflicting and merging elements of the three chief figures of the fable. The subsidiary characters are not sufficiently important or rounded to demand the time and attention they absorb. They are each set in their groove in the first half hour. They never emerge from the pattern to take on human proportions. The reiterated pattern of their false redemption and its death-dealing effect becomes tedious. Mr. O'Neill seems to underestimate the ability of the audience to grasp his idea, or perhaps more truly he has so fond a remembrance softened by time and distance of these denizens of his kingdom of despair that he cannot bear to tear up the sketches he has made in his mind's eye as he sat with them at marble-topped tables or leaned against mahogany bars in a hundred saloons the world over.

But the length of *The Iceman*, though it adds very little to the characterizations so boldly sketched in the first scenes, does permit an interesting orchestration of effects which Mr. Dowling has developed in this direction. The stage is almost continuously peopled by all the characters in the play at once. There is little movement; there is only an antiphonal development of themes. Besides the pipe-dream motive, which is developed in turn by each of the characters playing in groups of threes and fours, there is also the predominant, haunting theme of Death. O'Neill's bums are all in pursuit of forgetfulness, of sleep, of death. They spend most of their time in blissful or tormented alcoholic slumber. O'Neill uses this device to bring them in and out of the action without making them leave the stage. As the play progresses, the way the tables are grouped in the backroom and bar and the manner in which actors are grouped around them—slumped over asleep or sitting in a deathly daydream—provides a constant visual comment on the developing theme.

Mr. Dowling and the Theatre Guild have gathered a fine cast which gives as integrated a performance as has been seen in many a long day on the New York stage. Robert Edmond Jones has managed the miracle of making visible and at the same time expressive a sordid environment which is essential to the play but would lose its power were it merely photographic. Harry Hope's bar and backroom is indeed the very home of oblivion, a Sargasso Sea of human flotsam. It seems etched in dirt, dusty with despair—a place where wrecked mariners are kind to each other because this is the end and there will be no rescue. The derelict ship is captained by Harry Hope, superbly played by Dudley Digges to whom the role of this genial, testy, irascible, kindly saloon keeper is a mine of histrionic possibilities. James Barton has a more difficult assignment in Hickey, the genial salesman peddling a false redemption among his bottlemates. He acquits himself with vigor of a task that might conceivably be more subtly handled, doing full justice to the speech in which he tells his life history—the longest soliloquy yet heard on any New York stage. Larry, the philosophic bystander who discovers that he is not really as much in love with easeful death as he thought, is given substance and authority by Carl Benton Reid, while a young actor, Paul Crabtree, does a sound, workmanlike job with the role of the distraught youth tormented by a virulent Oedipus complex. Nicholas Joy and Russell Collins catch the essence of their simpler and more boldly sketched parts and present them with delightful clarity. Indeed it would be only fair to list the entire male cast, not excluding the explosive Italian barkeep (played by Tom Pedi) who strikes a welcome note of crude common sense and raucous humor in an atmosphere of boozy self-delusion and introspection. Ruth Gilbert as the youngest of the tarts contributes her shrill giggle and high sharp staccato chatter to a symphony played in a minor key. She is the most effective of the three girls, who, as is often the case in Mr. O'Neill's plays, lack reality. *The Iceman Cometh*, in fact, has many of Mr. O'Neill's old faults as well as his distinguished virtues—it shows his complete lack of humor, his sententiousness and sentimentality—but it is immensely rich and rewarding to the playgoer and serves the welcome purpose of stirring argument and contention in the theatre, as Mr. O'Neill has done all his life. It is good to know he has not lost his cunning and that we are to have other plays from him this year and next to remind us that the theatre is not all dumb show and noise.

Mary McCarthy

A MOON FOR THE MISBEGOTTEN

In the mid-Nineteen Forties this latest play of Eugene O'Neill's was tried out on the road by the Theatre Guild but never brought to New York. "Casting difficulties" were spoken of, which is generally a theatrical euphemism for loss of interest in a property. Yet the play, as it appears in book form, seems very much like the New England farm plays of the O'Neill apogee, and in particular like *Desire Under the Elms*, which was revived last winter in New York. The spectacle of a mature play by a renowned dramatist vainly haunting the managers' offices while revivals of his early successes close and open has a certain sardonic pathos, a note of Enoch Arden.

A Moon for the Misbegotten is *Desire Under the Elms* grown old and hoarse and randy. There is the familiar puritan triad of greed, land, and sexual repression. There are a demonic old man, a stony unrewarding farm, a vital Demeter of a woman. The finale is lit by an apocalyptic dawn, and the whole play is reddened by whisky, like a bloodshot eye. There is an opening which is really a prologue, with the cunning son (two in *Desire Under the Elms*) deserting the farm with a sum of money stolen from the miser father. This opening imparts to both plays a curious, desolate aspect, as if normal self-interest, in the person of the departing sons, had stealthily forsaken the vicinity; those who are left are survivors in a waste.

A Moon for the Misbegotten, however, is not laid in the period-past of the gold rush but in the golden bootleg Twenties, on a Connecticut tenant farm, an old box of a house raised up on blocks

---

From Sights and Spectacles *by Mary McCarthy, copyright 1946, 1956 by Mary McCarthy. Used by permission of the publishers, Farrar, Straus and Cudahy, Inc. and Lawrence Pollinger Limited. Published in London by William Heinemann, Ltd. Originally in* The New York Times Book Review, *August 31, 1952.*

of timber. The characters are not New Englanders of the original stock but Irish supplanters. The heroine is a gigantic young woman, one hundred and eighty pounds broad and tall, who carries a club to defend herself; as the daughter of a bootlegger and shifty, shiftless farmer, she is known throughout the neighborhood for her herculean sexual prowess. A sort of Olympian knockdown comedy is enacted between the trickster father and the virago daughter, but this comedy is at bottom sad, for the daughter is in actuality a virgin with a strong maternal heart and the father a grimy cupid with benevolent matrimonial plans for her.

These plans center on a middle-aged alcoholic of educated pretensions, the son of a well-known Thespian who owned farm property. Here the theme of puritanism suddenly appears, like an elemental blight. Behind the pagan façade of Irish boasting, drinking, and ribaldry is revealed a wheyey sentimentality and retching hatred of sex. With the nuptial couch all readied in the tar-papered leanto, James Tyrone, Jr., man of the world and Broadway rakehell, makes his true confession: he is a man who, like Stephen Dedalus, has wronged his dying mother, and wronged her again, a thousand times over, when escorting her body home on the train, he entertained a prostitute in his drawing-room while Mama was in the baggage car ahead. In his moment of opportunity, he sobs himself chastely to sleep, a guilt-sickened altar-boy.

This moment, in which the bootlegger's daughter discovers that this middle-aged man is really "dead," emotionally speaking—an exhausted mummified child—is a moment of considerable poignancy. The defeat of all human plans and contrivances is suddenly shaped in the picture of the titaness sitting staring at a stage moon with a shriveled male infant drunkenly asleep at her side. The image of the survivors takes on a certain grotesque epic form; the woman, stage center, like a gentle beached whale, appears for an instant as the last survivor of the world.

What disturbs one here, however, as in so many of O'Neill's plays, is the question of how far the author himself is a victim of the same sentimentality and self-pity that is exhibited clinically in the characters; how far, specifically, O'Neill himself is taken in by the "tragic" figure of James Tyrone, Jr., who is merely a pitiable wreck. My impression is that O'Neill himself does not know, that he puts the character forward like a question, which he hopes may be answered favorably. The crudity of the technique makes it hard to descry intention. Nevertheless, despite this, despite the tone of barbershop harmony that enters into all O'Neill's work, this play exacts homage for its mythic powers, for the element of transcendence jutting up in it like a great wooden Trojan horse.

Brooks Atkinson

THE ICEMAN COMETH

Since José Quintero's productions at Circle in the Square are always admirable, no one should be surprised by his latest achievement.

But it is impossible not to be excited by his production of Eugene O'Neill's *The Iceman Cometh*, which opened in Mr. Quintero's theatre yesterday. It is a major production of a major theatre work. Taking a long script with a massive theme, Mr. Quintero has succeeded in bringing every part of it alive in the theatre. Although he tells the story simply and spontaneously, he leaves no doubt about the value he places on O'Neill's place in the literature of the stage. Mr. Quintero seems to take him on the level of Ibsen, Strindberg, Gorky, and other modern masters of tragic writing.

If *The Iceman Cometh* seems to belong in Mr. Quintero's theatre, there is a good reason. For Circle in the Square was a night-club originally, and all four of the acts of the O'Neill drama are set in a saloon. The audience has the sensation of participating. The rows of seats are only an extension of David Hayes' setting of the battered, blowzy waterfront saloon and flophouse that is under the fabulous proprietorship of Harry Hope. A few tables and chairs, a squalid bar, a flimsy door leading into the street, a handful of fly-blown chandeliers and a few ranks of benches for the audience —they are all part of the same setting and closely related on that account.

In the circumstances, it is difficult to be objective about this melancholy, sardonic drama that pulls the rug out from under the whole structure of life. It seems, not like something written, but like something that is happening. Although it is terrible in its comment on the need for illusions to maintain an interest in life, it is

---

From The New York Times, *May 9, 1956. Used by permission of* The New York Times.

also comic. Some of the dialogue is pretty funny. On the surface, all the characters are comic, since they live in a world of befuddled fantasy and talk big to compensate for the puniness of their spirits.

But beneath them there is nothing more substantial than a void of blackness. These are creatures that once were men—very pungent and picturesque creatures, too, for O'Neill was a good deal of a romantic. But the tone of *The Iceman Cometh* is devastatingly tragic. Life is bearable, it seems to say, only when men contrive not to look at the truth.

The performance lasts four and three-quarter hours. For *The Iceman Cometh* is one of the O'Neill marathon dramas. No doubt it could be cut and compressed without destroying anything essential. But as a creative work by a powerful writer, it is entitled to its excesses, which, in fact, may account for the monumental feeling of doom that it pulls down over the heads of the audience.

The performance is a vital one. Mr. Quintero is a versatile conductor who knows how to vary his attack with changes in volume and rhythm; he knows how to orchestrate a performance. In one important respect, this performance surpasses the original of ten years ago. Jason Robards, Jr. plays Hickey, the catalyst in the narrative, like an evangelist. His unction, condescension and piety introduce an element of moral affectation that clarifies the perspective of the drama as a whole. His heartiness, his aura of good fellowship give the character of Hickey a feeling of evil mischief it did not have before.

Although the narrative is sprawling, the acting is vibrant in every part. Conrad Bain's fanatical philosopher who sees all sides of all questions and is therefore a futile human being is especially well acted. But it would be difficult to pick and choose among the others. Farrell Pelly's crusty but soft-hearted boss of the saloon; Addison Powell's bitterly-humorous relic of culture; William Edmonson's highly emotional Negro; Richard Bowler's cashiered British Army officer; Phil Pheffer's circus con-man; Peter Falk's cocky bar-keep; Paul Andor's left-wing intellectual; James Greene's degraded war correspondent; the tarts played by Dolly Jonah, Patricia Brooks and Gloria Scott Backé—are excellent character portraits.

In both the writing and the acting, *The Iceman Cometh* is a mighty theatre work. O'Neill is a giant, and Mr. Quintero is a remarkably gifted artist.

Harold Clurman

LONG DAY'S JOURNEY INTO NIGHT

Eugene O'Neill wrote this play in 1940. Since it is a painfully autobiographical work, he did not wish to have it published or performed until twenty-five years after his death. His wife, Carlotta Monterey O'Neill, to whom the play is touchingly dedicated, has consented to have it published here and performed in Sweden three years after his death. I believe she was right. Who knows what such a play—or any play—will mean twenty-five years after an author's death? At the present moment, the play is a precious gift to us—regardless of its ultimate value.

I say this, though on a first reading I cannot determine what I actually think of it as a work of art or simply as a play. I am moved and fascinated by it in a personal way. The fact that the Swedes were held by it and did not complain of its four and one-half hours of playing length indicates something about its theatrical viability. It is indisputable that O'Neill's plays are nearly always more impressive on the stage than on the printed page. I should very much like to see this play done on or off Broadway. If such a play is "impractical" for our theatre, so much the worse for our theatre. The play is the testament of the most serious playwright our country has produced.

To say this is not to set oneself down as an unqualified O'Neill admirer. O'Neill was a faulty craftsman; he was not a sound thinker. Though he probably read more extensively and profoundly than most of our playwrights, O'Neill could not by any "universal" standard be considered a cultivated man. His view of life is circumscribed, he is often raw, naive, sentimental and pessimistic in a somewhat adolcscent manner.

From Lies Like Truth *© Harold Clurman 1958. Used with permission of The Macmillan Company. Originally in* The Nation, *March 3, 1956.*

Yet to dwell on these shortcomings as if they negate the value of the man to our stage and to our culture is to confess one's own inadequate and bloodless response to the world we live in. For in a time and place where life is experienced either as a series of mechanistic jerks or sipped in polite doses of borrowed sophistication (when it is not dully recorded in a sort of statistical spiritual bookkeeping) O'Neill not only lived intensely but attempted with perilous honesty to contemplate, absorb and digest the meaning of his life and ours. He possessed an uncompromising devotion to the task he set himself: to present and interpret in stage terms what he had lived through and thought about—a devotion unique in our theatre.

What do we discover in *Long Day's Journey Into Night?* Not only the specific sources of O'Neill's suffering: the father, whom he hated and loved, an old-time star actor with the yearning of an artist and the confusion of an ignorant boy ruined by the stage and by the general environment of the gas-light era; the mother, an innocent woman, isolated and bereft of everything but conventional "protection" and finally resorting to the solace of drugs; an older brother whose only rebellion is in blasphemy and alcohol; O'Neill himself, a hypersensitive tubercular boy in quest of a God whose Word builds no true house and achieves no tangible body in the brick desert of the New York to which his father came from the famines of Ireland.

We find O'Neill trying to probe the meaning of all this, making an almost violent effort not only to understand but to forgive—to free himself from resentment, to fight the fate which, as in the Greek plays, seems to burden him unmercifully because of the antecedent crimes of his family heritage.

The family's Catholicism is not so much a faith as a guilt. Because he feels guilt, O'Neill shifts between a self-pity which he despises and a burning blame which he keeps trying in this play (and his whole work) to fight off. The accusation of his own guilt and obsessive desire to purge himself of it through blame nags at him: hence the repetitiousness of phrases and scenes; it is a planned repetitiousness, often wearisome to the reader (or the spectator) but organic to the author.

From this sense of guilt—all his characters suffer it in one form or another—and a corresponding sense that the guilt feeling is in itself a sin or at least a fatal blemish comes a constant alternation of mood. Every character speaks in two voices, two moods—one of rage, the other of apology. This produces a kind of moral schizophrenia which in some of O'Neill's other plays has necessitated an interior monologue and a speech for social use (*Strange Interlude*) or as in *The Great God Brown* and *Days Without End*, two sets of masks. In this everlasting duality with its equal pressures in several directions lies the brooding power, the emotional grip of O'Neill's work.

There are unforgettable speeches, and scenes in this play. One of them is the father's confession of how he was destroyed by the success of a romantic melodrama which he felt constrained to play almost throughout his career because it guaranteed him thirty to forty thousand a year. (The triumph and doom of James O'Neill's life was the endless run all over the country of *The Count of Monte Cristo.*) This is deeply perceptive as well as moving, because it not only touches off the usual case of the artist damaged by commerce, but because O'Neill shows how his immigrant father's fear of poverty led to a concern about money ("stinginess" his family called it) for which his sons hated him and which led to many disasters ostensibly remote from their point of origin. This is a dominant American (O'Neill) theme which finds many symbolic variant expressions in the plays: *Desire Under the Elms*, *The Great God Brown*, *Marco Millions*.

The father's confession leads to the boy's (the author's) own confession of what his youthful escapades at sea have meant to him: it is a dream of beatitude, a seeking for God and wholeness—as direct, unabashed and truly soulful as any ever to be written by an American dramatist. To which his father replies "Yes, there's the *makings* of a poet in you all right" and O'Neill answers "The *makings* of a poet . . . I couldn't touch what I tried to tell you just now. I just stammered. That's the best I'll ever do. . . . Well, it will be faithful realism at least."

O'Neill's work is more than realism. And if it is stammering —it is still the most eloquent and significant stammer of the American theatre. We have not yet developed a cultivated speech that is either superior to it or as good.

Henry Hewes

LONG DAY'S JOURNEY INTO NIGHT

Most people live in several planes of existence. There is the plane of impulse, in which we respond spontaneously and without reflection. There is the plane of society, in which we treat with, impress, and/or deceive other people. There is the plane of compromise, in which we tolerate the undesirable rather than risk a correction. There is the plane of contemplation, in which we search hopefully for the truth of what we are. And there is the plane of escape and dreams.

In *Long Day's Journey Into Night* the late Eugene O'Neill has shown himself, his elder brother, his father, and his mother as they slip back and forth from one plane to another in a grim dance of life. He doesn't sentimentalize. He doesn't moralize. He blames no outside agency for the family's collective failure. As he has his mother explain it in the play, "None of us can help the things life has done to us. They're done before you realize it, and once they're done they make you do other things until at last everything comes between you and what you'd like to be, and you've lost your true self forever."

Thus, *Long Day's Journey Into Night* is not so much a "play" as a continuously absorbing exegesis of Mary Tyrone's line, "The past is the present, isn't it? It's the future, too. We all try to lie out of that but life won't let us." O'Neill steers as far from conscious plots and phony resolutions as he can. In their place he offers character development. Each of the quartet advances from morning's surface jocularity into evening's soul-shaking revelations of self-truth. Each tries to blame others for his or her failures. Mary Tyrone takes to narcotics with excuses of her son's health, her husband's unwillingness to spend money on a good doctor in-

---

From The Saturday Review, *November 24, 1956. Reprinted by permission of the editors.*

stead of the quack who first gave her morphine after a difficult childbirth, and his failure to supply his family a decent home life. But by the time she's finished we realize that this simple convent-bred child was never equipped to face the terrors of life outside. Likewise, James Tyrone justifies his penury as wise and considerate, and then harks back to a poverty-stricken childhood. But though it is never quite stated we finally come to suspect that an incurable self-centeredness is the heart of this famous actor's trouble. As for the two sons, Edmund (pseudonym for the author) confesses that only on certain occasions at sea did he ever feel "the joy of belonging to a fulfillment beyond men's lousy, pitiful, greedy fears and hopes and dreams." He will always be "a stranger who never feels at home, who does not really want and is not really wanted, who can never belong, who must always be a little in love with death!" The other, Jamie, at the height of drunkenness reveals that while he loves his brother he also has the subconscious wish to destroy him.

For those who are familiar with some of the details of O'Neill's tragic life and with the twenty-five full-length plays that gained him his reputation as America's greatest playwright, this merciless autobiography is enormously interesting. But even for those who are not, there is a breadth to *Long Day's Journey Into Night* that may make it the most universal piece of stage realism ever turned out by an American playwright. For doesn't it expose the forces that work both to unite and to tear asunder all human groups? What family does not have its private disgraces, its nasty recriminations, its unforgotten grievances? What family is not obliged to put up with some sort of unreasonable behavior from its breadwinner, some self-centeredness from its dominant figure? What brothers or sisters do not possess a pinch of jealousy that pollutes their love of each other? What wife is not doomed to spend much time in the company of hired help or neighbors or associates that bore her? What family is not faced with some compulsive behavior which it must ignore, coddle, or excuse in order to avoid rupture? All these things O'Neill has put into this play, baldly and directly. The terror it inspires comes not from the day's events, but from the gradual intensification of its torment and violence as night moves in.

The greatness of the work is apparent when one compares it to other American plays that deal with the destruction of the conventional family. Written in 1940 it preceded Arthur Miller's *Death of a Salesman*, which implied that society and economics were crushing the modern family under indignity. Tennessee Williams' *Cat on a Hot Tin Roof* showed mendacity as the foul glue that keeps a family stuck together. Last season's *A Hatful of Rain*, by Mike Gazzo, resolved the problem by suggesting that a tough-minded decision is preferable to preserving an illusionary family relationship. *Long Day's Journey Into Night* takes all the arguments of these plays into account, but finds a greater realism by refusing to hang them on a suspenseful plot, and by showing up, as did O'Casey in *Juno and the Paycock*, the hopeless feeding of life on old arguments and old defenses. It also seems a larger-sized piece of work because of its constant recognition of man's quest for religious ecstasy.

Director José Quintero and a dedicated cast have done a remarkable job in performing the four-hour play with such inner concentration that we are seldom conscious of the time. Fredric March's James Tyrone is a miraculously sustained portrayal. He starts off as a man more-or-less resigned to the waywardness of his sons, but with cheerfulness maintained by the hope that his wife will not resume her narcotics habit; his narrow view of religion equates God and hope. Once she does resume Mr. March visibly resigns himself to going the rest of the way without faith, and the ashen way he walks offstage at the end of the second scene is great acting. Then, as he proceeds to anesthetize himself with whiskey, Mr. March avoids the flamboyance that has marked the drunk scenes we remember from former performances. Instead, he captures a true alcoholic saturation that he holds onto with complete discipline. Even in the wild and ridiculous moment when he jumps on top of the table to screw in three light bulbs, melodramatically shouting, "We'll turn them all on . . . The poorhouse is the end of the road, and it might as well be sooner as later," Mr. March does not abandon the characterization to indulge himself in a virtuoso stunt. Because his performance is relatively subdued, it becomes possible for Jason Robards, Jr. to explode and steal the show. Mr. Robards' drunken Jamie is loud and free-swinging; he not only expresses but demonstrates his ambivalent feelings for his younger brother Edmund.

Edmund is played sensitively by Bradford Dillman, who makes the poetic passages effective. Yet Mr. Dillman seems more a young Keats than a young O'Neill. As Mary Tyrone, Florence Eldridge is at her best when she nervously goes on the defensive about her addiction or when she gets a mad look in her eye as she describes her wedding gown. There are times, however, when we would like to see more feeling towards her sons, and other times when we are not as aware as we should be that she is under the influence of drugs.

Mr. Quintero has directed the play with great fidelity, resisting the getting of a dramatic impact at the expense of the production's total truthfulness. He begins the long day with the family normal and jovial. Indeed, one might assume that this was going to be a comedy about two "regular fellers" and their happily-married mom and dad. Mr. Quintero makes no attempt to rush a grim tone into the proceedings. He allows the mutual recriminations to develop slowly and naturally. Thus, everything that ensues seems a part of life in the Tyrone summer-house rather than scenes from a play. David Hayes' set is a beauty, changing character from day to night. And Tharon Musser's lighting is superb as it strengthens each important moment.

The thirty-two-year-old Mr. Quintero and his production associates can certainly be said to have lived up to the trust Mrs. O'Neill put in them when she accorded them the honor of giving *Long Day's Journey Into Night* its American première. If anything, they have perhaps felt too slavishly responsible to the stage directions of the late playwright. A production with more directorial invention and conscious "performing," like the one in Stockholm, is in some ways more memorable. But when one recalls that O'Neill used to say, "Actors generally get between me and the performance. I catch myself recognizing the technique all the time and what they are doing when they put over a point," one suspects that he would have been astounded and gratified to find that the young director had put almost nothing between the theatregoer and this great theatre work.

Henry Hewes

A TOUCH OF THE POET

Eugene O'Neill's *A Touch of the Poet*, now in its world première at Stockholm's Royal Dramatic Theatre, is a distinguished and vital example of demon-driven dramaturgy. While the four-hour work, written *circa* 1939, follows a conventional play form, its nature can only be described as a human comedy hovering dangerously near the fires of tragedy. Self-delusion obsesses the play's central figure, retired Major Cornelius ("Con") Melody. Con, though he is the son of an Irish innkeeper, fancies himself as a Byron standing in the crowd but not of it. Feeding this aristocratic illusion are the facts that he did fight bravely under Wellington at the Battle of Talavera and that he keeps a thoroughbred mare.

Con's pretensions to refinement cost his family dearly and make him a lonely man in the Massachusetts of 1828, where he operates a wayside inn. He won't mix with the "Irish scum" around Boston and he is not accepted by the Yankee aristocrats. While his wife and daughter secretly enjoy his pretensions, to some extent, they at the same time spoil them for him: his wife, Nora, because she has so worn herself out with menial work to support his fancy ways that her appearance constantly reminds him of his unaristocratic marriage; his daughter, Sara, because she wants to rise in the world and attacks Con for a self-indulgence that stands in her way.

The situation comes to a head when Sara sets her cap for the young Yankee aristocrat Simon Harford. Simon's father insults Con by trying to buy him off and Con furiously sets out to avenge his honor. Unfortunately, the days in which such affairs were settled by duels had just passed and Con finds his expedition of revenge degenerating into a Donnybrook. This so disillusions him that he shoots the symbol of his predilection for aristocracy, his

From the Saturday Review, *April 13, 1957. Reprinted by permission of the editors.*

thoroughbred mare. Then, much chastened, he joins his class and discards his extravagances while Sara becomes engaged to young Simon.

This plot, which recalls Ibsen's *The Wild Duck*, is only the bare bones of the play. O'Neill, who planned *A Touch of the Poet* as a part of an eleven-play cycle tracing the conflict between soul and matter through 150 years of American history, is concerned with the large questions of how European romance mixes with American materialism and of the impact of earthy immigrants on cold-blooded Yankees. As Nora points out, "When Con came here the chance was before him to make himself all his lies pretended to be. He had education above most Yanks and he had money enough to start him and this is a country where you can rise as high as you like and no one but the fools who envy you care what you rose from once you've the money and power that goes with it." O'Neill never shows much of the Yankee side of the picture.

Beyond a concern with social history O'Neill explores the relationship between pride and love; this is what moves contemporary audiences most. At the beginning of the play we learn that Con married Nora because he'd fallen in love with her, but was ashamed of her because her folks were only ignorant peasants. Later Nora tells Sara, "It's little you know of love and you nivir will for there's the same divil of pride in you that's in him and it'll kape you from ivir givin all of yourself and that's what love is." Sara argues, "I'll love—but I'll love when it'll gain me freedom and not put me in slavery for life." Nora replies, "There's no slavery in it when you love." This simple wisdom is proved in the fourth act when, after making love to Simon, Sara discovers, "I knew nothing of love or the pride a woman can take in giving everything—a woman can forgive whatever the man she loves could do and still love him, because it was through him she found the love in herself: in one way he doesn't count at all, because it's your own love you love in him and to keep that your pride will do anything." O'Neill finally celebrates the victory of love over false pride when, at the end of the play, Nora turns to Sara and says, "Shame on you to cry when you have love. What would the young man think of you?"

In the role of Con Melody, Lars Hansson rises to one of the great virtuoso performances of our day, alternating a deep romantic charm and maddened rage. He hypnotizes us with a masterful variety of actions. Who will forget the dashing way he takes his stance before the full-length mirror, flicks a speck of lint from his sleeve, slings with calculated casualness his imaginary cape over his shoulder, and proceeds to recite Byron? When stung by Sara's rebukes, what sadistic relish burns in his eyes as he cruelly reminds her that she has the coarse body of a peasant. When he argues with his daughter he does it with the punctuated intensity of a Spanish dancer. He does not speak lines, he generates sound. His hysterical laughter fills the theatre, and his agonized squeak of ego-exorcism sears the entire audience. He can be gloriously exultant too, as he speaks of the freedom he feels when riding his horse. While some of his acting is artificial, he never loses his potential to terrify us at will.

Though played in contrasting quietness, Sif Ruud's Nora is just as memorable. As a dumpy woman prematurely aged by overwork, worry, and maltreatment, Miss Ruud manifests an uncomplicated overflow of indestructible love that immunizes her to our pity. The role of Sara is a difficult one. She must be both coarse and beautiful, both sharing her father's pretensions and railing against them. If Eva Dahlbeck doesn't quite accomplish all this she does manage to glow marvelously in the scene after she has given herself to her love.

If *A Touch of the Poet* suffers somewhat from overexposition, too many vital scenes occurring offstage, and a plethora of old-fashioned melodramatic plot details, it at the same time foreshadows O'Neill's growth into his final great period. He bluntly refuses to bribe the audience with smooth and facile writing. He seems to be saying, "Here's your damned exposition and climaxes. They are arbitrary and unreal. The true drama lies in the moments of anguish and love. Someday I shall dare to write *Long Day's Journey Into Night*, which is pure anguish and love."

Henry Hewes

"HUGHIE"

Flying north from Paris on a serene Air France Viscount, I had some less than serene thoughts about "Hughie," the new Eugene O'Neill play being given its world première by Stockholm's Royal Dramatic Theatre. From the little I had heard about this short work, I had the impression that it was a leftover, an oddment that was now being presented only because it and *More Stately Mansions* (which may be destroyed) were all that was left of the great playwright's unproduced writing.

But the curtain was scarcely up when I realized that "Hughie" is top-drawer O'Neill. The play takes place in a shabby Times Square hotel at that hour of night when city life is at lowest ebb. A drab night clerk, who because he has never dared to do anything more ambitious, is serving his time behind the desk. To him the night—and life—are shortened by such idle games as doodling or watching the garbage men pick up cans. He daydreams about his suppressed hostility against a world he never made, and his vicarious desire to join, without risk, the more reckless doers of deeds.

Into the lobby stumbles Erie Smith, a small fry gambler and horse player, who lives in the hotel. He has been off on a drunk, mourning Hughie, the previous night clerk. Hughie is dead, but O'Neill allows Erie to bring him to life for us as he mumbles about their past relationship. Erie says: "Hughie was a sucker—the kind of sap you'd take to the cleaners a million times and he'd never wise up he was took." But gradually as Erie talks on about his affection for the little guy, we begin to see that Erie needed Hughie's admiration as much as Hughie needed the rub-off of phoney glamor Erie provided.

From the Saturday Review, *October 4, 1958. Reprinted by permission of the* Saturday Review.

Says Erie:

"We'd play with real jack, just to make it look real, but it was all my jack. He never had no jack. His wife dealt him four bits a day for spending money. So I'd stake him at the start to half of what I got—in chicken feed I mean. We'd pretend a cent was a buck, and a nickel was a finn and so on. Some big game! He got a big kick out of it. He'd get all het up. It gave me a kick, too—especially when he'd say, 'Gosh, Erie, I don't wonder you never worry about money, with your luck!'"

But the new night clerk isn't listening. He is preoccupied with all the things that reveal the smallness of his existence. Erie drones on revealing his own insecurity. He has lost his luck and his confidence without Hughie there to bolster them. And unconsciously he blurts out what he would never openly admit, "But Hughie's better off, at that, being dead. He's got all the luck. He needn't do no worryin' now. He's out of the racket. I mean the whole goddamned racket. I mean life."

Because this statement gives the clerk an opening to express his own ordinarily repressed opinion the two men make real contact for the first time. And this contact leads both of them back from despair to a live relationship which is similar to the one Erie enjoyed with Hughie. At the end of the play Erie is rolling dice with the clerk. His confidence has returned, and the racket of life is on again.

O'Neill in "Hughie" has written the whole cycle of life into a forty-minute piece. The wise guy and the sucker stand for all forms of human interdependence. The swing from naked truth to illusion, from isolation to communication, from bitterness to love are all basic to living. We alternate from one to the other, and this cyclic motion rather than the achievement of a goal is the stuff and richness of life.

His technique is somewhat Chekhovian, and he keeps the play happily free of any important plot. Furthermore, though there is the occasional overstatement that is characteristic of O'Neill there is more poetry than usual in the lines.

Unfortunately, some of the best things in the play have been written in the stage directions, where he has given the hotel clerk a plan of things to think about silently while Erie is talking. For example:

> The clerk's mind remains in the street to greet the noise of a far off El train. Its approach is pleasantly like the memory of hope; then it roars and rocks and rattles past the nearby corner, and the noise pleasantly deafens memory; then it recedes and dies, and there is something melancholy about that. But there *is* hope. Only so many El trains pass in one night, and each one passing leaves one less to pass, so the night recedes, too, until at last it must die and join all the other long nights in Nirvana, the big Night of Nights. And that's life.

It is not really possible for the actor to get all this across without speaking. However, director Bengt Ekerot has had the clerk count silently on his fingers as the El train passes—the action most essential to the drama. The role of Erie Smith presents a great challenge to the actor, but Bengt Eklund who plays it has truly begun to penetrate its potentialities. Departing from O'Neill's stage directions, Mr. Eklund plays Erie less as a cheap Broadway sharpie than as a crumpled victim of life's racket. It is an understated performance which sacrifices something in explosiveness and fire to bring credibility to a play whose dénouement might otherwise seem too mechanical. And its finest moments come between lines when Erie and the night clerk suddenly realize their isolation from each other.

For O'Neill, who wrote this perfectly-constructed work at about the same time as *A Moon for the Misbegotten*, as the first in a never-completed series of short plays to be entitled *By Way of Obit*, had come to believe that the interdependence of human beings, even when it is selfishly motivated, contains a divine element of love.

4

THE PLAYWRIGHT

AN INTERNATIONAL SYMPOSIUM

Early Recognition

AMERICAN

Clayton Hamilton

O'NEILL'S FIRST BOOK

A Review of THIRST, AND OTHER ONE-ACT PLAYS. 1915

Another playwright of promise is Mr. Eugene G. O'Neill —a son of the noted actor, Mr. James O'Neill—who has recently published five one-act plays under the title of *Thirst*. This writer's favorite mood is that of horror. He deals with grim and ghastly situations that would become intolerable if they were protracted beyond the limits of a single sudden act. He seems to be familiar with the sea; for three of these five plays deal with terrors that attend the tragedy of ship-wreck. He shows a keen sense of the reactions of character under stress of violent emotion; and his dialogue is almost brutal in its power. More than one of these plays should be available for such an institution as the Princess Theatre in New York.

From The Bookman, *April 1915. Used by permission of Gladys Hamilton.*

Barrett H. Clark

THE PLAYS OF EUGENE G. O'NEILL

A Review of THE MOON OF THE CARIBBEES, AND OTHER ONE-ACT PLAYS. 1919

When a few weeks ago, John Galsworthy asked me to name our most promising native dramatist I was at first unable to do so. I tried to think of some new star on the theatrical horizon and mentioned the names of two or three playwrights whose work seemed to me above the average.

It was not, however, until after I had exhausted the Broadway group that I thought of the one logical man. The name of Eugene G. O'Neill had not occurred to me at once in connection with Broadway, where Mr. O'Neill is practically unknown. My mind wandered to the Comedy Theatre and the Greenwich Village Theatre, where I had seen three plays that stood out above all other American plays that have come to my notice in recent years: "In the Zone," "Ile" and "The Rope."

I told Mr. Galsworthy that in Eugene G. O'Neill I felt there was something genuinely American, that he was not only "promising"—Heaven knows, Broadway is full of the "promising youngsters" of yesteryear—but that his actual achievement was considerable.

I have just sent Galsworthy *The Moon of the Caribbees, and Six Other Plays of the Sea*, and I am sure he will realize, as I do, that O'Neill's volume is a significant collection of one-act plays, the most significant that has been published in this country. . . .

Wherein are Mr. O'Neill's fifteen-odd plays different from the average native product? Why is Mr. O'Neill, if not our most versatile and "finished," so indisputably our most powerfully sincere dramatist?

The first reason, I believe, is that he is intent before all else upon depicting that segment of life which he knows and with

From the New York Sun, *May 18, 1919. Used with permission.*

which he sympathizes. He never seeks to construct an effective vehicle for a star; he never wastes a moment's time in effect for effect's sake. He makes you feel, even in his feeblest work, that he understands the secret springs in the men and women he sets before you: his simple sailors and farmers are thrillingly alive; his is the power to convince you at once of the authenticity of a situation primarily through the vitality of the characters involved.

The atmosphere with which his best plays are saturated is not factitious; it is not the result of a heaping up of the actual; he resorts to no Belasco tricks to beguile you into believing you are in the presence of life because a well copied suit of clothes or a stage full of "real" bric-a-brac is foisted upon you. A cheap set such as was used in his play "Ile" at the Greenwich Village Theatre was all that was necessary in the way of material equipment. To this day I feel the presence of mountains of ice outside that forecastle. O'Neill used his imagination where Belasco would have collaborated with the ice company.

Or take "In the Zone," which was produced by the Washington Square Players. A group of sailors in a forecastle, the tragedy of a man's life revealed to them, a touch of pity on the part of a few rough men for a fellow being. And for background the fateful sea of the submarine zone. Atmosphere? All one could ask for, but not one atom of it dragged in for effect. The situation demanded the atmosphere.

"Ile" I have already referred to. It is a stark picture of human misery at the mercy of human obstinacy. Here again is atmosphere —with a haunting sense of impending doom—but as always an integral part of the drama of humanity.

"The Moon of the Caribbees" is rather less a play of character than the others. At first sight the atmosphere seems to exist for its own sake, but on rereading it I am struck by the extraordinary artistry of the canvas, *as a background*. Here, amid the heat of the tropics, on shipboard in the harbor, is a scene of mad revelry; figures of men and women flit back and forth. Dim and insignificant at first, they gradually emerge just in time to play their petty parts and disappear.

This play does not grip one in quite the same way as does "In the Zone"; it is a broader canvas, in which the purely dramatic element does not predominate.

"The Long Voyage Home" is a heartbreaking little play; a Swedish sailor has hoarded his savings for years with the intention of returning to his aged mother, buying a farm and leaving the sea. Each time during the past that he has tried to carry out his determination he has taken too much drink and been robbed. In this play we see him ashore refusing whiskey but accepting a harmless "belly wash"—which is drugged. He is robbed and carried aboard an outward bound ship. An incident, scarcely more; but I can count on the fingers of one hand the full length plays I have seen during the past two seasons that are as truly dramatic.

"Where the Cross Is Made" is somewhat different from the plays I have just mentioned. Mr. O'Neill has seen fit to introduce a touch of the supernatural, and while he has succeeded in creating the desired effect I cannot help feeling that this play lacks the freshness of the others. It has not the direct power of "In the Zone" and "Bound East for Cardiff"—another stark specimen of the forecastle play.

The last play is "The Rope," a painful and bitter drama, the scene of which is the barn of a New England farm on the sea coast. It is a tragedy of greed, hatred and madness. Money lies at the bottom of it all. The touch at the end of the play is one Balzac would have appreciated. The little maid Mary climbs up on a chair to swing from the rope hanging from the loft; it comes loose and she pulls down a bag full of gold pieces. Spreading the coins on the floor, "she picks up four or five of them and runs out to the edge of the cliff. She throws them one after another into the ocean as fast as she can and bends over to see them hit the water."

These plays are the expression of a man of powerful imagination. They are written because of the "urge" of which Mr. O'Neill has spoken. Sincerity itself is nothing in art, of course; yet without it there is no art. But Mr. O'Neill has by the very force of his sincerity been able to mold the one-act play form to the requirements of his temperament. His technique—which is only another way of saying the medium of his expression—is exactly suited to what he had to say, and what more can we ask of any artist?

I have been privileged to see the MS of *Beyond the Horizon*, Mr. O'Neill's new three-act play, the production of which is announced for the fall. While I am not at liberty to describe it, I may say that the author of "In the Zone" is well able to handle a striking theme and living characters in a long play.

Having demonstrated his skill in the one-act form and, to me and his manager at least, in the three-act, I see no reason why O'Neill should fail to be recognized as our leading dramatist. O'Neill is not perfect, he is not free from defects of characterization and style, but he is better equipped than any other young American. He *promised* five years ago, with his *Thirst* and other plays; since then he has fulfilled his promise; he has now only to develop, to widen his vision of men and women and do his best, unhampered by the material success that is sure to come to him.

Isaac Goldberg

AT THE BEGINNING OF A CAREER

Properly to appreciate the promise and the performance of Eugene O'Neill as one of the youthful experimenters in the theatre, one has but to have gone through the thousands of pages that his contemporaries have written at home and abroad—the monodramatic extravagances of Evreinov, the lucubrations of the Italian "grotesquers," the mad confusion of half of the German Expressionists. To talk of "placing" O'Neill at this early date would be the worst of academic fatuousness; his work is plentiful, widely varying in quality, and his attitude, perhaps, as his production, is, of choice, experimental rather than settled. Seemingly he marks a new era in the drama of the United States; what one may do now is to examine, at the beginning of that career, the qualities and the works of which it is compounded, following it from the worst of melodrama to the best of realism, and thence to a freedom of structure that approaches Expressionism only in its disruption of conventional form. For, thus far at least, O'Neill has yielded to neither the formlessness nor the incoherence of the more extreme Expressionists; even when his contact with external reality seems least firm, he yet maintains his grip upon the roots of things. There are, in *The Emperor Jones*, for instance, elements of the monodrama, yet O'Neill never becomes metaphysically abstruse as Evreinov; his *The Hairy Ape* may suggest the later Kaiser and the youthful Hasenclever, but it is not of the self-willed, esoteric brood that is signalized by the misty productions of Oskar Kokoschka and his fellow-Germans. In this, the foreign critic, who has his labels as have our own, may be inclined to find a Yankee tendency to stick to facts and not fly too easily off on the wings of fancy or the back of a Pegasus who has broken the reins of the imagination and ranges wildly through stellar space. I rather find it in the man's own personality, in an elemental vigor that sees even phantoms clearly. For it is one of O'Neill's distinguishing traits that he lends a peculiar vitality even to his worst scenes—and there are bad ones even in his later productions.[1]

In his very first published work appear, in the rough, both the good qualities and the bad that are to haunt his later plays. For the light they throw upon the maturer artist, they repay something more than cursory examination. *Thirst, and Other One-Act Plays* comprises "Thirst," "The Web," "Warnings," "Fog," and "Recklessness."

"The Web" is melodrama at its worst, with all the outworn technique connoted by the name, but already there appears, in the sound of Rose's coughing as she is led away by the officers, O'Neill's predilection for the potency of pure sound upon the stage. Time and again this fondness for aural effects is evident; in the remaining plays of the volume, for example, there is the whining of the wireless in "Warnings," the steamer whistles and the dripping water of the icebergs in "Fog"; there are, in "The Web" itself, the falling raindrops. So in the later "Bound East for Cardiff," there is the whistle blowing through the fog at intervals of a minute and, in *The Emperor Jones*, the haunting crescendo of the tom-tom, beating faster and faster with the wild palpitation of terror.

"Recklessness," like "The Web," has all the earmarks of melodrama: the spying maid, the lying mistress, the treacherous chauffeur, the purloined letter proving the wife's guilt, the husband's cruel and sardonic revenge. "Warnings," the tale of a deaf wireless operator who fails to receive the message warning of a derelict, and who commits suicide on learning that the fault is his, requires two scenes for its setting; the first would not have been necessary in the hands of a dramatist more skilled than was O'Neill at the time; the second scene is better done and is in the nature of a foretaste of the later work. "Fog" is the tale of yet another wreck, brought

1. In the case of O'Neill I assume, of course, a knowledge of his latest pieces, which are readily accessible in print, if not on the stage. All but the first of the volumes (*Thirst, and Other One-Act Plays*, Boston, 1914) are published in New York. A special edition of *The Emperor Jones* is issued in Cincinnati.

about by a collision with an iceberg. Best of the collection, easily, is "Thirst," for the depiction of the raving, wrecked trio afloat on a boundless ocean with a raft for their world is accomplished with true psychological power, vivid scenic sense, and a flair for the abnormal passages in the lives of men and women. One thinks of this playlet as he reads the opening act of *Gold*.

What the earth was to Antaeus, the sea is to O'Neill in these early plays. He gathers strength from each new contact. On land, in these same products of his prentice days, he fairly wobbles like a sailor on shore leave after months and months on the deep. To be sure, the dialogue as often as not is a string of *clichés;* the characterization is uncertain; but even thus early we have a welcome infusion of the exotic element, a groping after the inscrutable powers that rule over land and sea, a vigorousness, a masculinity, whose muscles were strong with a strength that lacked direction and discipline.

"But the blind sky will not answer your appeals or mine," says the Gentleman in "Thirst." "Nor will the cruel sea grow merciful for any prayer of ours." Already, in the cannibalism of the negro, resurgent through the ravages of thirst, there is prefigured the regression, through fear, of the burly Emperor Jones—a psychological retracing that, by the way, was accomplished for the group in "In the Zone," as *The Emperor Jones* accomplishes it for the individual. Already, in "Fog," O'Neill, like the Dark Man of his play, finds the people in the steerage more interesting to talk to than the second-class passengers; the suggestion of a mysterious grinding power does not harmonize with the realism of the scene, any more than does the philosophical argument between the poet and the business man, but one may glimpse here the original suggestion of *The Hairy Ape*. In "The Web," O'Neill had spoken, in a stage direction, of an "ironic life-force"; in "Fog" there is talk of "poverty—the most prevalent of all diseases." By which tokens he had levied tiny tribute upon Shaw.

Intrinsically, these early pieces are of meager worth; they are, however, necessary to a fuller understanding of the man, containing, as they do, the suggestions of a number of his later plays.

The Moon of the Caribbees and Six Other Plays of the Sea, though published five years later than the little volume we have just considered, contains plays written between 1917 and 1919.

The melodramatic element, though refined, is still there; by now, however, O'Neill seems to have acquired a genuinely philosophic grasp upon his material. Before, he was outside his imaginary world, now he has broken in. Before, he revealed no firm grasp upon character; now he is able to create a little human comedy of the sea, in which the same personages, clearly differentiated, appear in the various plays and are readily recognized for the distinct men they are. "The Moon of the Caribbees" has color, mood, suggestion, action; "Bound East for Cardiff" has all these, and a simple pathos that is the voice of a whole philosophy:

> "This sailor life ain't much to cry about leavin'," says a dying comrade to his mate. ". . . Just one ship after another, hard work, small pay and bum grub; and when we git into port, just a drink endin' up in a fight, and all your money gone, and then, ship away again. Never meetin' no nice people; never gittin' outa sailor town, hardly in any port; travellin' all over the world and never seein' none of it; without no one to care whether you're alive or dead. . . . There ain't much in all that that'd make yuh sorry to lose it, Drisc."

No pretty language there; no romanticizing of the heaving billows and a life on the ocean wave; no stage rhetoric. This is the tongue of reality, with the clear-sightedness of actual contact. It is the language that *The Hairy Ape* is to speak, in harsher tones, down in his hole at the bottom of the ship which is the bottom civilization as well. Not so good is "The Long Voyage Home," with its tale of Olson of the *Glencairn* shanghaied in a London dive just as he is on his way home to a farm, after giving up sailoring for good. This melodrama of types, with its seduction, poisoned drink, robbery, and other familiar devices, is saved only by a tinge of irony, and only for a while. Of better stuff is "In the Zone," with its war-scarred crew in the mine zone suspecting the lovelorn Smitty of harboring a treacherous bomb in the box that treasures his harmless love letters. "Ile" inclines to melodrama, but is strengthened by its revelation of man's search for power in the face of woman's weakening love, while both "Where the Cross Is Made" and "The Rope" are spoiled by the author's unwillingness to forego the assistance of convention and coincidence. Else, why these foreclosed mortgages, these wills, this plentiful passing of information across the footlights, these maundering soliloquies? Yet there is vision in "Where the Cross Is Made," as the fulfillment of the theme in *Gold* has revealed. And, for that matter, is not the theme of "Ile" deeply akin to the struggle between man and wife in the selfsame *Gold?*

Beyond the Horizon, written in 1918, is the first of the author's longer plays to survive his destructive wrath. Even here, where the domestic tragedy is enacted upon the land, the roar of the sea is heard in the distance. Though the ever-present sea is oftener than not the "ol' davil" that Chris Christopherson is always calling it in *Anna Christie*, it yet may heal, as it does Anna herself, so long shielded from it by her obsessed parent. To Robert in *Beyond the Horizon*, as to Anna of the later play, the land proves a curse; but the sea that heals Anna is kept by the irony of fate from Robert, whom it would have cured doubly, by taking him from Ruth, who was not made for him, and by bringing him the romance that his poetic nature craved. At the end Robert speaks to his returned brother, Andrew, with the clear vision of the dying. He asks him to take care of Ruth, whom Andrew and not Robert should have married in the first place, and of the land, which Andrew and not Robert should have remained to till:

> You've spent eight years running away from yourself. Do you see what I mean? You used to be a creator when you loved the farm. You and life were in harmonious partnership. And now—(*He stops as if seeking vainly for words.*) My brain is muddled. But part of what I mean is that your gambling with the thing you used to love to create proves how far astray you've gotten from the truth. So you'll be punished. You'll have to suffer to win back—.

The play was hailed, upon its initial performance, as one of the master products of realism in the United States; O'Neill, who must since have disconcerted the ready prophecies of our pigeon-hole critics with his experiments in the new forms, was looked upon as the founder of a truly realistic drama. Yet from the standpoint of such a realism he has carried over, into the play, some of the less worthy devices of his early pieces. His dialogue is natural enough, the writing is well-modulated, there are high moments, and one feels something like an implacable fate hovering over these toys of the land and the sea. This is a domestic tragedy of might-have-been, permeated with that "ironic life-force" of which the prentice O'Neill had written. But to overpraise the play and the author in one's enthusiasm at our drama's final attainment of adulthood, is to be false to both. "O'Neill's future," Mr. Macgowan has written, "lies along the new way and he must follow it."[2] Nor is this mere partisanship of the new for novelty's sake. Realism, in the catalogue sense of the word, holds for O'Neill the traps of melodrama, of the artistically purposeless goings and comings of the dramatist's puppets. This appears in so good a play as *Beyond the Horizon*, in which Andrew, each time that he comes on a visit to the old farm, wishes to return at once to his distant business, the reason for this impatience being more the playwright's than the character's. It appears in *Anna Christie*, where her future lover, though he has been five days adrift with his shipwrecked companions, rowing them to safety, must begin to make love to her no sooner than he has been picked out of the water. It appears later in the play, in the inexcusable fourth act, wherein the author kicks his dramatic and artistic structure to bits by a sudden reversal of the situation. It appears, in a peculiar manner, in *Diff'rent*, by not appearing at all, so to speak. For *Diff'rent* is by implication a psychological contrast, yet the author presents only the outer ends of that contrast, with thirty years between the acts. The missing act, the one he did not write, was precisely that in which some hint of the process which changed the woman from a prim Sunday-school mistress to a silly flapper of fifty should have been presented.

Had O'Neill, for example, treated *The Emperor Jones* (produced in 1920) in the fashion of conventional realism—and there was, one may imagine, that possibility—he would have fallen short of a veritable triumph, not through the accidental use of an inappropriate technique so much as through failure to grasp the essence of his theme, which demanded the form—which was the form itself—that he employed. The Emperor, not to be slain except by a silver bullet, is killed by just such a bullet molded by his

2. *Vanity Fair*, April, 1922, page 16d. If I concur in Macgowan's opinion, it is not through definite allegiance to the new way as against the old. The worthy playwright transcends the limitations of any particular form, and the special form of a play is determined by the material as it shapes itself in the author's imagination, and by nothing else. That form is part of the matter—an aspect of it. O'Neill's outlook upon the world is a peculiar blend of vivid insight and spiritual groping; it violates itself in the molds of ordinary realism, as I try to show.

credulous vassals. So, too, are we slain by the very belief of others in our own deceptions. Here we have a masterly presentation of the degenerative process of fear. The Emperor, once he has fled the palace—the first step in his fear, despite all his bluster, which was a sign of fear in the first place—wanders through the forest in rapid regression to primitivity. The tom-tom effect is remarkable, and is the culmination of O'Neill's natural response to such sensory stimuli. This is no mere sound accessory, as it is in the early plays, with their fog whistles, their raindrops, their whining children, and the whirr of the wireless. The tom-tom is part and parcel of the psychological action; at first it is the call to war; then it merges into the Emperor Jones's vision of the slaves rolling to its beat; finally it becomes his own throbbing, feverish temples, and all the while it is our heart beating more and more rapidly as we follow his fate.

Is the play one long soliloquy, practically? But fear talks much to itself. The visions that rise before his eyes? They are such as fear beholds, and truer to genuine reality than would be a blank stage. It is the surge of the Emperor's speech that makes these specters live for us as they do for him. This part of the play is really of a piece with the monodrama, in that it achieves complete identification of the auditor with the actor, and presents surrounding reality not as it appears to those outside the action, but in subjective terms of the actor's self. There are hints of the cinema in the gradual unfolding of the past as the play progresses—a series of "flashbacks," as it were; but this is no mere imitation of a medium; it is inherent in the character of the play; it *is* the play, and could not have been presented otherwise. Here symbol and psychology merge; analysts have found it a remarkable study, fundamentally as true of the white man as of the black; the Emperor Jones is, in addition, or simultaneously, an unobtrusive symbol of man's vain boast of power.

Anna Christie, written in 1920, just before *The Emperor Jones*, was produced a year later. For three acts it presents another realistic study in the "ironic life-force"; the fourth, as we have said already, is inexcusable, except upon the frankly commercial desire to provide a happy ending at whatever cost to the artistic conscience. If Mr. O'Neill really believes in that final act, the three preceding ones, with their closely woven narrative, their pungent dialogue, their reality to the life they portray, must be a lucky accident. And one refuses to believe in such fortunate fortuities. Not from the man who has written the relentless scenes of *The First Man*, in which the creative soul that is the artist may tread even upon the creative body that is woman.

And so, from melodrama and external realism, through the novelty of *The Emperor Jones*, we come to the newest of O'Neill's productions, *The Hairy Ape*, a "comedy of ancient and modern life." The ancient life of the author's sub-title is that same ancient life which sprang into being in the successive downward steps of the Emperor Jones's terror, for in theme and scene *The Hairy Ape* is contemporaneous with the transatlantic steamship on which it takes place, at once realistic background and symbolic timeless token of caste and character. "The beginnings of it," wrote Mr. Woollcott in *The New York Times* on the day (April 16, 1922) preceding its initial production at the Plymouth Theatre, whither it had moved from the Macdougal Street home of the Provincetown Players, "can be traced back to the days ten or eleven years ago when O'Neill was an able seaman aboard one of the ships of the American Line and came to know a certain stoker on the same ship —a huge Liverpool Irishman, who drank enormously, relished nothing in all the world so much as a good knock-down-and-drag-out fight, and who had a mighty pride in his own strength, a pride that gloried in the heat and exhaustion of the stokehold which would drop the weaklings and leave him roaring with mirth at the sight of them carried out. He was just such a specimen, therefore, as the Yank Smith on whose immense shoulders the ominous, nightmare events of *The Hairy Ape* press down like the crowding phantoms in some fantastic picture of Despair.

In the mutual snobbery of the liner, O'Neill as a seaman could hardly exchange confidences with the stoker, but they got to know each other ashore in the greater democracy of Johnny the Priest's saloon down in Fulton Street just around the corner from West— the same saloon, probably, through whose grimy windows the light filtered on the gaudy hair and cheerless face of Anna Christie. There, over his beer, O'Neill was free to contemplate the immense complacency of the Irishman and his glowing satisfaction with what most folks would have regarded as an unenviable rôle in the world. The memory of that satisfaction furnished a curious background for the news which drifted up from the waterfront some years later—the tidings that one night, when the ship was plowing along in mid-Atlantic, the big stoker had stolen up on deck and jumped overboard. Why? What had happened to shake that Gargantuan contentment? What had broken in and so disturbed a vast satisfaction with the world that the big fellow had been moved to leave it? O'Neill never heard if anyone knew, but out of his own speculation there took shape at last the play called *The Hairy Ape*.

The Emperor Jones emphasized the individual's regression through fear; *The Hairy Ape* shows that same individual thwarted in his gropings after social significance, returning in his inarticulate rage to his savage ancestor of the forest. The "ironic life-force" again, tinged with a distinctly social meaning and attitude. As the Emperor, blustering in his consciousness of power before the fear connoted in his blustering begins to get the better of him, so Yank, the coal-heaver, bellowing his pride of position in the infernal heat of the stokehole—a pride, already from the first, instinct with the uncertainty of all exaggerated pride, already betraying the inevitable result when stokehole clashes with upper deck in the vision of a curious daughter of the rich, who would go a-slumming on the transatlantic and get a glimpse of life below decks.

Listen to the bluster of the hairy ape, Yank:

> Hell, sure! Dat's my favorite climate. I eat it up! It's me makes it roar. It's me makes it move. Sure, on'y for me everything stops. It all goes dead, get me! De noise and smoke and all de engines movin' de woild, dey stop. Dere ain't nothin' no more! Dat's what I'm sayin'. Everything else dat makes de woild move, somep'n makes it move. It can't move without somp'n else, see? Den yuh get down to me. I'm at the bottom, get me? Dere ain't nothin' foither. I'm de end. I'm de start! I start somp'n and de woild moves. It—dat's me! De new dat's moidern de old. I'm de ting in coal dat makes it boin; I'm steam and oil for de engines; I'm de ting in noise dat makes you hear it; I'm smoke and express trains and steamers and factory whistles; I'm de ting in gold dat makes it money! And I'm what makes iron into steel! Steel, dat stands for de whole ting! And I'm steel—steel—steel! I'm de muscle in steel, de punch behind it! (*As he says this he pounds with his fist*

against the steel bunk. All the men, roused to a pitch of frenzied self-glorification by his speech, do likewise. There is a deafening metallic roar through which Yank's voice can be heard bellowing.) Slaves, hell! We run de whole woiks. We're it, get me! All de rich guys dat tink dey're somp'n, dey ain't nothin'! Dey don't belong. But us guys, we're in de move, we're at de bottom, de whole ting is us, see? We belong.

But "belong" is precisely what Yank does not, and the eight scenes that comprise the play spell his disillusionment, until he meets a grisly end in the arms of a gorilla at the zoo. Ape has come back to ape.

It is *The Hairy Ape* and *The Emperor Jones* that are the cause of the linking of O'Neill with the German Expressionists. But, as we have seen, the resemblance is by no means identity. He shares their speed technique, but not the telescoping of time and space that is practiced by the extremists of Germany, together with their Futurist brethren in Italy. He shares with them, too, an inability to create a perfect fusion of his elements, though he has not so clearly broken away from the old technique, which has a habit of making disconcerting appearances even in his best work. Nor should we forget, in all such comparisons as these, that the term "Expressionism," applied to modern German dramatists, is quite meaningless unless modified by a knowledge of the playwright to whom it is applied.

This, then, is the sketch of a man who is but at the beginning. And with him and Susan Glaspell, it may be, begins the entrance of the United States drama into the deeper currents of continental waters. O'Neill flaunts no narrow, mistaken nationalism; he apotheosizes no "ism"; he digs down into the subsoil of common humanity. Already he has produced, in the new forms, a pair of pieces challenging comparison with the best that foreign youth has brought forth in the same time, and that emerges victorious out of the test. Every favor of circumstance is with him—the press, the critics, the playhouses. The rest is in him, and in his artistic duty not to be content, as heretofore he has been, with second- or third-best.

George P. Baker

O'NEILL'S FIRST DECADE

A fifth volume containing *The Great God Brown*, *The Fountain*, and seven one-act plays of much earlier date, has just been added to the four volumes already published of Eugene O'Neill's plays.[1] Now that we have these nine one-acts, two two-acts, and eleven longer plays, dating from 1916 to 1926, we have an adequate basis for judging what has been Mr. O'Neill's development in the ten years in which he has been more and more before the public as a dramatist. He first courted public attention in a volume of one-act plays, unproduced, I think, professionally. They are melodramatic in a certain over-straining of stage values and a greater feeling for theatric than for human qualities. Yet there was in them power and promise, if crude. With "Bound East for Cardiff," O'Neill proved that he was working out of situation with character, into studies of characters who created the situations in and of themselves. Atmosphere, too, understood, restrained, not over-supplied, appeared in this play. O'Neill's development has been just slow enough to be sure. He perfected himself in one-act plays before he became successful in longer plays. With the Washington Square Players, above all with the Provincetown group, he offered to the public one-act after one-act—swift, sure, full of atmosphere, with increasing mastery of character. When in "The Moon of the Caribbees" the atmosphere of the place, the sounds, became almost a force, even a character, it was clear that as situation had led O'Neill into character, now character was leading him to think of the forces, the subtlest influences, which work compellingly on men and women who believe themselves free agents.

Beyond the Horizon (1920), his first long play presented to the

From The Yale Review, *July 1926, copyright Yale University Press. Used by permission of the editors.*

1. *The Works of Eugene O'Neill*, 4 vols.; Boni & Liveright.

public, shows discernment, behind, underneath, this story of heartbreak and misery, of elemental emotion, of forces that are not man himself, at work. Dimly, too, the dramatist senses and suggests poetry in the grimness of his story. Since 1920, the long plays have followed one another rapidly, at least one a year, on the average. By no means all, however, have been successes—for instance, *Straw*, *Gold*, and *Welded* have had no long runs—but, success or failure, each play has shown certain qualities. Always there has been a relentless facing of the facts of life as O'Neill sees them, with no sentimentality, no shaping up of his material with box-office, or supposed feelings of the public, in mind. There has been so constant a sense in the dramatist of life's ironies, great and little, that his plays must be tragedies or, at least, sternly ironic comedies. There has been, too, a steadily increasing sense on his part of the mystery of human life, of human relations. More and more he has been going back of, under, the individual in an effort to discern and to present the forces producing conduct in man. Studying Fear, he writes *The Emperor Jones*. Feeling here the need of a freer form than the three-act or four-act play, he turns to scenes, and begins to substitute suggestion for photography.

That is, O'Neill becomes an experimentalist in form—a symbolist even at times—not in order to experiment, not as a follower of any vogue of the moment, but because, as any of the great dramatists have come to feel, not what can be easily illustrated in action, but what can at best be only suggested, hinted, symbolized, is ultimately the most discerning, the most honest picturing of the complicated mingling in human emotions of heredity, environment, a multiplicity of causes large and small. *The Hairy Ape* only does on a larger scale and in a slightly different way what *The Emperor Jones* had done—studies relentlessly a suffering mind and finds visualized emotional expression for what is discovered. It is the masks, so slightly used here, as symbols, though effectively, which prepare the way for *The Great God Brown*.

What proves that O'Neill's experimentation with forms is not for its own sake but for definite artistic ends, what proves his indifference to supposed public response to given subjects or treatments, is that *Diff'rent* and *All God's Chillun* are in two acts. It has been shown again and again that two acts rarely fill an evening and that when they do, the audience usually finds the act division over-long. But O'Neill saw his subjects in two divisions only. He would not spoil the handling of the material as he saw it, either by overcrowding it into one act, or by thinning it into three acts. "There is nothing predetermined about form," he seems to say again and again. "The end is all. This is the way I see these people, the way in which I sense their emotional conduct. This way I must write this play to get the effects I desire. If the public accepts my work, good: if not, I have at least been honest with myself." When the air was full of charges and counter-charges as to how O'Neill should have ended the last act of his *Anna Christie*, he wrote to a friend: "Nothing could gratify me more than to know that you 'got' my last act as I intended it to be. I had begun to fear that, although I knew my intent was there, there might be some serious flaw in my execution in that final scene. It took a bit of courage to write it that way. I foresaw the easy and delighted accusations of 'commercial prostitution' that were going to be slung about. It would have been so much easier for me to have 'doused their lights' in palpable tragic catastrophe." It was true that Mat Burke, from his early religious and social training, no matter how little he had regarded them in everyday life, would turn from Anna in angry disgust when he heard her confession, but truer still that, with the force of the attraction between them, he would come back to her, not to be "happy ever after," but for some happiness, frequent quarrels, final adjustment, or more probable parting—who can tell which?

O'Neill deals with men and women not as convention of the stage, not even as they should be, but exactly as he sees them, far too often creatures blindly, helplessly driven by forces they have not the character to withstand. It is a Greek view of tragedy, this of his, notably so in *Desire Under the Elms*. The mistake the public often makes in judging O'Neill is to assume that what he says of individuals he means to have expanded into truth about the majority or even a class. He understands fully that the drama deals best with the individual. Doing that, it has for centuries found adequate forms and revelatory processes. Only very recently has he tried more and more to dramatize the emotions of groups, of the masses, to visualize by other means than soliloquy the inmost contents of the mind in emotional experiences. Even this O'Neill has attempted in his most recently produced play, *The Great God Brown.*

Naturally, the play has confused many people and consequently annoyed some. Here, after some ten years of work, is the most mature accomplishment of O'Neill. It does not treat merely individuals, but rather human relations, great forces in conduct rather than individual characteristics. It is concrete, but only against a background of mysticism. Naturally, if the subject is experimental, form and method must correspond. Hence the masks—not used in mere imitation of the Greeks, but freshly, imaginatively, as a real means to an attained artistic end.

If O'Neill's growth began slowly, it has gone on with increasing speed. Today O'Neill's plays are eagerly anticipated. They are seen, read, discussed as contributions not merely to acted drama but to our understanding of our fellows, and all this by that part of the public which is most alive to the drama as one of the great arts. Moreover, Eugene O'Neill today is the best known in other countries of all our dramatists. Vienna, Prague, Dresden, Berlin, Paris, London, Rome—all the capitals of Europe have seen his finest plays, long and short, of the past, and wait eagerly for new ones when announced. Best of all, he is in mid-career and, as an artist, still growing. Social and intellectual discontent is at the very center of his writing. It urges him on to ever more accurate knowledge of the subtleties of human conduct and more imaginative handling of his material for the best presentation of what he feels and thinks.

Early Recognition

FOREIGN

Hugo von Hofmannsthal

REFLECTIONS ON O'NEILL

It was at the Salzburg Festival last summer that I first heard the name of Eugene O'Neill. Max Reinhardt was producing one of my plays there; a sort of mystery, a synthetic or symbolic handling of allegorical material, mounted in a church. There were a few Americans in our audience, who aroused my curiosity by relating merely the plots of *The Emperor Jones* and *The Hairy Ape*.

Some time after, I read both these plays; also *Anna Christie* and *The First Man*. These plays and a few others, I am told, have placed Eugene O'Neill in the position of the foremost living American playwright. Judging from those of his plays with which I am familiar, his work is throughout essentially of the theatre. Each play is clear-cut and sharp in outline, solidly constructed from beginning to end; *Anna Christie* and *The First Man* as well as the more original and striking *Emperor Jones* and *The Hairy Ape*.

Originally entitled "Eugene O'Neill," The Freeman, *March 21, 1923. Translation by Barrett Clark.*

The structural power and pre-eminent simplicity of these works are intensified by the use of certain technical expedients and processes which seem dear to the heart of this dramatist and, I may presume, to the heart of the American theatregoer as well; for instance, the oft-used device of the repetition of a word, a situation, or a motive. In *The Hairy Ape* the motive of repetition progresses uninterruptedly from scene to scene; the effect becomes more and more tense as the action hurries on to the end. Mr. O'Neill appears to have a decided predilection for striking contrasts, like that for instance, between the life of the sea and the life of the land, in *Anna Christie*, or between the dull narrowness of middle-class existence and unhampered morality, in *The First Man*. The essential dramatic plot—the "fable," that is—is invariably linked to and revealed by that visual element which the theatre, and above all, I believe, the modern theatre, demands. The dialogue is powerful, often direct, and frequently endowed with a brutal though picturesque lyricism.

In an American weekly publication I find the following judgment on Mr. O'Neill, written by an intelligent and very able native critic: "He has a current of thought and feeling that is essentially theatrical. Taken off the stage it might often seem exaggerated, out of taste or monotonous." To this just praise—for it is intended as praise—I can heartily subscribe. But the same writer goes on to say, however, that in this dramatist's best scenes there is a power in the dialogue that is found in only one work among thousands. Granting that this is true, it seems to me that the manner in which Mr. O'Neill handles his dialogue offers an opportunity for some interesting speculations of a general character on the whole question of dramatic dialogue.

In my opinion, granting the primary importance of the dramatic fable, or plot, the creative dramatist is revealed through his handling of dialogue. By this, be it understood, I do not mean the lyrical quality or rhetorical power; these elements are in themselves of little importance in determining the value of dialogue. Let us assume a distinction between literature and drama, and say that the best dialogue is that which, including the purely stylistic or literary qualities, possesses at the same time what is perhaps the most important of all: the quality of movement, of suggestive mimetic action. The best dramatic dialogue reveals not only the motives that determine what a character is to do—as well as what he tries to conceal—but suggests his very appearance, his metaphysical being as well as the grosser material figure. How this is done remains one of the unanswerable riddles of artistic creation. This suggestion of the "metaphysical" enables us to determine in an instant, the moment a person enters the room whether he is sympathetic or abhorrent, whether he brings agitation or peace; he affects the atmosphere about us, making it solemn or trivial, as the case may be.

The best dialogue is that which charges the atmosphere with this sort of tension; the more powerful it is the less dependent does it become upon the mechanical details of stage-presentation.

We ought not too often to invoke the name of Shakespeare—in whose presence we all become pygmies—but for a moment let us call to mind that Shakespeare has given us practically no stage-directions; everything he has to say is said in the dialogue; and yet we receive pure visual impressions of persons and movement; we *know* that King Lear is tall and old, that Falstaff is fat.

Masterly dialogue resembles the movements of a high-spirited horse; there is not a single unnecessary movement, everything tends towards a predetermined goal; but at the same time each movement unconsciously betrays a richness and variety of vital energy that seems directed to no special end; it appears rather like the prodigality of an inexhaustible abundance.

In the best works of Strindberg we find dialogue of this sort, occasionally in Ibsen, and always in Shakespeare; as fecund and strong in the low comedy give-and-take scenes with clowns and fools as in the horror-stricken words of Macbeth.

Measured by this high ideal, the characters in Mr. O'Neill's plays seem to me a little too direct: they utter the precise words demanded of them by the logic of the situation; they seem to stand rooted in the situation where for the time being they happen to be placed; they are not sufficiently drenched in the atmosphere of their own individual past. Paradoxically, Mr. O'Neill's characters are not sufficiently fixed in the past. Much of what they say seems too openly and frankly sincere, and consequently lacking in the element of wonder or surprise: for the ultimate sincerity that comes from the lips of man is always surprising. Their silence, too, does not always convince me; often it falls short of eloquence, and the way in which the characters go from one theme to another and return to the central theme is lacking in that seemingly inevitable abandon that creates vitality. Besides, they are too prodigal with their shouting and cursing, and the result is that they leave me a little cold towards the other things they have to say. The habit of repetition, which is given free rein in the plot itself as well as in the dialogue, becomes so insistent as to overstep the border of the dramatically effective and actually to become a dramatic weakness.

The essence of drama is movement, but that movement must be held in check, firmly controlled.

I shall not venture to decide which is the more important in drama, the driving motive-element of action, or the retarding or "static" element; at any rate, it is the combination, the interpenetration of the two that makes great drama. In Shakespeare's plays there is not a line that does not serve the ultimate end, but when one goes through the text to discover this for oneself, one perceives that the relation between means and end is by no means evident: the means seem tortuously indirect, often diametrically opposed to the end. Nineteen lines out of twenty in a comedy or tragedy of Shakespeare are (seemingly) a digression, an interpolative obstruction thrown across the path of the direct rays; retarding motives of every sort impede the onward march of events. But it is precisely these obstacles that reveal the plasticity, the vitality, of the story and character; it is these that cast the necessary atmosphere about the central idea of the work. As a matter of fact, the unity of the play lies in these diversified and apparently aimless "digressions."

If one goes through *Antony and Cleopatra* looking only for the chain of physical events, the hard outlines of the plot, and neglects the indescribable atmosphere of pomp and circumstance, the spectacle of the downfall of pride and the fulfillment of destiny, the contrasting colors of Orient and Occident, all of which is made manifest through the dialogue, what is left? Nothing more than the confusion and incoherence of nine out of every ten motion-picture dramas. Or if one consider the best pieces of Gerhart Hauptmann merely as samples of superficial naturalism, one would find them pedantic and weak in characterization. Or again, take the productions of the doctrinaire naturalist: a good example is the dramatizations of the Goncourt novels. Thirty years ago these played a role of considerable importance, so far as theatrical history is concerned; but there is no life in them, nor was there when they were first produced; they suffer from lack of fresh air. Hauptmann's best plays, on the other hand, are bathed in it; it unifies and breathes vitality into them because it is the breath of life itself, transfused by that secret process which makes all great art, be it drama or canvas, giving it richness, variety and contrast. This is what the painters call "le rapport des valeurs." The plays of Strindberg are unified in this wise, not because of the bare plot on which they are built, but through the medium of an indescribable atmosphere that hovers somewhere between the realm of the actual and the dream-world.

The European drama is an old institution, laden with the experience of years, but as suspicious and watchful as a venerable though not yet impotent human being.

We know that the dynamic element in drama is a vigorous element, eternally striving for ascendancy. But we also know that great drama is and always has been—from the time of Aeschylus down to the present—an amalgamation of the dynamic and (shall we say?) "static" elements, and we are therefore a trifle suspicious of every effort towards the predominance of one element over another. The nineteenth century witnessed many such efforts, and each time great drama disappeared during the process. There is a constant danger that action—whether it masquerade as thesis-play or play of ideas, problem-play or drama of intrigue, or simply as the vehicle of a virtuoso playing with an anecdote—may prevail over the subtle and difficult but indispensable combination of dynamic and "static," the inseparable oneness of plastic form and action.

Sardou, the heir of Scribe, created a type of play the ingredients of which were entirely dynamic; action took the place of all else, and for twenty years Sardou dominated the States of Europe, while his followers—the Sudermanns, the Bernsteins, the Pineros—have continued to dominate it to the admiration of the middle classes of all nations and the abomination of the artists! This was the type of play in which the personages were never guilty of any "irrational" exhibition of character: they were the fixed units in a sharply outlined plot, manipulated by the skilled hand of the playwright; and they passed their lives in rooms hermetically sealed against the breath of mortals.

Sardou coined an expression for his style of play: "Life through movement," which was turned against him by his critics, who retorted: "Movement through life." The critics were all true artists: Zola, Villiers de l'Isle-Adam and their followers, among whom was the young Strindberg; but the most influential was Antoine, a man of the theatre.

But the pendulum swung back, and for the time being, perhaps, the European drama has gone too far in the opposite direction. It may be that this is the reason why the plays of so powerful a dramatist as Hauptmann are not popular outside Germany; for a large part of the German public is ready and able to listen to plays in which the "static" element is predominant, dramas in which psychological characterization and lyricism are of more importance than plot. Possibly this tendency is even a little overdeveloped.

Judged from this point of view, Hauptmann's plays are the exact antithesis of the plays of Eugene O'Neill. Where Mr. O'Neill reveals the first burst of his emotions in powerful, clean-cut pictures that seem almost like simple ballads in our complex world, Hauptmann applies himself to making his characters plastic; he does this by throwing a half-light over his men and women and allowing the values to appear slowly, to emerge in new and true and wonderful aspects, gradually shown through an accumulation of tiny and seemingly unimportant incidents of everyday life. As a result, Hauptmann's plots do not progress with directness or force; and at first sight his scenes appear to possess neither dynamic nor even truly "static" elements; they seem somewhat confused. But what ultimately strengthens these scenes and gives them the rhythm of life is a steady and unremitting infusion of the essence of life, which is soul. Hauptmann's method is that of Rembrandt the etcher, who works with a fine steel needle. Since Hauptmann continues to work in this fashion, he must necessarily give little thought to his audience; and indeed he is in actual danger of losing sight of them altogether. Meantime, he manages to accumulate so much of the spiritual life of his characters that his last acts are filled with an almost explosive force, so that there is no need for the introduction of any mechanical tension. Ibsen has done the same sort of thing in the last act of *The Wild Duck*, and Ibsen is the master from whom Hauptmann has learned most.

In the case of Mr. O'Neill, however, his first acts impress me as being the strongest; while the last, I shall not say go to pieces but, undoubtedly, are very much weaker than the others. The close of *The Hairy Ape*, as well as that of *The Emperor Jones*, seems to me to be too direct, too simple, too expected; it is a little disappointing to a European with his complex background, to see the arrow strike the target towards which he has watched it speeding all the while. The last acts of *Anna Christie* and *The First Man* seem somewhat evasive, undecided. The reason for this general weakness is, I think, that the dramatist, unable to make his dialogue a complete expression of human motives, is forced at the end simply to squeeze it out like a wet sponge.

I have no intention of giving advice to a man of Mr. O'Neill's achievements; what I have said is not said by way of adverse criticism; it is rather the putting together of dramaturgical reflections inspired by a consideration of his plays. His qualities as a dramatist are already very great, and I have no doubt that he will make progress when, in the course of time, which is necessary to each man who creates, he shall have acquired better control over his materials, and above all over his own considerable talents.

Andrew E. Malone

EUGENE O'NEILL'S LIMITATIONS

The Arts have their fashions no less pronounced than those of the milliner. Impressionism, vorticism, cubism succeed each the other as the millinery of yesterday gives place to that of today, and that of today will be old tomorrow. Manet is dead, and those who have caricatured his method rule for the moment in what poses as the van of enlightenment. The Yeats who wrote "The Lake Isle of Innisfree" writes no more; Ezra Pound has pounded him into a new form. The Ibsen about whom such fierce fights raged twenty years ago is no longer the idol of the cliques or the claques in the theatre. Strindberg, Hauptmann, Sudermann, Wedekind, Synge, and perhaps even Shaw and Galsworthy, have passed into the history of the drama. They no longer rouse the enthusiasm of those in whose hands is the molding of reputation; youth no longer regards them as rebels in the vanguard of the fight for intellectual freedom and honesty. The figures in Max Beerbohm's famous cartoon have nearly all fallen from their tubs; they still preach, but they preach from the ground level, and their fervent congregations surround them no more. There are new preachers in the marketplace today; preachers whose voices are more strident, pitched higher to catch the ears of those whom ten years of war and distraction have rendered deaf to the ordinary tones of everyday. To catch the ear of the world today the voice of the preacher must be pitched so high that the aid of the broadcasting machine is not required. Violence is no longer extraordinary, the theatre audiences of today in all countries have been through blood and mud, and verbal violence is no longer a thrilling experience.

The violence of war has given place to the violence of words and the violence of movement. In the dance there is the Jazz, and

From the Dublin Magazine, *December 1923. Reprinted with permission.*

the music of the populace is the jazz-band. In painting and in poetry the vorticists, the cubists, and the rest reflect the movement of the jazz. In prose there is James Joyce, whose *Ulysses* makes even the life of a filthy slum seem clean and desirable. In the theatre there is vulgar, glaring revue—and Eugene O'Neill. Eugene O'Neill is the great discovery of the post-war drama. His is the star now in the ascendant, outshining Shaw, Synge, Galsworthy, Barrie, Robinson, and all the Continentals. Even Chekhov and Andreyev are outshone by this new star from America. In the drama of nearly all of these there was little action; all was argument about states of soul, or mind, or the social system. Nothing *happened* in a play by Chekhov or a play by Shaw. There are no catastrophes of a material, visible kind; only the words are of importance. Eugene O'Neill varies all that. In his plays things happen, things that all may see and understand. There are fights, there is drunkenness, there is violent language, swearing and blasphemies, with a piquant American accent. There is everything that is likely to appeal to the post-war mind and taste. The language that might have proven too strong for the theatre audience in 1914 is not likely to shock anybody in 1923, and O'Neill's language will probably seem mild enough to those who have been accustomed to the language of an infantry battalion. His language is something which will probably aid him to popularity with those who have been the battalions, but who are now the bulk of the theatre-going public. His language may, indeed, prove to be his greatest asset in the theatre.

It is notable that, though Eugene O'Neill had written and published plays before the war, his success should be achieved only now. A volume of his early plays was published in Boston in 1914, but it was only in 1919 that New York heard of him, and since that date many of his plays have been produced there. Some of these plays we are now privileged to read, but the play which brought him first prominently before the public has not yet been published. This play is *Beyond the Horizon*, and it can only be hoped that it will soon come within our line of vision. Apparently some twenty-one plays have been written, and in the three volumes recently published in London by Mr. Jonathan Cape there are thirteen of these. Twelve of the twenty-one are one-act pieces, and of the nine longer plays six have been published. There is, therefore, sufficient material upon which to base an estimate of Eugene O'Neill as a dramatist, and to endeavor to place him in the dramatic world of today. Of course, any such estimate can for the present be tentative only, as he is still a very young man, and much may be hoped for in the years to come.

Of the man Eugene O'Neill little evidently is known. He avoids towns, and has not yet come within the circle of the popular literary organs. It is known, however, that he is of Irish parentage, his name betrays that, and that he was born in New York on 16th October, 1888. His full name is Eugene Gladstone O'Neill, which suggests that his parents were followers of Parnell and adherents of the older Parliamentary Irish Nationalism who were grateful to William Ewart Gladstone. His father was James O'Neill, a popular actor and theatre-manager in the United States, who had been born in Ireland. His mother's maiden name was Ella Quinlan, and she also was of Irish extraction, though born in America. He was educated at various Roman Catholic preparatory schools, and at the age of seventeen he entered Princeton University, then under the presidency of Mr. Woodrow Wilson. He spent only one year at Princeton, leaving the University to enter upon that wide experience of the world and its work which furnishes the material for his plays. . . .

He is now thirty-five years old, and he has written twenty-one plays. Of the thirteen plays published in London eight have the sea and seamen for their theme. The others vary widely from *The Straw* and *The First Man* to the magnificence of *The Emperor Jones*. In the first volume are three plays—*The Straw*, in three acts, five scenes in all; *The Emperor Jones*, in eight quick-moving scenes, and *Diff'rent*, in two acts. The second volume contains seven one-act pieces—"The Moon of the Caribbees," "Bound East for Cardiff," "The Long Voyage Home," "Ile," "In the Zone," "Where the Cross Is Made," and "The Rope." In the third volume are *The Hairy Ape*, in eight scenes; *Anna Christie*, in four acts, and *The First Man*, in four acts. It is evident that in his ten years as a dramatist Eugene O'Neill has been very busy and has worked hard. Having determined to become a dramatist, he has already gone a very long way towards the achievement of his ambition. Already he has been hailed by Mr. St. John Ervine as "immeasurably the most interesting man of letters that America has produced since the death of Walt Whitman." Of *The Emperor Jones*, Mr. C. E. Bechhofer says: "If Mr. O'Neill can continue to write plays as excellent as this it seems certain that within a very short time he will be recognized as one of the greatest living writers of English drama." High praise, indeed, from men of such standing as critics of the drama, which, however, sounds somewhat extravagant when one has read the published plays. That there is very solid achievement cannot be denied—*The Emperor Jones* is there to prove that, that there is genius and promise of its fulfillment cannot be denied either, but Eugene O'Neill must fulfill the promise before he joins the list which contains the names of Ibsen, Strindberg, Chekhov, Shaw, Synge, and Galsworthy. He is still young enough to unveil genius greater even than theirs, and *The Emperor Jones* leads one to expect that he will do so ere many years have passed.

The Emperor Jones is one of the most remarkable plays in the entire history of the drama. Its form shows that O'Neill's year at Harvard did him no harm, but conversely it proves that it profited him little. It is practically a monologue in eight scenes; only in the first and last scenes do any characters but Jones appear, and even then they play little more than chorus to the tragedy of the negro gaol-bird turned emperor. Brutus Jones, Emperor of a West Indian Island, is an ex-convict reared upon a past of slavery and crime. He has a touch of greatness, but is none the less a robber and a rogue. Beset by a revolt of his subjects, the Emperor flees from his palace to the forest, hoping to elude their vengeance. In the forest he loses his way, and in gradually growing delirium he lives through the scenes of his past life. Always he hears the tom-toms of his pursuers ringing in his ears, but his pursuers depend upon the forest law which will bring him back to his starting-point. As his reason deserts him he, who taught his subjects English, and even learned their "lingo" so that he could rule them, slowly reverts to his primitive beliefs, and all the superstitious dread of his race re-asserts itself. All his greatness and his meanness, his dignity and his servility, his humor and his horror are portrayed by speech and action in the six scenes driving remorselessly towards the tragic climax. He had taught his subjects that only a silver bullet could kill him, and in his revolver he kept a silver bullet for himself. At the height of his delirium he uses it, and they find only his dead body. In the incidents of the flight one is reminded of Andreyev's method of externalizing states of mind by speech and action. If the stage can produce the illusion of the forest at night, the visions and the terror, as forcibly as O'Neill's stage directions produce it, *The Emperor Jones* should be one of the most wonderful things ever experienced in a theatre.

The Hairy Ape is Eugene O'Neill's second great achievement. It is the tragedy of a man who belongs "to the stokehold of an Atlantic liner, a man who is entirely out of place on land, known to his mates by the name of Yank. While the men are at work in the stokehold they are visited by Mildred Douglas, a passenger on a voyage to England. Mildred is the daughter of one of the directors of the steamship company coming to London to indulge her craving for the study of slum life. When she visits the stokehold, hears Yank's language and sees his beast-like form, she faints. A "filthy beast" she calls him; but this is afterwards translated by one of his mates into "hairy ape." The description wounds him deeply and he vows to avenge the insult. "I scared her," he says. "Why de hell should I scare her? Who de hell is she? Ain't she de same as me? Hairy ape, huh? I'll show her I'm better'n her, if she on'y knew it. I belong and she don't, see! I move and she's dead! Twenty-five knots an hour, dat's me! Dat carries her, but I make dat. She's on'y baggage. Sure! (*Again, bewildered*). But, Christ, she was funny-lookin'! Did yuh pipe her hands? White and skinny. Yuh could see de bones trough 'em. And her mush, dat was dead white, too. And her eyes, dey was like dey'd seen a ghost. Me, dat was! Sure! Hairy ape!" He tries to encounter Mildred as she leaves the ship, but he is prevented by the officers. Long, the ship's socialist orator, takes him ashore in New York in an effort to convince him that not Mildred only but her entire class is the enemy. Yank gets very drunk and is arrested in a street brawl. Having been informed in prison that the Industrial Workers of the World desires to blow up the great steel works owned by Mildred's father, Yank goes to the offices of that organization and offers his services for the job. He is suspected of being an *agent provocateur*, and is forcibly ejected from the offices. In the final scene he is found in the New York Zoo talking to the big gorilla. Having made the gorilla familiar with his philosophy and the results of his own experiences of the world, he opens the cage and releases the animal. "(*The gorilla scrambles gingerly out of the cage. Goes to Yank and stands looking at him. Yank keeps his mocking tone—holds out his hand.*) Shake—de secret grip of our order. (*Something, the tone of mockery perhaps, suddenly enrages the animal. With a spring he wraps his huge arms around Yank in a murderous hug. There is a crackling snap of crushed ribs—a gasping cry, still mocking, from Yank.*)" As he dies, Yank says: "Ladies and gents, step forward and take a slant at de one and only—(*his voice weakening*)—one and original—Hairy Ape from de wilds of . . ." *The Hairy Ape* is an extraordinary blend of weird fantasy and extreme realism. Yank, however, is the only character who really lives; all the others merely serve as a background against which he stands out. He resembles Brutus Jones in the primitiveness of his nature; but whereas the primitiveness of Jones is spiritual, that of Yank is entirely physical. Yank "belongs," and the world's movement depends upon him; all who do not "belong" have no interest for him. *The Hairy Ape* is a play that should give thrills in plenty to any theatre audience.

Anna Christie has been seen upon the London stage, and has had a very mixed reception from the critics. Its story is now too well known to need repetition. It is an ambitious play spoiled by its fourth act, which produces an effect of anti-climax. Throughout the play one finds a *motif* which seems to obsess O'Neill's mind, the idea that everybody envies the life and the work of every other body. The seaman hates the "ole davil sea" and desires an inland farm, while Anna Christie has fled from an inland farm for the life of the streets. It is probably true that most human beings are discontented with their lot. The theory of progress is founded upon such discontent; but O'Neill shows not progress but retrogression to be the result of change. Steadily downward go his people who change their jobs; but whatever be the result of the varied experiences of the dramatist, it is certainly not all the truth of human experiences.

In *The Straw* is the theme that love may cure where medicines fail. The scene is laid, for the most part, in a sanatorium for consumptives, where Eileen Carmody, whose disease is due to the drudgery of a household, is being treated. . . . One is left hoping that [a] cure may be effected, but with very little to base one's hope upon. This is the only play where one is left guessing what the end may be; it is also the only play in which O'Neill is a sentimentalist. In this play the character drawing is perfect. We know the girl's abominable relatives, her weakling fiancé, as we know herself and the self-centered Stephen Murray. What they do is the only thing they could do in the circumstances, and the circumstances are the best that could reveal their qualities. The scenes and the routine of the sanatorium are so real that they are experienced.

The First Man and *Diff'rent* are the least satisfying of O'Neill's longer plays. *Diff'rent* is a study in the psychology of sex, in which a woman rejects her lover because he is not quite so "diff'rent" from other men as she had expected, but thirty years later she is found playing the fool with her old, and constant, lover's nephew. It is true, as Mr. St. John Ervine says, that the play has a beginning and an end but no middle; but it is none the less true that it acts very well indeed. It has been acted in London and in Dublin, and in each place it has been very successful on the stage. *The First Man* is also a study in the psychology of sex. . . . The play will probably act very well, but in reading it is somewhat unreal. . . .

Of the short plays little need be said, though they contain some of O'Neill's best and most characteristic work. They are probably only chips from his workshop, mere thumbnail sketches for his larger work, but they contain character sketches in many instances superior to any in the more ambitious plays. Sometimes the same character is more vividly portrayed in the one-act play than it is when it re-appears in the longer plays. The short plays are more impressions than analyses. None is marked by profundity; they are all more concerned with the work and the surroundings of men than with their souls and their philosophy. This is particularly true of "The Moon of the Caribbees," "The Long Voyage Home," and "In the Zone"; but in "Where the Cross Is Made" and "The Rope" are contained stories, horrible stories, which are thrust upon one with a cumulative force that is amazing. "Ile" and "In the Zone" are, perhaps, the best of the one-act plays. In each of these there is a true balance between character and setting, and the dramatic intensity of each is very marked. In all these short plays O'Neill's grip of a story is very well exemplified. There is vivid imagination, retentive memory, dialogue that compels by its obvious truth, the whole fused to produce several little masterpieces. Even if they be merely prentice work—they are certainly the work of his earlier years as a dramatist—it is probable that many people will consider that they contain the best work that O'Neill has yet done with the exception of *The Emperor Jones*.

Of O'Neill's method there is not much to say, except that it is different in every play. Realist, sentimentalist, fantasist, he uses the method and the framework that best suits his story. In *The Emperor Jones* and *The Hairy Ape* he comes very close to the method of the cinema; but in all his plays he ignores the fact that Aristotle laid down rules and that Professor Baker taught those rules in the University of Harvard. His method is as changeable as the sea, and it is perfectly obvious that he has learned more from the sea than he did from Professor Baker. In the plays may be seen the strength of the sea as well as its fluidity. He is still experimenting, and in his experiments O'Neill may discover a form which in its apparent formlessness may be more intensely dramatic than anything the theatre has yet known. He is to the contemporary drama what James Joyce is to the contemporary novel—an experimentalist who jars sometimes, provokes often, but who interests always. He cannot be ignored even now, though his best work has in all probability yet to come. He may decide as he grows older that the rules of Aristotle are good rules and still useful to the dramatist; but even if he does it is certain that his work will never degenerate to the level of the machine-made drama which seems to be preferred by the managers of theatres.

If O'Neill has ignored Aristotle, he certainly has not ignored the modern drama and its writers. In his work may be found traces of many dramatists from Andreyev and Strindberg to Bernard Shaw; pervading his dialogue through and through is the work of John Millington Synge. In almost every play may the traces of Synge be found. It is no gentle echo either, but the full-throated voice of the master. In *The Hairy Ape*, *Anna Christie*, and *The Straw* may be found how much Eugene O'Neill owes to Synge. "Oh, to be scudding south again wid the power of the Trade Wind driving her on steady through the nights and the days! Full sail on her! Nights and days! Nights when the foam of the wake would be flaming wid fire, when the sky'd be blazing and winking wid stars. Or the full moon, maybe," says Paddy in *The Hairy Ape*. "Let you not be hiding from me, whoever's here—though 'tis well you know I'd have a right to come back and murder you," says Burke in *Anna Christie*. And Carmody, in *The Straw*, has the

Synge accent on every word he utters. And it is not the Synge accent only that O'Neill has acquired, he seems to have absorbed the entire Synge philosophy of the drama. "In countries where the imagination of the people, and the language they use, is rich and living, it is possible for a writer to be rich and copious in his words, and at the same time to give the reality, which is the root of all poetry, in a comprehensive and natural form. In the modern literature of towns, however, richness is found only in sonnets, or prose poems, or in one or two elaborate books that are far away from the profound and common interests of life. . . . On the stage one must have reality, and one must have joy; and that is why the intellectual modern drama has failed, and people have grown sick of the false joy of the musical comedy, that has been given them in place of the rich joy found only in what is superb and wild in reality. In a good play every speech should be as fully flavored as a nut or apple, and such speeches cannot be written by anyone who works among people who have shut their lips upon poetry." These words from the preface to *The Playboy of the Western World* summarize Synge's philosophy of the drama, and they summarize also the plays of Eugene O'Neill. In O'Neill's plays there is reality and there is joy, there is the reality of life and the joy of life; his vocabulary is rich with the richness of life and work, and his people have that wildness which civilization accentuates. His speeches are fully flavored as a nut or an apple, and they have the poetry of human endeavor and human suffering. There are people who may not like his full-flavored speeches, just as there are people who do not like nuts or apples, but, like them or not, they will compel attention by their exuberant power. O'Neill's plays will bring to the theatre reality and joy; they are the plays that Synge sought for, but which he could not find because such plays had not yet been written. Synge has been to O'Neill a guide, philosopher, and friend; his advice has been taken and magnificently vindicated in practice. O'Neill has lived among people who have not shut their lips upon poetry, and who are at the same time bound up in the profound and common interests of life. It is, of course, fitting that one Irishman, who has never set foot in Ireland, should be strongly influenced by another, particularly when that influence is exerted by the greatest of Irish dramatists. Bernard Shaw has also influenced O'Neill, but to a very much less degree; his influence does not permeate these plays as does that of Synge. It is somewhat remarkable that the dramatists who have made the English theatre familiar with strong speech should all be Irishmen. It was Lennox Robinson who first used the word "bloody" as an adjective in a modern play, and Bernard Shaw shocked England when he made Eliza Doolittle repeat the word. But Robinson and Shaw are mealy-mouthed when compared with O'Neill, and where Shaw merely shocked, O'Neill might horrify—but then the war has come between Bernard Shaw and Eugene O'Neill.

Rudolf Kommer

EUGENE O'NEILL IN EUROPE

Two years after the Armistice intellectual Germany sent its first explorer across the Atlantic to rediscover America. The name of the courageous traveller was Gustaf Kauder, a writer and journalist of distinction. He reported that the process of multiplication, so characteristic of American civilization, had continued during the dark years of the war at a rather increased pace. By doubling, trebling or multiplying all industrial and economic statistics one could bring the records of American evolution up to date. A presidential election was in full swing at the time. Just an election. Two candidates and no idea.

Wars, elections, and similar disturbances pass, but good plays last. Accordingly, Gustaf Kauder reported at length that a strange man had appeared on the American stage: Eugene O'Neill, the author of *The Emperor Jones*. A new epoch had started. The American drama had arrived.

One year later, Germany's most capricious critic, Alfred Kerr, visited these shores. His enthusiasm for *The Hairy Ape* was even more intense. He returned to the Fatherland with one piercing yell: Eugene O'Neill! Shortly afterwards Hugo Hofmannsthal wrote a most sympathetic, searching essay on the art of the new dramatist. Thus heralded by an impressionable journalist, a leading critic, and a great poet, Eugene O'Neill became the center of excited expectations.

Such was the overture. The first act, however, did not go so well. In one year a farce may conquer a world; a drama may well need a decade. It so happened that *Anna Christie*, the first of the O'Neill plays to cross the Atlantic, was brought from America to Germany by a Hungarian. Apart from his admiration of the play,

---

From the Greenwich Playbill, *1924–25 Season.*

his qualifications as literary go-between were limited to a Berlitz acquaintance with English and German. What he may have guessed in English, he was utterly unable to express in German. According to all my Hungarian friends, Hungarian is the most beautiful and the most expressive language in the world—but it is certainly not a favorable filter through which an American play should pass on its way into German.

Unfortunate as this translation was, the selection of *Anna Christie* was even more so. It was one of those astounding errors of judgment not infrequently perpetrated by theatrical managers. It is one of the earlier plays of O'Neill, and whatever its merits are, it is certainly not representative of those qualities of its author which carried his fame beyond the borders of his native continent. Anna Christie's vivacious past is the central theme of the play. Alas! virginity, lost or otherwise, has no longer any interest for the European playgoer. It is a problem exhaustively dealt with (if not at all solved) on the stage and in literature, and the pathetic disilusion of a trusting virginity-seeker is no longer a tragic theme. There are many issues dead in life and still alive in romantic literature, and there are others dead in literature and still very much alive in life.

Anna Christie seemed, therefore, an uninteresting belated descendant of those heroines of bygone Naturalism, of those ladies with a past and of the past. (Ah, where are the days when Ibsen's Nora was a destructive though charming revolutionary?) The play failed in Berlin and in Vienna, but it was received with unanimous enthusiasm by the critics in London; an enthusiasm that was not fully shared by the public.

The next play to reach the Continent was *The Emperor Jones*. In Paris the regisseur committed atrocities, difficult to believe even when reported by eye-witnesses. But the pathetic misunderstanding of things Anglo-Saxon has become a well-established tradition in France. In Berlin they produced Gustaf Kauder's excellent translation with a more than adequate cast, but they thought they could only cope with the primeval forest by entrusting its execution to a neo-expressionist of the most radical brand. The result was so perplexing that even an Elizabethan signboard, if added to the scenery, could not have convinced the audience that it was sitting in front of a forest. Furthermore, concentrating upon the spiritual side of the play, the producer overlooked that Jones's revolver was supposed to go off from time to time—and so it didn't. Strange are the ways of producers.

In the meantime S. Fischer, Germany's leading intellectual publisher (the sponsor of Gerhart Hauptmann, Bernard Shaw, Ibsen, Hofmannsthal, Schnitzler, etc.), had published *The Emperor Jones* and *The Hairy Ape* in his literary monthly, *Die Neue Rundschau*, as well as in book form. The two plays were read all over Central Europe, and no longer depended on the hazards of a theatrical production. Once again the book was mightier than the stage. O'Neill conquered in spite of the failure of his first producers. When these lines appear in print, *The Hairy Ape* will have been produced in Berlin. Max Reinhardt is going to stage *The Emperor Jones* in Vienna and in Berlin, to prove that it was the production that failed last year and not the play. The Volksbuhne in Berlin is preparing "The Moon of the Carribees." The Deutsches Theatre—Max Reinhardt again—will present *All God's Chillun Got Wings* this season. Cologne, Hamburg, Dusseldorf, Munich and many others are following.

The theatres in Vienna and Berlin are still the intellectual shop windows for Central, Eastern, and Northern Europe. Stockholm, Copenhagen, Prague, Budapest, and, last but not least, Moscow, are grappling with the production of O'Neill plays. Richard Ordynski translated *The Emperor Jones* into Polish and produced it in Warsaw, scoring a sensational success. And the European Eugene O'Neill literature is piling up.

To understand O'Neill's position in Europe one must try to realize the mentality of Europe at the conclusion of the war. Art and literature found themselves in a blind alley, into which they had been led even long before the war. Futurism, Expressionism, Imagism, Aboriginism, Dadaism, Vorticism and all the other pitiful attempts at something new were exploded. The curious chaotic anarchy prevailing in European art before the war (and mysteriously foreshadowing it) left a desolation behind that corresponded most significantly with the political and economic impasse. Most of the great personalities of Central Europe are still alive, but they have missed contact with the new time. Gerhart Hauptmann retired into the past of Mexico to find pale symbols for the defeated soul of Germany. The great Viennese—Arthur

Schnitzler, Hugo von Hofmannsthal, Hermann Behr—are still representing the charming culture of the Danube which, supposedly, had died with the Austrian Empire, and which will live forever—as the literary historians have it—in their books. Georg Kaiser, Carl Sternheim, Ernst Toller and the younger Germans are all esoteric in their way, expressing a particular faddism of style or of creed. Even the adored G. B. S. and his puritan Fabianism seem somehow out of tune. Amidst such ruins and splendors of a lamented past the young American appeared. The day is his because he is of today.

What does he mean to the Germans? In journalese he is being called the representative of American drama. He is nothing of the sort. He does not represent any group, any movement, any current or tendency. He does not announce any aesthetic formulas or dogmas, he does not stand for any particular political or religious creed, he is just a personality, human and creative, sincere and isolated. In spite of the alleged levelling influence of American democracy, all great Americans appear as solitary mountains. It is very characteristic that the foreign visitors to last year's P. E. N. congress were asked to witness a performance of *Abie's Irish Rose*, representing the American drama, or perhaps, statistically, the American theatre public.

O'Neill was not dropped from the skies. His European critics have detected in his plays traces of Strindberg, Wedekind, and Freud. But his technique, his atmosphere and the unexplainable essence of his dramatic genius are enthusiastically hailed as something entirely new, as American. No matter if the "Untergang des Abendlandes" will take place according to the schedule of Oswald Spengler or not—the heir of the European drama has appeared.

It is strange that the poet who has created a truly gigantic dramatization of pessimism—*The Hairy Ape*—should be sensed as American—but so it has happened. Edgar Allan Poe and Walt Whitman had and still have an overwhelming influence on European literature. Eugene O'Neill bids fair promise to become the third great gift of America to Europe.

Achievement

AMERICAN OPINIONS

Francis Fergusson

MELODRAMATIST

After Mr. O'Neill had spent several years travelling about the country with his father, James O'Neill, who was playing in *The Count of Monte Cristo*, and a few more bumming all over the world, he fell ill; and while recovering in a sanatorium, decided he wanted to write plays. His first plays, written while he was studying under Professor Baker at Harvard, and working with the young Provincetown Playhouse, are the product of his romantic youth and a desire to write for the stage. They are not complicated by the anxiety about his own soul which gets in his way later, and, more clearly than his later work, they show the real nature of his vocation to the stage. The first published volume, *Thirst*, is now repudiated. Mr. Barrett Clark, whose book[1] on O'Neill contains all the available information about his life and the origins of his

Originally entitled "Eugene O'Neill," Hound and Horn, *January 1930.*
Used by permission of Lincoln Kirstein.

1. *Eugene O'Neill, The Man and His Plays*, by Barrett H. Clark, 1929.

plays, says that the plays collected under this title are similar to those in the earliest preserved collection, *Moon of the Caribbees*, though cruder.

The first thing that strikes one on reading the latter collection, is the over-emphatic language. The characters, usually the crew of a tramp steamer, communicate almost entirely in profanity. Mr. Clark, who once made the crossing on a cattleboat, testifies that the dialogue is not inaccurate; but the more educated people in the later plays, while not so profane, also seem to be laboring to express the inexpressible, and achieving a similar flatness. I conclude that the fault is with the dramatist rather than with his material. This conclusion is borne out by the fact that, except in the "atmospheric" play, "Moon of the Caribbees," the author remains on a level with his characters. We are required to accept people with ineffable sorrows or longings as carrying the main burden of the play. And the plots and situations are built on a similar assumption of a vast emotion which cannot be put into words.

I understand that Mr. O'Neill has never liked "In the Zone"; but it seems to differ from the other plays in the volume we are discussing, chiefly in having a neater and more self-conscious technique. It may be that Mr. O'Neill thinks that this interferes with its sincerity; or it may be that I do him an injustice. The crew of a tramp steamer crossing the submarine-infested zone is nervously on the watch for spies. What a spy would be doing there is never satisfactorily explained. This does not prevent the men, in search of a scapegoat, from suspecting Smitty. This character is a recurrent figure in the early plays: a melancholy and solitary hobo "of the higher type." Someone discovers him reading a batch of letters one night; they tie him up in spite of his screams, and investigate. But instead of the telegrams from the Kaiser which they expected, they find letters from Smitty's lady-love, who rejected him years ago because he drank. One dried rose falls to the floor. At this sudden revelation of hidden sorrow the rough sailors, whose hearts are really of gold, are abashed and conscience-stricken.

This plot, which, however absurd it may sound in the telling never fails to move an audience, is really as helplessly bombastic as the language; a language of childish superlatives which are always trying to imply more than they succeed in stating. I take it that the essence of melodrama is to accept emotions uncritically; which, in the writing, amounts to assuming or suggesting emotions that are never realized either in language or action. Melodrama in this sense is a constant quality in Mr. O'Neill's work. It disfigures his middle period, when his feeling for a character is out of all proportion to that character's importance to the play, as well as his later period, when his attempt to deal with his own unattached emotion takes the unhappy form of a passion for some large idea. In fact it seems that Mr. O'Neill typically resorts to the stage, not to represent emotions through which he has already passed; which have been criticized and digested, and so may be arranged in patterns to form works of art: he resorts to the stage to convey a protest, the *first* cry of the wounded human being. His fundamental feeling for the stage, so clearly shown in these first plays, is not that of the artist, but of the melodramatist: the seeker after sensational effect.

Nevertheless his naive belief in emotion is related to a priceless quality, which one may call the histrionic sincerity, the essence of mummery. Every dramatist as well as every actor depends for his power over his audience on his own belief in what he is trying to put on the stage, whether it be an emotion, a character, or a situation. An audience is extremely malleable. It may be swayed by suggestion, hypnotized by the concentration of the stage figure. This complete concentration, which would be wrecked by a wakeful critical faculty or a touch of humor at the wrong time, Mr. O'Neill possesses in a very high degree. It is the secret of his success; and when it is joined to an interest in a character, it produces his best scenes.

2

After Mr. O'Neill had exhausted the vein of mood and atmosphere derived from his early experiences of bumming, he ceased to write melodrama for its own sake, and developed an interest in people he had known or heard about. His next plays begin with an interest in a character or characters. Mr. O'Neill thus explains[2] the origin of *Beyond the Horizon*, the earliest play of this type to be preserved: "I think the real life experience from which the idea of *Beyond the*

2. Quoted by Barrett Clark.

Horizon sprang was this: On the British tramp steamer on which I made a voyage as ordinary seaman, Buenos Aires to New York, there was a Norwegian A.B., and we became quite good friends. The great sorrow and mistake of his life, he used to grumble, was that as a boy he had left the small paternal farm to run away to sea. He had been at sea twenty years, and had never gone home once in that time. . . . Yet he cursed the sea and the life it had led him—affectionately. . . . I thought, 'what if he had stayed on the farm, with his instincts? What would have happened?' . . . And from that point I started to think of a more intellectual, civilized type . . . a man who would have my Norwegian's inborn craving for the sea's unrest, only in him it would be diluted into a vague, intangible wanderlust. . . . He would throw away his instinctive dream and accept the thralldom of the farm for—why, for almost any nice, little poetical craving—the romance of sex, say." Though we do not have Mr. O'Neill's account of the origins of most of his plays, I should say, from internal evidences, that *Gold*, *Anna Christie*, *Diff'rent*, *All God's Chillun Got Wings*, and perhaps *Desire Under the Elms*, started from a similar interest in a character, which was sometimes real, sometimes partly or entirely imaginary. I shall look at *All God's Chillun* as typical of this group. It shows his most characteristic failings as well as some of his very best results.

The first scene shows Ella, a white girl, and Jim, a sensitive little negro boy, having a childish love affair in their native slum. This scene, unnecessary for the main theme of the play, is typical of O'Neill. Its only possible relevance is as psychological and sociological background, for the important information is duplicated later. I shall have more to say later on about Mr. O'Neill's use of this type of realism. Meanwhile observe that the realism of the dialogue and the natural history of a stage full of children (which, I may say, is extremely difficult to do practically), are complicated by a kind of symbolism or super-realism of the set. The scene is a street-corner, one street being full of black faces and negro tunes, the other street full of white faces and *their* tunes. Aside from the sloppiness of leaving so much to the carpenter and the regisseur (which I shall also mention later), it may be doubted whether realism with a super-imposed symbolism of this kind is ever a success. Even Ibsen, with his "Wild Ducks" and his sea-ladies, has the greatest difficulty in making it seem anything but artificial, and Mr. O'Neill hasn't a tenth of his skill.

Ella falls in with tough companions and gradually degenerates, while Jim painfully acquires education and starts to study Law. Ella, disillusioned with her own kind, marries Jim in a moment of depression, as the only "white" man she knows. There is a good "symbolistic" scene showing the newly married couple emerging from the church between rows of hostile faces, white on one side and black on the other. And then the real drama begins: the struggle in Jim between his love for Ella and his ambition to succeed in the world; the struggle in Ella between her love for Jim and her hatred of him as the cause of her exile from her own people. The point of conflict is Jim's career: for his self-respect he needs to become a lawyer, while Ella, who has never really accepted Jim as her husband, needs to preserve her spiritual ascendancy by preventing him from passing his examinations. Tied together by their love and by their solitude, they alternately take refuge in each other's arms and fight for mastery or vengeance. The scenes throughout this middle part of the play, in spite of their inadequate language, are deeply convincing. But at the end they both give up: Jim agrees to play a little boy to Ella's little girl. In effect, they cease to strive for an adult relation of husband and wife and accept a childish one.

Now if the previous scenes mean anything, this conclusion marks a degeneration on both their parts. But Mr. O'Neill, under the necessity of ending his play, asks us to accept it as a hard won *Verklärung:*

Jim—Forgive me, God—and make me worthy! . . . Let this fire of burning suffering purify me of selfishness and make me worthy of the child you send me for the woman you take away!

Ella—Don't cry, Jim! You mustn't cry! I've got only a little time left and I want to play. Don't be old Uncle Jim now. Be my little boy . . . Come and play!

Jim—Honey, Honey, I'll play right up to the gates of heaven with you!

What is the reason for this extraordinary failure of Mr. O'Neill's to master his material? Between the untidy and unnecessary first scene and the bathetic and evasive finale, there are several scenes of really tragic significance. Beginning with a person, and proceeding with that complete concentration on the stage figure which I described above, Mr. O'Neill sometimes sees his people so deeply that they acquire overtones of universal import. One may sometimes feel Jim and Ella, through their excellent concreteness, as every pair of exiles in love, and their story as realizing certain profound truths about the relation between a man, his work, and his wife. But these jewels are so rare, and are imbedded in such a disheartening matrix of psychology, bathos, and cheap symbolism that they seem not only accidental but misunderstood when they appear. And the end finally persuades one that the author wrought better than he knew. He turns away from his tragic vision, and all is lost.

But did he ever have a tragic vision? The finale, so wrong for the middle scenes, is not inconsistent with the characters. The reason it jars is that it belies the point of view from which their struggles were seen as having a dignity and a significance beyond themselves. It might be appropriate in some terrible comedy, but the characters are not seen as in any sense comic figures. In fact, they are not seen "as" anything: if they at times reveal heights and depths, that is an accident, for Mr. O'Neill's relation to them is personal. They are for him friends and enemies, other individuals in an anarchical universe, not parts of any larger vision. He is prepared to echo their cry, "Can such things be?" It is all very well for a character in a play to demonstrate this emotion, but when an author shows it it means that he has not digested his material to the point where it becomes suitable for a work of art. Interested in his people's psychology, yes: hence the filling in of naturalistic background in scene I; but interested in the esthetic value of their destiny, no: and hence no possible ending for their story. Mr. O'Neill is right when he says,[3] "Life doesn't end, one experience is but the birth of another. Violent death is seldom the solution of anything, in life or in fiction. It is too often a makeshift device. . . ." Life doesn't end, but a work of art does; a work of art is a bounded whole, and Mr. O'Neill's unsatisfying endings are a proof that his interest in his people is not the disinterested and final one of the artist, but the developing and tentative one of a man among men.

But Mr. O'Neill's power of convincing an audience is vastly aided by the fact that his belief in his characters is so purely

3. Quoted by Barrett Clark.

naturalistic. Where there is no publicly established convention, the only way to make a character acceptable is to establish him naturalistically. An audience will believe in a character who used to play on a certain street-corner in Harlem, and whose father was in the coal business, but it will not believe in one who can only be identified by the qualities of his soul, and toward whom it is invited to adopt no personal attitude. The limitations of this type of realism have been admirably studied by Miss Virginia Woolf, in her essay, "Mr. Bennett and Mrs. Brown." It has this inestimable advantage of being publicly understood, but the most that can be said for it as an art form is that it may, as in this play of Mr. O'Neill's, lead to the accidental discovery of a few muddy diamonds. Mr. O'Neill himself has never been satisfied with it; he has never called himself a realist: we have seen that even in these plays of his middle period he resorts to symbolism. And finally he abandons his interest in character altogether and attempts to enunciate general ideas.

3

Beginning perhaps with *The Hairy Ape*, and continuing through *The Fountain*, *The Great God Brown*, *Marco Millions*, *Lazarus Laughed*, and *Dynamo*, Mr. O'Neill's character studies are interspersed with, and finally superseded by, plays in which the author shows no interest in the concrete, and assumes the rôle of prophet. It is as though he had ceased to interrogate his acquaintances about what he is to expect of "Life," and had begun to interrogate Nietzsche and other nineteenth-century philosophers. About the prophecies themselves Mr. Clark says the last word: "If O'Neill were a genuinely original thinker, or even a brilliant spokesman for the ideas of a brilliant thinker, we might argue as to whether we should be the losers if he were to give up writing plays altogether, but his ideas as contributions to contemporary thought are negligible; they are at best slightly varied forms of what we have all been reading during the past decade or so." Lazarus' Nietzschean exclamation is typical: "Men are also unimportant! . . . Man remains! Man slowly arises from the past of the race of men that was his tomb of death! For Man death is not! Man, Son of God's Laughter, *is!*" Mr. O'Neill is not a thinker, and we need not attempt to investigate his thought any further. It is true that Lazarus sounds a little like Mr. O'Neill's own fundamental cry, that "Life goes on"—implying, perhaps, some confusion between pessimism and the unhappy ending, which would affect his ability to write plays; moreover, it is doubtful whether Lazarus' generalized and rather hysterical optimism could ever be realized in live characters; but the question which concerns us more nearly, in our attempt to understand Mr. O'Neill as a playwright, is not so much the quality of the thought as the relation between the thought, the author, and the play.

Mr. O'Neill, we find, is more interested in affirming his ideas than in representing the experience in which they are implied. The example of Elizabethan drama seems to prove that an unsatisfying philosophy may underlie a great play. But there the play is the thing, and the philosophy may at most be deduced from it as from a direct experience of life. In *Lazarus Laughed*, on the other hand, there is little or no play at all, for Caligula, the anti-Lazarus, is no more credible than Lazarus himself, and their conflicts fail entirely to move us. The burden of the play is carried by two elements: by Lazarus' philosophical arias, and by spectacular effects of crowd movements and colored lights. About the first of these, enough has been said. With regard to the element of spectacle, Reinhardt has shown us what can be achieved in this line, especially in his production of Büchner's *Danton*. Gordon Craig[4] has hailed these departures as first steps toward a new form, his hypothetical "pure art of the theatre." As a form, it is related to the 17th Century Masque, and the modern revue. It seems to mean a dissolution of the classic partnership of actor and author, to which we owe most great drama, in favor of a third figure, the regisseur. A good regisseur may of course get artistically satisfying effects with well-trained crowds and carefully calculated light and sound effects—too often at the author's expense. When an author resorts to it, it usually means that he has ceased to be interested in mastering the medium of the stage. This is certainly true in *Lazarus Laughed:* the stage becomes Mr. O'Neill's lifeless megaphone. Nothing stands between the audience and Mr. O'Neill, shouting his views. For his relation to his ideas, in these prophetic plays, is the same as his relation to his characters in his middle period:

4. Cf. Hyatt Mayor: "The Ideas of Gordon Craig," *Hound & Horn*, Spring, 1929.

they are emotionally significant to him, they play a part in his equilibrium as a man. Attaining no vision outside himself, his plays remain attached to him by his eternal immaturity.

We are not surprised to find, therefore, that his audience is often more interested in the author than in his play: "It is salvation the agnostic playwright is seeking. One might trace his life like one of those dry southwestern roads where the Penitente Brothers have laid down the dead man they are carrying. O'Neill's plays are crosses. Follow the road he travels and you will often hear the sound of flagellation. Look and you will see that the whip is brought down by a tormented soul on his own back. But flowers grow on this desert track, and the mountains and the sunset lie *Beyond the Horizon*."[5] The very imperfection which connects the author with his play also connects the author with his audience. The one quality which his admirers agree in stressing is his sincerity. We have seen that he believes in his own mood in his early plays, and in the personal reality of his characters in his middle period, while in his latest plays he is in earnest in asserting some Nietzschean war-cry. As a person, he is sincerely interested in figuring out his life, and perhaps in attaining a stable point of view—though unconsciously. He has in fact never attained it. He has managed to recognize his emotional demands, but he has not reached the further heroism of accepting what becomes of them: of describing them with reference to some independent reality. He has a sense of human needs, but none of human destiny. He offers us the act of seeking, but no disinterested contemplation; himself, therefore, rather than his work. Only the dead cease to change; but by discipline it is sometimes possible to produce a work complete and independent of the suffering individual. Mr. O'Neill's failings may all be ascribed to the fact that he has never found any such discipline.

4

I do not intend, in this essay, to enquire directly to what extent Mr. O'Neill's failure to find a discipline through which to realize his talent is due to his own shortcomings, and to what extent to "conditions" beyond his control. A slight acquaintance with modern drama since Ibsen shows one how difficult it is to write plays of artistic as distinguished from sentimental or sociological

5. Elizabeth Shepley Sargent, in *The New Republic*, March 16, 1927.

interest. But to tackle the general question of Mr. O'Neill as a modern dramatist—and an American—would involve questions which I am not competent to treat. It seems more profitable to compare briefly Mr. O'Neill's career with those of two other American playwrights, Mr. George Kelly and Mr. E. E. Cummings, who followed very different paths to the stage, in the hope that some sense of Mr. O'Neill's place in the contemporary scene may emerge by implication.

Mr. O'Neill began to work about the time of the 1912 Renaissance. He belongs with Mr. Mencken, Mr. Sherwood Anderson, and Mr. Theodore Dreiser (who was in advance of his time). This was the generation that raised the hue and cry about Puritanism. They were, as a group, impatient of tradition and convention, and their great discovery was their emotional needs. They were more interested in a man's emotions than in a map of them; therefore, more interested in the man than his work! Most of them wrote fiction—a genre which is much better suited to this temperament than the stage; but they also gave birth to the Little Theatre, and Mr. O'Neill, whose first plays were produced by the Provincetown, is in many ways a Little Theatre product. This movement seems never to have had anything more positive than a dissatisfaction with Broadway, and an ambition. It was a revolt against narrow commercialism; it asserted that the theatre was an art; but, having no standards and no technique, it remained somewhat ineffectual in its new freedom.

Mr. George Kelly on the other hand is a product of the commercial, which is also the professional stage. He began as a vaudeville actor[6] and presently he was writing his own skits. He stood behind the scenes with a stop watch, and if the audience did not laugh soon enough, he rewrote the act. From vaudeville he graduated to the three-act comedy, and finally to the drama. His experience proves that a certain sense of craftsmanship is not incompatible with Broadway, rare though it is there: having set himself the comparatively modest problem of making the *honnête* Babbitts laugh, he was rewarded by the natural discipline which an actual audience and a particular stage can give. Assuming the viewpoint of "commonsense" where O'Neill urges some large idea;

6. A short biography of him appeared in an issue of *Theatre Arts* devoted to American dramatists.

accepting the realistic set and the realistic dialogue which he found publicly established, where O'Neill was always making strange demands on the carpenter and the electrician, Mr. Kelly's work was that of the artist: to master and refine a given medium to the point where it can be made to realize his vision. While Mr. O'Neill's freedom has resulted in a complete loss of bearings, so that he has of late almost ceased to be a dramatist, Mr. Kelly has bequeathed us several comedies which are complete, and refer to nothing outside themselves. If they are rather trivial, and if there are signs[7] that his homefolks, having moved to more expensive suburbs and learned to drink gin, are no longer to be satisfied with his neat little interiors, the fault is not with his method, which was after all the method of Shakespeare and Molière. Mr. Kelly seems to have encountered the limitations of the theatre as it exists with us here and now. It is doubtful whether a method, which depends upon an acceptance of the existing theatre, would ever prove the solution for a man of Mr. O'Neill's potential dimensions.

If the Little Theatre, in its revolt against commercialism, forfeited incidentally the discipline of the craftsman which a Kelly could work out for himself on Broadway, it never showed the slightest tendency to develop its own standards and its own conventions. A play with a "kick" has remained its ideal. We have seen that the personality of the author or the agony of some unassimilated "character" can satisfy its cravings for drama better than a formal and autonomous play.

Mr. E. E. Cummings, however, was a poet before he tried to write for the stage. That is to say, he had trained himself—with what success I shall not attempt to say: his method rather than his results concern us here—to see his material as an artist. His play, *him*, is evidently more "autobiographical" than any of O'Neill's and yet the characters at least of Him and Me are acceptable as parts of the pattern of the play without reference to the author. Without trying to judge the merit of the play as a whole, I should say that the scenes between Him and Me have all the qualities we have failed to find in Mr. O'Neill's work. The characters, the rhythm, and the sense of the stage are all of a piece, whereas in Mr. O'Neill's plays we find realistic dialogue, symbolis-

7. *Behold the Bridegroom*, the latest play, about Long Island, was a failure commercially.

tic settings, and characters which are unamenable to any pattern or underlying rhythm. In a real writer for the stage, language, character, and the sound and movement of the stage, spring from the same root conception. A Molière dialogue implies the stage empty save for a few spectators, a little furniture, and the actors; it implies a rhythm derived from the pantomime of the Commedia dell'Arte,[8] and a certain relation between actor and audience. A Cummings' dialogue implies a brief light interval between "black-outs," a certain rhythm derived from the vaudeville act, and an audience which good-humoredly challenges the performer to "put his stuff across." Mr. Cummings' work, in fact, has style. His solitary discipline has enabled him to work in stage terms, disinterestedly, and with a mastery which Mr. O'Neill, for all his experience, has never attained.

But Mr. Cummings, unlike Mr. Kelly, is an artist of the theatre without either theatre or audience. I have said that his style was derived from vaudeville, but no vaudeville actor could manage a speech of Him's and no vaudeville audience could understand his play. In spite of his very authentic feeling for the stage, and in spite of his ingenious and courageous effort to dramatize his very lack of connection with a live stage and audience (so neatly of a piece with the "stunt" feeling of his vaudeville style), Mr. Cummings' first play remains mere closet drama. It was in fact produced at Mr. O'Neill's native theatre; but the Provincetown's crowd of Greenwich Villagers, just the thing to relish a revival of "In the Zone" and "Moon of the Caribbees," were at a loss to deal with *him*. Mr. Cummings does not belong at the Provincetown. So far he does not seem to belong anywhere. But Mr. O'Neill indubitably belongs at the Provincetown, at the Guild, in the suburbs of London, in Berlin, and in Little Theatres all over the English-speaking world. The man O'Neill is very close to a vast audience.

8. Cf. M. Ramon Fernandez' *Molière*, in the series *La Vie Des Hommes Illustres.*

George Jean Nathan

OUR PREMIER DRAMATIST

> "And had you chosen Eugene O'Neill, who has done nothing much in the American drama save to transform it utterly in ten or twelve years from a false world of neat and competent trickery into a world of splendor, fear, and greatness, you would have been reminded that he had done something far worse than scoffing, that he had seen life as something not to be neatly arranged in a study, but as terrifying, magnificent and often quite horrible, a thing akin to a tornado, an earthquake or a devastating fire."
>
> *—Sinclair Lewis, in his Nobel Prize address to the Swedish Academy.*

Among the items in Mr. Lewis' disquisition which came in for waspish comment, both printed and oral, at the hands of American writers who didn't get the prize and who were consequently displeased with the intelligence of the Swedish Academy, this presented itself as perhaps the most riddled target. Facetiousness over both Mr. Lewis' rich encomium and the measure in which O'Neill had justified it, or rather not justified it, laboriously insinuated itself into at least one-half the clippings patiently scissored by the indefatigable Dr. Romeike. There was derision for Mr. Lewis' "world of splendor, fear, and greatness," and for O'Neill's tornadoes, earthquakes, and devastating fires. There was a mocking of Mr. Lewis' faith in the transformation of American drama, and of O'Neill's share in that transformation. There were amused hisses and boos and cat-calls, and not a few senile eggs and pre-Raphaelite tomatoes. In the midst of the ironic din, a critic of the drama may have been privileged to retire for a moment to

---

the peace of his chambers, there to determine what sense there was to the business.

After about a quarter of a minute's prolonged and studious meditation, the critic came to the conclusion that, despite the pardonable smiles induced by Mr. Lewis' conviction that the American drama had been transformed utterly in ten or twelve years from a false world of neat and competent trickery into a world of splendor, fear, and greatness, there nevertheless was a very fair relative degree of truth in his statement, and that certainly if anyone was responsible for any sort of transformation in the American drama, O'Neill was that person. The American drama may still be very far from what one might desire it to be; but that in the last decade it has got much nearer to that desideratum than ever it got before must be obvious to anyone not wholly blind or British. It would be pleasant to believe that this great change for the better had been of slow, steady and relentless growth, that it had come as a result of gradually seeping revolution, and that O'Neill was simply the man who had grabbed the flag from the hands of the forces that step by step had paved the way for him and had then accompanied him shoulder to shoulder on the valiant march. But, pleasant though it would be, it would not be true. For the truth of the matter is just what Mr. Lewis announced it to be to the Swedes, to wit, that O'Neill alone and singlehanded waded through the dismal swamplands of American drama, bleak, squashy, and oozing sticky goo, and alone and singlehanded bore out of them the water lily that no American had found there before him.

I do not argue, in my somewhat dubiously poetic metaphor, that O'Neill, since first he invaded the swamp, has always come out of it bearing the gift of a water lily. There have been times, as in the case of *Welded* and *Dynamo*, when what he has brought to shore has resembled rather more closely a cauliflower. But I do argue with Mr. Lewis that to O'Neill alone must go the credit for transforming the American drama, if not quite entirely into a world of splendor, fear, and greatness, at least into a world at length wholesomely free from fear and, thus freed, possibly on the way to splendor and greatness. When O'Neill came upon the playwriting scene, the American drama—even at its least hypocritical, at its least sentimental, and at its bravest—had still the air of a female impersonator removing his wig and implying his perfect masculinity in a movement of his jaws on an imaginary hunk of chewing tobacco. Such antecedents of O'Neill as Augustus Thomas ("dean of American playwrights") with his interpretation of life in terms of osteopathy and thought transference, as Charles Klein with his stenographers outwitting actors in the rôles of Rockefellers and Morgans, as George Broadhurst with his boy politicians putting an end to municipal corruption by the exercise of what are today known as wisecracks, as Eugene Walter with his Rector's restaurant tragedies, and as William Hurlbut with his studies of New York in terms of the violation of an ingénue's virtue and with his Ibsen distillations like *The Writing on the Wall*—such antecedents surely left no inspirational legacy to O'Neill. Life, as he saw and wrote of it when first he began to take pen in hand, may not always have been akin to a tornado, an earthquake, or a devastating fire, but at least it was never akin to a Belasco conservatory, a Liebler drawing-room, or a Broadway supper café.

With O'Neill's acceptance and success in the theatre, American playwrights suddenly took courage and proceeded, as best as in their fashion they could, to set themselves to a species of drama far removed from that to which they had been devoting their efforts. The newer and younger writers, led by O'Neill, threw off the shackles at once and tried to write honestly, faithfully and truthfully; the older ones—men like Owen Davis—at least temporarily abandoned the further confection of mush dishes and tried to follow the changing taste with imitations, very pathetic, of the O'Neill drama. Even criticism, long tied to the apron-strings of sentimentality, moral cowardice, and dramatic falsehood, began slowly to get onto its own legs, to wag its tail independently, and to bark loudly and defiantly in behalf of the new order. And audiences, growing steadily in receptivity and intelligence, joined in the barking.

The result is apparent. Where once—and not so long ago as the clock ticks—the American stage, even in its then most reputable aspect, was occupied by such stuff as *The Witching Hour*, *Paid in Full*, *As a Man Thinks* and *The Man of the Hour*, it has in the last ten years gained respectability with plays like *The Great God Brown*, *Strange Interlude*, *Craig's Wife*, *A Texas Nightingale*, *Street Scene*, *Chicago*, *Desire Under the Elms*, *Another Lan-*

guage, *What Price Glory?*, *Saturday's Children*, *The Hairy Ape*, *The First Year*, *Ambush*, *Rain*, *Sun-Up*, *The Green Pastures*, *Veneer*, *The Front Page*, *The Left Bank*, *Brief Moment*, *The Vinegar Tree*, and numerous others. Sinclair Lewis may have been guilty of second degree hyperbole, but down under it he knew pretty well what he was talking about.

While waiting for the haughty English reviews of O'Neill's *Mourning Becomes Electra*, which, following the arbitrary depreciation of almost everything American, will in all probability be coming along as soon as the play is produced in London, let us, in the new light of this, his most recent work, consider O'Neill's position among present-day English-speaking dramatists. That he is the most, in fact, the only important serious dramatist that this country can presently offer needs no restatement for Americans. But that, with the possible exception of Sean O'Casey, Great Britain can at the moment among its immediately active writers for the theatre offer no serious playwright his equal is a postulate that may call for some explication in behalf of both nations.

The erstwhile important serious older writers for the British stage have gone to pot in recent years. Shaw's later work has been merely a very feeble rehash of familiar materials; nothing that he has produced lately has come within hailing distance of his earlier efforts; he gives every sign of being played out, though—like some prinked and still hopeful elderly gallant in tête-à-tête with a piquant maiden—he continues to go through the various superficially realistic motions. Galsworthy's *Exiled* and *The Roof*, his latest works, provide a melancholy example of that once estimable dramatist's collapse. His plays have steadily become weaker and weaker, the fizzing of so many soda-pop bottles mistaking themselves for philosophical Bollinger. Pinero disappeared from the scene more than a decade ago with *The Thunderbolt;* his work since then has been utterly negligible. Among the younger men, Granville Barker, in the opinion of this critic, was never much better than a pretentious third-rater. The new-fledged Denis Johnston shows, in *The Moon in the Yellow River*, undeniably some promise, but we are here treating of the factual present, not of tomorrow's possible dispensations. The talented St. John Ervine, after achieving a highly merited reputation with several very excellent examples of the serious drama, has in later years devoted himself exclusively to light comedy and so volitionally removes himself from the catalogue with which we are immediately concerned. In the way of light comedy, incidentally, Great Britain offers a half dozen writers greatly superior to any that we can offer—Ervine, Ashley Dukes, Lennox Robinson, George Birmingham, and Maugham among them. No American has written a comedy of the quality of Dukes's *The Man With a Load of Mischief*, or Birmingham's *General John Regan*, or Maugham's *The Circle*, or Robinson's *The White-headed Boy*, to name but four. About the nearest that American comedy has come to the wholly reputable in recent years is Behrman's *The Second Man*, Lawrence's *Two Married Men*, and the Kaufman-Ferber collaboration, *The Royal Family*, although on one occasion Elmer Rice and on several others the aforementioned Lawrence have come a few feet within striking distance. The rest of what relatively commendable comedy writing we have had has been found to be largely half-distance writing: comedy that moves smoothly, gracefully and intelligently up to the middle point of an evening and then collapses because of insufficient wind. Of all the better comedies written by American playwrights in the last fifteen years, perhaps not more than a half dozen at most have managed to sustain themselves until their final curtains. It is not that their themes have dissipated themselves so much as their authors' hold on the comedic resources of the English language. It has been a case of shortage of verbal legerdemain rather than one of comic idea. Where such a talented Englishman as Dukes or Brighouse or Maugham is able to lay hold of a slender comedy idea and by the jugglery of word and phrase give it not only comedy body but even an aspect of size, the American—less apt at such magic—exhausts himself after he has pulled but half a rabbit out of the silk hat. And the American comedy, as a consequence, pretty generally gives the critic the impression of having been written up to ten o'clock by a perfectly articulate man and thereafter by the same man suddenly struck dumb and driven to a dramatic sign-language. In farce, it is a different story; the English have produced nothing in late years in the same class with the best American farces during the same period.

To return to the so-called serious dramatists and omitting the sole living British exponent of the purely poetic drama, John Masefield, who has not figured conspicuously or fortunately in the drama of the last ten years, and regrettably as well being forced to eliminate Dunsany and Yeats on the score of their inactivity—the latter's recent and meagerly poetic *The Cat and the Moon* certainly does not provide critical counterevidence—and while waiting, further, for the possible development of the talent of Denis Johnston, we find no one else in Britain at the present time writing serious drama of any consequence. Only O'Casey, whose *The Plough and the Stars*—to single out his best play—is one of the superbly fine things in modern drama, remains a figure of immediate and real importance. And it is thus, O'Casey alone excepted, that O'Neill at the moment looms head and shoulders above all the other serious dramatists of the two English-speaking nations. In the last half dozen years England has offered only O'Casey's work to compare with his, and aside from the O'Casey masterpiece mentioned it has produced nothing to compare with *Strange Interlude* or, now, *Mourning Becomes Electra.*

While presenting O'Neill in this encomiastic light, it must not be imagined, however, that one sees him as a compendium of all the virtues, a fellow purged of all sin, his head encircled with a critical halo and his nose magnificent with a brass ring. He has his faults as he has, more richly, his virtues. Of both, though of the latter more especially, *Mourning Becomes Electra* is an illuminating mirror. It once again discloses its author as the most imaginatively courageous, the most independently exploratory and the most ambitious and resourceful dramatist in the present-day Anglo-American theatre. It once again gives evidence of his contempt for the theatre that surrounds him and of his conversion of that contempt into drama that makes most other contemporaneous drama look puny in comparison. It dismisses the little emotions of little people in favor of emotions as deep, as profound, and as ageless as time. It opens the windows of the stage so habitually shut against the world of pity and comprehension, and terror, to that world again. But so heroic is its intention, its sweep, and its size, that its characters, like the characters in certain other plays by the same author, are themselves not always up to the sweep and size of their author's emotional equipment and emotional dynamics. In other words, it sometimes paradoxically happens that it is O'Neill, the dramatist as man, rather than his characters and quite apart from them, who agitates and moves an audience. In other words still, the characters that O'Neill creates are at times the after-images rather than the direct images and funnels of his torrential and unbounded emotional imagination. They are periodically too inconsiderable to contain him. They sometimes give one the impression that the load he has placed on their shoulders is too heavy for them to carry. They present themselves occasionally in the light of characters valiant, faithful, and obedient, yet not equal to the demands their creator has made of them. Thus, though *Mourning Becomes Electra* is indubitably one of the finest plays that the American theatre has known, its Greek emotions now and again embarrass the American characters into which the author, loosing the flood-gates of his copious emotional fancy, has projected them.

In the modern drama to which we are accustomed, the emotions of the characters are often more trivial than those of the members of the audience. It is a rare play nowadays that imposes anything more than the most superficial of emotional demands upon an audience. For it must be remembered that the theatre audience of today is a different audience from that of other years. It is, in considerable part, the intelligent, experienced and sophisticated residuum of the erstwhile heterogeneous mass of theatregoers that embraced the presently happily expatriated movie, talkie, radio, and other such elements. Its elected and most prosperous dramatic fare is no longer such stuff as *Strongheart*, *Classmates*, and *Brown of Harvard*, but *Strange Interlude*, *The Last Mile*, and *The Barretts of Wimpole Street*. The larger number of dramatic exhibits offered to this new audience by the commercial producers fail to satisfy it. It is a platitude that intellectuality has little more to do with drama than with music, poetry, or home-brewing and that, as with these other arts, it is largely a question of emotion or nothing. And the emotional content of forty-nine out of every fifty present-day plays is approximately that of a clam juice cocktail. As a consequence, they fail to stir an audience in the slightest degree, for the audience, as has been observed, is usually just about twice as dramatic and twice as emotionally competent as the plays. The average man and woman in the selected theatre audience of today have in their own lives, and consequently in their own theatrical imaginations, emotional resources considerably superior to those of the usual play characters that they waste three dollars to watch. They are thus not even vouchsafed the pleasure of enjoying a vicarious emotional experience, for the dramatic emotions which they attend are largely those of emotional fledglings and so are not only insufficient to provide them with any reaction but are, to boot, pretty often unintentionally humorous. It is no wonder, under the circumstances, that the intelligent theatregoer often presently patronizes music shows in preference to drama and that, when anything at all possible in the way of open and shut farce comes along, he gallops to it for the dose of catharsis usually denied him in the serious theatre.

Into this theatre and into this audience, starved for an emotional purge, O'Neill has come with the physic that both have longed for. Into a theatre that night after night has dribbled out the meager little emotions of ladies' maids dressed as grand ladies, of Cockney actors listed in programs as builders of empire, and of men and women generally with passions as persuasively incendiary as warmed gumdrops, he has brought, since almost first he began to write, a new full heat and fire. The little faint flickers of dramatic flame that now and then lap pathetically at the edges of the Anglo-American stage have been stirred by him into something more like a conflagration, whose incandescence has reached even beyond that stage to the stages of Scandinavia, Russia and Germany.

In *Mourning Becomes Electra*, an independent reworking in terms of modern characters and the modern psychology of the Greek Orestes-Electra legend of Aeschylus, Sophocles and Euripides, O'Neill has once again taken over the present-day theatre and made it his own. From five in the afternoon until close to midnight he harrows and mauls, taunts and tortures, prostrates and exalts his characters, set into the New England scene at the close of the Civil War, with the lash, and the blaze of his passionate inspiration. It is this inspiration, mighty and crimson, that transcends his characters and play and that, like the glow of a steel furnace against the heavens, impresses the vision, the feeling and the fancy even though the furnace itself be a mile away. The characters are metaphorically this furnace, sometimes remote, not always immediately actual and not always plausibly determinable—the affinity between the psychology of the son of Agamemnon and the son of a New England Yankee soldier, for example, is not always altogether convincing; but the glow, spreading over all, luminous and radiant, is the glow that is O'Neill.

A parenthetical observation in conclusion. To superficial critics of O'Neill's writing career, the trilogy idea is associated specifically with his more recent development. A study of his canon, however, reveals the fact that, from his earliest beginnings, his dramatic mind, if not always his actual dramaturgy, worked with and toward that idea. The trilogy impulse is readily to be detected in three of his short plays of the sea, published under the general title of *The Moon of the Caribbees. Beyond the Horizon*, as he himself now sees it in retrospect, was essentially a trilogy arbitrarily compressed within a single, regulation-length play. *Dynamo*, as is well known, was the first play of a trilogy the writing of which he abandoned. *Strange Interlude*, as he originally visualized it and as he outlined it to his friends years before he set himself to its execution, was a super-trilogy. There is even a hint of the trilogy sequence in the nature of the emotional philosophy and its development in the recurrent battle of the sexes and Mother Earth theme in certain of his other plays. The dramaturgical form that the volcanic emotionalism of *Mourning Becomes Electra* takes is thus simply a natural outgrowth of a seed that has been in his work since first he began to write.

Lionel Trilling

THE GENIUS OF O'NEILL

Whatever is unclear about Eugene O'Neill, one thing is certainly clear—his genius. We do not like the word nowadays, feeling that it is one of the blurb words of criticism. We demand that literature be a guide to life, and when we do that we put genius into a second place, for genius assures us of nothing but itself. Yet when we stress the actionable conclusions of an artist's work, we are too likely to forget the power of genius itself, quite apart from its conclusions. The spectacle of the human mind in action is vivifying; the explorer need discover nothing so long as he has adventured. Energy, scope, courage—these may be admirable in themselves. And in the end these are often what endure best. The ideas expressed by works of the imagination may be built into the social fabric and taken for granted; or they may be rejected; or they may be outgrown. But the force of their utterance comes to us over millennia. We do not read Sophocles or Aeschylus for the right answer; we read them for the force with which they represent life and attack its moral complexity. In O'Neill, despite the many failures of his art and thought, this force is inescapable.

But a writer's contemporary audience is inevitably more interested in the truth of his content than in the force of its expression; and O'Neill himself has always been ready to declare his own ideological preoccupation. His early admirers—and their lack of seriousness is a reproach to American criticism—were inclined to insist that O'Neill's content was unimportant as compared to his purely literary interest and that he injured his art when he tried to think. But the appearance of *Days Without End* has made perfectly clear the existence of an organic and progressive unity of thought in all O'Neill's work and has brought it into the critical range

Originally entitled "Eugene O'Neill," The New Republic, *September 1936. Used by permission of the editors.*

of the two groups whose own thought is most sharply formulated, the Catholic and the Communist. Both discovered what O'Neill had frequently announced, the religious nature of all his effort.

Not only has O'Neill tried to encompass more of life than most American writers of his time but, almost alone among them, he has persistently tried to *solve* it. When we understand this we understand that his stage devices are not fortuitous technique; his masks and abstractions, his double personalities, his drum beats and engine rhythms are the integral and necessary expression of his temper of mind and the task it set itself. Realism is uncongenial to that mind and that task and it is not in realistic plays like *Anna Christie* and *The Straw* but rather in such plays as *The Hairy Ape*, *Lazarus Laughed* and *The Great God Brown*, where he is explaining the world in parable, symbol and myth, that O'Neill is most creative. Not the minutiae of life, not its feel and color and smell, not its nuance and humor, but its "great inscrutable forces" are his interest. He is always moving toward the finality which philosophy sometimes, and religion always, promises. Life and death, good and evil, spirit and flesh, male and female, the all and the one, Anthony and Dionysus—O'Neill's is a world of these antithetical absolutes such as religion rather than philosophy conceives, a world of pluses and minuses; and his literary effort is an algebraic attempt to solve the equations.

In one of O'Neill's earliest one-act plays, the now unprocurable "Fog," a Poet, a Business Man and a Woman with a Dead Child, shipwrecked and adrift in an open boat, have made fast to an iceberg. When they hear the whistle of a steamer, the Business Man's impulse is to call for help, but the Poet prevents him lest the steamer be wrecked on the fog-hidden berg. But a searching party picks up the castaways and the rescuers explain that they had been guided to the spot by a child's cries; the Child, however, has been dead a whole day. This little play is a crude sketch of the moral world that O'Neill is to exploit. He is to give an ever increasing importance to the mystical implications of the Dead Child, but his earliest concern is with the struggle between the Poet and the Business Man.

It is, of course, a struggle as old as morality, especially interesting to Europe all through its industrial nineteenth century, and it was now engaging America in the second decade of its twentieth. A conscious artistic movement had raised its head to declare irreconcilable strife between the creative and the possessive ideal. O'Neill was an integral part—indeed, he became the very symbol—of that Provincetown group which represented the growing rebellion of the American intellectual against a business civilization. In 1914 his revolt was simple and socialistic; in a poem in *The Call* he urged the workers of the world not to fight, asking them if they wished to "bleed and groan—for Guggenheim" and "give your lives—for Standard Oil." By 1917 his feeling against business had become symbolized and personal. "My soul is a submarine," he said in a poem in *The Masses:*

My aspirations are torpedoes.
I will hide unseen
Beneath the surface of life
Watching for ships,
Dull, heavy-laden merchant ships,
Rust-eaten, grimy galleons of commerce
Wallowing with obese assurance,
Too sluggish to fear or wonder,
Mocked by the laughter of the waves
And the spit of disdainful spray.

I will destroy them
Because the sea is beautiful.

The ships against which O'Neill directed his torpedoes were the cultural keels laid in the yards of American business and their hulls were first to be torn by artistic realism. Although we now see the often gross sentimentality of the *S.S. Glencairn* plays and remember with O'Neill's own misgiving the vaudeville success of "In the Zone," we cannot forget that, at the time, the showing of a forecastle on the American stage was indeed something of a torpedo. Not, it is true, into the sides of Guggenheim and Standard Oil, but of the little people who wallowed complacently in their wake.

But O'Neill, not content with staggering middle-class complacency by a representation of how the other half lives, undertook to scrutinize the moral life of the middle class and dramatized the actual struggle between Poet and Business Man. In his first long play, *Beyond the Horizon*, the dreamer destroys his life by sacrificing his dream to domesticity; and the practical creator, the farmer, destroys his by turning from wheat-raising to wheat-gambling. It is a conflict O'Neill is to exploit again and again. Sometimes, as in "Ile" or *Gold*, the lust for gain transcends itself and becomes almost a creative ideal, but always its sordid origin makes it destructive. To O'Neill the acquisitive man, kindly and insensitive, practical and immature, became a danger to life and one that he never left off attacking.

But it developed, strangely, that the American middle class had no strong objection to being attacked and torpedoed; it seemed willing to be sunk for the insurance that was paid in a new strange coin. The middle class found that it consisted of two halves, bourgeoisie and booboisie. The booboisie might remain on the ship but the bourgeoisie could, if it would, take refuge on the submarine. Mencken and Nathan, who sponsored the O'Neill torpedoes, never attacked the middle class but only its boobyhood. Boobish and sophisticated: these were the two categories of art; spiritual freedom could be bought at the price of finding *Jurgen* profound. And so, while the booboisie prosecuted *Desire Under the Elms*, the bourgeoisie swelled the subscription lists of the Provincetown Playhouse and helped the Washington Square Players to grow into the Theatre Guild. An increasingly respectable audience awarded O'Neill no less than three Pulitzer prizes, the medal of the American Academy of Arts and Sciences and a Yale Doctorate of Letters.

O'Neill did not win his worldly success by the slightest compromise of sincerity. Indeed, his charm consisted in his very integrity and hieratic earnestness. His position changed, not absolutely, but relatively to his audience, which was now the literate middle class caught up with the intellectual middle class. O'Neill was no longer a submarine; he had become a physician of souls. Beneath his iconoclasm his audience sensed reassurance.

The middle class is now in such literary disrepute that a writer's ability to please it is taken as the visible mark of an internal rottenness. But the middle class is people; prick them and they bleed, and whoever speaks sincerely to and for flesh and blood deserves respect. O'Neill's force derives in large part from the force of the moral and psychical upheaval of the middle class; it wanted certain of its taboos broken and O'Neill broke them. He was the Dion Anthony to its William Brown; Brown loved Dion: his love was a way of repenting for his own spiritual clumsiness.

Whoever writes sincerely about the middle class must consider the nature and the danger of the morality of "ideals," those phosphorescent remnants of a dead religion with which the middle class meets the world. This had been Ibsen's great theme, and now O'Neill undertook to investigate for America the destructive power of the ideal—not merely the sordid ideal of the Business Man but even the "idealistic" ideal of the Poet. The Freudian psychology was being discussed and O'Neill dramatized its simpler aspects in *Diff'rent* to show the effects of the repression of life. Let the ideal of chastity repress the vital forces, he was saying, and from this fine girl you will get a filthy harridan. The modern life of false ideals crushes the affirmative and creative nature of man; Pan, forbidden the light and warmth of the sun, grows "sensitive and self-conscious and proud and revengeful"—becomes the sneering Mephistophelean mask of Dion.

The important word is *self-conscious*, for "ideals" are part of the "cheating gestures which constitute the vanity of personality." "Life is all right if you let it alone," says Cybel, the Earth Mother of *The Great God Brown*. But the poet of *Welded* cannot let it alone; he and his wife, the stage directions tell us, move in circles of light that represent "auras of egotism" and the high ideals of their marriage are but ways each ego uses to get possession of the other. O'Neill had his answer to this problem of the possessive, discrete personality. Egoism and idealism, he tells us, are twin evils growing from man's suspicion of his life and the remedy is the laughter of Lazarus—"a triumphant, blood-stirring call to that ultimate attainment in which all prepossession with self is lost in an ecstatic affirmation of Life." The ecstatic affirmation of Life, pure and simple, is salvation. In the face of death and pain, man must reply with the answer of Kublai Kaan in *Marco Millions:* "Be proud of life! Know in your heart that the living of life can be noble! Be exalted by life! Be inspired by death! Be humbly proud! Be proudly grateful!"

It may be that the individual life is not noble and that it is full of pain and defeat; it would seem that Eileen Carmody in *The Straw* and Anna Christie are betrayed by life. But no. The "straw" is the knowledge that life is a "hopeless hope"—but still a hope. And nothing matters if you can conceive the whole of life. "Fog, fog, fog, all bloody time," is the chord of resolution of *Anna Christie*. "You can't see vhere you vas going, no. Only dat ole davil, sea—she knows." The individual does not know, but life—the sea—knows.

To affirm that life exists and is somehow good—this, then, became O'Neill's quasi-religious poetic function, nor is it difficult to see why the middle class welcomed it. "Brown will still need me," says Dion, "to reassure him he's alive." What to do with life O'Neill cannot say, but there it is. For Ponce de Leon it is the Fountain of Eternity, "the Eternal Becoming which is Beauty." There it is, somehow glorious, somehow meaningless. In the face of despair one remembers that "Always spring comes again bearing life! Always forever again. Spring again! Life again!" To this cycle, even to the personal annihilation in it, the individual must say "Yes." Man inhabits a naturalistic universe and his glory lies in his recognition of its nature and assenting to it; man's soul, no less than the stars and the dust, is part of the Whole and the free man loves the Whole and is willing to be absorbed by it. In short, O'Neill solves the problem of evil by making explicit what men have always found to be the essence of tragedy—the courageous affirmation of life in the face of individual defeat.

But neither a naturalistic view of the universe nor a rapt assent to life constitutes a complete philosophic answer. Naturalism is the noble and realistic attitude that prepares the way for an answer; the tragic affirmation is the emotional crown of a philosophy. Spinoza—with whom O'Neill at this stage of his thought has an obvious affinity—placed between the two an ethic that arranged human values and made the world possible to live in. But O'Neill, faced with a tragic universe, unable to go beyond the febrilely passionate declaration, "Life is," finds the world impossible to live in. The naturalistic universe becomes too heavy a burden for him; its spirituality vanishes; it becomes a universe of cruelly blind matter. "Teach me to be resigned to be an atom," cries Darrell, the frustrated scientist of *Strange Interlude*, and for Nina life is but "a strange dark interlude in the electrical display of God the father" —who is a God deaf, dumb and blind. O'Neill, unable now merely to accept the tragic universe and unable to support it with man's whole strength—his intellect and emotion—prepares to support it with man's weakness: his blind faith.

For the non-Catholic reader O'Neill's explicitly religious solution is likely to be not only insupportable but incomprehensible. Neither St. Francis nor St. Thomas can tell us much about it; it is neither a mystical ecstasy nor the reasoned proof of assumptions. But Pascal can tell us a great deal, for O'Neill's faith, like Pascal's, is a poetic utilitarianism: he needs it and *will* have it. O'Neill rejects naturalism and materialism as Pascal had rejected Descartes and all science. He too is frightened by "the eternal silence of the infinite spaces." Like Pascal, to whom the details of life and the variety and flux of the human mind were repugnant, O'Neill feels that life is empty—having emptied it—and can fill it only by faith in a loving God. The existence of such a God, Pascal knew, cannot be proved save by the heart's need, but this seemed sufficient and he stood ready to stupefy his reason to maintain his faith. O'Neill will do no less. It is perhaps the inevitable way of modern Catholicism in a hostile world.

O'Neill's rejection of materialism involved the familiar pulpit confusion of philosophical materialism with "crass" materialism, that is, with the preference of physical to moral well-being. It is therefore natural that *Dynamo*, the play in which he makes explicit his anti-materialism, should present characters who are mean and little—that, though it contains an Earth Mother, she is not the wise and tragic Cybel but the fat and silly Mrs. Fife, the bovine wife of the atheist dynamo-tender. She, like other characters in the play, allies herself with the Dynamo-God, embodiment both of the materialistic universe and of modern man's sense of his own power. But this new god can only frustrate the forces of life, however much it at first seems life's ally against the Protestant denials, and those who worship it become contemptible and murderous.

And the contempt for humanity which pervades *Dynamo* continues in *Mourning Becomes Electra*, creating, in a sense, the utter hopelessness of that tragedy. Aeschylus had ended his Atreus trilogy on a note of social reconciliation—after the bloody deeds and the awful pursuit of the Furies, society confers its forgiveness, the Furies are tamed to deities of hearth and field: "This day there is a new Order born"; but O'Neill's version has no touch of this resolution. There is no forgiveness in *Mourning Becomes Electra* because, while there is as yet no forgiving God in O'Neill's cosmos, there is no society either, only a vague chorus of contemptible townspeople. "There's no one left to punish me," says Lavinia. "I've got to punish myself."

It is the ultimate of individual arrogance, the final statement of a universe in which society has no part. For O'Neill, since as far back as *The Hairy Ape*, there has been only the individual and the universe. The social organism has meant nothing. His Mannons, unlike the Atreides, are not monarchs with a relation to the humanity about them, a humanity that can forgive because it can condemn. They act their crimes on the stage of the infinite. The mention of human law bringing them punishment is startlingly incongruous and it is inevitable that O'Neill, looking for a law, should turn to a divine law.

Forgiveness comes in *Ah, Wilderness!* the satyr-play that follows the tragedy, and it is significant that O'Neill should have interrupted the composition of *Days Without End* to write it. With the religious answer of the more serious play firm in his mind, with its establishment of the divine law, O'Neill can, for the first time, render the sense and feel of common life, can actually be humorous. Now the family is no longer destructively possessive as he has always represented it, but creatively sympathetic. The revolt of the young son—his devotion to rebels and hedonists, to Shaw, Ibsen and Swinburne—is but the mark of adolescence and in the warm round of forgiving life he will become wisely acquiescent to a world that is not in the least terrible.

But the idyllic life of *Ah, Wilderness!* for all its warmth, is essentially ironical, almost cynical. For it is only when all magnitude has been removed from humanity by the religious answer and placed in the Church and its God that life can be seen as simple and good. The pluses and minuses of man must be made to cancel out as nearly as possible, the equation must be solved to equal nearly zero, before peace may be found. The hero of *Days Without End* has lived for years in a torturing struggle with the rationalistic, questioning "half" of himself which has led him away from piety to atheism, thence to socialism, next to unchastity and finally to the oblique attempt to murder his beloved wife. It is not until he makes an act of submissive faith at the foot of the Cross and thus annihilates the doubting mind, the root of all evil, that he can find peace.

But the annihilation of the questioning mind also annihilates the multitudinous world. *Days Without End*, perhaps O'Neill's weakest play, is cold and bleak: life is banished from it by the vision of the Life Eternal. Its religious content is expressed not so much by the hero's priestly uncle, wise, tolerant, humorous in the familiar literary convention of modern Catholicism, as by the hero's wife, a humorless, puritanical woman who lives on the pietistic-romantic love she bears her husband and on her sordid ideal of his absolute chastity. She is the very embodiment of all the warping, bullying idealism that O'Neill had once attacked. Now, however, he gives credence to this plaster saintliness, for it represents for him the spiritual life of absolutes. Now for the first time he is explicit in his rejection of all merely human bulwarks against the pain and confusion of life—finds in the attack upon capitalism almost an attack upon God, scorns socialism and is disgusted with the weakness of those who are disgusted with social individualism. The peace of the absolute can be bought only at the cost of blindness to the actual.

The philosophic position would seem to be a final one: O'Neill has crept into the dark womb of Mother Church and pulled the universe in with him. Perhaps the very violence of the gesture with which he has taken the position of passivity should remind us of his force and of what such force may yet do even in that static and simple dark. Yet it is scarcely a likely place for O'Neill to remember Dion Anthony's warning: "It isn't enough to be [life's] creature. You've got to create her or she requests you to destroy yourself."

Bernard De Voto

MINORITY REPORT

You will find the majority opinion in nearly any paper you may pick up. Unquestionably most of the critics and most of the public who think about literature at all will regard the award of a Nobel Prize to Eugene O'Neill as a gratifying recognition of a great dramatic talent. A minority will not, however, and because what may be a signal weakness rather than a great strength of our literature is involved, the *Saturday Review* cannot let the occasion pass without expressing that minority opinion. For the Nobel Prize, although it was once awarded to Rabindranath Tagore, is supposed to recognize only the highest distinction in literature, and Mr. O'Neill falls short of that. He falls short of it both absolutely and relatively. Whatever his international importance, he can hardly be called an artist of the first rank; he is hardly even one of the first-rate figures of his own generation in America.

Mr. O'Neill's good fortune has been his misfortune. He came to Broadway from the little theatre of cheese-cloth and mandolutes at the exact moment when the preciosities of coterie art in general were caught up on the impetus of a national movement. That impetus alone would have conferred success on the mechanical novelties that he brought with him from Washington Square—the off-stage tom-toms, the timed throb of engines and dynamos, the masks alleged to be ever so meaningful, the sirens blowing in the fog. But he also brought with him more important guarantors of success, a training in dramaturgy supervised by George Pierce Baker, and, even more important than this, an inherited instinct for the theatrically effective. Calling on all these, Mr. O'Neill composed some very good early plays; some of them remain among his

---

From the Saturday Review of Literature, *November 21, 1936. Reprinted by the author in his book* Minority Report (*Little, Brown & Co., 1943*). *Used by permission of Mrs. Bernard De Voto.*

best work but it would be absurd to call any of them great drama, and they cannot have figured in the Nobel award. A restless and extremely energetic intelligence, he was already beginning the experiments that were to confuse and confute him when his alliance with the Theatre Guild began.

It is not alleged against the Guild that it created that confusion, but that it contributed more than all other forces to the inflation of his reputation which is so disproportionate to his talents and achievements. There is such a thing as economic determinism of reputation and surely that has had a part here; but a much greater part was intellectual and social determinism. A foundation engaged in the development of dramatic art, the Guild was under every obligation of sense and sentiment to discover a great native dramatist. Need we be surprised that it discovered him in Mr. O'Neill? Its great prestige, its power to compel the admiration of multitudes, its lavish resources for spectacular presentation and for publicity no less, and its austere authority as an arbiter of judgment combined to elevate him to a grandeur which neither criticism nor the public has ventured to impeach. He has had every kind of success that a playwright can have: money, fame, the best directors and designers and actors of his time, a sumptuous collected edition, a critical acclaim so reverent that the more recent treatises discuss him in language usually considered sacrilegious when applied to the merely mortal, and now the Nobel Prize. Here is a great triumph, but a very large part of it is due to prestige and publicity. At best he is only the author of some extremely effective pieces for the theatre. At worst he has written some of the most pretentiously bad plays of our time. He has never been what the Guild and the Nobel jury unite in calling him, a great dramatist.

It is not a derogation but only a definition to say that workable theatricality is the measure of successful playwriting. In the theatre the test is not: Is this true to the realities of human experience? Instead the test is: Is this fictitious representation satisfactory to the artificial conditions of the theatre? With luck—or with genius—a play may pass both tests, but it must pass the second, and if they are in conflict, the first must yield. The theatre is under many limitations: the exigencies of space and time; the dictation of the literal, which requires an actual Peter Pan to swing through actual air on the end of an actual wire in the presence of practicable props; and especially the necessary conditions of people meeting together as an audience, the lowered intelligence, the lulled critical faculty, the enhanced emotionalism and suggestibility of a group, the substitution of emotional accord for the desire to experience and understand that is fed by other forms of literature. Under all these limitations, the theatre succeeds in its own terms. They are terms of the momentarily effective, not the permanently true or the permanently illuminating. Only small and superficial portions of human life can be honestly and thoroughly represented in such terms and under such limitations. Quite properly, the theatre does not care. Where honest and thorough presentation of life makes available material, the theatre will use it; where it does not, the theatre must and cheerfully will depart from it for the sake of the theatrical values. They, the theatrical values, are concerned with something else.

A great dramatist, I take it, is one who has somehow managed to transcend the limitations of the theatre and, while preserving the theatrical values that pass the second test, to add to them some profundity of human experience, human understanding, or human enlightenment that brings the art of the theatre into the same area as the highest art of fiction or poetry. Those who have transcended them—we need name no more than Shaw and Ibsen—have done so by reason of great intelligence, great imagination, and great understanding. The whole truth about Mr. O'Neill is that his gigantic effort to transcend them has been of an altogether different kind. He is a fine playwright who is not sufficiently endowed with those qualities to be a great dramatist but who has tried to substitute for them a set of merely mechanical devices.

Let us recall his career. The charmingly romantic one-act plays were young Greenwich Village. They revolted against the dead theatre of the day chiefly by means of sweetness. They were full of hairy chests, gentlemen rankers burning with despair, and a traditional rhetoric about the sea—the implacable enemy, the immortal lover who covets man, the inappeasable devourer, man's elder love, man's testing ground, the oldest mistress, the primal call. They had novelties of decoration but their effectiveness, like the dialects spoken by the sailors, came from time-honored tricks by which generations of playwrights had lifted the audience out of their seats for the tense half-second that means effectiveness in the theatre.

A group of miscellaneous plays followed, some expressionistic, some realistic, some successful on their own terms, some obviously tending toward the confusion that was soon to follow. Two of them, *The Emperor Jones* and *Anna Christie*, are among the best work that Mr. O'Neill has ever done; of his other plays, only *Ah, Wilderness!* is comparable to them. *Beyond the Horizon* was still youthfully romantic in its conception of disease as heroic, and still very Washington Square in its clichés about sex-starved New England. *The Emperor Jones* was a triumphant experiment in the drama of fantasy, which may last longer than anything else he has written. It was a very effective assault on the emotions, and that path, if followed to the end, might have led him well beyond such work of his colleagues as *Beggar on Horseback*. But in *The Hairy Ape* it began to be apparent that expressionism and Washington Square, the masks and the ballet, the attraction of the allusively and immensely vague, were betraying him: already they seemed subtly counterfeit. *Anna Christie* was something else. It remains his most effective play. But note carefully that its effectiveness is theatrical—of the theatre, not of life. The romantic conception of a prostitute, the Greenwich Village cliché of "dat ol davil sea," the flagrant falsification of life in the oath scene at the end were magnificent theatre, magnificent craftsmanship, but surely they were the very antithesis of great drama. It should be noted here, also, that with *All God's Chillun Got Wings* he began the use of insanity as a solution of all dramatic problems which makes for thrilling effects on the stage but falls short of explaining human life.

Mr. O'Neill then dived into the infinite. He undertook to transcend the theatre, to break the shackles of mortality, to work with the immortal urges and the eternal truths. His characters would not be men and women merely, they would be Man and Woman, they would even be Earth Man and Earth Woman. And this mighty effort to be a great dramatist inexorably proved that he lacked intellectual, emotional, and imaginative greatness. In the theatre he is a master craftsman. But in the cosmos he is a badly rattled Villager straining titanically with platitudes, and laboring to bring forth ineffabilities whose spiritual and intellectual content has been a farcical anticlimax to the agonies of birth.

Lazarus Laughed, *The Great God Brown*, *Marco Millions*, *Dynamo*—one or another of them must be the silliest play of our time. The gorgeous mounting which the Guild gave *Marco Millions* veiled the triviality of the play. Mr. O'Neill was trying to be a metaphysical Sinclair Lewis but he did not make the grade. The play echoes a hundred forgotten mellers, trying to transmute them to poetry and philosophy. But the immortal wisdom of the East comes out very much like Sidney Smith's laundryman in the *Chicago Tribune*, and oriental loveliness and mystery have a heavy odor of Fu Manchu. *Dynamo* will long fascinate connoisseurs of the incredible and contains some of the most amazing nonsense ever spoken seriously in the theatre. But one comes finally to the judgment that *The Great God Brown* is the worst of them. The design is once more to transcend, to Go Beyond—by means of Cybel the Earth Mother and Dionysus, the spirit of anarchic joy that treads down the stale conventions of this world, and the frustrate human spirit tortured and betrayed. But the result is uneasily one of a Model T Euripides—and a feeling that if George White ever set out to do a March of the Earth Mothers, it would look very much like this.

Mr. O'Neill has called himself a poet and a mystic. In these plays he is trying to press beyond the theatre into great drama by means of poetry and mysticism focused through symbolism. But it is the very essence of symbolism that the meaning symbolically conveyed must be a distinguished meaning—a meaning profound and exalted—or the result will be preposterous. And Mr. O'Neill has no such meaning to convey. He has only a number of platitudes which would be comfortably accommodated to the one-acters of Washington Square from which he graduated, or to Dads' Night at a prep school drama festival, but which come out flat and unchanged through as elaborate a mechanism as was ever devised to amplify inanities.

The same lack of profundity, subtlety, and distinguished imagination is quite as clear in the next cycle where, turning from symbolism, Mr. O'Neill occupied himself with racial myths and the unconscious mind. Probably the Nobel award was based on *Strange Interlude* and *Mourning Becomes Electra*, and yet these plays only emphasize what the others had made clear. Here all the strains meet and blend—the novelties of the little theatre substituting for knowledge of the human heart, dodges and devices, a fortissimo assertion of significance, and a frantic grappling with what seem to be immensities but turn out to be one-syllable ideas and mostly wrong at that. The biggest wind-machine in our theatrical history is used to assist the enunciation of platitudes. Mr. O'Neill is dealing with ideas that elude him and straining for achievements beyond his power. Now it may well be that what he tries to do in these plays cannot be done in the theatre at all. But a more flagrant point is that the significances he announces to us are elementary and even rudimentary. The intention is again cosmic but the meaning is very simple indeed, and though the effects are sometimes marvelously successful as theatre they are false as life. Many times these plays reach the highest possible level of theatrical effectiveness, by reason of a superb craftsmanship working for the ends of the theatre in the theatre's terms. (With an overtone from many generations of sure-fire stuff, and the ghost of Monte Cristo raising a finger aloft and intoning "One!") But it is just that—it is not something more. Malicious animal magnetism destroying an unloved husband, a box of poison pills on papa's corpse—that is an expert playwright bringing the audience out of its chairs for the golden half-second. But it is not a sudden flood of light cast by genius into the dark recesses of the soul—it is not great drama giving us understanding more abundantly. Mr. O'Neill intended it to be that, and the burden of the Nobel award is that he succeeded. But what does he tell us, what does he show us, that we did not know before? Wherein is his wisdom, his revelation? Nowhere do we encounter the finality or the reconciliation of great art, nowhere is any fragment of human life remade for us in understanding and splendor. What he tells us is simple, familiar, superficial, and even trite—and because of a shallow misunderstanding of Freud and a windy mysticism, sometimes flatly wrong. It is not great drama for it is not great knowledge. You may add a new volume to the Rover Boys series by setting the action in the unconscious mind, but they will still be the Rover Boys.

Mr. O'Neill has given us many pleasurable evenings in the theatre, though he has also given us some pretty tiresome ones. But he has never yet given us an experience of finality, of genius working on the material proper to genius, of something profound and moving said about life. Just why, then, the Nobel Prize?

Homer E. Woodbridge

BEYOND MELODRAMA

The award of the Nobel Prize in literature to Eugene O'Neill will hardly add to his fame, for his fame already is world-wide. This has been true of perhaps two-thirds of the earlier awards in literature, the rest having gone to writers who were comparatively little known outside their own countries. It is perhaps a question whether in these days of quickened communication international popularity means as much as it once did; it never, of course, was a sure criterion of literary quality. But it is still rare enough to serve as a rough test of achievement. And if the prize was destined to an American playwright, Mr. O'Neill's title to it, quite apart from his European reputation, is indisputable. His plays have been popular and influential at home, both on the stage and in book form; they stand the test of reading, as good plays must. He is easily the foremost of American dramatists, and he is the first and still the only one of them to become widely known outside of America. His plays are translated, acted, and read in most European countries; some of them have been produced even in Japan. Mr. O'Neill is only forty-nine, but he has already done more important and memorable work in the theatre than any American before him.

This is not as high praise as it sounds; for drama has always been the weak spot in American literature. Up to the Great War we produced almost no plays of more than immediate contemporary interest—almost none which had literary value or prospect of permanence. In 1917 Professor Arthur Hobson Quinn, who probably knows as much about American drama as any man living, published a collection of *Representative American Plays*. The book in-

Originally entitled "*Eugene O'Neill,*" South Atlantic Quarterly, *January 1938. Reprinted by permission of Mrs. Homer Woodbridge and Duke University Press.*

cludes seventeen pieces of various periods, from Thomas Godfrey's *Prince of Parthia* in 1767 to Rachel Crothers' *He and She* in 1911. The result is depressing. Not more than four or five of the plays have any distinction as literature; perhaps only one, William Vaughan Moody's *The Faith Healer*, bears the mark of genius. Professor Dickinson's *Outlines of Contemporary Drama*, which includes a survey of the nineteenth century, gives just one rather short paragraph to American drama before 1900, characterizing it as "colonial," and one still shorter to American drama of 1900–1910. To get up much interest in the American theatre before O'Neill one must consider it from the historical or sociological point of view.

Among the Lilliputians Gulliver was a giant, and unquestionably O'Neill's apparent stature has been increased by the mediocrity of the writers with whom we naturally compare him. Because he is the most interesting and original figure who has appeared in the American theatre he has been extravagantly praised. So good a critic as Mr. J. W. Krutch, for instance, can find no one but Shakespeare and the Greeks with whom O'Neill at his best can be compared. "O'Neill," he says, "is almost alone among modern dramatic writers in possessing what appears to be an instinctive perception of what a modern tragedy would have to be." At *Mourning Becomes Electra*, he thinks, "we sit amazed by the height and depth of human passions, by the grandeur and meanness of human deeds." As compared with *Hamlet* and *Macbeth* it lacks only magnificence of language; and for this lack our prosaic age, and not Mr. O'Neill, is to blame. Some voices have been raised in protest, but they have generally erred almost as far on the other side. Thus Mr. H. G. Kemelman, in the *Bookman* for September, 1932, argues at length that O'Neill's plays can be dismissed as mere melodrama. His conclusion is: "The intelligentsia whose patronage has raised O'Neill to his present eminence . . . mistake extravagant purple passages for poetry and a maudlin pathos for power. In short, they call that tragedy which is merely violent and unbalanced melodrama." One trouble with Mr. Kemelman's article is that it is a prosecuting attorney's brief; it presents the evidence for one side of the case, and minimizes or ignores evidence which points in other directions. Anyone who has read O'Neill's plays thoughtfully or seen them in the theatre must have been aware of certain elements of melodrama in them, but there are elements of melodrama in *Macbeth* and *King Lear*. What is needed is an analysis which should attempt to determine how far melodrama enters into O'Neill's work, with what other elements it is combined, and in what proportions. Such an analysis should offer a basis for a fair judgment of the playwright's achievement.

The first necessity is a definition of melodrama, not as a historical form, but as a trait characteristic of the historical form, which appears in plays of different kinds. Melodrama occurs when the playwright sacrifices truth to life (consistency, verisimilitude) in either character or events, for the sake of theatrical effect.[1] This sacrifice of truth often involves violence in language or action; but it does not necessarily include violence, and it is important to recognize that violent words and deeds are by no means always or necessarily melodramatic. Lear's curse upon Goneril is violent and theatrically effective, but not melodramatic, because it is what a man like Lear would say in Lear's situation. So with Othello's murder of Desdemona, and with most of the deeds of violence in Shakespearean tragedy; they are not melodramatic because they are the natural results of character and situation. So with a good deal, though by no means all, of the violent language and action in O'Neill's plays—for instance, the murder of Adam Brant in *The Hunted*. In the recent *Bookman* essay to which I have referred, the author vitiates his conclusions by assuming in his definition that all or nearly all violent speech or action is melodramatic.

The point would not need stressing, except that this confusion between melodrama and violence is so common. Historically, of course, violence has been quite as necessary to tragedy as to melodrama. Let me quote two or three sentences about the essential elements of tragedy: "Tragedy at its best is a vision of the heart of life. The heart of life can only be laid bare in the agony and exultation of dreadful acts. The vision of agony, of spiritual contest, pushed beyond the limits of the dying personality, is exalting and cleansing. . . . Our playwrights have all the powers except that power of exultation which comes from a delighted brooding on excessive, terrible things." This sounds a good deal like a justification of some of O'Neill's plays; it might almost be one of the playwright's own attempts to explain his idea of tragedy. Actually

1. This is substantially Professor Baker's definition.

it is from John Masefield's preface to the *Tragedy of Nan*, and was written in 1911, before Mr. O'Neill had produced a play. The fact is, of course, that no great tragic writer has ever been afraid of violence.

Apart from melodrama, the conspicuous elements in Mr. O'Neill's work are naturalism and symbolism. By naturalism I mean that form of literary art which aims to represent the surfaces of life accurately, and deals by preference with the uglier aspects of life, emphasizing primitive instinct as a motive force in human behavior. Naturalism is a specialized form of realism. By symbolism I mean the use of any part of a play—character, incident, stage business, scene setting—to suggest an idea not obviously necessary to the surface story. What critics usually call O'Neill's expressionism is really his use of symbolism to project the inner life—the "behind-life" as he calls it—of his characters, and convey it to his audience.

It is obvious that two of the three basic elements in O'Neill's work are antagonistic to the third. Melodrama and symbolism are both hostile to naturalism; melodrama because it tends to sacrifice all kinds of truth to life to stage effects; symbolism because it often sacrifices the illusion of reality to the projection of an idea. Many of the inconsistencies and weaknesses of O'Neill's plays are accounted for by these fundamental antagonisms among the elements out of which they are created. He succeeds at times by sheer imaginative force in blending these hostile materials, but the blend is never quite perfect. There are always cracks and flaws.

A natural line of division in Mr. O'Neill's career is the production of *Beyond the Horizon* in 1920 (the play was apparently written two years earlier). Up to this time, he had been learning to use the tools of his craft, and had written only one-act plays. With *Beyond the Horizon*, his first full-length play to be produced, it became clear that he had finished his apprenticeship and had arrived as a playwright to be reckoned with. Let us look first at the one-act plays of the prentice period, which appeared in the volumes entitled *Thirst, and Other One-Act Plays* (1914) and *Moon of the Caribbees* (1918).

Most of the traits of Mr. O'Neill's later work appear, in varying proportions, in one or another of these short pieces. In general, the one-acters may not unfairly be described as naturalistic melodramas; they are naturalistic in style, melodramatic in substance. The substance was probably determined by Mr. O'Neill's temperament (he has a natural liking for what he calls "strong stuff with a kick in each mitt"); the style was determined in part by the fashion of the time among "advanced" lovers of drama. Naturalism, it will be recalled, arrived in the American theatre about a generation after its appearance in Europe. The plots of such plays as "The Web," "Recklessness," "The Rope," and "Where the Cross Is Made" are essentially melodramatic. In "Recklessness," for example, the heroine, Mrs. Baldwin, is in the arms of her chauffeur, when her maid "appears noiselessly"—for no reason at all—"in the doorway from the veranda. They are looking raptly into each other's eyes and do not notice her. She glares at them for a moment, vindictive hatred shining in her black eyes. Then she disappears, as quietly as she came." Of course the jealous girl reports the affair to her mistress's husband, who is a regular melodramatic villain. "His face is puffy and marked by dissipation and his thick-lipped mouth seems perpetually curled in a smile of cynical scorn. His eyes are small with heavily drooping lids that hide their expression." He chokes the tale-telling maid, shouting, "You lie! You lie! Tell me you lie, damn you, or I'll choke you to hell!" But she is supplied with evidence in the form of a purloined letter, and Baldwin proceeds to plot the murder of the handsome chauffeur. Pretending that his wife has been taken suddenly ill, he sends him after a doctor, in a car which he knows has something wrong with the steering gear, telling him to "drive like hell!" Contrary to all probability, but strictly according to the villain's plan, Fred is killed before he has got down the hill to the main road, and his mangled body is brought in later before the eyes of the guilty wife, who at first shrieks and faints, and after recovering runs upstairs and shoots herself. This is the most purely melodramatic in plot of the one-act plays, though several others are not far behind. But among the early one-acters there is much better stuff than this. "Warnings" (the tale of the radio man who goes deaf) is unsatisfactory in construction and slightly melodramatic at times, but deals sympathetically with a really tragic situation. "Fog," certainly the best piece of writing in the earlier volume, is reminiscent of Maeterlinck in its creation of atmosphere and in its use of symbolism; it marks the first appearance of this important element in

O'Neill's work. Stronger and finer work in both characterization and atmosphere is found in "Moon of the Caribbees," the title-piece of the 1918 volume. Here two characters are tellingly sketched in the talk on the deck between the English sailor Smitty and the hard-boiled Donkeyman. In the distant chanting of the negroes on shore Mr. O'Neill uses effectively a device similar to the beating of the tom-tom in *The Emperor Jones*. The play gives the impression of a dramatic poem in rough prose; it is a striking instance of O'Neill's occasional imaginative and poetic use of coarse and ugly speech. "Bound East for Cardiff" and "In the Zone" are bits of honest and vivid naturalism, unmarred by melodrama. "The Long Voyage Home," another powerful little piece, brutally naturalistic at times, is touched with melodrama only in the unnatural perfection of the dramatic irony.

In "Ile," which is sometimes (I think mistakenly) regarded as the best of the one-act plays, I find the other and more objectionable type of melodrama—that in which verisimilitude of character is sacrificed for stage effect. The theme, it will be recalled, is the struggle in Captain Keeney's mind between his determination not to turn his ship homeward until her hold is filled with "ile," and his love for his wife, which we are to believe is genuine and deep. His crew is on the point of mutiny, and he sees that his wife is in imminent danger of going insane unless he turns southward. He is on the verge of yielding, when the news of clearing weather and whales beyond the ice to the north hardens him, and in his resolution to get that "ile" at any cost he scarcely seems to notice that his wife's mind has given way. Here we have the first significant instance in O'Neill's work of the fascination which an obsession exercises over him. The captain becomes for him a symbol of blind will; and the symbol so dominates the playwright's imagination that he loses sight of the captain's humanity. The captain's hardness is under the circumstances incredible; and the upshot is that the character is ruthlessly sacrificed for the glory of the symbol and the splendid theatrical "punch" of the conclusion, where the captain goes off in the boat leaving his wife insanely fingering the keys of the organ. Dr. Johnson said that to Shakespeare a pun was the fatal Cleopatra, for which he was well content to lose the world; to O'Neill an obsession is the fatal Cleopatra, for which he counts all kinds of truths to life well lost. It is not merely the illusion of surface reality that is destroyed by such obsessions; it is the inner truth of character. And we shall find them again and again in O'Neill's later plays—in *The Hairy Ape*, and *The First Man*, and *Diff'rent*, and *Dynamo*, and *Lazarus Laughed*, and to a less degree in *Strange Interlude* and *Mourning Becomes Electra*. Symbolism, developing from obsession and leading to melodrama —that is the formula of O'Neill's besetting sin.

These early pieces show, then, that O'Neill began as a writer of naturalistic melodrama, that he soon developed a talent for characterization and the evocation of atmosphere, and in two or three plays shook himself free of the shackles of melodrama; that in "Ile," the most characteristic of his early plays, his fondness for obsession led him to a kind of symbolism, and coalesced with his love of striking stage effects to create a new variety of melodrama. In his later work the element of naturalism tends to diminish, though it never quite disappears (except, perhaps, in *Lazarus Laughed*); the element of symbolism tends to increase, though very irregularly; and the element of melodrama remains approximately constant, though it appears in various forms. On the whole, though the symbolism greatly heightens the imaginative appeal of some of the plays, it is more often a curse than a blessing, and it is disastrous when it gets out of control. In most of the stronger and finer plays—*The Emperor Jones*, *Anna Christie*, *Strange Interlude*, *Mourning Becomes Electra*—it is subordinated and used chiefly to create overtones; in some of the weakest or most questionable—*The Fountain*, *The Great God Brown*, *Dynamo*, *Lazarus Laughed* —it becomes dominant, and, sometimes in alliance with melodrama, wrecks the play. It is powerfully used in *The Hairy Ape* through most of the piece; but when near the end it takes control, reality and emotional appeal fade away.

Of the full-length plays, *Gold*, which in composition belongs to the same year as *Beyond the Horizon*, may conveniently be glanced at first. I have no wish to stress the weaknesses of the play, especially as Mr. O'Neill has repented of it among his sins (along with *The First Man*, *The Fountain*, and *Welded*). But it happens to illustrate rather aptly the two kinds of melodrama which we have found in the one-act pieces. The first act gives us the melodrama of improbable events—shipwrecked sailors in the South Seas at the point of death from thirst, the discovery of supposed treasure, scantily motivated murder. Act II shows Captain Bartlett, like Captain Keeney in "Ile," sacrificing his wife to his obsession. The later acts show the influence of the Captain's fixed idea upon his impressionable son, who acquires the obsession in his turn. The play is artistically a failure, but its defects are significant of certain weaknesses of the author.

Beyond the Horizon shows us strong drama emerging from rural melodrama. In the conventional rusticity of its setting, in the type characters of Farmer Mayo and his wife and the purely typical stage figures of the sea captain uncle and the doctor, in the country love idyl, the play is strongly reminiscent of *Way Down East* or *Shore Acres*. Melodramatic touches of the more distinctive O'Neill sort appear in the occasional outbursts of emotion too violent for the situation; for instance, in the brutal violence of some of Andy's speeches to Ruth after Robert's death. Yet the main action of the play is finely conceived, and the relation between the two contrasted brothers is strongly and skillfully handled. The play falls short of greatness, chiefly because even the best drawn characters remain types; they are never quite individualized. *Diff'rent*, the two-act piece produced in the same year, has a good naturalistic first act, but turns melodramatic in Act II. Here two of the leading characters, Captain Williams and Emma, are the victims of obsessions which lead to theatrical and highly improbable suicides.

Anna Christie is the best of O'Neill's naturalistic plays, and perhaps the most moving of all his plays on the stage. The play is not free from melodramatic traits, of which the hardest to defend is the change in the character of Anna. If one stops to consider, it is not easy to believe that the soul of a prostitute could be cleansed and ennobled by being exposed to the influence of the sea while she is living for a few weeks on a coal barge. The dramatist manages the transition so skillfully, however, that this improbability is scarcely felt in the theatre. For the so-called "happy ending," which has been criticized as melodramatic, Mr. O'Neill's own defense seems perfectly valid: it is not really an ending at all, but a pause, a "comma" in the action, during which the forces hostile to Anna and Mat are gathering themselves for a new attack. Anna's father, old Chris, is a triumph of naturalistic characterization, a really great and memorable figure. The rather slight symbolical elements in the play are strictly subordinated to the characters and the story.

The Emperor Jones, *The First Man*, and *The Hairy Ape*, unlike as they are in other respects, all deal with obsessions. *The Emperor Jones* is a masterly study in fear. Here we have an obsession which does not lead to melodrama, and an entirely successful use of the "expressionistic" method, through which the individual and racial memories of Jones are objectified. The play is a *tour de force* of a very special and limited type; but it is an almost perfect example of that type. Though it lacks elements of greatness which appear in some of O'Neill's later plays, it remains probably his most complete and satisfactory artistic achievement. *The Hairy Ape* is only a partial success; *The First Man* is by common consent a failure. What are the reasons for the wide differences in achievement among these plays?

One reason undoubtedly is that in *Jones* the playwright's objective was more sharply limited, and hence more attainable. But the chief reason, I believe, is that in the negro play the obsession remains a mere obsession; it does not swallow up the character. The line that divides hallucination from objective reality is kept clear. *The Hairy Ape* is measurably successful because until the last scenes Yank, too, remains a man—a sort of modern Caliban, produced by our industrial society, disowned by it, and rebellious. In the last scenes, however, he becomes a symbol; and it is as a symbol that he lets the gorilla out of the cage, and claims brotherhood with him. In these scenes symbolism leads straight to melodrama. In *The First Man*, Curtis Jayson, the anthropologist, likewise becomes so dominated by his "humor" of zeal for exploration that he, too, loses his humanity and becomes a mere idea in coat and trousers. Hence his melodramatic behavior after the birth of his child.

At about this point (1922) or a little later, Mr. O'Neill seems to have become conscious of the difficulty in blending symbolism and naturalism; and his later plays tend to be differentiated, either largely naturalistic, or largely symbolic. To the first group belong *Desire Under the Elms*, *Strange Interlude*, and *Mourning Becomes Electra;* to the second *The Fountain*, *The Great God Brown*, and *Lazarus Laughed*. In *All God's Chillun Got Wings* and *Dynamo*, however, he again attempted a fusion of the clashing elements; in neither case with much success. Throughout the playwright remains faithful (in his fashion) to his old love Melodrama; he seems never to feel any difficulty in combining this with either naturalism or symbolism. Examples of Mr. O'Neill's fidelity to melodrama are Ella's inadequately motivated violence in *All God's Chillun Got Wings* and her mental breakdown; Abbie's incredible murder of her baby in *Desire Under the Elms;* the theatrical climax to Act VI in *Strange Interlude*, where Nina, after asserting her claim to her three men, kisses each one in turn as she goes out; and Reuben's shooting Ada and throwing himself upon the dynamo in *The Dynamo*. In this last we have another instance of a character who through an obsession becomes a symbol, and then plunges to a melodramatic end. The heroines of *Strange Interlude* and *Mourning Becomes Electra* show symptoms at times of the disease which might be called "symbolitis"; thus Nina almost becomes a personification of what Albany called "the undistinguished space of woman's will"—the boundless range of female lust; and Lavinia at one time becomes almost a symbol of revenge. In proportion as the two heroines approximate these personified abstractions, they tend to act melodramatically. But fortunately neither of them ever quite turns into a mere symbol; and because they remain human, though at times on the uttermost verge of humanity, *Strange Interlude* and *Mourning Becomes Electra* are stronger and better plays than, for example, *The Hairy Ape*.

It is for these two remarkable plays, I believe, along with *The Emperor Jones*, *Anna Christie*, and two or three of the one-act pieces, that Mr. O'Neill seems at present most likely to be remembered. In the plays which are romantic in spirit, such as *The Fountain*, and *Marco Millions*, and in those which he tried to make chiefly symbolic, such as *The Great God Brown* and *Lazarus Laughed*, he is handicapped by his lack of an appropriate style. The only idiom of which he is really a master is the naturalistic idiom. In *Lazarus Laughed* and to some extent in *The Great God Brown* he tried to create a poetic style to fit his theme; but though we must respect the sincerity of his purpose, we cannot feel that he succeeded. The materials are too obdurate. Even Ibsen, who had been a great poet in his time, felt that he had failed to blend perfectly his symbolism and poetry with his realistic idiom in *The*

Master Builder; and Mr. O'Neill has never attained command of a poetic style. He is therefore at his best when, as in *Strange Interlude* and *Mourning Becomes Electra*, he works with naturalistic themes. Neither play is free from melodrama; neither is a great or perfect masterpiece. But *Strange Interlude* is a fascinating dramatic novel, much better to read than to see on the stage; and *Mourning Becomes Electra* is a powerful naturalistic tragedy in which Mr. O'Neill's technique has gained much from the study of his Greek models, in simplicity and economy of structure, in steady advance toward an inevitable end. The play is Mr. O'Neill's best piece of dramatic story-telling. It is not a great tragedy, partly because it is at times melodramatic, partly because the leading characters, as in so many naturalistic dramas, are motivated almost solely by hate and lust, so that they cannot command our sympathy. The chief melodramatic elements are furnished by the heroine, Lavinia, who dominates the action. Perhaps the most startling instance occurs when, after sending her brother to his death, she makes excited love speeches to Peter while she waits impatiently for the pistol-shot that will announce Orin's suicide. Here plainly, it seems to me, verisimilitude of character is ruthlessly sacrificed to stage effect; Lavinia is quite incredible in this scene. *Mourning Becomes Electra* belongs in substance not with *Oedipus* or the *Oresteia*, nor with *Othello* or *Lear*, but with such Elizabethan plays as *The Maid's Tragedy*, *The Revenger's Tragedy*, and *'Tis Pity She's a Whore*. In style, of course, through their superior command of great imaginative phrase, through the appeal of poetry, which partly redeems their ugliness, these decadent Elizabethan tragedies have a great advantage over Mr. O'Neill's. But thanks to modern Freudian psychology, *Mourning Becomes Electra* is more elaborately motivated than any of them; like them it is marred by melodrama, and like them it has what Mr. Masefield called "the power . . . of delighted brooding over excessive, terrible things."

The last two plays, *Ah, Wilderness!* and *Days Without End*, show Mr. O'Neill in contrasted moods, one of them new, the other a development of a mood familiar in his earlier work. *Ah, Wilderness!* has affinities in style with some of his earlier plays, notably with *Beyond the Horizon* and the first act of *Diff'rent;* like them it presents an American scene with straightforward realism. But in spirit it differs widely from these plays and from all Mr. O'Neill's previous work. It is a comedy of family life, written in a mood of genial and tolerant sympathy. Its humor, never subtle and sometimes rather too heavily underlined, is none the less genuine and hearty. Nat Miller, the father of the family, is one of the most individual and vital characters Mr. O'Neill has drawn; he will be remembered, I think, with old Chris Christopherson and perhaps Marco Millions. The young people in this story, especially Richard, recall Booth Tarkington's portraits of adolescence, though they are outlined with a rather heavier hand. All of them are substantial youngsters, with no taint of morbidity, and the central theme of the play, the fifteen-year-old Richard's love affair, is treated directly and honestly, and with more sympathy than calf love generally gets in the theatre. All the more important people in the story are likeable, and evidently Mr. O'Neill liked them himself. It is partly for this reason, perhaps, that *Ah, Wilderness!* is the truest picture of American life that Mr. O'Neill has painted. He has again bewildered some of his critics, this time by writing a play which contains nothing morbid and nothing sensational, but which relies for its effects on shrewd and sympathetic observation of a group of normal human beings. The scene is in Connecticut, but it might have been almost anywhere in the northern half of the United States; the dialogue impresses me as savoring more of the Middle West than of New England.

Days Without End deals with a theme which has long haunted the dramatist—the religious quest for reality. He has treated other aspects of it in *The Great God Brown*, *Dynamo*, and *Lazarus Laughed*. In *Days Without End* he has achieved for it a clearer and stronger dramatic form; he has seen the fundamental issue more distinctly, and has embodied it in a better planned and more dramatic plot. Mr. O'Neill calls the piece "a modern miracle play"; it is rather a modern morality. The subject is the fight for a man's soul between his better and worser selves. The technique is realistic, with one exception: the divided personality of the hero is symbolized by the two figures of John, the better self, and Loving, the Mephistopheles-self ever at his elbow, who wears a mask identical with John's face. Loving is seen only by the audience. Persons on the stage hear his speeches, but believe that they come from John. The story is an ingenious one, involving the plot of a novel which John Loving is preparing to write, and which parallels the events of his own life. Eventually, through sin, suffering and repentance, John conquers Loving, who dies rather melodramatically as John kneels before a crucifix in a church.

It is true that in this play as in others where Mr. O'Neill has tried to fuse symbolism and realism, they prove refractory. But the significance of the *alter ego* Loving is so obvious and simple that we can accept him much more easily than the complicated mask symbolism in *The Great God Brown*. Mr. O'Neill asks us to make only one impossible supposition, and though that remains an alien element in the play, we can reconcile ourselves to it for the sake of seeing what the dramatist will do with it. What he does is to use it skillfully as a dominant note in an interesting story. For me John Loving never becomes quite a credible character, because I do not believe that a personality is ever divided quite so sharply in just this way between a good self and a bad self. But he is more nearly credible and more nearly normal than Stevenson's Dr. Jekyll-Mr. Hyde, since the two selves are represented not as alternating in control, but as constantly in combat. It is not, perhaps, a great play, but it is the best morality we have produced in America.

In their different fashions, the two plays are significant of a change in Mr. O'Neill's thinking. He has been on a quest for human values; and like Mr. Chesterton's imaginary explorer, he has sailed around the world and discovered what he was seeking at home. *Ah, Wilderness!* reveals as hearty an enjoyment of the simple and normal human relationships as you can find in Mr. Tarkington or Miss Cather: *Days Without End* is as sincerely orthodox as *Everyman*. Mr. O'Neill seems at last to have come out on the side of the angels.

His failures and imperfect successes are due partly, as we have seen, to the inherent difficulty of the tasks he has attempted. They are also due in part to certain individual limitations and defects of his talent. Perhaps his most obvious limitation is the inadequacy and intermittent appearance of his sense of humor. He has, indeed, a rather grim irony; *Marco Millions* shows satiric power, and *Ah, Wilderness!* a broad recognition of humorous values. But a richer sense of humor would have preserved him from many melodramatic extravagances, and from such defects as the crude treatment in *Diff'rent* of the results of sex suppression; also from the intolerably mechanical laughter of *Lazarus Laughed*. Second, his grasp on character is uncertain. How few people in his plays do we remember as individuals!—Emperor Jones, old Chris, Marco, perhaps Lavinia in *Electra*, Nat Miller in *Ah, Wilderness!*—not many more. As Halsted Welles says: "O'Neill's portraits are done in wood block; no fine lines, but striking masses of black and white." Third, he lacks the power of happy memorable phrase; he seldom or never gives final form to an idea in words. There are few or no lines in his plays that will become familiar quotations. Fourth, he lacks control, and does not distinguish between force and violence. He has the ex-invalid's love of strong words and violent deeds—what Dean Briggs used to call "false robustness." Thus he often spoils his effect by laying on his colors too thick.

These are heavy handicaps, and it is evidence of O'Neill's genius that in spite of them he triumphs. His great and central merit is that he is a serious and generally sincere artist in drama. He has never compromised with box-office demands, but has won his success without tampering with his artistic conscience. G. J. Nathan, in his *Notebooks*, quotes a saying of one of our old-school popular playwrights, Augustus Thomas: "The first principle of playwriting is to bear in mind the entertainment of the masses." Nathan compares this with a recent utterance of O'Neill: I would put it beside a sentence or two which O'Neill wrote in 1922. "I intend to use whatever I can make my own . . . and I shall never be influenced by any consideration but one: 'Is it the truth as I know it, or better still, *feel* it? If so, shoot, and let the splinters fly where they will. If not, not.' " O'Neill has always, I think, been faithful to his vision, such as it is; and this is the root of all good writing. In the second place, O'Neill has at his best a fine sense of dramatic values, and a penetrating insight into emotion. His imagination has a fiery heat which sometimes fuses the discordant elements of which his work is composed, and makes us forget all his defects. Finally, he has always shown a splendid artistic courage. He has dared to try new things, and to do old things in new ways. He has greatly widened the range of our theatre.

John Gassner

HOMAGE TO O'NEILL

For some years now I have felt that the most distressing aspects of the current American theatre are its easy conscience concerning neglect of O'Neill's plays and the apparent indifference with which he is regarded by the young. There would be less reason for dismay if the neglect were a decision of intelligent criticism or, better still, if O'Neill had been supplanted by one or more playwrights of comparable stature whose idiom happened to be more "modern." Such, however, is hardly the case. The representatives of a younger generation than O'Neill's who have been incisively critical of him have had too little influence to stand in the way of professional revivals of his work or to set the young against him. Nor are the young actually set against him; perhaps they are even vaguely impressed when they read his plays—which is never the same thing as seeing them, since "theatre" even more than "drama" was his special endowment. They are merely lackadaisical in accepting his significance; his importance to them appears to be more a matter of academic fiat than of enthusiasm for his published work.

As for the displacement of O'Neill by fresher talent, it is true that a few newspaper reviewers in the nineteen-thirties, notably the late Burns Mantle, ventured the opinion that the glory had descended upon Maxwell Anderson while others placed O'Neill's laurels on the fiery young head of Clifford Odets. And more recently a few have supported the candidacy of Arthur Miller and Tennessee Williams for the honor. Yet it must be apparent that no one has arisen in two decades to take O'Neill's place. When the work of the aforementioned playwrights is reviewed, can more be said than that it is possible to set against his substantial output of drama one single play by Anderson (*Winterset*), one by Miller

From Theatre Time, *Summer 1951. Reprinted by permission of the author.*

(*Death of a Salesman*), and perhaps two pieces by Williams, *The Glass Menagerie* and *A Streetcar Named Desire?* These and other American playwrights who have made an impression since O'Neill delivered *Mourning Becomes Electra* in 1931 remind me in some respects of the neo-classic playwrights who succeeded the "noble brood" of Shakespeare and his fellow-Jacobeans after 1660. They are free from the awkwardness of the giants, but they are not giants.

As O'Neill wasted by disease lies in a Boston hospital a thin shadow of himself, and as it is unlikely that he will write again, I feel a pang not merely for the suffering of a fellow man, but for the playwright who, along with Shaw, gave my former organization, the Theatre Guild, much of the importance it possessed in its pioneering years. I also feel a sharp twinge for the professional theatre which, except for the Theatre Guild production of *The Iceman Cometh* in 1946 and of an out-of-town tryout in 1947, has not produced his work for well over a decade—a condition that could never have arisen in the European repertory theatre in the case of one of its major playwrights except in war-time. And I feel sorry for the new generation that has been deprived of the opportunity of experiencing his kind of theatre, of the element of discovery or rediscovery in it, and of the reaching out, or even the fumbling for, greatness that his work represented. As for those of us who grew up in the theatre of the nineteen-twenties when he became our major dramatist, it can be said with certainty that he served us as a symbol of our trust in the greatness and splendor of our theatre's future. We are not necessarily blind to his shortcomings and only pardonably nostalgic when we recall the sense of exaltation that suffused us with the appearance of many of his plays. We cannot help feeling that a mighty presence has receded from our somewhat bleary view. Our mood cannot but be elegiac. We feel the force of what Rupert Brooks wrote in his youthful book on the late Elizabethan playwright John Webster, to whom contemporaries referred as "crabbed Websterio" very much as some people declared O'Neill to be crabbed. Like Webster, O'Neill seems to us a receding titan, "the last of Earth," even if he occasionally merited the reproach Bernard Shaw leveled at Webster when he called that sultry dramatist of extreme passions a waxwork show-man—a "Tussaud laureate."

It is difficult to recover for the young our original rapture, which in many instances perhaps has diminished even for us. Although the American theatre, no doubt, has as many youthful enthusiasts and aspirants now as it had in our green years, their hopes for the theatre as a temple of art are, with good reason, considerably more temperate. We were just building a new stage that would accommodate the aims and achievements of the men who founded the modern drama and theatre in Europe. We came somewhat late to this dispensation of modernity, it is true. But our sense of discovery, transforming itself at that time into exploration and settlement, was exhilarating. And in practice we saw ourselves—and chiefly in the mirror of O'Neill, the Provincetown Players, and the young Theatre Guild—as pioneers of "art theatre" in the Western hemisphere. We were celebrants, if not indeed practicing priests, of springtime rites by means of which we tasted the bread of Naturalism and the wine of Symbolism for the salvation of our souls and of theatrical art. It is difficult as well to engage the young in our pristine interests. We sought self-expression while present concerns are properly with survival. We wanted to be free artists whereas the young of the present period, again quite understandably, want to strike roots in a profession—and as quickly as possible. We despised security whereas they, very sensibly, seek it and count themselves fortunate if they can find it. We *left* our homes whereas they want to *build* homes. We wanted to "live dangerously." They on the contrary, have had their fill of recent danger since the start of the Second World War and are most directly affected in a world that is again turning into a holocaust.

We were, in short, romanticists, and O'Neill—whether he wrote technically realistic or expressionist dramas—was a romanticist with us. The young of today are, by comparison, realists, and O'Neill's metaphysical gloom and dismay may strike them as curious and extravagant. He may strike them as a man tilting at windmills in a self-induced nightmare while they have to push against barriers and barbed wire put in their way by others than themselves. In 1912, the notable Spanish man of letters Miguel de Unamuno wrote *The Tragic Sense of Life*, which had considerable vogue here in the early nineteen-twenties. He made anguish of the soul a condition for rising above the uninspiring life of modern society and declared an insatiable thirst for transcendental truth to be the heroic fate of man. The Salamancan professor concluded his farewell to the reader of the book with the sentence: "And may God deny you peace, but give you glory!" It seemed like a good prayer to our generation of rebels against Main Street complacency and materialistic values. One rather suspects that today most people would gladly forego the "glory" and settle for the "peace"—if they could have it.

Primary for O'Neill was a cosmic anguish. It was anguish over the inscrutability of fate and over the search for the faith he personally lost in abandoning Catholicism and that others had lost in abandoning the various religions into which they had been born. The twist of the tragic rack on which our Eugene O'Neill placed both his dreamers and his materialists—whether in *Beyond the Horizon*, *Desire Under the Elms*, *The Great God Brown*, or *Days Without End*—was loud in the theatres where his plays were performed. The rack could be love and life frustrated by possessiveness or twisted into hate by failure, lust, or environment. The rack upon which he stretched his characters could be past life and the sense of devouring fate—Chris Christopherson's "ole davil sea" in *Anna Christie*. The torment could come from man's sense of being separated from nature and not yet attaining complete humanity, of not "belonging" in the universe, as in *The Hairy Ape;* or of not belonging to either the old supernatural god and the new scientific god represented by the machine, as in *Dynamo;* or of not belonging to oneself and of not quite belonging to any all-fulfilling love, as in *Strange Interlude;* or of wanting to belong, incestuously, to a forbidden object, as in *Mourning Becomes Electra.* Wherever the tension came from, the suffering blackened man's horizons in O'Neill's dramas while the worshippers of material comfort rode the crest of optimism under Presidents Harding, Coolidge, and Herbert Hoover.

O'Neill cast a weird shadow on the easeful life, on money-bought comfort and specious consolations. He stood stonily unreconciled in the land of plenty and promise. He was heroically saturnine. When he smiled for more than a fleeting moment in his plays, it was mainly to smile to scorn the American Babbitt he incarnated in a Venetian one, the Marco Polo of *Marco Millions.* Not until 1933, in recalling the beginning of our tragic century in

Ah, Wilderness!, was his smile genial, steady, and conciliatory to life and to a father-image. His major theme was man's disorientation, man's bedevilment from within and from without. O'Neill made himself the dramatist of ironic Fate and of the psychological tensions Freud's interpreters and misinterpreters were then communicating to us in books and lectures. And the young and the brave of the nineteen-twenties found exhilaration in his confronting the bitter "truth" for them so stalwartly—even if many of them were more inclined to make parlor palaver rather than drama out of it, unless they made melodrama out of it by drinking themselves into a frenzy during the years of the "noble experiment." The important point, of course, is that O'Neill made strong drama and exciting theatre out of this "truth." He took for his masters the Greek tragedians of fate, to whom he ultimately paid the tribute of imitation in *Mourning Becomes Electra*, and Strindberg, the Scandinavian dramatist of man's division and search for reunification, to whom he also paid the tribute of imitation in *Welded* and *Strange Interlude*.

O'Neill was not unaware of society and its effects, I hasten to add, although neither his anti-political nor his leftist critics have cared to concede this fact. Surely his ironic romance *Marco Millions* made an explicit reckoning of the era of Prosperity and of the mounting stockmarket. His "hairy ape," the stoker Yank, was Worker as well as Man. The society he presented in *The Hairy Ape* with the slumming heiress Mildred Douglas and the spats-wearing automatons of the Fifth Avenue Easter parade scene had what the leftists of the nineteen-thirties called "social significance." He also took sharp notice of racial discrimination and slum life in *All God's Chillun Got Wings*, of poverty and prostitution in *Anna Christie*, of grinding and narrowing impoverished farm life in *Beyond the Horizon*, and of the loneliness and sorry satisfactions of sea-faring men in the *S. S. Glencairn* one-act cycle. The tensions produced by New England patriarchal authority and the struggle for land figured in *Desire Under the Elms*. Brahmin family pride, joy-denying puritanism, and mercantile possessiveness were the correlates of the love drama and incest tragedy of *Mourning Becomes Electra*.

Deny it who can! O'Neill, who contributed to the Socialist *Call* in his early days of journalism and who mingled with the political vanguard of liberals associated with the Provincetown Players, was a social critic of sorts. And more important to art is the fact that he rendered life and speech in his realistic plays authentically. He did not abandon colloquial dialogue until late in the nineteen-twenties, and then only for good reasons—and he returned to it in 1939 with the writing of *The Iceman Cometh*. He depicted environment scrupulously. And he was virtually the first serious American dramatist of any standing to bring characters from all walks of life on to the stage, noting their origins of race and background with sympathy and understanding. It would not be difficult to sustain the point that he gave us social pictures and socially-conditioned, if not altogether socially-determined, actions with greater credibility and vitality than most "social dramatists" of the nineteen-thirties and since then. He is, indeed, historically important as the first American to make naturalist art prevail on our stage.

Nevertheless, he was not a "naturalist," and struck out, in fact, against the belief that mere transcriptions of life were the province of art. He fused naturalistic detail with symbolist mood, suggestiveness, and symbol. And taking his cue from his admired Strindberg, he resorted to the "expressionist" dramatic style of distortion of action, speech, and scene, as in the weird calvary of his Emperor Jones through the jungle and in the Fifth Avenue scene of *The Hairy Ape*. Tireless in his search for theatrical means of projecting the inner life and the metaphysical idea, he used interior monologue—speech on different levels of consciousness—in *Strange Interlude*, and he experimented with masks as a method of dramatization—with partial success in *The Great God Brown* and with virtually none in *Lazarus Laughed*. He even employed monologue in one highly effective scene of so realistic a comedy as *Ah, Wilderness!*, and he split the protagonist of *Days Without End* into two characters who had to be played by two actors. This constant, if not indeed always satisfactory, experimentation, is actually another important feature of O'Neill's work. It was his role to open all the stops of theatre art in America, and we have reason to be grateful to him.

The well known restiveness of his personal life had its correlate in his restiveness as an artist which made him seek new forms of expression even after succeeding in one particular style, and the unpredictability of his style added to the excitement that his playwriting brought to an increasing number of playgoers. To contend that this tendency to shift the artistic base of his work prevented O'Neill from completely perfecting himself on one basis is legitimate. To protest that he should not have done so is absurd. He acted under artistic, as well as psychological, compulsion in the flux of his life and in the flux of the transitional civilization apparent in both drama and fiction after 1914. He entertained extremely high expectations for the theatre which the success of motion pictures and radio, as well as high production costs, had not yet dampened for the profession; and he had high, sometimes recklessly high, ambitions for himself as a dramatist. In *Strange Interlude* and *Mourning Becomes Electra*, as well as later in *The Iceman Cometh*, O'Neill even violated the sacred right of the playgoer to discharge his obligations to the stage in two hours and a half of theatre attendance. He resorted to epic dimensions, taking some risk of introducing elephantiasis into playwriting. *Strange Interlude* acquired some of the qualities of a large impressionist or expressionist novel. *Mourning Becomes Electra* brought back the spaciousness of the Aeschylean trilogy.

He also aspired to the estate of a poetic dramatist, and he rightly sensed that his artistic necessity and the requirements of his matter and point of view would be unfulfilled unless he became one. Whether he succeeded is debatable. It is a strongly held opinion that he lacked "language" equal to the reach of his non-verbal powers. This was noted with particular justice in the case of *Mourning Becomes Electra*. Granted the validity of the charge, it is nonetheless possible and only right to modify and moderate it. As long as he wrote about common life—of sailors and farmers and social outcasts—he managed his language securely, often with strong effect, sometimes with poetic overtones appropriate to his subject. When he set out to be deliberately poetic, he failed—sometimes embarrassingly. When he turned to middle-class or upper-class society, he missed fire in those parts of his plays in which he tried to generalize a feeling or an idea. Yet it may be conceded that even then he could achieve a poetic effect of low degree through the full rhythms of his sentences, if not through cadences and imagery.

If my memory serves, he was once referred to as a "prose Shakespeare." His plight, apart from personal reasons of insufficient endowment and of insufficient control over slang and colloquialisms (as in the constant harping on "pipe-dreams" in *The Iceman*), was due to the modern division between prose and dramatic poetry—a large subject which cannot be explored here. If, because of his turbulence and reiterations of an idea, he also appeared to lack "taste," it is questionable whether he really lacked it. It is sufficiently present, for example, in *Ah, Wilderness!;* and it is difficult for me to believe that I am the only one who found a considerable measure of it in *Desire Under the Elms*, in my opinion his best play. He simply did not bother about "taste" or balance when the surge of conflict and anguish was strong. Those who press the charge of want of "poetry" in the man should be reminded, moreover, that he got his "poetry," as other modern playwrights have done, not from verbal beauty but from the breadth and reach of his imagination, mood, or feeling, and especially, from his theatrical—at times exaggeratedly theatrical—sense. If he was not felicitous in creating verbal poetry, he often created a "poetry of the theatre"—this in effects of which a few examples are the tom-toms in *Emperor Jones*, the firemen's forecastle and the Fifth Avenue nightmares of *The Hairy Ape*, the mask and transformations effects of *The Great God Brown*, the evocation of the farmhouse and land in *Desire Under the Elms*, and the Greek colonnade, the chanty refrain, and Electra-Lavinia's tragic closing of the doors upon herself in *Mourning Becomes Electra.*

O'Neill did not become the full-fledged tragic poet he evidently aspired to be. And want of language was only one reason. Another was his tendency to set up abstract personalities and issues, as most conspicuously in *Dynamo* and *Lazarus Laughed*, or to schematize characters and deprive them of some of their life—this in order to develop a psychological conception or an argument. This tendency can be found in *The Great God Brown* and even in *Strange Interlude* and *Mourning Becomes Electra.* Perhaps he took ideas *per se* with too much of the seriousness of those who have only recently discovered "ideas." He sometimes took these in too simplified a form, and in too rarefied a form for drama—an error not committed by Sophocles and Shakespeare, though committed by other dramatists of distinction such as Euripides and Shaw under the pressure of an "intellectual" climate. He also tended to give a passion a bear hug instead of an austere embrace, which is the more usual way with master-tragedians. And one may reflect, finally, that he did push too furiously toward catastrophic consummations and drive his characters too hard toward their destiny, thereby eliciting the charge of writing melodrama rather than tragedy. On this score, however, it must be said that he had company among the late "minor Elizabethans," who also piled horror upon horror. He bore, in fact, a resemblance to them in his susceptibility to extremes of passion, will, and affliction, as we may note in John Webster's *The Duchess of Malfi* and John Ford's *'Tis Pity She's a Whore*.

I believe that O'Neill wrote tragedy of a naturalistic-poetic kind in *Desire Under the Elms* and that he approached, if he did not quite reach, the altitude of high tragedy in *Mourning Becomes Electra*. Generally, moreover, if he failed to write tragedy, as he plainly intended in much of his work, he achieved a noble tragic mood—and this in a context of exciting drama. I believe this will be found to be the case in such plays as *Beyond the Horizon*, *Anna Christie*, *The Hairy Ape*, *All God's Chillun Got Wings*, and *The Iceman Cometh*, regardless of what faults can be ascribed to them. And if the quality of his mind prevented him from securing a maximum of meaning from many of his plays, he at least secured a maximum of tension—which is or contains a meaning of some sort not lightly to be dismissed in the kind of theatre we have had since 1914. He was hardly ever as sharp as Strindberg in scoring his points, and he lacked the agility of a Pirandello in dealing with them. But he was virtually the only American playwright to confront ideas on more than an elementary level and to wrestle with them "tragically"—heroically. He often set loose a mighty smoke with his fire, and consequently the fire was obscured, especially when it was the fire of an idea. But the smoke came from dramatic heat, and it created an atmosphere of dramatic feeling and conception which few other American playwrights have been able, or have seemed disposed, to create. Many of their plays, even their acceptable ones, in consequence, seem located solely in the theatre rather than in the life of the soul. O'Neill, perhaps the most theatrical of them all, actually wrote from a core of drama within himself, and there is a sultry questing in his work that suggests a large, if not necessarily always a keen or wise, soul in the work. Europe, too, recognized him as a major figure in the Western theatre, and produced his work frequently and with skill.

We men of the nineteen-twenties are not disposed to invalidate his rightful claim to being the only major dramatist of our theatre thus far. And we believe that the young generation would do well, too, if they drew closer to his work, not necessarily with reverence and awe but with the respectful attention that high purpose and intense wrestling with formidable demons or phantoms rather than with pigmies deserve. We may have a difficult time of it trying to convince the clever Eliot disciples. But surely, as T. S. Eliot himself can tell them, cleverness in art is not enough. There must be a real man with a real, if not always intellectually reducible, passion behind the art. O'Neill, we maintain, was such a man. As a matter of fact, he is still such a man to those of us who feel close to him in his present wrestling with the demon whom medical science seems unable to vanquish and who can be vanquished only by the soul's fortitude, which we are confident does not fail O'Neill even now.

Eric Bentley

TRYING TO LIKE O'NEILL

It would be nice to like O'Neill. He is the leading American playwright; damn him, damn all; and damning all is a big responsibility. It is tempting to damn all the rest and make of O'Neill an exception. He *is* an exception in so many ways. He has cared less for temporary publicity than for lasting and deserved fame. When he was successful on Broadway he was not sucked in by Broadway. The others have vanity; O'Neill has self-respect. No dickering with the play doctors in Manhattan hotel rooms. He had the guts to go away and the guts to stay away. O'Neill has always had the grownup writer's concern for that continuity and development which must take place quietly and from within. In a theatre which chiefly attracts idiots and crooks he was a model of good sense and honor.

In 1946 he was raised to the American peerage: his picture was on the cover of *Time* magazine. The national playwright was interviewed by the nationalist press. It was his chance to talk rot and be liked for it. It was his chance to spout optimistic uplift and play the patriotic pundit. O'Neill said:

> I'm going on the theory that the United States, instead of being the most successful country in the world is the greatest failure . . . because it was given everything more than any other country. Through moving as rapidly as it has, it hasn't acquired any real roots. Its main idea is that everlasting game of trying to possess your own soul by the possession of something outside it too. . . .

Henry Luce possesses a good many things besides his own soul. He possesses *Life* as well as *Time*, and in the former he

---

Reprinted from In Search of Theater *by Eric Bentley, by permission of Alfred A. Knopf, Inc. and also appears in Vintage Books edition.*

published an editorial complaining of the lack of inspiration to be found in the national playwright. In *The Iceman Cometh* there were no princes and heroes, only bums and drunks. This was "democratic snobbism." Henry Luce was evidently in favor of something more aristocratic (the pin-up girls in his magazine notwithstanding). Inevitably, though, what the aristocrats of *Time Inc.* objected to in O'Neill was his greatest virtue: his ability to stay close to the humbler forms of American life as he had seen them. It is natural that his claim to be a national playwright should rest chiefly on a critical and realistic attitude to American life which they reject. Like the three great Irish playwrights, O'Neill felt his "belonging" to his country so deeply that he took its errors to heart and, although admittedly he wished his plays to be universal, they all start at home; they are specifically a criticism of American life. *Marco Millions* is only the bluntest of his critical studies. Interest in the specifically American pattern of living sustains his lightest work *Ah, Wilderness!* New England patterns are integral to *Desire Under the Elms* and *Mourning Becomes Electra*, the latter being an attempt at an *Oresteia* in terms of American history, with the Civil War as an equivalent of the Trojan War. The protagonist of *The Iceman Cometh* is a product of Hoosier piety, a study much more deeply rooted in American life than Arthur Miller's of a salesman going to his death. It would be nice to like O'Neill because the Luce magazines *dis*like him—that is, because he is opposed to everything they stand for.

Last autumn, when I was invited to direct the German language *première* of *The Iceman*, along with Kurt Hirschfeld, I decided I should actually succeed in liking O'Neill. I reminded myself that he had been honored with prefaces by Joseph Wood Krutch and Lionel Trilling, that he had aroused enthusiasm in the two hardest-to-please of the New York critics, Stark Young and George Jean Nathan, and so forth. I even had a personal motive to aid and abet the pressure of pure reason. My own published strictures on O'Neill had always been taken as a display of gratuitous pugnacity, amusing or reprehensible according to my reader's viewpoint. Under a rain of dissent one begins to doubt one's opinions and to long for the joy that is not confined to heaven when a sinner repenteth. Now it is a fallacy that drama critics are strongly attached to their own opinions; actually they would far rather be congratulated on having the flexibility to change their minds. In short, I would have been glad to write something in praise of O'Neill, and I actually did lecture—and speak on the Swiss radio—as an O'Neillite. If this seems disingenuous, I can only plead that I spoke as a director, not as critic, and that it is sometimes a great relief to do so. There is something too godlike about criticism; it is a defiance of the injunction to men: Judge not that ye be not judged; it is a strain. And if it would be subhuman to give up the critical attitude for mere liking and disliking, the directorial, interpretative attitude seems a more mature and challenging alternative.

Both critic and director are aware of faults, but whereas it is the critic's job to point them out, it is the director's job to cover them up, if only by strongly bringing out a play's merits. It is not true that a director accepts a play with its faults on its head, that he must follow the playwright even into what he believes to be error. He cannot be a self-respecting interpreter without following his own taste and judgment. Thus, Hirschfeld and I thought we were doing our best by O'Neill in toning certain things down and playing others full blast. Specifically, there seemed to us to be in *The Iceman Cometh* a genuine and a non-genuine element, the former, which we regarded as the core, being realistic, the latter, which we took as inessential excrescence, being expressionistic. I had seen what came of author-worshipping direction in the Theatre Guild production, where all O'Neill's faults were presented to the public with careful reverence. In order to find the essential—or at least the better—O'Neill we agreed to forego much O'Neillism.

Our designer, Teo Otto, agreed. I told him of Robert Edmond Jones's Rembrandtesque lighting and of the way in which Jones, in his sketches, tried to create the phantasmagoria of a Strindberg dream play, but Otto, though we discussed various sensational ways of setting the play—with slanting floors and Caligari corridors or what not—agreed in the end that we were taking O'Neill's story more seriously if we tried simply to underline the sheer reality, the sheer banality and ugliness, of its locale. Instead of darkness, and dim, soulfully colored lights, we used a harsh white glare, suggesting unshaded electric bulbs in a bare room. And the rooms *were* bare. On the walls Otto suggested the texture of disintegrating plaster: a dripping faucet was their only ornament. A naked girder closed the rooms in from above. And, that this real setting be seen as setting and not as reality itself, the stage was left open above the girder. While Hirschfeld and I were busy avoiding the abstractness of expressionism, Otto made sure that we did not go to the other extreme—a piddling and illusion-mongering naturalism.

To get at the core of reality in *The Iceman*—which is also its artistic, its dramatic core—you have to cut away the rotten fruit of unreality around it. More plainly stated: you have to cut. The play is far too long—not so much in asking that the audience sit there so many hours as on sheer internal grounds. The main story is meant to have suspense but we are suspended so long we forget all about it. One can cut a good many of Larry's speeches since he is forever re-phrasing a pessimism which is by no means hard to understand the first time. One can cut down the speeches of Hugo since they are both too long and too pretentious. It is such a pretentiousness, replete with obvious and unimaginative symbolism, that constitutes the expressionism of the play. Hugo is a literary conception—by Gorky out of Dostoevsky.

We cut about an hour out of the play. It wasn't always easy. Not wishing to cut out whole characters we mutilated some till they had, I'm afraid, no effective existence. But we didn't forget that some of the incidental details of *The Iceman* are among O'Neill's finest achievements. Nothing emerged more triumphantly from our shortened, crisper version than the comic elements. With a dash of good humor O'Neill can do more than with all his grandiloquent lugubriousness. Nothing struck my fancy more, in our production, than the little comedy of the Boer general and the English captain. O'Neill is also very good at a kind of homely genre painting. Harry's birthday party with its cake and candles and the whores singing his late wife's favorite song, "She Is the Sunshine of Paradise Alley," is extremely well done; and no other American playwright could do it without becoming either too sentimental or too sophisticated. We tried to build the scene up into a great theatric image, and were assisted by a magnificent character actor as Harry (Kurt Horwitz). It is no accident that the character of Harry came out so well both in New York and Zurich: the fact is that O'Neill can draw such a man more pointedly than he can his higher flying creations.

I am obviously a biased judge but I think Zurich was offered a more dramatic evening than New York. The abridging of the text did lay bare the main story and release its suspense. We can see the action as presumably we were meant to see it. There is Hickey, and there is Parritt. Both are pouring out their false confessions and professions and holding back their essential secret. Yet, inexorably, though against their conscious will, both are seeking punishment. Their two stories are brought together through Larry Slade whose destiny, in contrast to his intention, is to extract the secret of both protagonists. Hickey's secret explodes, and Larry at last gives Parritt what he wants: a death sentence. The upshot of the whole action is that Larry is brought from a posturing and oratorical pessimism to a real despair. Once the diffuse speeches are trimmed and the minor characters reduced to truly minor proportions, Larry is revealed as the center of the play, and the audience can watch the two stories being played out before him.

A systematic underlining of all that is realistic in the play did, as we hoped it would, bring the locale—Jimmy the Priest's—to successful theatrical realization, despite the deletion of much of O'Neill's detail. It gave body and definition to what otherwise would have remained insubstantial and shapeless; the comedy was sharpened, the sentiment purified. I will not say that the production realized the idea of the play which Hirschfeld, Otto, and I entertained. In theatre there is always too much haste and bungling for that. One can only say that the actuality did not fall further short of the idea in this instance than in others.

And yet it was not a greater success with the public than the New York production, and whereas the New York critics were restrained by awe before the national playwright, the Swiss critics, when they were bored, said so. My newly won liking for O'Neill would perhaps have been unshaken by the general opinion—except that in the end I couldn't help sharing it.

I enjoyed the rehearsal period—unreservedly. I didn't have to conceal my reservations about O'Neill out of tact. They ceased to exist. They were lost in the routine, the tension, and the delight of theatre work. I don't mean to suggest that you could lose yourself thus in any script, however bad; there are scripts that bear down on a director with all the dead weight of their fatuity. But in an O'Neill script there are problems, technical and intellectual, and every one a challenge. I gladly threw myself headlong into that mad joy of the theatre in which the world and its atomic bombs recede and one's own first night seems to be the goal toward which creation strives.

The shock of the first night was the greater. It was not one of those catastrophic first nights when on all faces you can see expectancy fading into ennui or lack of expectancy freezing into a smug I Told You So. But, theatrically speaking, mild approval is little better. Theatrical art is a form of aggression. Like the internal combustion engine it proceeds by a series of explosions. Since it is in the strictest sense the most shocking of the arts, it has failed most utterly when no shock has been felt, and it has failed in a large measure when the shock is mild. *The Iceman* aroused mild interest, and I had to agree that *The Iceman* was only mildly interesting. When I read the critics, who said about my O'Neill production precisely what I as critic had said about other O'Neill productions, my period of liking O'Neill was over.

Of course there were shortcomings which could not be blamed on O'Neill. We were presenting him in German, and in addition to the normal translation problems there were two special ones: that of translating contrasting dialects and that of reproducing the tone of American, semi-gangster, hardboiled talk. There was little the translator could do about the dialects. She wisely did not lay under contribution the various regions of Germany or suggest foreign accents, and her idea of using a good deal of Berlin slang had to be modified for our Swiss public. One simply forewent many of O'Neill's effects or tried to get them by non-verbal means—and by that token one realized how much O'Neill does in the original with the various forms of the vernacular spoken in New York. One also realizes how much he uses the peculiarly American institution of Tough Talk, now one of the conventions of the American stage, a lingo which the young playwright learns, just as at one time the young poet learned Milton's poetic diction. In German there seems to be no real equivalent of this lingo because there is no equivalent of the psychology from which it springs and to which it caters. And there is no teaching the actors how to speak their lines in the hardboiled manner. Irony is lost, and the dialogue loses its salt. This loss and that of dialect flavor were undoubtedly great deficiencies. But not the greatest. I saw the production several times and, in addition to the flaws for which we of the Schauspielhaus were responsible, there stood out clearer each time the known, if not notorious, faults of O'Neill. True, he is a man of the theatre and, true, he is an eloquent writer composing, as his colleagues on Broadway usually do not, under the hard compulsion of something he has to say. But his gifts are mutually frustrating. His sense of theatrical form is frustrated by an eloquence that decays into mere repetitious garrulousness. His eloquence is frustrated by the extreme rigidity of the theatrical mold into which it is poured—jelly in an iron jar. Iron. Study, for example, the stage directions of *The Iceman*, and you will see how carefully O'Neill has drawn his ground plan. There everyone sits—a row of a dozen and a half men. And as they sit, the plot progresses; as each new stage is reached, the bell rings, and the curtain comes down. Jelly. Within the tyrannically, mechanically rigid scenes, there is an excessive amount of freedom. The order of speeches can be juggled without loss, and almost any speech can be cut in half.

The eloquence might of course be regarded as clothing that is necessary to cover a much too mechanical man. Certainly, though we gained more by abridging the play than we lost, the abridgement did call attention rather cruelly to the excessively schematic character of the play. Everything is contrived, *voulu*, drawn on the blackboard, thought out beforehand, imposed on the material by the dead hand of calculation. We had started out from the realization that the most lifeless schemata in this over-schematic play are the expressionistic ones but we had been too sanguine in hoping to conceal or cancel them. They are foreshadowed already in the table groupings of Act One (as specified in O'Neill's stage directions). They hold the last act in a death grip. Larry and Parritt are on one side shouting their duet. Hickey is in the center singing his solo. And at the right, arranged en bloc, is everyone else, chanting their comments in what O'Neill himself calls a "chorus."

It would perhaps be churlish to press the point, were O'Neill's ambition in this last act not symptomatic both of his whole endeavor as a playwright and of the endeavor of many other serious playwrights in our time. It is the ambition to transcend realism. O'Neill spoke of it nearly thirty years ago in a note on Strindberg:

> It is only by means of some form of "super-naturalism" that we may express in the theatre what we comprehend intuitively of that self-obsession which is the particular discount we moderns

> have to pay for the loan of life. The old naturalism—or realism if you will (I wish to God some genius were gigantic enough to define clearly the separateness of these terms once and for all!)—no longer applies. It represents our fathers' daring aspirations towards self-recognition by holding the family kodak up to ill-nature. But to us their audacity is blague, we have taken too many snapshots of each other in every graceless position. We have endured too much from the banality of surfaces.

So far, so good. This is only a warning against that extreme and narrow form of realism generally known as naturalism. Everyone agrees. The mistake is only to talk as if it followed that one must get away from realism altogether, a mistake repeated by every poetaster who thinks he can rise above Ibsen by writing flowerily (e.g. Christopher Fry as quoted and endorsed by *Time* magazine). Wherever O'Neill tries to clarify his non-realistic theory the only thing that is clear is lack of clarity. For example:

> It was far from my idea in writing *The Great God Brown* that the background pattern of conflicting tides in the soul of man should ever overshadow and thus throw out of proportion the living drama of the recognizable human beings. . . . I meant *it* always to be mystically within and behind them, giving them a significance beyond themselves, forcing itself through them to expression in mysterious words, symbols, actions they do not themselves comprehend. And that is as clearly as I wish an audience to comprehend *it*. *It* is Mystery—the mystery any one man or woman can feel but not understand as the meaning of any event—or accident—in any life on earth. And it is this mystery which I want to realize in the theatre.

I have italicized the word *it* to underline the shift in reference that takes place. The first two times "it" is "the background pattern of conflicting tides in the soul of man." The third time "it" is just a blur, meaning nothing in particular, exemplifying rather than clearing up the mystery which O'Neill finds important. An event can be mysterious, but how can its mystery be its meaning? And how can we know that its mystery is its meaning if we do "not understand" it? And what would constitute a "realization" of such a phenomenon in the theatre?

In a letter to Thomas [sic] Hobson Quinn, O'Neill tries again. He has been seeking to be a poet, he says,

> and to see the transfiguring nobility of tragedy, in as near the Greek sense as one can grasp it, in seemingly the most ignoble, debased lives. And just here is where I am a most confirmed mystic too, for I'm always, always trying *to interpret Life in terms of lives, never just lives in terms of characters.* I'm always acutely conscious of the Force behind (Fate, God, our biological past creating our present, whatever one calls it—Mystery certainly) and of the one eternal tragedy of Man in his glorious, self-destructive struggle *to make the Force express him instead of being, as an animal is, an infinitesimal incident in its expression.* And my profound conviction is that this is the only subject worth writing about and that it is possible—or can be—to develop [syntax?] a tragic expression in terms of transfigured modern values and symbols in the theatre which may to some degree bring home to members of a modern audience their ennobling identity with the tragic figures on the stage. Of course, this is very much of a dream, but where theatre is concerned, one must have a dream and the Greek dream in tragedy is the noblest ever!

I have italicized this time phrases where we expect O'Neill to say something, where we even think for a moment that he *has* said something. Reading them several times over, we find that we could give them a meaning—but without any assurance that it is O'Neill's. What is interpreting "Life in terms of lives" and what is "mystical" about it? What does it mean to be "expressed" by a Force—as against being an incident in "its expression"? Isn't O'Neill comforting himself with verbiage? For what connection is there—beyond the external ones of *Mourning Becomes Electra*—between his kind of drama and the Greek? How could one be ennobled by identifying oneself with any of his characters?

It is no use wanting to get away from realism (or anything else) unless you know what you want to get away *to.* Raising a dust of symbols and poeticisms is not to give artistic expression to a sense of mystery. It is merely, in O'Neill's case, to take your eye off the object. (Cf. Ibsen: "To be a poet is chiefly to see.") It seems to me that O'Neill's eye was off the object, and on Dramatic and Poetic Effects, when he composed the Hickey story. Not being clearly seen, the man is unclearly presented to the audience: O'Neill misleads them for several hours, then asks them to reach back into their memory and re-interpret all Hickey's actions and attitudes from the beginning. Is Hickey the character O'Neill needed as the man who tries to deprive the gang of their illusions? He (as it turns out) is a maniac. But if the attempt to disillude the gang is itself mad, it would have more dramatic point made by a sane idealist (as in *The Wild Duck*).

Does O'Neill find the meaning of his story by looking at the people and the events themselves or by imposing it on them? There are ideas in the play, and we have the impression that what should be the real substance of it is mere (not always deft) contrivance to illustrate the ideas. The main ideas are two: first the one we have touched on, that people may as well keep their illusions; second, that one should not hate and punish but love and forgive. The whole structure of the play is so inorganic, it is hardly to be expected that the two ideas would be organically related. The difficulty is in finding what relation they do have. In a way the truth-illusion theme is a red herring, and, as in *Cosi è (se vi pare)*, the author's real interest is in the love-hate theme. Pirandello, however, presents the red herring *as* a red herring, relates his "false" theme to this real one. O'Neill is unclear because he fails to do so. A high official of the Theatre Guild remarked: "the point is, you aren't *meant* to understand." In Pirandello this is indeed the point of the Ponza/Frola story. Pirandello *makes* the point, and in art a point has to be made before it can be said to exist. For O'Neill it is merely a point he might have made. As things are, it is his play, and not life, that is unintelligible.

The Iceman, of course, has big intentions written all over it. Most of O'Neill's plays have big intentions written all over them. He has written of

> the death of an old God and the failure of science and materialism to give any satisfying new one for the surviving primitive religious instinct to find a meaning for life in, and to comfort its fears of death with. It seems to me [he adds] anyone trying to do big work nowadays must have this subject behind all the little subjects of his plays or novels.

In other words, O'Neill's intentions as a writer are no less vast than Dostoevsky's. *The Iceman* is his version of crime and punishment. What is surprising is not that his achievements fall below Dostoevsky's but that critics—including some recent rehabilitators—have taken the will for the deed and find O'Neill's "nobler conception" of theatre enough. "Conception" is patently a euphemism for "intention" and they are applauding O'Neill for strengthening the pavement of hell. In this they are not disingenuous; their own intentions are also good; they are simply a party to a general gullibility. People believe what they are told, and in our time a million units of human energy are spent on the telling to every one that is spent on examining what is told; reason is swamped by propaganda and publicity. Hence it is that an author's professions and intentions, broadcast not only by himself but by an army of interested and even disinterested parties, determine what people think his work is. The realm of false culture thus created is not all on one level; brows here, as elsewhere, may be low or high. No brows are higher indeed than those of the upper stratum of the subintelligentsia. They spend their time seeking sublimities, works which provide the answers to the crying questions of our time, impassioned appeals for justice, daring indictments of tyranny, everything surefire. Seek and you shall find: a writer like O'Neill does not give them the optimism of an "American century" but he provides profundities galore, and technical innovations, and (as he himself says) Mystery. Now there is a large contingent of the subintelligentsia in the theatre world. They are seen daily at the Algonquin and nightly at Sardi's. They don't all like O'Neill, yet his "profound" art is inconceivable without them. O'Neill doesn't like *them*, but he needs them, and could never have dedicated himself to "big work" had their voices not been in his ears telling him he was big. The man who could not be bribed by the Broadway tycoons was seduced by the Broadway intelligentsia.

At one time he performed a historic function, that of helping the American theatre to grow up. In all his plays an earnest attempt is made to interpret life; this fact in itself places O'Neill above his predecessors in American drama and beside his colleagues in the novel and poetry. He was a good playwright insofar as he kept within the somewhat narrow range of his own sensibility. When he stays close to a fairly simple reality and when, by way of technique, he uses fairly simple forms of realism or fairly simple patterns of melodrama, he can render the bite and tang of reality or, alternatively, he can startle and stir us with his effects. If he is never quite a poet, he is occasionally able—as we have seen in *The Iceman*—to create the striking theatric image.

But the more he attempts, the less he succeeds. *Lazarus Laughed* and *The Great God Brown* and *Days Without End* are inferior to *The Emperor Jones* and *Anna Christie* and *Ah, Wilderness!*. O'Neill has never learned this lesson. The idea of "big work" lured him out into territory where his sensibility is entirely inoperative. Even his most ardent admirers have little to say in favor of *Dynamo*, the only play where he frontally assails the problem of "the death of an old God and the failure of science." A hundred novelists have dealt more subtly with hidden motives than O'Neill did in his famous essay in psychological subtlety, *Strange Interlude*, a play which is equally inferior as a study of upper-class Americans. Then there is his desire to re-create ancient tragedy. Though no one is more conscious than he that America is not an Athens, the "Greek dream"—the desire to be an Aeschylus—has been his nightmare.

The classic and notorious problem about tragedy in modern dress has been that the characters, not being over life-size but rather below it, excite pity without admiration and therefore without terror. Though O'Neill has talked of an "ennobling identification" with protagonists, he has only once tried to do anything about it: only in *Mourning Becomes Electra* are the characters over life-size. Unhappily this is not because of the size of their bones but, as it were, by inflation with gas, cultural and psychological.

The cultural gas is the classic story. The use of classic stories has been customary for so long, and has recently come into such vogue again, that writers have forgotten their obligation to make the stories their own. They figure that the Aeschylean names will themselves establish the dignity and identity of the subject, while they—the modern adaptors—get the credit and draw the royalties. They are not necessarily conscious opportunists. They probably assume, with some psychologists and anthropologists, that archetypal patterns of myth elicit profound responses of themselves, irrespective of presentation; if this were true the poet would be unnecessary; it is a belief not to be discussed by a critic since the very act of criticism presupposes its falsity. If we ask what difference it makes that Orin and Lavinia are versions of Orestes and Electra the answer is that they thereby acquire an artificial prestige. They have become more important without any creative work on the author's part. We now associate them with the time-honored and sublime. They are inflated with cultural gas. It's like finding out that your girl friend is the daughter of a duke. If you are impressionable, you are impressed; she will seem different from now on, clad in all your illusions about nobility.

We are told that myth is useful because the audience knows the plot already and can turn its attention to the how and why. To this I would not protest that all adaptors, including O'Neill, change the mythic plots, though this is true; what I have in mind is, rather, that they do not always change them enough. Events in their works have often no organic place there, they are fossilized vestiges of the older version. We ask: why does this character do that? And the answer is: because his Greek prototype did it. In *Mourning Becomes Electra* the myth makes it hard for O'Neill to let his people have their own identity at all, yet to the extent that they do have one, it is, naturally, a modern and American identity, and this in turn makes their ancient and Greek actions seem wildly improbable. Heaven knows that murders take place today as in ancient times; but the murders in O'Neill are not given today's reality.

Instead, the characters are blown up with psychological gas. O'Neill has boasted his ignorance of Freud but such ignorance is not enough. He should be ignorant also of the watered-down Freudianism of Sardi's and the Algonquin, the Freudianism of all those who are ignorant of Freud, the Freudianism of the subintelligentsia. It is through this Freudianism, and through it alone, that O'Neill has made the effort, though a vain one, to assimilate the myth to modern life. Now what is it that your subintellectual knows about Freud? That he "put everything down to sex." Precisely; and that is what O'Neill does with the myth. Instead of reverent family feeling to unite an Orestes and an Electra we have incest. *Mourning Becomes Electra* is all sex talk. Sex *talk*—not sex lived and embodied but sex talked of and fingered. The sex talk of the subintelligentsia. It is the only means by which some sort of eloquence and urgency gets into the play, the source of what is meant to be its poetry. The Civil War never gains the importance it might have had in this telling of the story, it is flooded out by sex. "New England," surely a cultural conception with wider reference than this, stands only, in O'Neill, for the puritanic (i.e. sexually repressive) attitude.

O'Neill is an acute case of what Lawrence called "sex in the head." Sex is almost the only idea he has—has insistently—and it is for him *only* an idea. Looking back on what I wrote about him a few years ago, I still maintain that O'Neill is no thinker. He is so little a thinker, it is dangerous for him to think. To prove this you have only to look at the fruits of his thinking; his comparatively thoughtless plays are better. For a non-thinker he thinks too much.

Almost as bad as sex in the head is tragedy in the head, for tragedy too can decline into a doctrine and dwindle into an idea. And when the thing is absent its "idea" is apt to go soft. Tragedy is hard, but the idea of tragedy ("the tragic view of life," "the tragic sense of life" etc.) is seldom evoked without nostalgic longing. And the most decadent longing is the longing for barbarism, *nostalgie de la boue*, such as is voiced by our tragedy-loving poets:

> Poetry is not a civilizer, rather the reverse, for great poetry appeals to the most primitive instincts. . . . Tragedy has been regarded, ever since Aristotle, as a moral agent, a purifier of the mind and emotions. But the story of *Medea* is about a criminal adventurer and his gun-moll; it is no more moral than the story of Frankie and Johnny; only more ferocious. And so with the yet higher summits of Greek Tragedy, the Agamemnon series and the *Oedipus Rex;* they all tell primitive horror stories, and the conventional pious sentiments of the chorus are more than balanced by the bad temper and wickedness, or folly, of the principal characters. What makes them noble is the poetry; the poetry and the beautiful shapes of the plays, and the extreme violence born of extreme passion. . . . These are stories of disaster and death, and it is not in order to purge the mind of passions but because death and disaster are exciting. People love disaster, if it does not touch them too nearly—as we run to see a burning house or a motor crash. . . .

Aristotle's view of tragedy is humane, this one—that of Robinson Jeffers—is barbaric without the innocence of barbarism; it is neo-barbaric, decadent. O'Neill is too simple and earnest to go all the way with Jeffers. Puritanism and a rough-hewn honesty keep him within the realm of the human. But *Mourning Becomes Electra* does belong, so to speak, to the same world as Jeffers' remarks, a world which titillates itself with tragedy in the head. Your would-be tragedian despises realism, the problem play, liberalism, politics in general, optimism, and what not. Hence *Mourning Becomes Electra* is unrealistic, unsocial, illiberal, unpolitical, and pessimistic. What of the *Oresteia?* It celebrates the victory of law over arbitrary violence, of the community over the individual. It is optimistic, political, social and with permissible license might be called liberal and realistic as well. *O tempora, o mores!*

If one does not like O'Neill, it is not really he that one dislikes: it is our age—of which like the rest of us he is more the victim than the master.

Achievement

FOREIGN OPINIONS

Julius Bab

AS EUROPE SEES AMERICA'S FOREMOST PLAYWRIGHT

I consider Eugene O'Neill the most interesting and important dramatist who has appeared since the World War. But he is interesting particularly as an American dramatist.

Although in poetry and in the novel America has long since established itself in Europe, it had not, before the war, issued a dramatic coinage which had currency among Europeans. But soon after the Armistice O'Neill became known in England, France, and Germany. And since then we have been aware that America is beginning to express itself through the theatre.

It is significant that O'Neill appeared just when he did. For during the almost perpetual revolution which followed the war it has become clear to all Europeans that their future would be determined by the two great powers of East and West—Russia and the United States. But the revolutionary striving of the Russians

From the Theatre Guild Magazine, *November 1931. Reprinted by permission of* Theatre Arts *Magazine.*

hovers about a new "art of the theatre" because they lack a theatre of their own. The plays which have come out of Russia in the past twelve years are only a naive imitation of very old European forms. But the contemporary striving of America to attain a new art of the theatre appears much more promising. We Europeans are already acquainted with many notable plays by such writers as Elmer Rice, Paul Green, Maxwell Anderson, and Susan Glaspell. The most vigorous personality in this group, however, is unquestionably Eugene O'Neill.

O'Neill was, so to speak, born in the American theatre. He is the son of one of the most successful American actors. He did odd jobs in the theatre with his father and learned the stage thoroughly. Yet—he deserted the theatre. He became an apprentice in a mercantile house and a gold-digger in Honduras; he shipped as a sailor to South America, to Africa, to Europe; he was a college student (and was expelled); he was a reporter, a railway conductor. In scores of ways he learned to know his fellow Americans, and identified himself with the misery of their lives.

But seven months in a sanatorium were, as he has testified, decisive in his life. It was there that he began to understand that his concern was not with the physical but with the spiritual existence. And, with his Irish inheritance, he began to study the lessons of his very typically American apprenticeship.

He wrote short plays—very unskillful ones. Then he did what few Europeans would do—he went to school and learned under Professor Baker how to write plays. And then he went to Provincetown, where a group of amateurs were putting on plays for their own amusement, and served as playwright, director, and actor. A happy beginning consonant with the oldest traditions of the theatre.

Today O'Neill unquestionably belongs among those few who study foreign models in order to learn, yet by studying do not make themselves imitators but free themselves to create something new. Certainly the will to create is central in this man's development. To be sure, not all the forty or so plays which he has written are masterpieces. Even the twenty odd which have been published are of very unequal merit. But in all that he has written there is a drive which makes his total work more important than any single play. He has a restlessness, a courage to experiment, which makes his dramas more interesting than those of any other new playwright in any other language.

At first O'Neill wrote only one-acters—character or atmosphere pieces. He tried a few experiments in the American metropolitan underworld. Then, fully conscious of what he was doing, he wrote of the experiences of his *Wanderjahre*. The "old devil ocean" is the true hero of all these early plays. It is the uncanny, fateful ocean which inspires them. They have no action, but they eloquently express the "feel" of the sea.

In these early works of O'Neill it is the subject-matter, the stuff of American life, which interests us Europeans, rather than the artistic expression. The profounder psychological problems which he essayed in *The Great God Brown* and *Strange Interlude* are perhaps more interesting for Americans than for us. For we have had such characters, with their Christian-Pagan conflicts and their thirty-year life-spans, on our stage for decades; in Ibsen, in Hauptmann, in Schnitzler. What interests us especially is the form, the new mode of expression, the technique with which O'Neill attacks his themes. In *The Great God Brown* it is the attempt to use masks to express the interplay of two distinct personalities within the same human being. In *Strange Interlude* it is the amazing device of the double dialogue, which presents a new and formidable problem to the art of the theatre. The tireless curiosity with which O'Neill explores all theatric and dramatic forms promises a fascinating American drama in the future.

Early in his career O'Neill wrote a one-acter after the model of Strindberg's *The Stronger*. "Before Breakfast" is a self-contained monologue drama which projects the fates of two human beings. *Desire Under the Elms* is a *Bauernstück*, a drama of property-lust which admirably catches the sodden mood of those who are bound to the soil. Then *The Fountain*. And, after the two problem plays which I have mentioned, *Marco Millions*—a more individual adaptation of the Shavian ironic-serious mode of history-writing than any European author has yet been able to achieve.

Both *Strange Interlude* and *Marco Millions* are extremely long, and *Mourning Becomes Electra* is nothing less than a trilogy. Such recklessness in space and time is characteristically American; (it would be a hindrance to us less heroically fashioned Europeans). But in his evolution from his earlier one-act plays to these more recent monster-pieces O'Neill has developed a new form whereby he creates an artistic unity by means of a series of crisp, powerful scenes following rapidly on one another.

Yet the best of O'Neill's plays is not *Anna Christie*, a not very original story of the fallen woman; not the somewhat violently monotonous character-study *Gold;* not the all too complex soul- and love-dramas, *Beyond the Horizon*, *Welded*, and *Diff'rent*, nor even the Negro tragedy *All God's Chillun Got Wings*, which in its simple and powerful scenes presents the unbridgeable chasm between the races in America. The most significant and compelling of O'Neill's works up to now are—in my judgment and in the judgment of many other Europeans—*The Emperor Jones* and *The Hairy Ape*.

The Emperor Jones begins as a lengthy dialogue between a Negro who has made himself emperor of a Negro island and the London tradesman Smithers. And at the end ensues another dialogue between Smithers and the old Negro chieftain Lemm, who has finally vanquished the tyrant with his silver bullet. But in between, Jones is alone, in uninterrupted conversation with the spooks of his conscience, with the demons of the primeval forest, and with the ceaseless drum-beat of his Negro enemies in the distance. And it seems to me that O'Neill has here created something noteworthy—this picturing of a man and his fate, the past life and career of a crafty and brutal bully and the wrecking of his power. This Negro is only an insolent tyrant in a Caribbean island; yet the collapse of his criminal egomania, the defeat of his extraordinary vitality by the imaginings of his own brain—these are represented so magnificently, so movingly, that the play seems to me to offer a complete parallel with Shakespeare's *Macbeth*. I believe that one need only see *The Emperor Jones* once played by an actor of the first rank to feel that this comparison is by no means too bold; both plays deal with the downfall of a powerful man who has lived beyond his strength; the end of a despot.

Yet still more significant (and I believe the most important of all O'Neill's works hitherto) is *The Hairy Ape*. Here the theme, which is handled with equal artistic mastery, is closer to the core of modern life. *The Hairy Ape* is the tragedy of the proletariat, seized at the point where it is still tragic—that is to say, before politics enters in. With politics begin the struggle of faction and interest and the play of calculation. O'Neill has admitted that he once had a socialistic bent but no longer believes that anything important for mankind can be won by this approach; so he has never written crass propaganda plays. Here he presents the proletarian, so to speak, as he really is (without the admixture of politics)—a man who "has lost his harmony with nature and not yet found harmony in his soul."

This giant stoker Yank is happy and confident in his existence, is proud of his strength, longs for nothing beyond what he possesses. But in a second his self-respect is shattered when he talks with an elegant young lady of the ruling class. He begins to make comparisons, to fume, to seek revenge. It is characteristic that the final bankruptcy of his self-esteem occurs in the office of the Workers' Party, among proletarians already bitten by the political bug, who naturally take this naive revenge-seeker for a spy and throw him out. He is a child of nature and exactly for that reason he feels the tragedy of the proletarian's exile from all the charms of culture. A hairy ape they call him, and finally he ends in the cage of a gorilla, the one being towards which he feels a fraternal kinship. It is this hairy ape who kills him. The rejected of man, who ends in an animal's cage, is a daring and a terrible symbol. Yet this symbol is completely alive, thanks to the splendid power with which the eight scenes are constructed. There is no more decisive test of creative ability than the task of making a man without intellect and education speak his own language, yet withal be alive. This task O'Neill has here performed with a mastery which definitely fixes his rank as playwright.

We in Europe have, so far as I know, but one play which presents the tragedy of the proletariat with equal clearness and sweep—*Wozzek* by the German writer Georg Büchner, who died in 1837 at the age of twenty-three. But those scenes of the soldier Wozzek, who was abused by everybody until "nature came to him" and he turned murderer, were written before the beginning of the proletarian movement. It is O'Neill's triumph that in the midst of our politics-mad age he has created a type which projects the fate of the proletariat with tragic clearness. All the multitude of other dramatists who in all languages have sought to put the worker and his existence on the stage, have failed to rise above speech-making and picture painting.

The dramatist who wrote *The Hairy Ape* is a master, and a crumb of immortality is his because of this work alone. But we must not forget that we are speaking of a man of but forty years or so, one who presumably has the most fruitful portion of his artistic career ahead of him. And if O'Neill's more recent and more elaborate experiments lack the power which resides in *The Emperor Jones* and *The Hairy Ape*, they are still so rich in substance and interest, they are so certain an indication of a restless searching for new tasks, that we feel justified in expecting from this vigorous American more dramatic masterpieces of fine and original stamp.

Camillo Pellizzi

IRISH-CATHOLIC ANTI-PURITAN

Eugene O'Neill is recognized without dispute as the greatest American dramatist of our time, but the attribute *American* is not enough to define him, and one could almost say it was unnecessary. He is a writer with a very decided, singular and rebellious personality, of Irish descent and affinities, but restless and variable in inspiration and technique, as his work, by now very considerable, shows. One might say that humor and a sense of the comic are not a spontaneous part of his artistic nature, and observe that he has certain constant psychological characteristics, above all that of *passionateness*. Although the very striking genius of this author can be recognized in each of his works, one cannot yet say that there exists an "O'Neill style," and this is perhaps the greatest praise one can give him. . . .

"Bound East for Cardiff" shows a sailor, Yank, dying in his bunk as the result of a fall in the hold, while his rough companion, Driscoll, attends him and tries to comfort him as much as he can in his rude way. The tramp steamer is making slow progress through the sea fog, and every other minute the blast of the whistle is heard. Other sailors, sketchily portrayed, come in and out of the dim cabin in their dripping oilskins. The strange, broken, coarse dialogue of the two friends is among the noblest and most beautiful things in modern drama: their slang acquires a rhythm and a swing which make one think of Synge, by whom O'Neill was certainly influenced. The drama lies wholly in the contrast between these poor human creatures and the hostile elements which *live* all around them, between the spark of soul they reveal and their monotonous, brutal and obscure fate, between their timid, confused

---

From Rowan Williams' translation of English Drama: The Last Great Phase *by Camillo Pellizzi, copyright 1935. Reprinted by permission of Macmillan & Company, Ltd. Title supplied by the editors.*

longing for affection and the death which takes place in the midst of the fog, without tears or lament. This is the drama, and yet, as also in Verga, the ultimate artistic effect of the dialogue is *epical;* it is a confession, a pure poem, a song, which expresses the author's feeling in a fresh and ingenuous way.

Anna Christie being better known, at least on the screen, let us examine *The Emperor Jones*. The hero is a sort of negro tyrant who is seen, in the first act, enthroned in his palace; he is petulant and solemn, a mixture of the cruel and the grotesque. His enemies force him to leave the palace and flee into the jungle. In the six successive scenes we see him alone in the forest, a prey to ancient, atavistic fears. "They are," says a critic, "six progressive stages of his rising terror. They are expressionistic rather than realistic, each one a vision his brain conjures up as terror more and more overwhelms him, each one a vision going farther back into his racial past, to the slave market, the slave ship, and then the black superstition of the African jungle" (W. P. Eaton, *The Drama in English*, p. 334). All through these six scenes there is nothing but Jones's monologue, his rising madness, which, before these apparitions, these silent groups, pervades the scene. In the distance is heard the uninterrupted beat of the tom-tom of his enemies. At the end Jones comes out of the jungle at the same place where he went in, and here his enemies await him and kill him.

The tom-tom in *The Emperor Jones* can be compared to the repeated blast of the whistle in "Bound East for Cardiff"; some would call them stage devices to excite the nerves of the audience. In reality they are symbolical elements dramatized; they represent, in both cases, a brooding Fate, a predestination. Since we have already spoken of predestination with regard to English and Scotch Protestant writers, we may observe the form it assumes with an American of Irish and Catholic origin: whether O'Neill is dealing with ancestral terrors latent in the soul, as with Jones, or with a strange, cruel Nature, as in all his sea dramas, man's destiny, here, always depends on a terrible, unequal struggle between man and a *created* reality from which he is sharply distinguished. If Providence does not intervene and assist man with a power which is not wholly human, we know already that he will succumb. This attitude can be found even in the subsequent psychological and psychoanalytical plays. O'Neill, irreligious in his beliefs, does not perhaps perceive that, in his own particular form of anti-Puritanism there is implied a Catholic outlook in the strictest sense—the acceptance of the positive, powerful reality of evil, and the existence of grace and the miraculous. Fate, even when it interweaves itself with man, is always a *different thing* from man, who presses and struggles against it with all the violence of passion; with O'Neill, therefore, the tragical is hardly ever the contrast of distinct and opposed personalities, but the unequal and desperate struggle of each character against an *objective* reality which hangs over him. In this atmosphere the psychological elements also become the *object*, or tragic fate; and in this can perhaps be found the reason for O'Neill's *tragic* superiority over all other living Anglo-Saxon writers (and also the reason for his scant popularity in Protestant, alternative-seeking England), in the fact that he does not confuse man with his destiny, his internal passions or his follies; he sees man as a subject who is *struck*, even if it be in his most inward and secret fibers, by these passions, disasters and follies. At the most, if there occasionally figures in his plays a man of destiny, he will be a type of old American Quaker, a product of Puritanism. Such, for instance, is the father in *Desire Under the Elms*, a strict, miserly, despotic old man, who at his second wedding marries a young girl, and she fatally, irresistibly, falls in love with his son.

Even when O'Neill, as in *Strange Interlude*, resolutely attacks a theme dear to psychoanalysts, that of "frustration," he extracts tragedy from it; for the heroine, Nina, who has lost her lover in the war and will remain all her life a woman unsatisfied in her profoundest needs and instincts, is still always a *subject*, a personality, a free human soul; and the frustration is like a disease, a profound impression which is made on her by outward circumstances, from which she will never be able to free herself, and against which, eternally defeated, she will eternally rebel. This play, in nine acts, takes six hours to perform; the author has also attempted to give dramatic expression to what the Freudians call the "subconscious": the action continually stops while this or that character, looking into space, expresses out loud his or her inward, unconfessed, unspoken thoughts. It is, in fact, the *aside* of the old school, reinstated with a very new function. All those who read the play before it was acted swore that no public would be able to stand such a work, but, on the contrary, *Strange Interlude* was a great success. O'Neill's technical audacities, after all, always adhere strictly to the subject he is treating, and are not thought out separately and then added; for that reason the audience generally accepts them readily, even if at first it loses its bearings for a few minutes.

The trilogy *Mourning Becomes Electra* resembles a great classic model in its general outline. Here the hostile gods are replaced by the Freudian complexes, especially the "Oedipus complex," which compels the son and daughter of old Mannon, an American Brigadier-General of very ancient descent, to love respectively their mother and father. When the mother, in order to elope with her own lover, murders her husband, the children pursue the fugitives and in their turn murder the lover, and finally perceive that they are bound to each other by a latent incestuous passion: it is the Oedipean love, which first bound the son to the mother, the daughter to the father, and now unites the brother and sister, who find in each other the same features and characteristics as in their parents. The action ends with the suicide of the brother, which follows that of the mother, and with the return of Lavinia, the daughter, to the ancestral home, full of ghostly memories.

In this ancient tragic chain, seeming strangely audacious in these times, the Catholic, anti-Puritan Irishman is revealed again, the enemy of the Anglo-Saxon race and religion, which dominated in Ireland, the country of his origin, and predominates in his adopted country. The terrible Mannons, whom such a pitiless nemesis seems to overshadow, are really representative of the oldest race of English Nonconformist settlers, transplanted centuries ago into New England, and uncompromising in their religious, social and economic dogmas; they are the "man-eaters" of the new America, the tyrants who are always thinking of death and pray to God according to Calvin. It is not that O'Neill has quarrels to pick, or social arguments to support; nevertheless, he always remains the best exponent of the rebellion of a new America, more original and eclectic, against the old, on which certain imprints received at the time of its origin are still deeply stamped.

We have seen that O'Neill, in *The Emperor Jones* and other works, has touched on the negro theme, and how he made use of the small experimental and provincial theatres to start his career.

To the experimental and "little" theatres must be added those of the universities, very numerous in America, which have largely helped towards the development of American drama in the last twenty years. This is a necessary reaction to the commercial theatre and the dictatorship of the Broadway public, who are easily swayed by advertisement and inclined to overestimate those stage elements which produce an immediate effect but are of little artistic value. Yet in these enterprises there is the danger that they may end by attracting a restricted public of initiates, resulting in a total loss of contact between the author and the masses, and, since the masses represent the average common reality of an epoch, between the author and that reality. O'Neill's triumph and success both with the masses and with the initiates can be explained also by his defects: he is capable of easily losing contact with culture, though not so easily with reality, in the simplest and most elementary sense of the word. He is wanting in finish, artistic restraint, humor and self-criticism; he is like a force of nature, obscure, disordered and confused, but so rich and spontaneous that the public is carried away and submits to him. By this I mean the American public; the English public, for example, remains suspicious and irritated after seeing these plays; its moral sense and its fineness of taste rebel against accepting them as anything more than interesting manifestations of a paradoxical and abnormal genius. Cultured Europe, in fact, has to make an effort to return to its own forgotten origins, to an atavistic simplicity and rudeness of heart, in order to appreciate this form of art which the Americans, on the other hand, have accepted with a relative ease and readiness.

Anonymous

MR. EUGENE O'NEILL: AN ICONOCLAST IN THE THEATRE

It has long been the habit of criticism to say of Mr. Eugene O'Neill, and to say with more truth than is common in such avoidances, that his powers and reputation are so much in flux that no inclusive estimate of him can now be attempted. Being not yet forty-nine, he has, one may hope, many years of work before him; but it is not this alone, or chiefly this, that holds judgment of him in suspense. The significance, the aesthetic form, of other writers has generally been established before their attainment of his age. Criticism has been able to say of them that what is to come will be a development of a known maturity; surprises will be surprises of degree, not of kind—such a surprise as Bridges gave to the world when in his old age he published "The Testament of Beauty." The splendor, the depth and the vitality of that poem were astonishing, not its authorship, for it proceeded evidently from a known past; the parent had excelled himself, but the marks of legitimate parentage were upon the offspring. O'Neill, on the contrary, may at any time produce a sport. He has an extraordinary boldness, an unaccountable rashness; he rushes at dramatic experiment without counting and, it would seem, without fully understanding the cost; he has the kind of ambition, at once lovable and absurd, that might drive an undergraduate headlong at an epic of which the first sentence came into his mind at breakfast this morning. In brief, he has not reached a maturity on which either he or his critics can build with assurance. For all that, he is the leading dramatist in America, he has been awarded the Nobel Prize for Literature, his plays are familiar in our theatre and a dozen volumes of them are published in London. There is material and reason enough for a study of so remarkable an immaturity.

The similitude of a very young man struggling with passionate impulse to compose an epic has not been used scornfully but as a pointer to what is most valuable, as well as most perilous, in his genius. To read any of his plays, from the early one-acters of the sea to the tortured symbolism of *The Great God Brown*, *Strange Interlude* and *Days Without End*, is to perceive that O'Neill, as a man and as a writer for the theatre, is afraid of nothing except of being, or appearing to be, afraid. This is, indeed, courage, but courage with a dangerous flaw. Brave soldiers, attacking frontally an enemy whom they might have out-manoeuvered or circumvented, have lost battles by reason of it. All O'Neill's theatrical disasters have been due to it, but so has his success been, his freedom, his emancipating influence on the American stage. The good he has done has been done by virtue of that very rashness which those whom caution makes barren are inclined to condemn. No man has had greater temptations to play for commercial or, alternatively, for academic safety, for his father was a popular actor-manager and O'Neill himself was at one time an earnest student of Professor Baker's playwriting class at Harvard. But there was a spirit of defiance in the young man that has never died or—to present the contrary aspect of the same truth—been disciplined. If wisdom meant acceptance of either the naturalistic convention or the limitations of space, time, humor, and reticence fashionably imposed upon dramatists, he would be determinedly unwise. He would decide for himself what was "good theatre" and what was not. He would choose his own subject and force the dramatic medium to serve it. Thirty years ago, across the assembly hall of the Naval College at Osborne, there was set up in brass letters, for the encouragement of young officers, the following sentence: "There is nothing the Navy cannot do." Cadets were taught that this was not the tempting of Providence that it seemed to be, for it was to be interpreted to mean only that, in the Service, there was no such word as "can't" to excuse disobedience to an order or refusal of an attempt. O'Neill's battle in the theatre has been fought in the same spirit.

Not until the appearance of *Days Without End*, which describes a tormented man's estrangement from, and reversion to Roman Catholicism, the faith of his childhood, was the significance of O'Neill's early life made clear. In a preface, written fifteen years ago, to *The Moon of the Caribbees*, Mr. St. John Ervine, having said that Eugene Gladstone O'Neill was born in New York on October 16, 1888, drew attention to the racial and political implications of the name. The father, James O'Neill, was a native of Ireland; and mother, Ella Quinlan, was of Irish stock:

> "O'Neill" by itself [said Mr. Ervine] might as easily be worn by an Orangeman as by a Sinn Feiner—many O'Neills have been high in the counsels of the Ulster Unionists—but when it is preceded by the name of "Gladstone," there can be little doubt that its wearer had a pre-Sinn Fein Nationalist for a father who carried his affectionate respect for the first author of a Home Rule Bill to his son's baptismal font.

When these words were written O'Neill was thirty-four years old; and, discerning of the future though the preface was, Mr. Ervine could not then know, what only later development of O'Neill's work has indicated, that, in the parents, the element of ultimate importance to the son was less their race or their politics than their religion. Not that O'Neill is, or has ever been a Roman Catholic writer. On the contrary, he appears to have been all his life an ardent and variable heretic; but his plunges into the doctrines of Nietzsche, into atheism, anarchism, and scientific materialism, have had that restlessness and violence which do not spring from coldly rational intellect. What he is seeking, or from what he is fugitive, is as yet undetermined; but the heat of the quest and the flight affects his art for good and evil, and affects it more and more as he grows older, preserving in it a remarkable force of unpremeditation, of having been written with youthful blood, and, at the same time, giving to it sometimes an air of unselective, revivalist tub-thumping which might well prove intolerable if the authenticity of the impulses behind it were not understood.

These, then, are the two aspects of O'Neill with which criticism is principally concerned—his experimental craftsmanship in the theatre, and the faith, religious in essence though often seemingly anti-religious in form, which he is struggling to discover and express. If the questions here implied can be answered by a student of his work, the answers, however tentative, may be the basis of a foreseeing of O'Neill's delayed maturity. To estimate the value of his technical experiments is relatively easy, but to decide what he "stands for" is hard for us because so evidently it is hard for him. "We may honor him for his high aim," Mr. Barrett H. Clark has written, "but we cannot trust his judgment or believe in the validity of his self-criticism." That is true, and its truth lies at the root of the difficulty. But Mr. Clark, who has proved himself to be a friendly and discerning critic of O'Neill, makes elsewhere what is from him an astonishing remark:

> If O'Neill were a genuinely original thinker or even a brilliant spokesman for the ideas of a brilliant thinker, we might argue as to whether we should be the losers if he were to give up writing plays altogether, but his ideas as contributions to contemporary thought are negligible; they are at best slightly varied forms of what we have all been reading during the past fifteen years.

How odd is the implied belief—the besetting sin of modern criticism—that there is a real distinction between thought and "contemporary thought," and that no one is "a genuinely original thinker" who does not cancel out each Monday morning the sum of wisdom attained by the human race on each preceding Sunday night. So fashionable is the pursuit of iconoclasm that men—O'Neill himself has been among them—indulge in it for its own sake, and call it, alternatively, "debunking" or, with capital letters, Contemporary Thought. By such enthusiasts we shall hardly be understood if we say of O'Neill's ideas that, though not revolutionary, they are yet not valueless, being at their best slightly varied forms of what we have all been thinking since the death of Socrates and the crucifixion of Christ. There is nothing new under the sun and no reason that there should be—nothing new except each new man's slow, unwilling application to himself of the ancient and inexorable laws.

It is true that O'Neill has by the tone of many of his writings given encouragement to those who would have him be, in the narrow sense, a "contemporary" thinker. He is always at pains to dress up in smart new clothes what his parents taught him. Of one of his plays, *Dynamo*, he wrote as follows, and Mr. Clark quotes him:

> It is a symbolical and factual biography of what is happening in a large section of the American (and not only American) soul right now. It is really the first play of a trilogy that will dig at the roots of the sickness of today as I feel it—the death of an old God and the failure of science and materialism to give any satisfying new one for the surviving primitive religious instinct to find a meaning for life in, and to comfort its fears of death with. It seems to me that anyone trying to do big work nowadays must have this big subject behind all the little subjects of his plays or novels, or he is simply scribbling around on the surface of things and has no more real status than a parlor entertainer.

That is not enough, or is too much, for Mr. Clark. "O'Neill," he says, "was certainly worrying too much about God and his own soul." What else, on earth, is an artist to "worry about"? The objection to religion as a subject for art is, presumably, that God antedates Sunday night and can no longer be regarded as "contemporary" on Monday morning; and O'Neill himself, in this passage, is as cocksure of the divine death as an undergraduate with his first atheistical pamphlet in his hand. But compare with it the continually significant *Days Without End*. Here a Roman Catholic priest, uncle to the principal character, John Loving, describes his nephew's salad days; it is impossible to believe that the description is without reference to O'Neill himself:

> First [says Father Baird], it was Atheism unadorned. Then it was Atheism wedded to Socialism. But Socialism proved too weak-kneed a mate, and the next I heard Atheism was living in free love with Anarchism, with a curse of Nietzsche to bless the union. And then came the Bolshevik dawn, and he greeted that with unholy howls of glee and wrote me he'd found a congenial home at last in the bosom of Karl Marx. He was particularly delighted when he thought they'd abolished love and marriage, and he couldn't contain himself when the news came they'd turned naughty schoolboys and were throwing spitballs at Almighty God and had sup-

planted him with the slave-owning State—the most grotesque god that ever came out of Asia!

Later in the same play the movement of O'Neill's mind since he wrote the comment on *Dynamo* which we have quoted above is clearly indicated. John Loving in sardonic and bitter mood, has denounced freedom as "merely our romantic delusion." We must "create new goals for ourselves, ends for our days!"

JOHN: A new discipline of life will spring into being, a new will and power to live, a new ideal to measure the value of our lives by! . . . We need a new leader who will teach us that ideal, who by his life will exemplify it and make it a living truth for us—a man who will prove that man's fleeting life in time and space can be noble. We need, above all, to learn again to believe in the possibility of nobility of spirit in ourselves! A new Saviour must be born who will reveal to us how we can be saved from ourselves, so that we can be free of the past and inherit the future and not perish by it!

This obsession by the word "new"! This helpless, adolescent desire to be "free of the past" and to dissociate the creeds of Sunday night from the Messiah of Monday morning! But, in this play, O'Neill knows what he is at. He writes of John Loving with regretfully satirical sympathy as though, having at last outgrown him, he were half-sorry for having done so; but that he has outgrown him is not to be questioned, for he permits to the priest the expected reply:

FATHER BAIRD: You are forgetting that men have such a Saviour, Jack. All they need is to remember Him.

The play, with its hysterical conclusion, is not among the dramatist's best. It has all the crudity of a tract, but the tract is nearer to maturity than the former rebellious pamphlets.

Whether maturity of style is approaching as rapidly as maturity of thought is open to doubt. It is O'Neill's greatest handicap that he is so little a writer. A writer is one to whom words are an intuitive means of defining a mental process; an aid to the mind, not an obstruction to it; a disciplined instrument of lucidity. Words to O'Neill are something in which his mind is entangled and from which it is forever struggling to break free. When he tries to speak straightforwardly and without decoration, as he does in his comment on *Dynamo*, and wishes to say that materialism has provided nothing to satisfy mankind's religious instinct, he speaks instead of "the failure of science and materialism to give any satisfying new (god) for the surviving primitive religious instinct to find a meaning of life in, and to comfort its fears of death with" —a sentence that is shocking, not because it is ugly but because one cannot understand how any writer, wishing to express clearly an idea that he valued, could leave it on paper in such unbuttoned confusion.

In his dramatic dialogue O'Neill suffers from corresponding disabilities. His language is at its best when its effect is that of keyhole reporting—for example, in certain early plays of the sea—and even here it is damaged when Synge chants in the listener's ear. When he puts on the robes of a seer his sentences at once become like mounds of shingle up which the reader must walk, sliding back resoundingly at each step. Poetic exaltation, which is again and again demanded of him by the subjects of his later plays, produces on O'Neill's undisciplined prose the effect of heady liquor on a man untrained to carry his wine. All this because he is afraid of being afraid; because to seek the precise and pregnant phrase seems to him niggling, cowardly, old-fashioned. He will destroy whole plays because they do not satisfy him; a generous boldness appears to him in such deeds of sacrifice; but, in the plays he keeps, he will not choose one among a dozen phrases that approximate to his meaning, and concentrate on the perfecting of it. He prefers to retain the redundant eleven, vaguely hoping that truth will struggle through the fog.

How woolly his writing is when it attempts poetic flights may be shown by a single quotation, chosen because its origin is a play, *Strange Interlude*, which by many is regarded as his masterpiece and does in fact survive its defects. Marsden, in the ninth act, comes in noiselessly and sees a man and a girl kissing each other. He thinks aloud—for this is the play in which O'Neill first made general use of soliloquy:

> MARSDEN (*Scandalized as an old maid—thinking*): I must say! . . . his father hardly cold in his grave! . . . it's positively bestial. (*Then struggling with himself—with a defensive self-mockery*) Only it wasn't his father . . . what is Sam to

> Darrell's son? . . . and even if he were Sam's son, what have the living to do with the dead? . . . his duty is to love that life may keep on living . . . and what has their loving to do with me? . . . my life is cool green shade wherein comes no scorching zenith sun of passion and possession to wither the heart with bitter poisons . . . my life gathers roses, coolly crimson, in sheltered gardens, on late afternoons in love with evening . . . roses heavy with afterblooming of the long day, deserving evening . . . my life is an evening . . . Nina is a rose, my rose, exhausted by the long, hot day, leaning wearily towards peace. . . .

This, which might have been written in the nineties by some unfledged imitator of Wilde, illustrates with precision the difficulty by which O'Neill is confronted in his attempt to give direct, as distinct from implied, expression to the forces which to his vision, are manifest behind the appearances of life. Direct expression in this kind is possible only to lyrical and mystical poets. O'Neill has not their nature or their language.

But to quote the passage would have been a vain unkindness if it indicated only its author's defect. Its interest is that the play of which it forms a part holds a theatre until the ninth act. *Strange Interlude* has a hundred faults. The uses of soliloquy are confused. Spoken thoughts are used sometimes legitimately and with profound effect to illumine the minds of the speakers, but almost as frequently they are a delaying commentary on the action or a means of telling the audience what has happened during an interval. The dramatist has rushed at his idea of reviving soliloquy without thinking out the principles on which his experiment should have relied. Yet the play holds a theatre as valueless work could never hold it, and we are forced to ask what is this quality in O'Neill which makes him a dramatist in spite of the inadequacy of his language and the uncritical confusion of his thought? It is that he can create life in his people and that he has something of value to reveal. What is the nature of the life he creates? By what means peculiar to him is it created? What is the vision, behind his nebulous rhetoric and poeticism, which, like a half-darkened sun, gives such promise of warmth and light to his scene that we are aware of it, and look up, and wait, and inquire.

He has, in the first place, a way of considering men and women that is rare among dramatists faced by the requirements of the modern stage. His judgment of them is, as it were, continuously suspended, like his judgment of himself, but of them he is patiently observant. One feels that their hand is upon him, not his upon them. This was not always so. In some of his earliest pieces in one-act, character is subservient to an action planned beforehand, to the demands of plot; but in the later plays character is free. Here O'Neill's rashness has been his salvation. Refusing to be bound by theatrical convention he has been able to grant free will to the people of his stage. No one, in his presence, is likely to commit the first folly of dramatic criticism—the folly of saying: "A woman of that kind would not have behaved in that way"; for beings are not ruled off by O'Neill into categories so rigid that their futures are ascertainable. In *Strange Interlude*, which is in effect a history of the seven ages of woman, Nina's growth is not a growth by plot nor an obedience to any theatrical expectation, but a natural movement, year by year and hour by hour, which is inevitable only as life itself is inevitable and might, in terms of plot, have taken a different direction at any moment. The audience would not have been surprised because O'Neill himself would not. Very seldom, even in his relatively "well-made" plays such as *Mourning Becomes Electra* or the straightforward comedy *Ah, Wilderness!* are the characters at any point manipulated. They are watched and recorded. O'Neill does presumably plan their actions before he begins to write; for plays, of which the structure is necessarily more rigid than that of novels, could not otherwise be written at all. The secret underlying the extraordinary liberty of his effect is, probably, twofold: first that the imaginative process antecedent to the making of a structural plan is a process in terms of life and not in terms of the theatre; secondly, that, even after the course is begun on paper, he gives his people their heads, accepting from a phrase that he hears them speak knowledge of them which he did not before consciously possess.

To point a contrast with Mr. Coward, whose imaginative world is framed by a proscenium arch, may help to define the quality in O'Neill. Everything said or done in any piece of Coward's is related to a scale of theatrical values. That is why, in his own sphere, he succeeds, for his life is of the theatre; while others are laboriously learning to swim in the theatrical pool, he takes to it like a duck. O'Neill does not take to it at all; he wades through it, causing it to overflow its banks. His imagination works outside the theatre, permitting to mankind the measure of free will that Providence allows. The result is often something that can by no means be fitted into three acts of naturalism, but O'Neill goes his way. There shall be nine acts or twenty-seven; his people shall speak their thoughts aloud, or split their individualities visibly into component parts, or wear adjustable masks for his convenience. The theatre shall conform to his people's free will, not they, as he has imaginatively perceived them, to the restriction of the theatre.

He is claiming for the stage the liberties that are the novel's natural inheritance. The cautious, who say that this is a dangerous confusion of media, have on their side all the arguments, but one—and that as yet hypothetical. If O'Neill's struggle succeeds, they will be answered; a great revolution in the theatre will have been accomplished. The dramatist is reported by Mr. Clark to have said that he is saving up material for a cycle of plays that he hopes to do some day. "There'll be nine separate plays, to be acted on nine successive nights; together they will form a sort of dramatic autobiography, something in the style of *War and Peace* or *Jean Christophe*." He has spoken of this work as "the Big Grand Opus," adding that "it will have greater scope than any novel I know of." Every spine of resentment is inclined to bristle against a man who says that he proposes to write "something in the style of *War and Peace*," as though Tolstoy's masterpiece were a hat on a peg; but O'Neill's ingenuousness is a part of his value, and when it is he who says such a thing one sits back to await the miracle.

Not without hope: for, although he may not be, in the American sense, a contributor to contemporary thought, he is something of much greater value—a man who is not self-sufficient, who distrusts his own cleverness, whose very defiances, when they seem most arrogant, are least so, being the acknowledgment, by a spirit pursued and at bay, of spiritual forces greater than its own. It was not by chance that he drew attention, by quoting Francis Thompson in *Days Without End*, to that "modern miracle play's" debt to *The Hound of Heaven*. Whether he submits finally to capture by any creed is of less importance than that he feels himself to be pursued, and that there is behind his work a tension of flight and longing which, if he can communicate it, will establish his masterpiece and justify all his endeavors. He comes nearest to full communication where he is least hasty to expound and proclaim—in two deeply contrasted pieces, *Desire Under the Elms* and *Mourning Becomes Electra*, which have in common their acceptance of the discipline of form and their reliance upon natural appearances as a means of implying abstract truths. In brief, to revert to Strindberg, who has exercised a powerful influence on O'Neill, *The Father* and *Miss Julie*, not *Towards Damascus* and *The Dream Play*, are his profitable models. Anything that may be called *Expressionism* encourages in O'Neill all his faults. His way to greatness is in self-control and reserved pressure; his way to humiliation is in *folie de grandeur* and in the delusion that an undisciplined soldier is of value in a rebel army.

Anonymous

COUNSELS OF DESPAIR

Mark Twain, when he was told that the Pilgrim Fathers had landed on Plymouth Rock, fervently wished that Plymouth Rock had landed on the Pilgrim Fathers. The wine of veneration for these pioneering puritans was even then turning to vinegar, and now there is not a newly naturalized immigrant from the slums of Europe who will do them reverence or refrain from thumbing his nose at them. Yet it was they who made America safe for Mr. Ben Hecht. What a paradox it is that America, where energetic enterprise and undauntable individuality are more highly esteemed than elsewhere, should deride the Pilgrim Fathers and applaud, as its greatest playwright, Mr. Eugene O'Neill, whose whole belief about life contradicts his country's! All his plays are contemptuous of people and denunciatory of human existence; a commination service without a hymn. He has no zest for life: it disgusts him; and he may be described as the last of the Cathari, that singular sect of Christians, who loathed life, refused fertility, in principle if not in practice, and gave their greatest admiration to suicide. Larry Slade, in his latest play, *The Iceman Cometh*, is a typical *credens* Cathar: one who professes, but does not practice, the faith in its extreme form. He has no will to live, nor any will to die; and he drifts down to Harry Hope's squalid bar to become one of its dreariest inhabitants; a dismal drunkard who has not the courage of his futile convictions, and can commit suicide only by deputy.

Mr. O'Neill is as puritanical as Mr. Shaw, but his puritanism, unlike Mr. Shaw's, unlike Milton's, unlike Andrew Marvell's, has no grace or geniality. It is sour stuff, and makes a Pilgrim Father, in comparison with Mr. O'Neill, seem a blood relation of Sir Toby Belch. Yet no one denounces puritans so frequently and so ferociously as Mr. O'Neill, who spits and spews upon their tombs as if they had done him personal injury. A man has only to mention that he is a Methodist minister to receive the entire contents of Mr. O'Neill's vast vials of wrath. The Rev. Hutchins Light, in an incoherent piece, *Dynamo*, catches it severely; and a minister's son, Theodore Hickman, the protagonist of *The Iceman Cometh*, rails against his father as if he were the original owner of horns and hooves. His fury against puritans is so fierce that it appears to be pathological. Hickman, who has been created in the fallacy, refuted by fact, that the children of the clergy generally go to the devil, tells the dreary sots in Hope's bar that his home was "like a jail." If it was, we may well believe that he made it one.

The puritanical Milton was not the first of our poets to say:

The mind is its own place, and in itself
Can make a Heav'n of Hell, a Hell of Heav'n.

That roistering Elizabethan, Marlowe, slain in such a "dive" as Harry Hope's, was equally certain that each of us makes his own hell. Mephistopheles, when Faustus inquires where hell is, replies:

Where we are is hell,
And where hell is, there must we ever be.

Mr. O'Neill's drunken "drummer," accusing his father of his own fault, describes a home which in no way, save that of being a minister's, resembles the one so lovingly portrayed by Thomas Lamont in his charming reminiscences, *A Boyhood in a Parsonage*, nor is his description reconcilable with the extraordinary number of great men and women, in America and Great Britain, who were born in rectories and manses. Mr. F. C. S. Lowell, in *Munsey's Magazine* for September, 1907, shows that "nearly one in 12 of the Americans who have risen to distinction are clergymen's sons." They include Emerson and Oliver Wendell Holmes.

Our own list is not negligible. It contains Addison, Matthew Arnold, Jane Austen, F. H. Bradley, the Brontës, John Buchan, Coleridge, Cowper, Crashaw, Cudworth, Drake, Froude, Mrs.

Gaskell, Goldsmith, J. R. Green, T. H. Green, Hallam, Warren Hastings, Hobbes, Hazlitt, Jenner, Keble, Charles Kingsley, Marvell, Nelson, Sir Joshua Reynolds, Cecil Rhodes, Henry Sidgwick, Tennyson, the Wesleys, Sir David Wilkie, Wolfe, Sir Christopher Wren and several hundred others. This nation would be greatly reduced in mental status if our rectories and manses had been barren. Students of the drama who are constrained by earnest teachers in co-educational schools to pore upon the works of Mr. O'Neill as if they were the Holy Writ might well wonder how he, the son of devout Irish Roman Catholics, and brought up in a well-found theatrical family, knows anything about clerical homes, where means are usually small, and can assert with so much violent emphasis that they are sinks of iniquity where children are certain to be damned. Hickman is the only minister's child who frequents Hope's bar. What damned the rest of them to that? We can recall only one man with a load of clerical ancestors, and on both sides too, whose prospects of salvation have been hopelessly, if willingly, compromised: Karl Marx.

The question is not idly raised. It is strictly germane to Mr. O'Neill's philosophy, if, indeed, philosophy is a word which is applicable to the mass of undisciplined emotions and jejune opinions which appear in his plays. This Cathar differs from his predecessors, from Manichee to Tolstoy and Ruskin, in a fundamental respect. They despaired of this life; he despairs of any. All other Cathari, Manicheans, Albigensians, and what not, loathed human life because they had a profound faith in a better one, and counted time spent here as wasted. The wise Cathar was one who quickly rid himself of humanity so that he might enjoy eternal felicity. But Mr. O'Neill, the neo-Cathar, has no hope of anything better, here or hereafter. The world is futile and so are its inhabitants. There is no other world, and this one had better be ended. Let us therefore drink ourselves to death if we have not enough courage to blow out our brains. The people who frequent Harry Hope's bar are of different nationalities: American, Afrikaaner, English, German, Irish, Italian, Scottish, and Negro; but they are all sots and spongers. The only workers among them are the barmen, who are pimps. The three women are prostitutes. That, according to Mr. O'Neill, is mankind. There is nothing here of courage and endurance, nothing of unflinching faith, nothing of self-sacrifice deliberately made. The O'Neill world is a dirty pub, frequented by drunks and disorderlies and shiftless loafers; and periodically raided by corrupt cops.

Into this assembly of despair comes Hickman, the breezy boozer, who visits the bar occasionally for an orgy. But he is now a changed man: he has acquired a belief, and, after the fashion of converts, is eager to proselytize. They must all do what he has done, confront fact, and acknowledge themselves to be what they are. If the pimp will admit that he is a pimp, if the prostitute will confess her occupation, if the sot and sponger will own up . . . then their misery will end. They undergo against their will some sort of conversion, but their regeneration renders them more futile than before; and when they learn that Hickman has solved his problem by murdering his wife, they relapse with relief. The swine return to their swill. They are, Slade asserts, converts to death.

The Iceman Cometh is not a brief decline into despair by an idealist who loses heart when he compares people as they are with people as he wishes them to be. Mr. O'Neill is not Shakespeare writing *Timon of Athens*, with *The Tempest* still in his head. The Mr. O'Neill who wrote *Beyond the Horizon* in 1920 is the Mr. O'Neill who wrote *The Iceman Cometh* in 1946; and we must take him with some seriousness, since his countrymen applaud him loudly, calling him their greatest playwright and placing him in august company. He has received the Pulitzer Prize three times. He was awarded the Nobel Prize in 1936, when he was forty-eight; a prize which has been capriciously awarded since 1914. Mr. Shaw had to wait for it until he was sixty-nine. It was withheld from Thomas Hardy and H. G. Wells, but given to Mr. Sinclair Lewis and Mrs. Pearl Buck. Mr. O'Neill's work has now been published and performed in many countries, although it has been less warmly received in Europe, and especially in France, than it has been in America. He is entitled, therefore, to be judged by the highest standards; and since *The Iceman Cometh*, the twenty-ninth of his plays to appear in Great Britain, seems to sum up his beliefs, its publication justifies us in attempting to estimate his rank. Is he, as many of his countrymen assert, of the same stature as Aeschylus and Shakespeare? He himself has not disclaimed the comparison. He has, indeed, insisted on it by using themes they used.

The most obvious difference between Aeschylus, Shakespeare, and Mr. O'Neill is that the two former loved mankind, but the last feels only contemptuous pity for it. The strongest passion animating his characters is hate. A Desert Father was not more disdainful of existence than Mr. O'Neill, who finds nothing inspiring in the sight of Caliban looking up to the beautiful Miranda. There is no sign of nobility in the characters who populate his plays. Not one of them has been made in the image of God. All of them bear the mark of the beast. The best of them are only negatively good, inertly abstaining from evil as if they were less in love with virtue than terrified of vice. Wandering through his underworld, and holding our noses as we wander, we have difficulty in believing that even it could have existed without one positively good and likeable inhabitant. Nobel, in his will, laid down a law to guide adjudicators in awarding his Prize for Literature. It should be given "to the person who shall have produced in the fields of literature the most distinguished work of an idealistic tendency." The word *idealistic* is susceptible of various interpretations. It can be made applicable to Swift, even when he is writing about the Houyhnhnms, but one must stretch and strain it severely to find its applicability to Mr. O'Neill, whose world is a bestiary full of vulpine animals and crushed worms.

His characters are ineffectual egotists, whining for opportunities they are incapable of using. The most virile of them, the sailors and stokers in the early sea-plays, are mindless creatures, clawing and clutching like dying dinosaurs; and those who show some signs of contact with intelligence are impotent. In spite of the difference in their color and physique, Yank, in *The Hairy Ape*, and Robert Mayo, in *Beyond the Horizon*, and the Negro student, Jim Harris, in *All God's Chillun Got Wings*, are closely akin; equally inept and empty. The leading characters in such plays as *The First Man*, *Welded*, *The Great God Brown* and *Days Without End*, who may be called "intellectuals," are embarrassingly puerile, causing us to wonder how they managed to keep out of asylums. Marco Polo, in *Marco Millions*, and Juan Ponce de Leon, in *The*

Fountain, are fustian figures, as futile and dispiriting as Emma Crosby in *Diff'rent*. Man, Mr. O'Neill invites us to believe, is a puny creature who vainly dreams of high achievements, but is dogged by disaster. The desponding Gael has overpowered Mr. O'Neill; and where there might have been poetic acclamation, there is only shrill and petulant complaint. It was Mommsen who said "the Celts have shaken all states and have founded none." Mr. O'Neill, in his despondent drama of despair, seems eager and ambitious to prove him right.

"Of the thirty-seven O'Neill plays I have seen or read," Mr. Barrett Clark remarks in a hasty survey of them, "there are only five in which there is no murder, death, suicide or insanity. In the others, I find a total of eight suicides and one unsuccessful attempt, twelve important murders (not counting incidental episodes); twenty-six deaths, nearly all due to violence; and eight cases of insanity." Mr. Clark's calculation was made in 1933. His figures can now be increased. Preoccupation with violence, however, is not Mr. O'Neill's prime fault. An estimate of violent deaths in Shakespeare would make the Newgate Calendar seem pure as undriven snow. At the end of *Hamlet*, the stage is strewn with dead bodies, all of them violently done to death. Eight persons in that play are murdered. The heroine goes out of her mind and is drowned. Even Mr. O'Neill has not indulged in so much slaughter in a single work. His supreme defect is his morbidity and febrile despair, his pathological contempt for people. Mr. Somerset Maugham is not so disdainful of mortal motives as Mr. O'Neill; is, indeed, less cruelly, because he is more cynically, contemptuous of them. There is greater pity for people in Mr. Maugham than in Mr. O'Neill, but neither of them seems to have noticed man's nobility, or to have observed his incessant efforts to rise to finer conditions, or to feel the slightest admiration for his courage under adversity. Mr. O'Neill, indeed, has a perverse and sadistic desire to invert the nobility other men have seen. Shakespeare shows us a Caliban lifting up his eyes from the slime in which he flounders to gaze on loveliness and grace, but Mr. O'Neill, in *The Hairy Ape*, finds his Caliban no more than a vicious gorilla, disguised as a man, who is infuriated by the fear and contempt he inspires in a multi-millionaire's degenerate daughter. His Miranda never meets a Ferdinand who makes her exclaim:

> *O wonder!*
> *How many goodly creatures are there here!*
> *How beauteous mankind is! O brave new world,*
> *That has such people in it.*

She is, her aunt declares, "a natural born ghoul," whose dilettante slumming is an excuse for indulging her morbid craving for sensation. When she sees Yank, the hairy ape, she faints with horror, murmuring, "Oh, the filthy beast!" Yank, enraged by her disgust, swears to revenge himself, but he never sees her again, nor does she re-enter the play, where she appears only in two short scenes. Her insignificance is a cardinal defect in it. The hairy ape begins a futile war on society. But his end is casual. He visits the monkey house of New York Zoo, where he sees a gorilla, and enters its cage, and is crushed to death in its arms. The gorilla then escapes to ravage! . . . Here, as always, Mr. O'Neill is surprisingly insufficient. Shakespeare superbly surpasses him in *The Tempest.* There is more mind in H. G. Wells's *Food of the Gods.*

There was a fog on the night in 1916 when Mr. O'Neill's first play to be publicly performed, a short sea-piece entitled "Bound East for Cardiff," was produced in a fish-shed on a wharf in Provincetown, on the coast of Massachusetts. The fish-shed had been transfigured, and was now The Wharf Theatre, with a "capacity" of ninety persons: a little smaller than the bandbox in Bergen in which Björnson and Ibsen learned their craft. The cast included the author, who, however, failed to convince his audience that his father lived again on the stage. The salt tide swept through holes in the floor as the band of unsophisticated Greenwich Villagers, who had fled from the disenchantments of New York to settle on that bleak and solitary coast, to regenerate the drama and enrich the minds of artless fishermen with news of *Das Kapital*, watched the birth-pangs of America's greatest dramatist. The fog entered Mr. O'Neill's soul that night and has remained there ever since. "Fog, fog, fog, all bloody time," cries

Anna Christie's Swedish-American father as he shakes his fist at the universe. "You can't see vhere you vas going, no!" And Anna herself, embittered, drab, sums us up. "We're all poor nuts," she moans. The fog has thickened in *The Iceman Cometh;* a thick, yellow, suffocating fog; and it makes Larry Slade, the spineless Celt, a convert to death, too cowardly to seek the end he craves. When Faustus, in Marlowe's play, summoned Alexander the Great and Helen of Troy from the grave, they came, but did not speak. Like Bottom, they had been translated, and the mind of man could not conceive what they had seen. But when Mr. O'Neill, in *Lazarus Laughed*, summons the brother of Martha and Mary from the tomb, Lazarus comes in a fit of the giggles. Even the giggles have ceased for Larry Slade. There is nothing left for him but a delusive bottle and the hope that he will one day die of delirium tremens.

Karl-Ragnar Gierow

EUGENE O'NEILL'S POSTHUMOUS PLAYS

During all these years of seclusion, O'Neill was working on projects which, if he had had the physical strength and the time to finish them, would have been dramatic frescoes on a scale never before seen in any theatre. The least of these was a series of eight one-act plays entitled *By Way of Obit*. Only one was completed, "Hughie," a psychological sketch, almost a monologue, based on New York Bohemian circles in the 1920's. This is now at the Royal Dramatic Theatre in Stockholm awaiting its performance.

The main projects were two separate dramatic sequences; the one having the development of the United States during 150 years as its background and theme; the other being an autobiography which he called "a dramatic *Jean-Christophe*." To the latter belonged *The Iceman Cometh*, with motifs from his youth, *A Moon for the Misbegotten*, concerning his elder brother, and perhaps his finest play, the posthumous masterpiece *Long Day's Journey into Night*.

O'Neill evidently had plans for several plays in the autobiographical series, but it was to the historic series, the "cycle" as he called it, that O'Neill devoted the lion's share of his energies. One play from this has reached the public, *A Touch of the Poet*, which was first performed in March of this year at the abovementioned Stockholm theatre and was published by the Yale University Press this autumn. Confusion exists regarding this cycle, not only because O'Neill constantly changed his plans but because he altered the names of the plays within the sequence. *A Touch of the Poet* was at first the title of the whole cycle, not a single play.

From World Theatre, *Spring 1958, a quarterly review published by the International Theatre Institute with the assistance of UNESCO. Reprinted by permission of the author and publishers.*

Mr. Gierow is manager of the Dramatiska Teater—the Royal Dramatic Theatre—of Stockholm.

The play now published was at that stage called *Hair of the Dog*. In the final sketch for the whole enormous work, this last-mentioned title is given to the concluding part while the cycle itself is now called *A Tale of Possessors Self-Dispossessed*. On a scrap of paper dated December 18th, 1941 he has noted down what is apparently the definitive plan for the sequence as follows:

1. *The Greed of the Meek.*
2. *Or Give Us Death.*
3. *A Touch of the Poet.*
4. *More Stately Mansions.*
5. *The Calm of Capricorn.*
6. *The Earth's the Limit.*
7. *Nothing Lost But Honor.*
8. *The Man on Iron Horseback.*
9. *Hair of the Dog.*

The cycle did not include, on the other hand, two other important projects for which O'Neill had had time to make quite complete drafts before the pen dropped from his hand. The first was called *The Career of Bessie Bolan* (the name occurs in different spellings), a play in two parts whose plot, with the boom of the motor-car industry as its background, begins in the 1890's and takes us up to 1928. The second, sometimes called *The Last Conquest*, sometimes *The Thirteenth Apostle*, seems to have been a play on the metaphysical plane, with Christ and Satan as the main protagonists and, according to what Mrs. Carlotta Monterey O'Neill once told me, a finale "with all the world's church bells ringing."

The dramatic sequence begins on Evan Harford's farm in Massachusetts one Spring morning in 1775. A note shows that with *The Man on Iron Horseback* the cycle had reached the 1880's. From the opening scene in *Greed of the Meek* the author had, with endless revisions, got so far that the first six plays of the sequence were completed although not perhaps in their final form, when his illness led him to destroy the manuscripts. One of these, as mentioned above, he found worthy of the stage and spared. Thousands of sheets of paper, with abstracts, sketches for characters, genealogies, stage scenery and thematic notes, remain as traces showing the road he took towards the goal he never reached. But the plays are gone. Only the names remain.

It has been discovered however, that one more manuscript remains intact, *More Stately Mansions*. It is uncertain why this play escaped the destruction that overtook the others—it may have been an oversight. But possibly, in spite of all, O'Neill may have hoped that a temporary improvement might give him the strength to complete this play also. It picks up precisely where *A Touch of the Poet* leaves off; its first scene is cast in the same place, at Con Melody's Inn, whither his daughter Sara, for some years now Mrs. Harford, has come to attend her father's funeral. In its present form, however, the play is earlier than the final version of *A Touch of the Poet;* this fact emerges from a number of discrepancies in the two plays. Apart from this, *More Stately Mansions* is an uneven work, where scenes of savage dramatic power alternate with sections which do not seem to have been finally shaped. O'Neill himself drew up a detailed plan for the revision and condensation of the play, and the copy is at present at the Royal Dramatic Theatre. The question has to be decided whether another writer could possibly revise this work which ill-health compelled O'Neill to abandon.

5

SPECIAL STUDIES

The Quest for Belief

Harry Slochower

EUGENE O'NEILL'S LOST MODERNS

> POLICEMAN: What you been doin'?
> YANK: Enuf to gimme life for! I was born, see? Sure, dat's de charge. . . . (addressing the gorilla): On'y youh're lucky, see? Yuh don't belong wit 'em and yuh know it. But me, I belong wit 'em—but I don't, see? . . . I ain't on oith and I ain't in heaven, get me? I'm in de middle tryin' to separate 'em, takin' all the worst punches from bot' of 'em.
>
> *The Hairy Ape*

Through the character of John Loving in *Days Without End*, O'Neill recapitulated his own stormy development from anarchic defiance to pious recantation. O'Neill's vogue in America, similar to that of Hauptmann in Germany, stems from the representative character of his shifting allegiances. The difference between O'Neill and Hauptmann consists in the more realistic and passionate statement of these vacillations by the American dramatist.

From No Voice Is Wholly Lost *by Harry Slochower, copyright 1945 by Harry Slochower. Used by permission of the publishers, Farrar, Straus and Cudahy, Inc. and the author. Published originally in* The University Review, *Autumn 1943.*

Lionel Trilling has noted the religious tenor of O'Neill's work. One should add that it has a "modern" quality in that it contains a minimum of religious submissiveness. The passion of O'Neill's characters is not the passion of Christ. It is the passion of business, ownership and acquisitiveness. "Somethin' " drives them on to seek freedom. But it is a freedom which disturbs, unsettles, demanding a restless pace. Where the Greek man might find release in esthetic or ethical catharsis, and the medieval man might place it all in the lap of God, O'Neill's skeptical and disillusioned moderns can find no such resting points. Their appeal is to science and to psychoanalysis. But the "Dynamo" does not answer, and analytic probings only render communication more confusing. When they try the way "downward" toward innocence, they discover that it is too late for that. They have been driven out from the naïve plane, and know too much to be content with not knowing enough.

The specific nature of O'Neill's problem derives from his concern with characters who stand in an unsteady midway position. In fear of losing their power, they are nervous, fretful, discontented. In Chekhov (where this group never played a leading rôle) they just talk about it apathetically. In Odets they react forcefully to the threat but are finally released after they have lost their illusions of power. O'Neill's people cling to their positions tenaciously. Hence, where in Chekhov the characters develop passively, and in Odets they are transformed radically, in O'Neill their transformation is partial, jittery and interrupted. Where it is thorough it remains barren because they lack the substitute norms which save the characters of Odets. The efforts of O'Neill's people are concentrated on rising to or holding on to their middle position. Brutus Jones and Jim struggle against being driven back to their original color lines. Yank accepts the embrace of death rather than sink back to his pit of not "belonging." In Nina and Lavinia the will to power is so extreme and insistent as to reach near hysteria.

Brutus Jones, Yank, and Jim reach out from "below," Nina and Lavinia from "above," with Brown, Dion Anthony, and John Loving occupying an intermediate position on the intellectual-poetic level. But their rebellion, being incomplete or negative, proves inadequate to cope with their situation. The result is that these characters are invaded by doubts which split their personalities. It was O'Neill's startling innovation to give *theatrical* form to the dissociated personality through the visions in *Emperor Jones*, the masks in *The Great God Brown*, the "double talk" in *Strange Interlude*, the change of personality in *Mourning Becomes Electra* and the *Doppelgänger* motif in *Days Without End*. Brutus Jones repudiates and is repudiated by both blacks and whites. What is here projected through the twilight consciousness of one person is dramatized in the later plays, where O'Neill extends the technique of dissociation to the point where it becomes a *naturalistic form*. In *The Great God Brown* he would have us *see* the split in his characters by their use of masks; in *Strange Interlude* he would have us *hear* the evidence of their duality, and in *Dynamo* and *Days Without End* we are both to *hear and see* the absolutes toward which O'Neill's desperate people finally veer. In the one we hear and see the Dynamo refusing to give up its secret; in the other we hear Loving's prayer that he may find peace. And in the silent Christ statue we see the "granting" of the prayer.

In O'Neill's two major plays, *Strange Interlude* and *Mourning Becomes Electra*, the action pivots on a war scene which serves as the background for the inner wars of the characters. Nina rebels against her father's intervention which kept her from consummating her love for Gordon; Lavinia and Orin trespass all natural boundaries in defiance of their father's strict morality. But their warlike challenge is wild, explosive and blind. Nina would transvaluate all values. Deprived of love, she rejects love itself, giving herself to men and marrying without love. Even her child is conceived in loveless "scientific" planning. Having freed herself from all outer authority, Nina is trapped by the authority within herself. Her desire for possession ends in herself being possessed. Each new act only leaves her more a prey to guilty feelings. They are the Erinyes of middle-class conscience.

In *Strange Interlude* the characters still manage to live and talk themselves out. Nina enjoys afternoons with her lover Darrell, bears a son and stays married to Sam Evans. In *Mourning Becomes Electra*, all expression is turned inward. Here, love is for oneself, sinful and guilty love of daughter for father, son for mother, brother for sister. It is the sunset stage of the "upper" development. (All the events in this play occur toward evening or at night.) "We've renounced the day, in which normal people live—or rather it has renounced us. Perpetual night-darkness or death in life—

that's the fitting habitat for guilt!" The "rich exclusive Mannons" feel guilty in no longer being capable of productive love. They snatch at love stealthily from those below, from Marie Brantome, the nurse girl with the joy of life (reminiscent of Regina in Ibsen's *Ghosts*), and her son, Brand. Nina was still able to produce "in secret." The Mannons cannot do even that. The war has maimed them, and after the public civil war is over they continue a private civil war within themselves. Even as they succeed in keeping the murders from becoming public, the acts carry on their secret "publicity" within the characters themselves. The result is the *secular* tragedy in which suffering constantly mounts without alleviation. Lavinia, the master will in all three murders, hopes by her acts of "removal" to free herself for simple love. But what Lavinia cannot control is the effect of the action on herself. With each physical removal, she adds to her inner burden. The dead souls rule the living ones. She retains her willfulness to the very end, refusing to atone, but the confession and atonement take place nonetheless in the form of her self-rejection. "There's no one left to punish me. I'm the last Mannon. I've got to punish myself." With these words she enters her church of hell to practice love of hatred on herself.

In Nina and Lavinia, O'Neill presents the ultimate in self and social alienation. Both are the masochistic products of modern rationalistic probing. Both attempt to wield and possess people's lives, as if they were "god and had created them." Nina renounces at the end. Lavinia remains defiant even in her acceptance of suffering. Her very self-surrender and self-immolation have the character of challenge and insubordination. She remains in the grip of the Furies.

In the midst of their sophisticated schemings, O'Neill's characters yearn for the state in which there is no knowledge of sin, where man is not tormented by "dreams of greed and power." But this return to innocence is thwarted, for it is inevitably invaded by the modern spirit of doubt. The conversion is rather the other way. "Have I done this to you already, Peter?" Lavinia cries, as she notes that his eyes have taken on a suspicious look through contact with her.

One of O'Neill's characters, Marco Polo, does begin and end in innocence. In the Epilogue, Marco is shown as having seen a performance of O'Neill's play about himself. He appears dressed as a thirteenth-century Venetian merchant, still "sure of his place in the world." In his preface, O'Neill states that he wanted to exonerate Marco Polo as a liar and adventurer. He shows him as the "best" in the bourgeois ethic. Marco lives in the immediate present, has no imagination for love or death, has no secrets and no fears, knows no passion or loneliness. In short, he lacks soul and spirit. And it is only because he has a minimum of conscience that he can accept life and his commercial ethic uncritically. To be sure, if this Renaissance hero lacks the Faustian metaphysical drive, he is also incapable of Mephistophelian plotting. Because he has remained "pure," he can be neither spiritual nor treasonable. He keeps his promises because he does not "know" any better. He holds to his bargain of simply watching over the beautiful princess, keeps the promise made to his girl, marries her even though she is no longer young or beautiful. In short, O'Neill's "happy" story is made possible by isolating his "worldly" character from the world.

The business characters in O'Neill's later plays become problematical in that they question their status. Brown doubts that he is "the great God Brown"; Sam Evans inherits Marco Polo's innocent acquisitiveness, but his success is illusory and planned for him by the sensitive and guilty characters, Nina and Darrell. He himself no longer enjoys the robust health of Marco, and while the insane streak in his family passes him by, he dies a sudden, "non-natural" death. What was an "instinct" of acquisitiveness with Marco Polo becomes neurosis with Nina and Lavinia. What was simple reasoning with him becomes tortured self-analysis. Marco Polo was intent on accumulating information and goods. The modern characters having gathered them, question their meaning, want to know what lies "behind" them.

Dynamo presents the inadequacy of the answer given by modern science and Protestantism. The Fife house of "science" and the Light house of Protestant religion are seen simultaneously with both their living-rooms and bedrooms exposed to the public. Theirs is an open world in which there are a few secrets. Reuben Light leaves his father's home to discover the new god, electricity. But his "protesting" upbringing leads him to ask for its hidden formula. Yet although the new god is the product of man's reason and the nature of science is to give precise and complete answers, the dynamo remains incommunicable. Reuben's demand for *absolute* knowledge is answered only by the unbroken *continuity* of the rhythm of the dynamo.

But the state of living with two faces is painful. As Cybel tells Brown: "You've got to go to sleep alone." Most of O'Neill's people at last confess that they are in need of grace, not "justice." Brown died with Cybel's prayer, "Our Father, who art." Reuben's final cry is, "I only want you to hide me, Mother." Nina tires of the attempt to enjoy father, lover, and husband all in one, is "contentedly weary with life," as she delivers herself to the fatherly protection of "good old Charley." Only Lavinia refuses to bow, remaining "woodenly erect" in her defiance. In the Greek drama the Erinyes are followed by the Eumenides which augur the beginning of a new age. But O'Neill lacks the faith of a new order. This appears in O'Neill's dramatic technique. With few exceptions, the end of his characters is foreshadowed at the beginning. They begin with a "curse" from which they cannot escape. Locked up in their original sin they have recourse to original faith.

In this sense, *Days Without End* is the sequel to *Dynamo* and *Mourning Becomes Electra*. From the secular church of the Dynamo and the secular purgatory of the Mannon house, O'Neill returns to the "old" church. He would resolve the ever-mounting despair of the Electra theme by religious grace. John Loving takes the path of O'Neill's other characters, going through the "seven periods of life," as they are characterized in *Lazarus Laughed:* the simple, the eager, the self-tortured, the proud, the hypocritical, the revengeful, the resigned. But here resignation is complete and final. John Loving finds refuge in the walls of the church against his own and the world's fires of revolt. Beginning in extremest negation, he ends in absolute affirmation.[1]

The final scene in *Days Without End* recalls Hauptmann's *The Assumption of Hannele*, where a heaven is naturalistically projected on the stage. In both the technique is one of *physical* demonstration. In Hauptmann's play verisimilitude is gained by the fact that the character who imagines herself to be in heaven is a little girl. John Loving's conversion to simple faith is less convincing, inasmuch as he has gone through the stages of doubt.

1. The church as the universal "Mother" suggests the function of the letter "M" which recurs in O'Neill's plays from the universal "openness" of *Marco Millions* to the universal "closedness" of the Mannons.

The unification granted to him omits all the complexities of his situation. It is a kind of Christian idyl on the religious plane corresponding to the pagan isles which O'Neill's characters have never been able to get to. The peace achieved is unreal. Behind the silence and submission there remains the underground passion of O'Neill's men and women, the dynamite of Yank and the power of Reuben's Dynamo.

Doris Alexander

EUGENE O'NEILL AS SOCIAL CRITIC

"I'm going on the theory that the United States, instead of being the most successful country in the world, is the greatest failure,"[1] said Eugene O'Neill in 1946. Clearly O'Neill is a critic of American society and society as a whole. But what are his standards for criticism? Why does he castigate the status quo in *Marco Millions* only to sentimentalize over it in *Ah, Wilderness!?* Why, since he criticizes the whole structure of modern society, has he never espoused even mild reform, let alone revolutionary movements? The theory according to which O'Neill criticizes society is complex, but nevertheless it is a theory, and may be formulated by working backwards from the plays it affected.

Perhaps the best starting point for analysis of O'Neill's social criticism is *The Hairy Ape*, for it gives the main outlines of his social theory as no other one play does. *The Hairy Ape* presents an extremely negative view of the state, of mechanized America, where the worker best adjusted to the system is a "hairy ape," and where the "Capitalist clarss" is even more terribly dehumanized, for it has lost all connection with life, is simply "a procession of gaudy marionettes."[2] According to *The Hairy Ape*, both government and religion are devices for maintaining the status quo. The church substitutes political conservatism for Christianity, substitutes bazaars, methods of making money, for a concern with the meaning of life and death. Government is equally at the

---

From the American Quarterly, *Winter 1954. Reprinted by permission of the author and editor.*

1. John S. Wilson, "O'Neill on the World and 'The Ice Man,'" *PM*, September 3, 1946, p. 18; also in Barrett H. Clark, *Eugene O'Neill: The Man and His Plays* (New York: Dover, 1947), p. 152. Hereafter Wilson, *PM;* Clark, *O'Neill.*

2. *The Hairy Ape*, scene v, p. 236. All references to *The Hairy Ape* are to *The Plays of Eugene O'Neill*, 3 vols. (New York: Random House, 1941), III.

service of the marionettes. On the legislative side, it is exemplified by the windy oratory of Senator Queen, glorifying the status quo and denouncing with ignorant terror any threat to it like the I. W. W. On the enforcement side, it is exemplified by police who function to keep the workers from disturbing the wealthy. On the whole, the state, as pictured in *The Hairy Ape* is a device for dehumanizing its citizens, and for preventing change.

O'Neill presents his own reaction to the modern state through his central character Yank, for Yank is, according to O'Neill, "every human being."[3] O'Neill faces Yank with three possible attitudes toward modern society. The first is his own at the beginning of the play: complete acceptance of industrialized society, identification with speed and power. As Yank puts it, "I'm smoke and express trains and steamers and factory whistles."[4] This attitude becomes impossible for Yank the moment he sees how he appears to a cultivated sensibility, and, more important, realizes that he is owned and controlled by the men who own the steel.

The second attitude toward modern society is represented by Paddy, the chantyman, who longs for the days before society became industrialized, the days with "sun warming the blood of you, and wind over the miles of shiny green ocean like strong drink to your lungs. Work—aye, hard work—but who'd mind that at all? Sure, you worked under the sky and 'twas work wid skill and daring to it." Yank does not object to the idea of returning to the past, but he is contemptuous of it as an impossible "dope dream." He tells Paddy, "All dat tripe yuh been pullin'—Aw, dat's all right. On'y it's dead, get me?"[5]

The third attitude toward modern society with which O'Neill faces Yank is that of Long, the radical. O'Neill gives a clear ac-

3. Mary B. Mullett, "The Extraordinary Story of Eugene O'Neill," *The American Magazine*, XCIV (November 1922), 118. Despite his superficial bestiality, Yank shows in all of his important attitudes and ideas, a striking resemblance to O'Neill. For instance, even Yank's love of speed is a trait of O'Neill's. In France, O'Neill owned a Bugatti racing car. Ward Morehouse reported, "He's a fool about motoring and always was. To him the Bugatti is a joy. When let out it will do 106." (Ward Morehouse, "The Boulevards After Dark: Four Hours from Paris in His French Chateau Eugene O'Neill is Writing American Drama," New York *Sun*, May 14, 1930, p. 24.) Other, more significant parallels between Yank and O'Neill will be demonstrated in the course of this paper. Hereafter Mullett, *American Magazine*.

4. *The Hairy Ape*, scene i, p. 216.

5. *Ibid.*, scene i, pp. 214–15.

count of what Long (as well as the I. W. W.) thinks is wrong with society, and what he considers to be the remedy. Long starts with the same assumption that underlies the whole play: the structure of society is rotten. The cause of this rottenness, for Long, is the economic system: "They dragged us down 'til we're on'y wage slaves in the bowels of a bloody ship, sweatin', burnin' up, eatin' coal dust! Hit's them's ter blame—the damned Capitalist clarss!" Since the basic evil is capitalism, the workers, according to Long must be educated to a knowledge of the economic structure of society. As he tells Yank, "I wants to awaken yer bloody clarss consciousness. Then yer'll see it's 'er clarss yer've got to fight, not 'er alone." Long fights with strictly legal means. He tells Yank, "Remember force defeats itself. It ain't our weapon. We must impress our demands through peaceful means—the votes of the on-marching proletarians of the bloody world!"[6]

O'Neill, through Yank, agrees with Long's diagnosis of the social problem, but not with his solution to it, nor with his method of achieving a solution. The one idea of Long's that Yank accepts is the idea that he is enslaved by capitalism. To Long's comment on Mildred's father, " 'Er old man's a bleedin' millionaire, a bloody Capitalist! . . . 'E makes arf the bloody steel in the world! 'E owns this bloody boat! And you and me, Comrades, we're 'is slaves!" Yank replies, not with his usual contempt for Long, but with bewilderment, "Is all dat straight goods?" By the end of this scene, Yank shows that he has accepted Long's statement, by saying, "She grinds de organ and I'm on de string, huh?"[7] Yank's final analysis of his relationship to Mildred's father is entirely in line with Long's: "Sure—her old man—president of de Steel Trust—makes half de steel in de world—steel—where I tought I belonged—drivin' trou—movin'—in dat—to make *her*—and cage me in for her to spit on! Christ!"[8] In diagnosis, at least, Yank agrees with Long and the I. W. W.

Why, then, doesn't he accept the rest of their program? A partial answer lies in an interview O'Neill gave on *The Hairy Ape*, where he looked back, even as Paddy, to the old days of the sailing

6. *Ibid.*, scene i, p. 212; scene v, pp. 235–36.
7. *Ibid.*, scene iv, pp. 228, 231.
8. *Ibid.*, scene vi, p. 244.

ships. Then, as he saw it, men were controlled by "love of the ship":

> This feeling, by the way, does not exist so strongly now. Labor leaders have organized the seamen and have got them to thinking more about what is due *them* than what is due *from* them to the vessel. This new type of sailor wants his contract, all down in black and white; such and such work, so many hours, for so many dollars.
>
> Probably some abuses have been corrected by this new order of things. But under it there has been lost the old spirit. It was more like the spirit of medieval guilds than anything that survives in this mechanistic age—the spirit of craftsmanship, of giving one's heart as well as one's hands to one's work, of doing it for the inner satisfaction of carrying out one's own ideals, not merely as obedience of orders. So far as I can see, the gain is over-balanced by the loss.[9]

Obviously, O'Neill does not take the idea of progress for granted. He sees no great hope for mankind in improved methods of production. Nor does he see any correlation between a man's satisfaction in his work and the material rewards he gets from it. Rather, he assumes that poor food and overwork are not sufficient to dim the sailor's love for his work, whereas an over-concern for his own physical needs is.

For O'Neill, then, the truly vicious effects of the capitalist state are not physical, but spiritual. The smoke and heat of the stokehole have no power to make Yank question the justice of the status quo. He is infuriated by Long's complaint at "sweatin', burnin' up," in the stokehole. "Yuh ain't got no noive," he tells Long. "Yuh're yellow, dat's what. Yellow, dat's you."[10] Nor does O'Neill present this idea simply as the naïve comment of a complacent stoker. Undoubtedly O'Neill too shares the idea that an objection to poor working conditions stems from weakness, for he characterizes Long throughout the play as a weakling, a coward. Moreover, in one of his early poems on the sea, O'Neill expressed an attitude very like Yank's:

9. Mullett, *American Magazine*, p. 118.
10. *The Hairy Ape*, scene i, p. 212.

I grant you the feed is passing bad,
And the labor great, and the wages small,
That the ways of a sailor on shore are mad
But they're part of the game and I loved it all.[11]

Nothing could be more paralyzing to the impulse for social reform than the attitude, expressed here, that there is a kind of manly virtue in enduring poor food and low pay, or at least in not being concerned with the quality of one's food or the amount of one's pay. For O'Neill, only the non-material satisfactions of work matter. As Yank puts it, "Dis ting's in your inside, but it ain't your belly."[12]

Of course, Long too is concerned with non-material values, as his indignation at Mildred's "hinsults to our dignity as 'onest workers" shows.[13] But he sees a solution of the spiritual problem in a solution of the physical problem. He believes that if you "change the unequal conditions of society"[14] you will solve the problem, or achieve the necessary conditions for a solution of the problem. In his concern for the spiritual answer, Yank, however, has rejected entirely any hope in an alteration of the physical conditions. Although he is against the organization of the state and the economic system as is, he is contemptuous of any hope in a changed social or economic system. In his final comment on the I. W. W., Yank rejects any hope of bettering man by bettering society: "Dey're in de wrong pew—de same old bull—soap-boxes and Salvation Army—no guts! Cut out an hour offen de job a day and make me happy! Gimme a dollar more a day and make me happy! Tree square a day, and cauliflowers in de front yard—ekal rights —a woman and kids—a lousy vote—and I'm all fixed for Jesus, huh? Aw, hell! What does dat get yuh?"[15]

Thus Yank rejects the solution to his problem offered by Long and the I. W. W., and he also rejects their method of attaining it.

11. "Ballad of the Seamy Side," in Ralph Sanborn and Barrett H. Clark, *A Bibliography of the Works of Eugene O'Neill* (New York: Random House, 1931), p. 158. The poem originally appeared in the New London *Telegraph* in 1912. Hereafter Sanborn and Clark, *Bibliography*.

12. *The Hairy Ape*, scene vii, p. 250.

13. *Ibid.*, scene iv, p. 228.

14. *Ibid.*, scene vii, p. 248. The words are spoken by the Secretary of I.W.W., but his ideas are identical with Long's.

15. *Ibid.*, scene vii, p. 250.

Both Long and the I. W. W. believe in using legal means to abolish the old order and establish the new. Yank sees no new society he wants to establish and can see only one way of getting rid of the old—dynamite. Once he has realized that Mildred's father, president of the steel trust, owns him, Yank reasons: "He made dis—dis cage! Steel! *It* don't belong, dat's what! Cages, cells, locks, bolts, bars—dat's what it means!—holdin' me down wit him at de top! But I'll drive trou! Fire, dat melts it! I'll be fire—under de heap—fire dat never goes out—hot as hell—breakin' out in de night—"[16] Later he explains to the leader of the I. W. W. his program for social change. "Dynamite! Blow it offen de oith—steel—all de cages—all de factories, steamers, buildings, jails—de Steel Trust and all dat makes it go."[17] Extreme as it is, Yank's advocacy of wholesale destruction of the status quo is almost identical in ideology and imagery to a poem "Submarine" that Eugene O'Neill wrote for the *Masses* in 1917, the year he wrote the short story on which *The Hairy Ape* is based:[18]

My soul is a submarine
My aspirations are torpedoes.
I will hide unseen
Beneath the surface of life
Watching for ships,
Dull, heavy-laden merchant ships,
Rust-eaten, grimy galeons [sic] of commerce
Wallowing with obese assurance,
Too sluggish to fear or wonder,
Mocked by the laughter of waves
And the spit of disdainful spray.

I will destroy them
Because the sea is beautiful.

That is why I lurk
Menacingly
In green depths.[19]

16. *Ibid.*, scene vi, p. 244.
17. *Ibid.*, scene vii, p. 248.
18. Reference to this unpublished short story appears in a chronology of his plays by O'Neill in Richard Dana Skinner, *Eugene O'Neill: A Poet's Quest* (New York: Longmans, Green, 1935), p. viii.
19. In Sanborn and Clark, *Bibliography*, p. 120.

O'Neill in the poem, like Yank in *The Hairy Ape*, wishes to destroy the "grimy galeons of commerce," although he sees nothing with which to replace them, except the beautiful sea. Of course, in the poem it is O'Neill's "aspirations" which are the torpedoes, while in the play Yank literally wishes to dynamite the Steel Trust, but the conception behind both is essentially the same. If labels serve as clarification, O'Neill's attitude in both the play and poem is anarchistic—individualist anarchism that sees the structure of society as evil, assumes therefore that any social structure will be evil, and so sees salvation in purely destructive terms.

Yank, O'Neill's Everyman, never goes beyond his desire to destroy what is. His last decision is his offer to the gorilla: "We'll put up one last star bout dat'll knock 'em offen deir seats!"[20] O'Neill gives Yank no other solution than this. Nor does he have faith in the possibility of this solution. He wishes to destroy the status quo, but he sees no hope for doing so. The only answer Eugene O'Neill can find for "every human being" is death. *The Hairy Ape*, then, presents a profoundly pessimistic social philosophy which rejects entirely the status quo, but sees no answer for man in a better society, and no hope for destroying the existing society.

In 1921, the year O'Neill wrote *The Hairy Ape*, he also conceived the idea for *Marco Millions*,[21] an ideological sequel to *The Hairy Ape*. In *Marco Millions* O'Neill concentrates, not on the problems of "every human being," but on a satirical portrait of the "Capitalist clarss," the "grimy galeons of commerce," through a typical specimen, Marco Polo. Clearly, Marco Polo, as presented by O'Neill, is an American businessman of the present, not a thirteenth-century Venetian merchant. Marco's values and his political philosophy are a parody of the American businessman's point of view.

In 1924, O'Neill spoke of the United States as "the most reactionary country in the world."[22] Certainly, it was with this judgment in mind that he designed Marco's program as mayor of Yang-Chau. To the appalled Kublai Kaan, Marco boasts of the "unprecedented amount" of taxes he has "sweated out" of the local citizens, and cxplains how he has done it. "I simply reversed the old

20. *The Hairy Ape*, scene viii, p. 253.
21. Clark, *O'Neill*, p. 107. *Marco Millions* was completed in 1925.
22. "Eugene O'Neill Talks of His Own and the Plays of Others," New York *Herald Tribune*, November 16, 1924, Sections VII and VIII, p. 14.

system. For one thing I found they had a high tax on excess profits. Imagine a profit being excess! Why, it isn't humanly possible! I repealed it. And I repealed the tax on luxuries. I found out the great majority in Yang-Chau couldn't afford luxuries. The tax wasn't democratic enough to make it pay! I crossed it off and I wrote on the statute books a law that taxes every necessity in life, a law that hits every man's pocket equally, be he beggar or banker!"[23] Just as Marco's plan for taxation is aimed at making the rich richer, so his whole economic philosophy is single-mindedly directed toward the same end. When he returns to Venice he tells blithely of how "millions of contented slaves labor unremittingly"[24] in the silk industry. His whole attitude toward the workers is typified by his cheerful announcement that his ship's cargo has been loaded before schedule: "We killed six slaves but, by God, we did it!"[25]

Marco's economic program leaves the citizens of Yang-Chau no political liberty. Marco responds to Yang-Chau's petition against his "gross abuse of power" very much as Senator Queen of *The Hairy Ape* responds to the I. W. W. He tells the Kaan, "That's the work of a mere handful of radicals—" When the Kaan goes on to protest, "They complain that you have entirely prohibited all free expression of opinion," Marco justifies himself as follows: "Well, when they go to the extreme of circulating such treasonable opinions against me, isn't it time to protect your sovereignty by strong measures?"[26] If Marco's rule of Yang-Chau was meant as a parody of the businessman's rule of the United States, then clearly O'Neill considered America no stronghold of political liberty. That O'Neill had such a parody in mind is evident, for instance, in this stage direction for Marco, which obviously is not an aid to the actor, but a gratuitous expression of O'Neill's opinion: "His . . . face is carefully arranged into the grave responsible expression of a Senator from the South of the United States of America about to propose an amendment to the Constitution restricting the migration of non-Nordic birds into Texas. . . ."[27]

In *Marco Millions*, Eugene O'Neill adds to his criticism of the

23. *Marco Millions*, Act II, scene i, pp. 391–92. All references to *Marco Millions* are to *The Plays of Eugene O'Neill*, II.
24. *Ibid.*, Act III, scene i, p. 431.
25. *Ibid.*, Act II, scene ii, p. 405.
26. *Ibid.*, Act II, scene i, p. 392.
27. *Ibid.*, Act II, scene i, p. 390.

state, a criticism of the relations between states. Perhaps the most appalling aspect of Marco's program is his formula for international relations. He tells the Kaan how to gain peace, to end war: "There's only one workable way and that's to conquer everybody else in the world so they'll never dare fight you again!"[28] The same idea is expressed by General Bayan, who, as a General, is eager for a war, any war, and suggests to the Kaan a preventive war, which he justifies in lofty moral terms as a war against Christian idolatry. The Kaan, however, suggests a practical war: ". . . there is a group of islands whose silk industry is beginning to threaten the supremacy of our own." General Bayan takes up this cause with enthusiasm, announcing to his staff: "His Majesty's benevolence and patience have been exhausted by the continued outrages against our silk nationals perpetrated by unscrupulous Japanese trade-pirates who, in spite of his protests, are breeding and maintaining silkworms for purposes of aggression!"[29] O'Neill's ideas here on the commercial origins of wars are essentially the same as those he expressed in a poem, "Fratricide," which appeared in the New York *Call*, May 17, 1914. In "Fratricide" he wrote of how the blaring bands call "Come, let us rob our neighbor's farms" to the "army of the poor," who must do the fighting for the "plutocrats" and "jingoes":

"A good war haloes any cause."
What war could halo this cause, pray?
The wise man's words had given pause
To him, were he alive today
To see by what unholy laws
The plutocrats extend their sway.
What cause could be more asinine
Than yours, ye slaves of bloody toil?
Is not your bravery sublime
Beneath a tropic sun to broil
And bleed and groan—for Guggenheim!
And give your lives for—Standard Oil![30]

Not the least of O'Neill's criticism of the modern state is his attack on it for manufacturing wars.

28. *Ibid.*, Act II, scene i, p. 394.
29. *Ibid.*, Act III, scene i, p. 422.
30. In Sanborn and Clark, *Bibliography*, pp. 113–16.

Marco Millions, then, confirms the rejection of capitalism in *The Hairy Ape*, giving a fuller expression of its material evils than the earlier play presented. However, *Marco Millions*, like *The Hairy Ape*, is chiefly concerned with the spiritual evils of the modern state. O'Neill's reading of Marx[31] is evident in his analysis of the material evils of the capitalist state, but it was his reading of Nietzsche[32] that determined his most consistent criticism of the state—its spiritual sterility. As a matter of fact, a summary of Nietzsche's view of the state might serve as an explanation of O'Neill's picture of the state in *The Hairy Ape*.

> The State is the Devil who tempts and intimidates man into animalic conformity and thus keeps him from rising into the heaven of true humanity; the Church is the Antichrist who has perverted Christ's original call to man to break with father and mother and become perfect: she has sold Christ to Caesar and become the chief accomplice of the State in compelling uniformity.[33]

Nietzsche was bitter, too, about the chief goal of the citizens of the modern state—the acquisition of wealth. "Wealth they acquire and become poorer thereby. Power they seek for, and above all, the level of power, much money—these impotent ones!"[34] Nietzsche saw the source of this search for wealth, power, in personal weakness. "The weak, lacking the power for creation, would fain shroud their slave souls in a royal cloak and, unable to gain mastery of themselves, seek to conquer others. Men dedicate their lives to the accumulation of riches; nations make wars to enslave other nations."[35] O'Neill's depiction of those who seek after wealth, power, always reflects these ideas of Nietzsche. Marco Polo, for instance, whose one pursuit in life is the acquisition of money, is particularly satirized by O'Neill for his spiritual impotence. As the Kaan remarks in final judgment of Marco, "He has not even a mortal soul,

31. Clark, *O'Neill*, p. 14.
32. *Ibid.*, pp. 14, 25.
33. Walter A. Kaufman, *Nietzsche: Philosopher, Psychologist, Antichrist* (Princeton: Princeton University Press, 1950), p. 150. Hereafter Kaufman, *Nietzsche*.
34. Friedrich Nietzsche, "The New Idol," "Thus Spake Zarathustra" in *The Philosophy of Nietzsche* (New York: Modern Library, 1927), p. 51.
35. Kaufman, *Nietzsche*, p. 224.

he has only an acquisitive instinct."[36] *The Great God Brown*, completed in the same year as *Marco Millions*, presents a similar picture of the American businessman in the character of Billy Brown. O'Neill's own comment on Brown states his criticism explicitly. "Brown is the visionless demi-god of our new materialistic myth—a Success—building his life of exterior things, inwardly empty and resourceless, an uncreative creature of superficial preordained social grooves. . . ."[37]

O'Neill particularly stresses the personal weakness of those who strive for wealth. Billy Brown is helpless without the creative strength of Dion Anthony. Marco Polo becomes despondent when lack of external activity forces him to think. Sam Evans, the successful businessman of *Strange Interlude*, is totally without inner resources. "How weak he is!" his wife thinks early in the play. When he gains power, it is purely external: "What a fount of meaningless energy he's tapped! . . . always on the go . . . typical terrible child of the age."[38] In an earlier play *Lazarus Laughed*, O'Neill showed that the craving for political power is also a compensation for inward weakness, emptiness. The depraved, power-mad Caligula is above all, weak, frightened, spiritually dead. After murdering Tiberius, he cries savagely to the empty amphitheatre, "Kneel down! Abase yourselves! I am your Caesar and your God!" But, a moment later, he becomes aware of his loneliness, and ends by "groveling in a paroxysm of terror."[39]

All those who seek wealth, power over others, in the plays of Eugene O'Neill, do so out of personal weakness. When they do gain power, wealth, they are "poorer thereby." This interpretation of financial, worldly success, was behind O'Neill's declaration that the United States is "the greatest failure." As he explained, "We are the greatest example of 'For what shall it profit a man, if he shall gain the whole world, and lose his own soul?' "[40] O'Neill's most

36. *Marco Millions*, Act II, scene i, p. 387.

37. "Eugene O'Neill Writes About His Latest Play, 'The Great God Brown,' " New York *Evening Post*, February 13, 1926, in Clark, *O'Neill*, p. 105.

38. *Strange Interlude*, Act IV, p. 69; Act VI, p. 122. References to *Strange Interlude* are to *The Plays of Eugene O'Neill*, I.

39. *Lazarus Laughed*, Act IV, scene ii, pp. 370–71. References to *Lazarus Laughed* are to *The Plays of Eugene O'Neill*, I.

40. Wilson, *PM*, p. 18; Clark, *O'Neill*, p. 153.

bitter condemnation of the status quo is thus based on his Nietzschean philosophy. Both O'Neill and Nietzsche believe that the state produces soulless conformity, that those who seek worldly power, money, do so out of inner weakness and sterility.

Apparently, O'Neill applied this philosophy without reservation to all members of society. He was, it seems, as contemptuous of a stoker's desire for edible food and decent pay (*The Hairy Ape*) as he was of Marco Polo's striving to add several more million to his millions. Thus, though he could castigate the rich, as in *Marco Millions*, for milking the poor, he could not side with the poor in any struggle to be less poor. Nor could he back any movement to establish a new form of state. Very revealing of his cynicism regarding all social structures, church and state alike, is a letter he wrote to Barrett Clark in the later nineteen thirties.

> A true play about the French Revolution ought to make a grand satire on the Russian one. Or . . . a play or novel depicting the history of any religion would apply rationally in the same way. God with a change of whiskers becomes the State—and then there's always a Holy Book—dogmas—heresy trials—an infallible Pope—etc.—etc., until you become sick. It appears we apes always climb trees—and fall out of them—with a boringly identical behavior pattern![41]

Moreover, O'Neill applies the Nietzschean psychology of compensation for weakness to all who work for a goal beyond their own individual perfection. As a result, he sees the social reformer or revolutionary in the same light as the capitalist, as striving for power over others to compensate for inner failure. For instance, Hugo, the anarchist editor of *The Iceman Cometh*, reveals, under the destructive influence of Hickey, his true motives:

> Hello, leedle peoples! Neffer mind! Soon you vill eat hot dogs beneath the villow trees and trink free vine—(*Abruptly in a haughty fastidious tone*) The champagne vas was not properly iced. (*With guttural anger*) Gottamned liar, Hickey! Does that prove I vant to be aristocrat? I love only the proletariat! I vill lead them! I vill be like a Gott to them! They vill be my

41. In Clark, *O'Neill*, pp. 144–45.

> slaves! (*He stops in bewildered self-amazement—to* LARRY *appealingly*) I am very trunk, no, Larry?[42]

It is no wonder, then, that O'Neill never was able to put his faith in any solution to the social problem, since any social leadership was for him automatically suspect.

Where, then, with his bitter condemnation of the status quo and his rejection of all social programs and methods for changing the status quo, did O'Neill see the answer for humanity? O'Neill, like Nietzsche, looked for his answer in the individual soul of man. Like Nietzsche he believed that salvation is a "question for the single one."[43] His comment on the depression of the thirties, through John Loving in *Days Without End*, is typical of his individualist point of view. John rails at the "stupid cowardice" of the people, who want nothing but "to start the merry-go-round of blind greed all over again."

> They have lost the ideal of the Land of the Free. Freedom demands initiative, courage, the need to decide what life must mean to oneself. To them, that is terror. They explain away their spiritual cowardice by whining that the time for individualism is past, when it is their courage to possess their own souls which is dead—and stinking! No, they don't want to be free. Slavery means security—of a kind, the only kind they have courage for. It means they need not think. They have only to obey orders from owners who are, in turn, their slaves![44]

O'Neill believed that individuals must gain the "courage to possess their own souls" before man can begin to think of establishing a just society. As Larry Slade of *The Iceman Cometh* puts it, "The material the ideal free society must be constructed from is men themselves and you can't build a marble temple out of a mixture of mud and manure. When man's soul isn't a sow's ear, it will be time enough to dream of silk purses."[45] For O'Neill, then, it is not a better state that makes better men, but better men who make a better state.

42. *The Iceman Cometh* (New York: Random House, 1946), Act III, p. 169.

43. See Kaufman, *Nietzsche*, p. 140.

44. *Days Without End*, Act III, scene ii, p. 542. References to *Days Without End* are to *The Plays of Eugene O'Neill*, III.

45. *The Iceman Cometh*, Act I, p. 30.

What hope does O'Neill have that such better men will appear? Part of his difficulty lies in knowing what is a better man. Exactly what does it mean to possess one's own soul? O'Neill is very much in the position of Kublai Kaan in *Marco Millions*, who asks Marco to "tell your Pope your example has done much to convert me to wisdom—if I could find the true one!"[46] O'Neill finds no difficulty in rejecting the status quo; the question is what to replace it with. There is no indication in his plays that he has ever answered that question to his own satisfaction. In *Lazarus Laughed*, where he showed a Nietzschean savior come to teach men how to possess their own souls, the savior was killed, and the weak, soulless, depraved Caligula remained in final power. All of O'Neill's statements on the future of mankind show profound pessimism. For instance, in his letter to Barrett Clark on the state, he ended with the P.S.: "The last of the above sounds pessimistic—whereas I feel full of hope these days. For, noting the way the world wags, I am sure that Man has definitely decided to destroy himself, and this seems to me the only truly wise decision he has ever made!"[47] In his press interview in 1946, O'Neill expressed the same attitude. "If the human race is so damned stupid that in two thousand years it hasn't had brains enough to appreciate that the secret of happiness is contained in one simple sentence which you'd think any grammar school kid could understand and apply, then it's time we dumped it down the nearest drain and let the ants have a chance."[48] So, in 1946, O'Neill saw no more hope for "every human being" than he had seen in 1921, when he wrote *The Hairy Ape*. The only solution O'Neill sees for mankind is death.

If this is the ultimate conclusion of Eugene O'Neill's social philosophy, the question then arises, how could this same O'Neill give a lyric acceptance of the status quo such as appears in *Ah, Wilderness!* or, for that matter, *Days Without End?* A clue to this riddle may be found in one of O'Neill's earliest efforts at playwriting, *Servitude*, written in 1914. In this play O'Neill argued against the Nietzschean individualism which later became the predominant element in his philosophy. *Servitude* tells how Mrs. Frazer leaves her stockbroker husband, rejecting all his values, including "his

46. *Marco Millions*, Act II, scene i, p. 397.
47. Clark, *O'Neill*, p. 145.
48. Wilson, *PM*, p. 18; Clark, *O'Neill*, p. 153.

business in all its hideousness,"[49] in order to follow an ideal she has learned from the playwright Roylston: ". . . the ideal of self-realization, of the duty of the individual to assert its supremacy and demand the freedom necessary for its development."[50] She appears in Roylston's house late one night to learn from him whether she has been right to follow the philosophy of his plays. What she sees of Roylston's family life convinces her she was wrong, and she tells him what she thinks of him: ". . . you were on such a high pedestal—I thought of the superman, of the creator, the maker of new values. This morning I saw merely an egotist whose hands are bloody with the human sacrifices he has made—to himself!"[51] From Roylston's Nietzschean individualism, Mrs. Frazer turns to the philosophy of the self-sacrificing Mrs. Roylston, telling her: "How much you have taught me! Happiness, then, means servitude?" Mrs. Roylston replies: "Love means servitude: and *my* love is *my* happiness."[52] With this precept in mind, Mrs. Frazer goes back to live happily ever after with her stockbroker husband. The interesting thing about this play is that O'Neill connects a critique of the system with Nietzschean individualism, and connects an acceptance of the status quo with a philosophy of love for others. In order to reject the "hideousness" of the social structure exemplified by the stock exchange, Mrs. Frazer must reject love, and a philosophy of sacrifice for others. In order to accept love and self-sacrifice, she must also accept capitalism, the stock exchange, the status quo.

This coupling of the status quo with brotherly love is not simply an accidental meaning in *Servitude*. It was, for O'Neill, a fundamental way of looking at life. Apparently he could not connect a criticism of society with the idea of love, self-sacrifice. Had he been able to connect criticism of the status quo with belief in love, in social responsibility, he might have achieved some positive hope for humanity. But O'Neill could never connect the negative concept of social criticism with the positive concept of love for others. His criticism of the state extended to the people in the state, and when he rejected hope for the state, he rejected hope for humanity, and thus was left with a total negativism, so that nothing was left

49. *Servitude*, Act I, p. 80. In *Lost Plays of Eugene O'Neill* (New York: New Fathoms, 1950).
50. *Ibid.*, Act I, p. 82.
51. *Ibid.*, Act III, p. 123.
52. *Ibid.*, Act II, p. 113.

for him but annihilation, death. When he sought love, he could see it only in the context of total acceptance, conformity to the very status quo that he despised.

This curious division is strikingly evident in *Days Without End*, where, as in *Servitude*, he again preaches a philosophy of love. Here he shows the division in his own mind by splitting his main character into a negative and a positive principle. The central character, John Loving, is represented in the play by two people: John, the positive principle, the one who loves, and Loving, the negative principle, who appears as "the death mask of a John who has died with a sneer of scornful mockery on his lips."[53] At one time, the negative, critical principle had been most powerful, so that, as Loving's business partner describes it: ". . . I can remember when I couldn't pick up an advanced-thinker organ without running into a red-hot article of yours denouncing Capitalism or religion or something."[54] However, after many years of criticizing society and searching for an answer to life, John had at last found love. With his engagement to Elsa, he gave up social criticism to enter Eliot's firm "and make some money."[55] Like Mrs. Frazer of *Servitude*, John Loving accepts a love that is linked inextricably to acceptance of the status quo. Nevertheless, part of him, Loving, continues to be critical of the state, of conventional religion, to accept nothing, not even love. Loving is entirely negative, and offers no solution to the problem of life other than the solution O'Neill offered to "every human being" in *The Hairy Ape:* ". . . the warm, dark peace of annihilation."[56] John Loving is torn between the impulse toward love and acceptance of the status quo on the one hand, and death and criticism on the other. Throughout the play these two alternatives war with one another until finally love wins, and John Loving, no more divided, ends with an acceptance of conventional religion.[57]

In the midst of his work on *Days Without End*, O'Neill took time off to write *Ah, Wilderness!*[58] The two plays are subtly re-

53. *Days Without End*, Act I, pp. 493–94.
54. *Ibid.*, Act I, p. 497.
55. *Ibid.*, Act I, p. 496.
56. *Ibid.*, Act III, scene i, p. 534.
57. In the light of O'Neill's earlier criticism of the church, Loving's acceptance of conventional religion is equivalent to Mrs. Frazer's acceptance of the stock exchange.
58. Clark, *O'Neill*, p. 137.

lated. In *Days Without End*, John's wife, Elsa, who has brought love to him, is said "to live in some lost world where human beings are still decent and honorable."[59] *Ah, Wilderness!* depicts such a world, and it is not surprising that this world is a thoroughly bourgeois world. Nat Miller, the small town American newspaper editor of *Ah, Wilderness!*, is a model of all that is "decent and honorable." As Sid puts it, ". . . everyone knows you're an old sucker, Nat, too decent for your own good."[60] Nat's son Richard is equally the soul of honor. His father says, "I've never known him to lie to me." Richard holds back the truth only on one occasion because, "I'd have to snitch on someone—and you wouldn't want me to do that."[61] Also, as John in *Days Without End* was "an old-fashioned romantic idealist"[62] at heart, Richard is tenfold a romantic idealist. In this atmosphere of decency and honor, love abounds. Nat Miller sums up the atmosphere of the play in the last act, when he says, ". . . we seem to be completely surrounded by love!"[63] Just as in *Days Without End*, so in *Ah, Wilderness!*, the victory of love is accompanied by the triumph of the status quo. In *Ah, Wilderness!* radical ideas, social criticism, are simply an adolescent revolt "against all authority"[64] to be looked upon with smiling indulgence. Love and bourgeois conventions live happily ever after.

O'Neill could kill Loving, the principle of criticism, in one play, *Days Without End*, and suppress him in *Ah, Wilderness!*, but he could not rest permanently on his philosophy of love, since to do so necessitated blinding himself to his own life-long criticism of the status quo. His later plays, as well as his later comments on the world, show that he returned to his predominant attitude of criticism.

The main trend in Eugene O'Neill's social criticism is negative. He condemns the capitalist state, but sees no hope for man in any other kind of a state. Whatever hope he sees for man lies in individuals who may have the courage to possess their own souls.

59. *Days Without End*, Act II, p. 518.
60. *Ah, Wilderness!*, Act I, p. 204. References to *Ah, Wilderness!* are to *The Plays of Eugene O'Neill*, II.
61. *Ibid.*, Act I, p. 206; Act IV, scene iii, p. 294.
62. *Days Without End*, Act II, p. 522.
63. *Ah, Wilderness!*, Act IV, scene iii, p. 292.
64. *Ibid.*, Act I, p. 202.

Most individuals, however, he sees as hopelessly dehumanized, and O'Neill's heroes who are searching for new values are so ingrown, tormented, and doomed, that they are not likely to lure one into following their example. Most of O'Neill's really pleasant characters are his conventional, unthinking bourgeois, for at least they are capable of affection for others, and have some sort of social ethic in personal relationships, however ruthless they may be in pursuit of their highest value—money. But they are manifestly empty souls.

Ultimately, Eugene O'Neill's social criticism cancels itself out, for he not only condemns all of society as is, he rejects all solutions for making it something better. He accepts no answer to life, but death.

Oscar Cargill

FUSION-POINT OF JUNG AND NIETZSCHE

The Great God Brown (1926) created discussion aplenty, but a good deal of it was ill-informed. Hawthorne has a short story which describes the consternation that settled upon a whole community when its minister assumed a black veil but this fictive fright was as nothing compared with the storm created in critical circles when the characters of *The Great God Brown* employed masks. As usual, the contemporary explanation occurred to nobody, though O'Neill was explicit enough. Even when he wrote, in 1932 in *The American Spectator*, defending the use of masks as "the freest solution of the modern dramatist's problem as to how—with the greatest possible dramatic clarity and economy of means—he can express those profound hidden conflicts of the mind which the probings of psychology continue to disclose to us . . . (those) adventures of 'free wills,' with the masks that govern them and constitute their fates" no one apparently grasped what O'Neill was talking about.

Now this may indicate how superficially we were touched by Freudianism, after all, for Jung[1] rather than Aeschylus, illuminates *The Great God Brown*. The mask is the face which the Conscious presents to the world—the thing which Jung calls the *persona*. It is the direct opposite of a balancing expression in the Unconscious, whence the dualism of O'Neill's characters. For example, the mask

---

1. Like Nietzsche, Carl Jung is frequently drawn upon by O'Neill. His most original play, and one of his greatest, *The Emperor Jones*, is a study of the involuntary regression of an individual consciousness through the stages of its own history to the racial or collective unconscious. From the artistic point of view, how far O'Neill subscribed to the Jungian thesis is immaterial; he used it imaginatively to create an amazingly poetic fantasy for the theatre, in which Charles Gilpin played the title role with a bravura I will never forget.

of Dion Anthony is "a fixed forcing of his own face—dark, spiritual, poetic, passionately supersensitive, helplessly unprotected in its childlike, religious faith in life—into the expression of a mocking, reckless, defiant, gayly scoffing and sensual young Pan."[2] When Margaret marries Dion in the play, it is the *persona* she loves, the deliberately immature thing which she thinks of as "my own Dion, my little boy." Anthony knows the difference between the face which he presents to the world and the inner man, and bitterly laments, "Why am I afraid of love, I who love love? . . . Why must I be so ashamed of my strength, so proud of my weakness? . . ." There is a splendid touch of irony in the fact that Margaret, who is masked as "a girl" (the typical American girl), is afraid of the buried Anthony and altogether prefers the capering, irreverent, boyish Dion. Of course, a marriage in which the wife insists on regarding her husband as her oldest child (see the opening lines of Act I) cannot be a success, and Dion Anthony's immaturity in this vital relationship affects his whole life. Margaret assumes the management of their finances, and when all other resources fail, it is she who appeals to Billy Brown (Dion's rival) to give her husband a job in his office as an architect. We are not surprised at all that the suppressed Anthony should finally have found his way to Cybel, prostitute and earth spirit, who insists that he be himself: "Stop acting. I hate ham fats."

The job in Brown's office and the simultaneous friendship with Cybel alter both the mask and the natural face of Dion Anthony; the Pan-like *persona* has now "a diabolical Mephistophelean cruelty and irony" while the true features have become those of "an ascetic, a martyr." Yet the marks of self-torture and pain are illumined by the glow of spiritual calm and human kindliness within —the result of Cybel's release of the true man. The racy wisdom of Cybel is one of the best things, in fact, in the play. "Life," she tells Anthony, "can cost too much even for a sucker to afford." She is at once—this great American whore—a native humorist of the Artemus Ward-George Ade school and a Freudian confessor for both Anthony and Brown. The Anthony whom she releases draws the acceptable designs for a cathedral before a final "bender" stills

2. O'Neill obviously is playing with the names of Dionysus, the wine-god, and of St. Anthony, the founder of monasticism, in naming Dion Anthony, to symbolize the antithetical dualism of his nature.

forever his jaded heart. Then the envious Brown, the "regular fellow," "the Big Brother, the Friend" who has still continued to love Margaret—but whose bovine, clean American personality has no attraction for her, seizes the mask of the dead Dion, and clapping it on assumes the dual rôle of Margaret's husband and William Brown, president of his architectural firm. Thus O'Neill enforces his observation that Margaret, the typical American wife, will accept only the conventionalized youth, the character whom she may mother, as husband. And this, of course, destroys the Great God Brown as it had destroyed Dion Anthony.

The trouble with *The Great God Brown* is that the spectator, rather than the actor, needs a prompt book—an interlinear one (filled out from Jung) in order that he may understand the play. The audience went away from performances (to which there were distributed a great many free tickets) puzzled by the constant clapping on and snatching off of masks—assumptions of character which, if referred to the proper psychological authority, were in every case reasonable and which genuinely heighten the effect of the action. Of course, if the analytical psychology of Jung is totally discarded, there yet remains a considerable interest in *The Great God Brown*, for the observation that we are all aliens to each other is an immutable fact, liable to outlast time itself and to give the play a permanency for readers, if not for theatregoers. One is inclined to think, despite some glorious exceptions to the generalization, that O'Neill's comment on the immaturity of most American marriage relations and the facelessness of our Great God Browns is valid criticism. The fact that all types of Anthony, artists and mystics, are generally regarded by the American public *and their own families* as immature children is so just a stricture of the national intelligence that one regrets it is lost in the Freudian labyrinth of this play, where only the Freudian archeologist and excavator can dig it out. *The Great God Brown* in some respects is an excellent social tract, just as, in others, it is a poor play—fundamentally weak because Dion Anthony, Margaret, and Brown are stalking theories and not human beings.

Jung helps in the interpretation of *Lazarus Laughed* (1927), the supreme piece of drama of modern times, as well as with *The Great God Brown*. It is the *Psychological Types* volume, however, to which *Lazarus Laughed* must be referred, rather than to Jung's earlier studies of the introvert and the extravert. Of course, O'Neill has his own names for the types of personality which Jung recognizes, and rather better names they are than Jung's. For example, the crowd at the home of Lazarus in Bethany is made up of people portraying the seven periods of life and these periods in turn are represented by characters wearing seven types of mask: (1) The Simple, Ignorant; (2) the Happy, Eager; (3) the Self-Tortured, Introspective; (4) the Proud, Self-Reliant; (5) the Servile, Hypocritical; (6) the Revengeful, Cruel; and (7) the Sorrowful, Resigned. An eighth type is possibly later supplied by the followers of Lazarus, whose masks reveal a fearless faith in life and whose mouths are shaped by laughter. This pattern is afterwards reworked with the Athenian and Roman crowds awaiting the coming of Lazarus. Caligula, the antagonist of Lazarus in the play, is wholly portrayed in terms of the inferiority complex—a boyish cruelty, encouraged as a manly attribute in the camps where he was reared, has determined the character of the *persona*, beneath which kicks a weak whimpering thing, his real self. In many respects Caligula is the best character O'Neill has drawn under the influence of the popular psychology, a shrewd reconstruction of what Crassus calls "the camp brat" and incidentally a comment on Roman civilization. Highly technical is the representation of the courtiers of "the old buck goat" Tiberius: not only do the young men wear the dress and curled hair of the women, while the young women are attired in the robes of men and wear their hair in a boyish mode, but also there is "the stamp of an effeminate corruption" on all the male masks and a "bold masculine expression" on all the female. Even though the characterization comes directly from Jung, one doubts if the utter rottenness of Caesar's court could be better suggested. Pompeia, the emperor's mistress, wears a mask of evil beauty and perverted passion, but her girlish mouth which may be seen beneath "is set in an expression of agonized self-loathing." Thus the *animus* balances the *persona* in the formation of her character. And the evil Tiberius Caesar himself is shown as wholly the product of his mother's ill-conceived ambition for him, a creature of staggering cruelty and great personal loneliness.

Yet *Lazarus Laughed* transcends far more completely the formulas of Jung than does *The Great God Brown.* The story of

Lazarus' victory over death, the stilling character of his presence upon unruly mobs, his reaching affection for the most depraved of mortals, the intoxicating character of his laughter, and the great wind of joy from the hilarious crowds sweep this play on to as complete a dramatic triumph as the theatre affords. With utter contempt for the nay-sayers we may pronounce *Lazarus Laughed* as much superior to all other dramatic conceptions in its day as were *Faust*, *Hamlet*, and *Oedipus Rex* to the contemporary drama of their times. *Lazarus Laughed* has been performed only once, in the Community Playhouse, in Pasadena, California, on April 9, 1928, and though we know not what skill and courage went into that enterprise, we cannot believe that it exhausted the possibilities of the play. Who has ever seen *Hamlet*, *Faust*, and *Oedipus Rex* performed wholly to his satisfaction? *Lazarus Laughed*, like these other plays, is so stimulating to the imagination, the lines offer such a wide variety of possibilities in interpretation, there is so great an opportunity to develop in a new way almost every situation that this drama will never be played wholly to anyone's liking, that is, to the satisfaction of anyone possessing imagination of the mimetic kind. We will never agree as to how the role of Miriam should be interpreted. Why does she age with Lazarus' increasing youthfulness? If her attitude is maternal, why does she not rejoice in this? Can Tiberius Caesar be played to elicit any sympathy, as his story seems to demand? And is it not likely that the death of Lazarus at the hand of Caligula will provoke as much discussion as the madness of Hamlet? How did he summon the courage to kill Lazarus? How did he overcome his laughter? Was Caligula mad? Americans, who are so deferential to the work of the writers of other nations, may rejoice in *Lazarus Laughed*, for here we have a theatrical masterpiece, one of the touchstones in dramatic art.

What has been said about the dramatic qualities of *Lazarus Laughed* need not deter us from a cavil at its philosophy. This is not the lusty, naive paganism of Cybel, the Earth Mother of *The Great God Brown*, who declared, "Life is all right if you let it alone." This is a decadent hedonism, not dissimilar to that which we find in Waldo Frank, but possibly more seductive, since it is glorified as a sort of selflessness. Its roots are as much in O'Neill's reflections as in Nietzsche's brilliant essay, "The Birth of Tragedy," from which there were two considerable quotations in the playbill of *The Great God Brown*, but which O'Neill had not adequately digested at that time for it to mark legibly the earlier play. When *Lazarus Laughed* was written, however, O'Neill had reflected sufficiently upon "The Birth of Tragedy" to select precisely what he wanted from it and to reject the rest. To us *Lazarus Laughed* seems a better "tragedy" in the Nietzschean sense—a better combination of form and rhythm, of dreams and drunkenness, of the Apollonian and the Dionysian—than anything the philosopher cites. Undoubtedly the germinal idea for the play is Nietzsche's observation that "all the celebrated figures of the Greek Stage—Prometheus, Oedipus, etc., are but masks of this original hero, Dionysus." In Lazarus, O'Neill has restored Dionysus to the stage. It is that third coming of Dionysus, prophesied by Nietzsche and evoked by the epopts. Such a god teaches that all the sorrow in the world comes from the splitting up of Nature into individual men; such a god promises a return of universal "oneness" and assures us of the joy behind phenomena—"that, in spite of the flux of phenomena, life at bottom is indestructibly powerful and pleasurable." So Lazarus is to O'Neill the soul of recurring seasons, of living and dying as processes in eternal growth; so Lazarus teaches oneness, "Believe in the healthy god called Man in you . . . men are unimportant! Men pass! . . . Man remains!"

If men are unimportant, then morals which touch men in relation to each other are unimportant, too. Hence O'Neill, like Jung and Nietzsche, denies the existence of evil and protests that there are only sickness and health. This makes it possible for his healthy Lazarus to sympathize with and to pity his sick Tiberius and Caligula. But Caligula and Tiberius are monsters, and the attempt to excuse their vice as unhealth is gross sentimentalism. Unlike Nietzsche, O'Neill has mixed a great many Christian ingredients into his Dionysus. For example, O'Neill asserts flatly that "Love is Man's hope—love for his life on earth, a noble love above suspicion and distrust! . . ." It is a specious love for man, however, which permits license to the destroyers of men, to the Caligulas. Underlying Nietzsche's picture of Dionysus and O'Neill's representation of Lazarus is a deadly resignation and nihilism. Nietzsche tells how a companion of Dionysus was asked what was most desirable for men and how he replied, "What is best for all is forever beyond your reach: not to be born, not to be, to be nothing. The second best for you, however, is soon to die." In the resigned love of Lazarus for life, in his refusal to designate evil, in his glossing of his attitude with the appearance of love for man (abstractly considered), there is not so much confusion as hedonism—hedonism turning ascetic, again as in the Cyrenaic school. No wonder that one of the effects of Lazarus' laughter is to make men grovel and spit, to derange their intellects so that they go berserk and destroy. It is significant that the followers of Lazarus in Rome disarmed their appointed slayers and with the soldiers' swords took their own lives. Again let us recall that Hegesias was nick-named "the persuader to die." And so Lazarus and his laughter.

Doris Falk

THE WAY OUT: THE MANY ENDINGS OF DAYS WITHOUT END

Learning, at last, to accept a moral order in which the only consolation for suffering is inherent in the suffering itself may be the mark of a tragic hero, but what about the bewildered, alienated, unheroic man who needs a more absolute order, a resurrection beyond the fall? His intuitive "hopeless hope" will keep him searching for escape from duality—for some peaceful *via media* between the heights and depths, some end to ambivalence in integrated release from the cell of mirrored masks. And death must not be the only answer. Nina's peace ought, somehow, to come while she is actively alive. Lavinia should—somehow—be able to avoid locking the door of her Mannon self behind her.

From 1931 to 1934 O'Neill struggled with his own despair and hope in his search for the "somehow." The result was *Days Without End*, completed after eight tortured drafts, in 1934. O'Neill's only other finished work in these years represented a month's vacation from the third draft of *Days Without End*. In that month he conceived, sketched, and completed his one comedy, *Ah, Wilderness!* Even this had a serious purpose; O'Neill wanted, he said, to write a play true to the spirit of the American large small-town at the turn of the century. Its quality depended upon atmosphere, sentiment, an exact evocation of the mood of the dead past. To me, the America which was (and is) the real America found its unique expression in such middle-class families as the Millers, among whom so many of my generation passed from adolescence to manhood.[1]

From Eugene O'Neill and the Tragic Tension, *Rutgers University Press, 1958. Used with permission of the author and publisher.*

1. *The Plays of Eugene O'Neill*, Wilderness Edition, 12 vols. (New York, 1934) III, pp. xi, xii.

Perhaps the greatest compliment we can pay to the dramatic excellence of *Ah, Wilderness!* is to say that its objectivity makes it relatively insignificant for this study—much less significant than the deeply personal and dramatically inferior *Days Without End*. The affectionate tone of *Ah, Wilderness!* hints that O'Neill felt that there must be a way out of the trap of self—or, at least, that some people are hopelessly tormented by the masks of themselves. Fate still springs out of the family, but it is not necessarily a tragic fate. The comedy breathes a gentle if not exulting optimism, a feeling that life isn't so bad after all—even with our neuroses.

Days Without End, however, which strives so desperately to affirm not only optimism, but faith—a positive solution to the "sickness of today"—is an unconvincing drama and a philosophical whistling in the dark. Man is still born broken, and his hope for mending is literally the grace of God.

Man's name here is John Loving, whose broken self is played by two actors rather than by one with a mask. The self called "John" is "handsome with the rather heavy, conventional type of good looks. . . ." "Loving," his double, invisible to the other characters in the play, wears a mask "whose features reproduce exactly the features of John's face—the death mask of a John who has died with a sneer of scornful mockery on his lips." (Act I, *Plays*, III, pp. 493–494.)

The conflict in *Days Without End* is, of course, between these two selves. The hero begins life as a devout Catholic, loving both life and God. However, at the death of his parents, in circumstances which seemed to be unjust, he dedicates himself to hatred. The "devil of hate" to whom he has sold himself is designated by his double, called, ironically, "Loving." John seeks for some kind of faith to take the place of that which he has lost. After trying many systems of philosophy, each of which is ultimately unsatisfying, he falls in love, marries, and thinks he has found the answer in human love. However, this kind of love alone is not enough to overcome the "devil of hate," for John begins to hate his dependency on and his possession by his wife—to "hate love." He tries to free himself, to kill his love by infidelity. The result is that his "good" self is now tortured by guilt at the blasphemy of his new faith, while the "evil" self secretly wishes for his wife's death and, hating life, for his own. His wife, divining his hatred of love and his secret wish for her death, determines upon suicide. As she lies dying from a partly self-induced illness, John, faced with unbearable guilt and agony, is driven back to the church of his parents for help. At the foot of the crucifix he begs forgiveness for his past hatred. As he does so, his double, still arguing, grows gradually weaker, until John, receiving a "sign" of forgiveness from Christ's figure on the crucifix, cries out "Thou art the Way—the Truth—the Resurrection and the Life, and he that believeth in Thy love, his love shall never die!" At these words, the figure of the demonic self falls dead at the foot of the cross, and John becomes unified as John Loving. News arrives that his wife will live, and John answers with much the same words as those of Lazarus, "Life laughs with God's love again! Life laughs with love!" (Act IV, Scene ii, *Plays*, III, pp. 566–567.)

Days Without End is O'Neill's version of the Faust legend. One of the *Memoranda on Masks* reads as follows:

> Consider Goethe's *Faust*, which, psychologically speaking, should be the closest to us of all the Classics. In producing this play, I would have Mephistopheles wearing the Mephistophelean mask of the face of Faust. For is not the whole of Goethe's truth *for our time* just that Mephistopheles and Faust are one and the same—*are* Faust?[2]

O'Neill's psychological interpretation of the Faust-Mephistopheles conflict is closely parallel to Horney's. The hero has sold his soul, the real self, to Loving in exchange for Loving's mask, the false image of himself as the cynical, all-knowing intellect. The price he pays is disintegration, the loss of true identity in the rending conflict between John, the submissive, childlike lover, and this sophisticated hater.

The only way he can recover the lost self is to relinquish the evil image—the magic of intellectual godhead which ravished Dr. Faustus. He must vanquish the force of reason in order to return to faith in intuition and emotion—the love with which, O'Neill says, God laughs.

So far, the psychological meaning of the play is completely consistent with O'Neill's view of life, but that consistency is lost

2. Eugene O'Neill, "Memoranda on Masks," *American Spectator Yearbook* (New York, 1934), p. 162.

when John finds his solution not only in love, but in the supernatural—in Christianity or, even more specifically, Catholicism. The melodramatic ending, when the face of Christ on the crucifix lights up, the news of Elsa's recovery arrives, and John sings his hymn of praise, was unconvincing to most audiences, and to O'Neill himself. He told Nathan that "the hero's final gesture calls for alteration." Barrett Clark, who quotes O'Neill's comment, questions whether O'Neill meant the dramatic gesture or the " 'mental' gesture in returning to the Catholic faith."

O'Neill meant both. This was the very conclusion he had tried to avoid from the time when the play was conceived as a sequel to *Dynamo*. Originally, under its first title, *Without Ending of Days*, it was intended as the second play in a trilogy of which *Dynamo* was the first. (The third, never written, was to have been called *It Cannot Be Mad.*) *Days Without End* is almost as desperate and hysterical in its search for faith in the supernatural as is the hero of his *Dynamo* in his effort to find solace in materialism. In many of O'Neill's earlier plays (especially *Welded*), the solution to the dilemma of integration is a Christian one in the sense that self-sacrifice and acceptance of the tragic opposites of life is an "Imitation of Christ"—Christ's example and his humanity are central. In *Days Without End*, however, acceptance of formal Christianity is the only redemption.

O'Neill knew that John Loving's Kierkegaardian leap to "faith which resolves contradictions" was itself a contradiction of the steadfast belief in life solutions to life problems which O'Neill had maintained in all his previous work. Even when the answer was a mystical one, O'Neill had always interpreted that mysticism as a psychological phenomenon, not a supernatural one. He had been disillusioned early in the Catholicism which, as his parents' religion, represented his parents to him. In the autobiographical *Long Day's Journey Into Night* he defines his mother's Catholicism as an escape from reality, back to an illusory child's world of innocence and peace. His father's Catholicism (in that play) is mechanical and dogmatic; his pride in it serves only to mask feelings of social inferiority.

Whatever unconscious sense of a renegade's guilt may have dogged O'Neill, it was still for him just another source of alienation, another symbol of his failure "to belong." The Church could, theoretically, provide absolution, security, love, one-ness—but only for true believers. O'Neill could never believe, but consciously or not he had been tempted. In the manuscript notes and drafts[3] of *Days Without End* he has left us a fascinating record of the temptation, of the struggle with his own defenses, of his resistance and ambivalence. Follow these and you will see him at every turn rejecting the supernatural for the natural, while each step only brings him closer to his final reluctant and skeptical capitulation.

The very earliest notes for a play to be entitled either *On to Hercules* or *Without Ending of Days* begin with a Jungian analysis of the hero (here called Russell), who finally commits suicide. O'Neill's manuscript jottings for the end of the play read in part as follows:

> Mother worship, repressed and turned morbid, ends by becoming Death-love and longing—thus it is statue of Virgin and child, identification of mother and Elsa with Her, himself with child, longing for reunion with them through Mother Goddess that really drives him to suicide before statue of Virgin—while at the same time it is his old resentment against mother, against Elsa as mother substitute (infidelity) that keeps him from giving in to Catholicism—longing, confession. . . .

In another early note (dated November 29, 1931), when O'Neill had decided to call the play *Without Ending of Days*, we find him taking a further step toward the Christian solution, but with reservations:

> Make (if possible) religion less definitely Catholic. At the end Russell does not commit suicide, nor does he arrive at faith in the supernatural—what does come to him in the church is a sudden mark (?) of identity, brotherhood with Christ, the man, this Son of Man crucified heroically on the Cross of Life—and this gives him courage to go on, a yea-saying of bound (?) submission to inevitable fate, a conviction that this symbol of Man accepting crucifixion in order to save men from themselves is a proof of the spiritual nobility which can be attained and which can make life a noble end in itself.

3. These are in the Yale University Library.

This is Christianity in the sense in which O'Neill usually refers to it, as symbol and example; nevertheless, he was uncomfortable even in this carefully qualified suggestion of salvation. In the first completed version of the play (the one O'Neill calls the fourth draft) he discards the Christian or Catholic solution altogether. Elsa dies, and Loving is not saved, but ends cursing God, with neither love nor faith to sustain him:

LOVING: (*Chokingly*) She's—dead? (*The doctor nods without speaking. Loving stares at Elsa's face with a horrible anguish*) Dead! (*Then suddenly a frightful rage convulses his face and he shakes his fists above him as if he were aware of some malign murderous fate in the air*) I curse you, God damn you! I curse you.

STILLWELL: (*Sharply*) Loving! Stop it!

LOVING: (*Stares at him bewilderedly—then flings his arms about the dead woman and pulls her to him, pressing his face to her breast, sobbing hysterically*) Elsa! Elsa!

The Faust motif with the Mephistophelean double is introduced in the fifth draft, or the second complete manuscript version of the play. Here John's disintegration becomes explicit in his portrayal as two men. He finds his integration, however, not in faith, but in death. Only in the final throes of the death-struggle with himself (Loving) does he gain insight into the meaning of the crucified Christ as poor broken and divided man, but it is too late for this knowledge to save him. His last speech before the crucifix is: "Oh Son of Life, oh Brother, I see now! Forgive my blindness! Forgive thy poor damned fool!"

So far the play has progressed from "Mother-worship" and "Death-love," through renunciation and defiance of God, to the concept of integration through Christ's example. In the sixth draft—or the third complete manuscript—O'Neill takes another step toward his ultimate solution. John becomes integrated, alive, as John Loving. He curses God first, as in the first complete version, but at the moment of cursing realizes that he believes in God and has always believed and that his hatred should have been love. "But if I curse, I must believe! I must have always believed! (*He gives a laugh that is half sob*) I see now! I see! Oh Lord, forgive thy poor damned fool!" Elsa lives, as in the final version, and John's last speech is almost that of the version which O'Neill eventually published. "I know. Love lives forever. There is a God —who laughs with love!"

In the next version—actually the last, except for a few minor changes—the earlier conception of Christ as a symbol of suffering man merges with the belief in the existence of God, becoming a belief in Christ as God. The progression from faith in the subconscious, "the mother of all gods and heroes," to faith in Christianity, in Catholicism, is complete.

If O'Neill had been writing in his usual vein, the cessation of strife between the two selves of John Loving would have meant the ending of all struggle, movement, and growth for him, or death. Loving is a "finder," but he does not discover acceptance of inevitable disunity; he thinks he has found unity. O'Neill was unhappy about Loving's final gesture because it appeared to be conclusive, to suggest that one can escape the tragic tension between opposites and still lead a rich life. John's return to the faith constitutes a withdrawal from life, and no amount of protestation in the form of stage symbolism nor of exclamatory affirmation can convince us otherwise. Nothing could make this clearer than comparison of *Days Without End* with Strindberg's play on the same subject, with essentially the same conclusion, *To Damascus*.

The conflicting selves of Strindberg's protagonist are represented by several characters—the Stranger, the Beggar, the Doctor, the Tempter. The first three of these form a conglomerate character comparable to John, while the Tempter is the voice of rationality and experience—Loving. There is even an all-knowing "Confessor," comparable to Father Baird of *Days Without End*. The protagonist has struggled with the same problems in his search for significance in life as has John, seeking the solution first in one political or scientific creed, then in another, and has reached the same crucial point—he finally believes that the answer is in the love of a woman, but is unable to accept the ambivalent nature of love in which resentment of her possessiveness and his dependence breeds hate. (Here Strindberg, of course, makes the woman a more active source of evil than does O'Neill, but even Strindberg sees the blame as, on the whole, equally divided.) The dramatic ending of Strindberg's play is different from O'Neill's, in that Strindberg's hero renounces earthly love completely and goes into a monastery—the only place where he can find integration of his divided selves—where portraits may be painted with one face, because there "we have no opinions, we believe." His solution is a frank withdrawal from life—a symbolic death. In the final scene of the play, a few seconds before the curtain falls on the entire trilogy, the Stranger in a dialogue with his double, the Tempter, affirms the tragic opposites of love and life, but denies his own strength to endure them and withdraws into the monastery. Every word of this finale sheds light on the similarity of, and the deviation between, the two plays:

(*A woman, with a baptized child, passes across the stage.*)

THE TEMPTER: See, there is a little mortal, destined to suffer!

THE STRANGER: Poor child!

THE TEMPTER: The first chapter in the history of man. (*A pair of newly-weds cross the stage.*) And there—the loveliest—the bitterest! Adam and Eve in Paradise, in eight days in Hell, in fourteen, once more in Paradise. . . .

THE STRANGER: The loveliest! The most illuminating! . . . The first, the only, the last thing that gives value to life! . . . Once I sat in the sun—a spring day, on a veranda—under the first green tree, and a little halo crowned a head, and a white veil lay like a faint morning-mist over a face, which was not that of a human being . . . Then darkness came!

THE TEMPTER: Where from?

THE STRANGER: From the light itself! . . . If not from the light then I don't know.

THE TEMPTER: It must have been a shadow, because shadow requires light, while darkness . . .

THE STRANGER: Stop! Or we will never come to the end!

(*The Confessor and The Chapter appear in procession.*)

THE TEMPTER: Goodby! (*He disappears.*)

THE CONFESSOR: (*with a large black pall*). God, give him eternal peace!

THE CHOIR: And may the everlasting light shine upon him!

THE CONFESSOR: (*wraps The Stranger in the pall*). May he rest in peace!

THE CHOIR: Amen![4]

Like Strindberg's Stranger, O'Neill knew that the only escape from the oppositions of light and shadow, from the fluctuations of the natural cycle, is in death. In *To Damascus*, of course, this is a ritual death, signifying a death to the world and rebirth in faith. O'Neill, prior to *Days Without End*, had always assumed that faith was itself a phenomenon of this world, the expression of a universal psychological need. Belief in the supernatural was an illusion, a "pipe dream" to keep men alive when other values were gone. He returned to this conception in his subsequent work, and never betrayed it again.

4. Part III, Act IV, scene iii, August Strindberg, *To Damascus*, trans. by Sam E. Davidson, *Poet Lore*, XLII (1933–35), p. 264. (The quotation is complete, the punctuation that of the translation; the dots are not ellipses.)

Bryllion Fagin

EUGENE O'NEILL CONTEMPLATES MORTALITY

Eugene O'Neill has been very prolific. He has utilized old themes and new ones. He has written good plays and merely fair ones. He has received enthusiastic acclaim and bitter condemnation. This is not another attempt to evaluate his contribution to American drama. A complete appraisal of O'Neill's dramatic activity would require much more space and a wider perspective. The aim of this article is to focus attention upon one theme that has stimulated O'Neill to creative work, one problem with which O'Neill has wrestled as a man and as an artist. It is a fundamental, a universal problem, never before exploited by American dramatists—excepting Mackaye. It is the problem of man's insignificance, of man's mortality.

In at least five plays, O'Neill contemplates man's mortality, not merely by implication, but deliberately and boldly. The first play upon this theme was *The Fountain. The Fountain* tells the story of Juan Ponce de Leon's search for the spring of youth. Juan is an adventurer, strong, active, arrogant. Youth and love are but glittering commonplaces to him—until youth passes and he is "sick with years." Then it is that he asks bitterly "Why have I lived?" and prays: "O Son of God . . . Show me Thy miracle—a sign—a word—a second's vision of what I am that I should have lived and died! I have striven for what the hand can grasp. What is left when Death makes the hand powerless? . . . O Mighty Relaxer of hands, have you no vision for the graspers of earth?" His words carry the tragedy of man's decay and the pathos of his helplessness. He calls pitifully: "What are you, Fountain? That from which all life springs and to which it must return—God! Are

---

From The Open Court, *April, 1931.*

all dreams of you but the one dream? (*Bowing his head miserably*) I do not know. Come back, Youth. Tell me this secret!"

"What are you, Fountain?" O'Neill repeats this question in *The Great God Brown*, in *Marco Millions*, in *Strange Interlude*, in *Lazarus Laughed*. He changes his words, modulates his voice, restrains or yields to his intensity, but the question remains essentially the same. Like Everyman, in the medieval Morality by that name, and before and after that Morality, confronted with the termination of his brief span of burning activity, O'Neill fumes and frets, cowers and trembles, rants and curses and whines and pleads, and broods brokenly upon the great enigma. He fumbles amid the welter of symbols he has constructed and gropes in the chaos of their emotions toward some sort of clarification, only, in the next play, to repeat his question over again.

The Great God Brown is a dramatization of the ancient conflict between Puritanism and Hellenism, between asceticism and hedonism. It contains eleven scenes and a prologue and an epilogue. Some of the characters are masked to indicate the duality of their natures. Even their names are symbolic. Margaret—the Eternal Feminine; Cybel—Mother Earth. But the play centers about Dion Anthony, who, it is easy to see, is Mr. Eugene O'Neill, of New York and New England, masked. Weary with the conflict between Dionysus the playboy and Antoninus the austere, O'Neill comes once more to Mother Cybel to be comforted. And Cybel strokes his hair maternally and laughs at his weakness. "You were born with ghosts in your eyes," she tells him, "and you were brave enough to go looking into your own dark—and you got afraid." A good diagnosis of the case of the artist in our midst. Yet he remains afraid before the dark curtain hiding the endless void. "Into thy hands, O Lord," he prays *with ascetic fervor*. (*Then suddenly, with a look of horror*) "Nothing. To feel one's life blown out like the flame of a cheap match . . . ! To fall asleep and know you'll never, never be called to get on the job of existence again!" And Cybel *pats his head maternally:* "There, don't be scared. It's borne in the blood. When the time comes, you'll find it's easy." But evidently he does not find it easy, for when she kisses him good-by he begins to sob. Even her admonition, "Remember, it's all a game, and after you're asleep, I'll tuck you in," does not help. His last word is a *choking, heart-broken cry:* "Mother!" And Cybel remains murmuring the old riddle: "What's the good of bearing children? What's the use of giving birth to death?"

And not only Dion Anthony trembles like a little child as he faces dissolution, but even the more practical William Brown himself. He too comes to Cybel battered and weary and snuggles gratefully against her, finding that "The earth is warm." Cybel tucks him in, and whispers soothingly, "Ssssshh! Go to sleep, Billy." "Yes, Mother," Brown responds. (*Then explainingly*) "It was dark and I couldn't see where I was going and they all picked on me." "I know," says Cybel.

In *Marco Millions* O'Neill started out to write a satire of our modern commercial civilization and its representative "wise man," Marco Polo, but the play ends as a poignant tragedy of man's quest for happiness and understanding and his ultimate defeat. Marco is convinced that he is immortal. He will not confess that his soul is but a stupid invention of his fear and that when he dies he will be "dead as a dead dog is dead," yet he trembles at the prospect of having his head cut off, for he cannot imagine his death. But Marco is too insignificant to make the contemplation of his mortality dramatic. Death becomes tragic only when it affects the existence of a sentient personality. It is only when O'Neill begins to contrast the ancient wisdom and the sadness and resignation of the East with the brashness and purposeless activity of the West that his play acquires the deep overtones of great drama. The death of the beautiful princess Kukachin, the Little Flower, "the golden bird singing beside a black river," and the unavailing lament of Kublai Kaan transmute the sordid history of Polo's acquisitiveness into a play full of exquisite poetry. The last scene reverberates with the intolerable burden of the unanswerable question. The priests of the East—Taoist, Confucian, Buddhist, Islamic—can answer Kublai only with the assertion of the chorus: "Death is." And the Chronicler intones resignedly:

We lament the shortness of life. Life at its
longest is brief enough:
Too brief for the wisdom of joy, too long for
the knowledge of sorrow.

. . . .

Our sobs stifle us, our tears wet the ground,
our lamentations sadden the wind from the West.
Yet we must bow humbly before the Omnipotent.

The same sadness of resignation marks the end of O'Neill's *Strange Interlude*. After nine acts crowded with human events—a "tangled mess of love and hate and pain and birth"—Nina settled down to "rot in peace." Ned Darrell leaves, praying to God to teach him to be resigned to be an atom, and Nina remains with the conviction that life is only a Strange Interlude. All "lives are merely strange dark interludes in the electrical display of God the Father!"

Lazarus Laughed chronologically came before *Marco Millions* and *Strange Interlude*. It is, of all O'Neill's plays the most rigidly concerned with the problem of mortality. Lazarus has risen from the dead and all that behold him seek to know: "What did you find beyond there, Lazarus?" He gently rebukes them: "O Curious Greedy Ones, is not one world in which you know not how to live enough for you?" But man's quest for the secret goes on. "What is beyond?" comes the refrain of the chorus. It is echoed in one form or another by the ragged multitude and the powerful Roman legions, by the lecherous Tiberius and the cowardly Caligula, who knows, even before Lazarus tells him, that he is but "a bubble pricked by death into a void and mocking silence." Lazarus has been beyond and he has brought back a strange laughter. His compassion embraces the entire race of men, "whose lives are long dyings! They evade their fear of death by becoming so sick of life that by the time death comes they are too lifeless to fear it. Their disease triumphs over death—a noble victory called resignation!" Most men, however, are not resigned; they cling to the few certainties they possess and, like Tiberius, they do not wish to die. Unlike Tiberius they might not even admit that "If I were sure of eternal sleep beyond there, deep rest and forgetfulness of all I have ever seen or heard or hated or loved on earth, I would gladly die!" Only Lazarus is sure, and he laughs a joyous laughter. He knows the secret. And O'Neill knows.

For himself at least, Eugene O'Neill has found an answer to the question of mortality. In these five plays in which O'Neill views the transcience of human existence, he not only poses dark riddles, but he presumes to point a way, to strike a heartening harmony. Out of the depths of fear and doubt and despair into which he has imaginatively gone down he returns, like Lazarus, with a joyous laughter in his heart, and exultation not the less triumphant because it encloses the vast sadness of the world. He could not remain passively whining at the inevitable doom of extinction; out of his fearful intimations of mortality he has forged a shining armor for man, a bold consciousness of survival with which to meet the devouring riddle of time.

Like Lazarus, O'Neill has found the answer to death. It is: "There is no death!" Only fools and madmen, cowards like Caligula, who kill out of a terrible fear of death, believe in death. In reality:

There is only life!
There is only laughter!

Lazarus who died returns with an affirmation, a thundering Yes, of the indestructibility, the endlessness of life. Man as dust is "eternal change, and everlasting growth, and a high note of laughter soaring through the chaos from the deep heart of God! Be proud, O Dust!" Lazarus calls. "Then you may love the stars as equals!" Because man thinks only in terms of his temporary form rather than of the agelessness of his dust he walks this earth in aching loneliness and dies of self-pity. If he would but say with Lazarus: "Millions of laughing stars there are around me! And laughing dust, born once of woman on this earth, now freed to dance! New stars are born of dust eternally. The old, grown mellow with God, burst into flaming seed! The fields of infinite space are sown—and grass for sheep springs up on the hills of earth! But there is no death, no fear, nor loneliness! There is only God's Eternal Laughter!" Alas, that man forgets the laughter of Lazarus, the eternal rhythm of rotating dust, the deep, soft laughter of being and becoming!

O'Neill's conception of immortality can be termed biological. Birth and death, growth and decay, are the unending cycles of existence. "Always spring comes again bearing life!" Mother Earth, Cybel, speaks over the body of Billy Brown. "Always again! Always, always forever again!—Spring again—life again!—summer and fall and death and peace again!—but always, always love and conception and birth and pain again—spring bearing the intolerable chalice of life again!—bearing the glorious blazing crown of life again!" And O'Neill's use of the term God is biological, naturalistic. God is, as Time is, as Dust is. And man's pain and travail are normal phases in the unchanging changes of being. Billy's last words are not words of lamentation. As he approaches his earthly habitation his words rise with the wisdom of Lazarus: "The laughter of Heaven sows earth with a rain of tears, and out of Earth's transfigured birth-pain the laughter of Man returns to bless and play again in innumerable gales of flame upon the knees of God!"

There is a good deal of Eastern philosophy in O'Neill's attitude toward life and death. If he has not been able to acquire the serenity of the East, he has at least accepted inevitability and resignation. He has accepted the Eastern view of life as "an interlude, of trial and preparation, say, in which our souls have been scraped clean of impure flesh and made worthy to bleach in peace." In fact, Charlie Marsden, who speaks these lines, has been more victorious by standing aloof and waiting with Buddha-like patience, than either Nina or Darrell by yielding to the fever and fury of their passions. In the end all three realize the inevitability of bleaching, except that Charlie comes to the anodyne of peace much earlier. The cycle is now continued by young Gordon, who flies "away into another life."

O'Neill's discovery of the endless continuity of life and of its perpetual metamorphosis in external form tempers the tragic brooding of his plays. A poetic flame lights up the rebellious futilities of his heroes. Their efforts become ennobled and their defeats become victories in the march of eternity. Everywhere the voice of the Fountain bursts into song:

Life is a field
Forever growing
Beauty a fountain
Forever flowing
Upward beyond the source of sunshine
Upward beyond the azure heaven,
Born of God but
Ever returning
To merge with earth that the field may live.

Ponce de Leon dying hears "the rhythm of eternal life." He sees the "Fountain everlasting, time without end! Soaring flame of the spirit transfiguring Death! All is within! All things dissolve, flow on eternally!" He prays to the "aspiring fire of life" to sweep the dark soul of man, and that he might burn in its unity. Ponce de Leon, the bold adventurer, dies exulting that "God is a Fountain of Eternity," that "He is the All in One, the One in all—the Eternal Becoming which is Beauty." He dies hearing the earth and youth and love and the Fountain sing "*an all-comprehending hymn of the mystery of life as the curtain falls*."

And the beautiful princess Kukachin, hearing the chorus of women chanting her earthly career:

The lover comes,
Who becomes a husband,
Who becomes a son,
Who becomes a father—
In this contemplation lives the woman.

responds with the terse summary of O'Neill's answer:

I am not.
Life is.

Helen Muchnic

THE IRRELEVANCY OF BELIEF: THE ICEMAN AND THE LOWER DEPTHS

When in *The Odyssey* the companions of Odysseus are changed by Circe into swine, they are not deprived of human consciousness; but in Milton's reworking of the episode in *Comus* the men are transformed so thoroughly that they have lost all notion of what has happened to them, and are completely brutish and contented in their pleasures. Milton, that is, in a way consistent with the severity of Puritanism, changed the pathos of a state in which human beings suffer from a sense of their depravity into the greater moral tragedy of a condition so depraved as to make such suffering impossible.[1] Eugene O'Neill's *The Iceman Cometh* and Maxim Gorky's *The Lower Depths* are, it seems to me, a modern instance of much the same contrast. But, although a comparison of these two plays seems clearly indicated, the fullest one that I have seen so far is but a brief discussion in the Russian journal *Zvezda;*[2] there, in the course of a long, and generally scornful, article on current American literature, Vladimir Rubin concludes that, "If Gorky's play asserts: 'Man—that has a proud sound,' then O'Neill's *The Iceman Cometh* seems to be saying: 'Man—that has a low and infamous sound,' for "the gloomy moral" of his play "debases man infinitely . . . as a pitiful, will-less toy of fate." It marks, he says, "the final 'spiritual capitulation' of this veteran of American drama." This, of course, is the opinion one would expect from Soviet criticism today; and there is, to be sure, a shade of truth in it. By comparison with Gorky's view of man,

---

From Comparative Literature, *Spring 1951. Originally entitled "Circe's Swine: Plays by Gorky and O'Neill." Reprinted in this revised version by permission of the author and editor. Parts of the article have appeared in a book by the author,* From Gorky to Pasternak, *Random House, New York, 1961.*

1. This comparison was made some years ago by Marjorie Nicolson in one of her lectures at Smith College.

2. Aug. 1948, p. 200.

O'Neill's is indeed a pessimistic one. But this shadowy truth dismisses with too casual a brutality the realms of concepts here involved. The whole matter is deeper and of a different order than that indicated by Mr. Rubin's remarks.

On the face of it, the plays are very much alike, not only in setting, plot, and structure, but in aesthetic conception; for they seem to be, and yet are not, "slices of life." They are, more accurately, parables of life; and the social outcasts who people Harry Hope's "cheap ginmill of the five-cent whiskey, last-resort variety" and the "cellar, resembling a cave," owned by Kostilev, are not, despite the naturalism of their portraiture, pictures of real men, but symbolic figures in a parable on man's fate. As such they are exceptionally well chosen; the "dregs of society," as the mark of extreme failure, are distress signals which urge inquiry into the nature of human disaster and the responsibility for it. Both plays are plays of dialogue rather than action, and what is done in them, reversing the usual method of drama, is an illustration of what is said. In each, a group of individuals, loosely bound together by a familiarity which breeds tolerant indifference and boredom and with enough in common to represent mankind by and large, is confronted by a solitary outsider who considers himself, and is considered by the group to be superior—to this extent, at least, that he is in a position to preach and to exhort them to a new way of life. In both plays this solitary individual is the repository of a "truth" unknown to the others, and in both, after a brief show of impressive authority, he leaves the scene of his activities in the same, or somewhat worse, condition than he had found it. Is the joke, then, on him? Are the tables turned? Is the prophet false, or at any rate, inadequate? And are the benighted souls whom he had tried to save in possession of a reality which his supposedly superior wisdom has not touched? Who, then, is better, and who is right? Who is to be blamed for the melancholy outcome of events, the prophet or those who refuse to become his disciples? The plays strike deep, deeper than their spoken arguments concerning the nature of truth and the value of illusion. Implicit in them are comparisons between theories of life and actual living, between idealism and reality: demands exacted by the mind and those made by the body, hope imposed by the spirit and the limits to hope set by the circumscribed potentialities of man; questions about the nature and the power of the will; and a search for an ethics that might be accepted as both just and possible in a human situation which is seen to be desperate. But here, with the kind of questions posed and the way they are examined, the similarities end. The answers given are amazingly different, and as one studies them one becomes aware that even the questions are not so similar as at first supposed.

Each play is constructed around a central character, and its meaning hinges on the interpretation of this man and of what he preaches, for he comes with a well-defined faith to correct his fellows; it is to him that they are constrained to respond individually and as a group, it is on him that thoughts and emotions converge. He is, in short, a test of moral principles, and the spectator must decide to what degree he should respect and trust him. In their natures, the two characters are entirely different. Gorky's Luke is a wanderer who, not from any newly found faith but from an accumulated store of sanctified dogma, hands out good advice wherever he happens to be to whoever will listen to him. He clucks sympathetically over men's complaints, tells little moral tales by way of illustrating his precepts, and, when the wretches he has been "saving" are drawn into a perilous situation and he himself is in danger of being caught and questioned by the authorities, slips out unperceived; for, with all his show of self-effacing, greathearted sympathy, he is not unmindful of his own safety—and he happens to be traveling without a passport. Hickey, on the other hand, enters with a program of reform, determined to make his friends happy, now that he himself has found happiness; and until the end, when he becomes a self-convicted felon, he has been a respected member of society. Nor is his scheme a ready-made concoction of untested, pious maxims; his recipe is drastic, and he has first tried it on himself. In the case of Hickey, there is no question of hypocrisy, but there is in the case of Luke.

When *The Lower Depths* was first performed in 1902, Luke was presented as a saintly character, and the play was interpreted as a lesson in brotherly love. That had not been Gorky's intention, as he himself explained in interviews at the time and in an article of 1933 in which—having described four types of "consolers," the sincere (an extremely rare variety), the professional, the vain, and finally "the most dangerous, clever, well-informed, and eloquent" of them all, the coldhearted men who cared about nothing so much as their own peace and comfort and consoled only because they could not be bothered with complaints—he declared that Luke belonged in the last division. "In our days," he added, "the consoler can be presented on the stage only as a negative and comic figure."

Gorky had intended Satin to be the real hero, but muffed the effect by leaving him off stage in some of the crucial moments of the play. Satin is in every respect at opposite poles from Luke, whom he appraises with his native acumen and honest incivility. "Pulp for the toothless" he calls him, but admits that in theory, at least, the wanderer has the right idea about man: namely, that man is large and free and must not be hampered. Satin, who sneers when he is sober and is eloquent when drunk, who is not apart from but very much of the group, on the spot when he is needed, sensible, and, above all, realistic in his understanding of what his fellowmen can and cannot do, has an undemonstrative, genuine sympathy which is infinitely more valuable than Luke's facile, soft-hearted, self-protecting kindliness: "You know how to do better than pity," Kleshch says to him, "you know how not to insult." And his rhetorical speech about man, which begins, "What is man? It is not you, not I, not they . . . no! It is you, I, they, the old man, Napoleon, Mahommed . . . all in one! Do you understand? It is—immense . . . ," is the culminating point of the play and the one that states its meaning. From Satin's standpoint Luke's pampering consolations, when they are not positively harmful—as in the case of the Actor, for whose suicide Satin holds the old man responsible—are insulting to man.

In *The Iceman Cometh* Satin's counterpart is Larry, "the only occupant of the room," according to the stage directions, "who is not asleep" when the curtain goes up, and who indeed remains terribly wide awake throughout the play, who speaks "sardonically," with "a comical intensity," considers himself aloof from all human affairs, "in the grandstand of philosophical detachment," but cannot help responding to the sufferings of "the breed of swine called men" with a sensitiveness and passion he would gladly suppress. He is discriminating and stern in his judgments and penetrating in his grasp of motives. He is not given to long pronouncements, does not try to influence men, but his influence is felt in what he is and in what he makes people do when they compel him to direct them; and, when he talks, it is with the aptness, wit, and brevity of poetry: "their ships will come in, loaded to the gunwales with cancelled regrets and promises fulfilled and clean slates and new leases"; "when man's soul isn't a sow's ear, it will be time enough to dream of silk purses"; and it is he who finds the right name for the Iceman, when he calls him the Iceman of Death. At the beginning of the play he makes a little speech that could be taken as the theme song of both *The Iceman Cometh* and *The Lower Depths:*

> What's it matter if the truth is that their favoring breeze has the stink of nickel whiskey on its breath, and their sea is a growler of lager and ale, and their ships are long since looted and scuttled and sunk on the bottom? To hell with the truth! As the history of the world proves, the truth has no bearing on anything. It's irrelevant and immaterial, as the lawyers say. The lie of a pipe dream is what gives life to the whole misbegotten mad lot of us, drunk or sober.

The "pipe dream" is the obvious leitmotif of *The Iceman Cometh*, as it is also that of *The Lower Depths*, the real theme of which, according to a splendid analysis by the Soviet critic Iury Iuzovsky,[3] is the question "What is Truth?" The characters of Gorky's play, this writer points out, are divided into well-marked groups with respect to the kind of truth they believe in: those, like the Actor, Pepel, Natasha, and Nastya, for whom illusion is truth; those, on the contrary, who believe only in the "truth of facts," like Bubnov, Kleshch, and the Baron, all of whom delight in pricking, variously, the bubble of man's hope—Bubnov with quiet satisfaction, Kleshch with bitterness, the Baron with a kind of sensual delight, "sneering out of envy," as Luke says of him; and, lastly, Luke and Satin who belong to neither category, and whose position Iuzovsky explains by a reference to Lenin's article, "What Is To Be Done?"—written in the same year as Gorky's drama. "One must day-dream," says Lenin in this article, and, quoting the nineteenth-century nihilist critic, Pisarev:

> My day-dream may be of such a kind as to catch up with the natural course of events, or it may go off completely at a tangent to where the natural course of events can never arrive.

3. Iuzovsky, Iury, *Dramaturgia Gor'kovo*, Chast' I (Moscow-Leningrad, 1940), pp. 61–161.

> In the first instance, the day-dream does no harm; it may even support and strengthen the energy of toiling mankind . . . In such day-dreams there is nothing that can prevent or paralyze the strength of workers . . . When there is a point of contact between the day-dream and life, then everything is going well . . .

comments that of the latter kind of day dream there is unfortunately too little in his time. *The Lower Depths*, says Iuzovsky, seems to give symbolic form to this distinction; Luke's is a daydream of slavery and leads to a dead end; Satin's is of freedom and opens a way out; the one goes off at a tangent, the other has contact with reality.

Nevertheless, whether they believe anything or not, the inhabitants of *The Lower Depths* retain, as individuals, a sense of their humanity and they suffer because of it; Circe has not deprived them of consciousness, and, even though they do not do very much, they retain the possibility of action. With the frequenters of Harry Hope's saloon the case is different. They are contented enough in their sodden stupor and are miserable only when, for a brief space, they are jerked into consciousness, for this robs their liquor of its potency to "paralyze." Once they are made to face themselves, the good-natured Americans, thrown into inward conflict by the sudden demonstration that their long-cherished beliefs about themselves are lies, become acrimonious and belligerent; the Russians, even the "romantic" ones, had been too sober and too unhappy from the start for any kind of pretense of mutual regard and general affability. In both plays, it would seem, amicable relations can exist only on the superficial basis of convenient indifference, the "live and let live" philosophy of those who have not chosen, but have been driven, to live together. The Russians have, indeed, much less sense of group solidarity than the Americans; all but wholly unaware of one another and much more callous, they appear to have theories about society but little capacity or desire for social living.

The real difference between the characters in the two plays, however, is not that of social relationships but of the kind of illusion they cherish and the nature of the "truth" they are invited to adopt. If both plays can be said to deal with illusion and reality, these terms have different meanings for their authors. "Truth" or "reality" for Gorky is not a metaphysical but a humanist concept; it involves not so much a recognition of that which is or may be, immutably, as of that which may or may not be done at a given moment. Freedom of will is here based simply on a practical view of possibilities. O'Neill's position is more sophisticated and complex; for him there is no distinction between useful and useless illusions, and no naive presentation of men as fully expressed by their beliefs. From an objective point of view, the "pipe dreams" here are all useless, but all are tragically inescapable and necessary to those who hold them; they are drawn not from the human consciousness of Circe's victims, nor from their idealistic hopes, but from painful, suppressed memories, the persistent iteration of recurrent images in troubled dreams. Here every man has been involved in something he wants to forget. Circe has helped him to oblivion, and the one real victory of his life is his capacity to forget. These men—all but one—unlike Gorky's, do not complain of the miserable state they are in. Parritt, the notable exception, commits suicide. The men of *The Lower Depths* are vaguely aware of some great solution to existence which they have not yet discovered, and the play exhorts them to seek a way that will lead them to discover it; those of *The Iceman Cometh* have no thought of anything beyond their individual well-being, which by now has been reduced to the form of drunken senselessness, and the play turns out to be a study of the impossibility of getting at the truth, indeed, a warning of the danger of going after it.

It is in keeping with this condition that the "leaders" differ as they do—that the American "prophet" is a salesman, peddling salvation as he peddles wash boilers, required to persuade a sales-resisting audience of the usefulness of his product, while the Russian is a wandering holy man, who preaches and consoles, leading despairing men who are only too ready to believe him along the path of human kindness, soothing them with assurances that their dreams are attainable. Both men are evil, Gorky's shrewdly and irresponsibly, O'Neill's, even in his noxiously commonplace sentimentality, rather pathetically and goodheartedly; for, whereas Luke's words are words only, Hickey is disastrously involved in what he preaches. Comically enough, neither accomplishes what he sets out to do—comically, because our sympathies are not with them. If the tone of the plays is on the whole tragic, the tragedy inheres not in the doom of the central characters but in the pathos of various episodes, and even more in implications, in what is not, rather than in what is, done or said. But if Luke and Hickey fail as prophets, it is not because they have misunderstood the values by which their audiences live—a passion for faith on the one hand, a desire for individualistic self-assertion on the other. Nor is it these premises, but something else, that is proved false in their failure.

What is at issue in Gorky's play is the relative usefulness—and *usefulness* is here the same as ultimate good—of two ideals: one, the Christian ideal of tender, pitying humility and inactive faith, the other, the materialist doctrine of forceful, self-reliant, practical action. In O'Neill's play the issue is the nature rather than the practicability of ideals. Social activity is the sphere of Gorky's thought, self-knowledge of O'Neill's. Though both are concerned with happiness, in *The Lower Depths* happiness is looked on as derivative, dependent on an intellectual grasp of values: let a man become conscious of his dignity and capacity, let him adopt an ideal which is possible for man, and he will realize it as an individual. In *The Iceman Cometh* happiness is seen to be immediate and primary; larger concepts may be valid only as abstract formulations of what men have done: let a man believe only what he has achieved—otherwise he will be ridiculous, self-deceived, and dangerous. The reason Luke fails is that he is neither serious nor honest in his relations with men; but Hickey fails because, in his desire to rouse Circe's victims to their original status as human beings with insight into themselves, he has attempted the impossible, for most of them cannot be roused, and those who can will kill themselves once they have understood what they are. Gorky's "message" is seriously meant as a program of conduct; O'Neill's is a poetic statement of disaster, presented only for the contemplation of those who care to look below the surface of human activity.

Murder is central to both plays; but in *The Lower Depths* it is accidental, based on passion, and is generally conceded to be regrettable, while in *The Iceman Cometh* it is more or less premeditated, rationalized to appear as an act of love, and is not a mere episode but the essence of the play. In fact, *The Iceman Cometh*, the latest of O'Neill's inquiries into the paradoxes of existence, is a prophecy of doom, of the willful and calculated murder by man of what he thinks he loves, a revelation of his unconscious hatreds and desire for death. Always concerned with illusion, O'Neill has presented it in many ways: in pictures of individuals pathetically or tragically frustrated because of some initial mistake they make about themselves or that others make about them, as in "Bound East for Cardiff," "Before Breakfast," "The Rope," *Beyond the Horizon*, *The Straw*, and *Diff'rent;* in symbols not of individuals but of man overwhelmed by the force of unconscious primitivism latent in him, as in *The Emperor Jones* and *The Hairy Ape;* in parables concerning the ethics of Western civilization, as in *The Fountain*, *Marco Millions*, and *Lazarus Laughed;* or in psychological probings of man's soul, as in *Desire Under the Elms*, *The Great God Brown*, *Strange Interlude*, and *Mourning Becomes Electra.* Despite great variation in focus and interest, certain factors remain constant enough throughout the plays to make O'Neill's work appear as a continuous philosophic investigation of the riddle of falsehood at the core of life, in the process of which several partial solutions have been reached, but no definitive one as yet. His plays are eerie with the ghosts of terrible dissatisfactions and of desperate guilt; and their darkness is hardly relieved by a hovering conviction that there is power in love and that an ultimate beneficent grandeur exists beyond the groping and raging consciousness of man, for it is in tragedy itself that men are shown to have attained their desires. Jones, in death, preserves the magnificent isolation he had wanted; Yank, in the brotherhood of monkeys, "belongs" at last; Ephraim Cabot's desolate farm is still "jimdandy"; Lavinia Mannon, who has dedicated herself to the punishment of a wrong, shuts herself away from life as the final phase of her life work—and so on. In an ironic way, death and suffering are always the price of attainment, while back of this human scene is "an infinite, insane energy which creates and destroys without other purpose than to pass eternity in avoiding thought," and is sometimes called God. A primitive, necessary, unthinking, intangible essence that insures perpetuity is shown to exist in opposition to the will of man, who desires extinction. "We're always desiring death for ourselves or others," says Nina Leeds. "Our lives are merely strange dark interludes in the eternal display of God the Father!"

The Iceman Cometh, perhaps more clearly than any of the other O'Neill plays, is a morality play, a variation on the ancient motif of the Dance of Death, with its modern, paradoxical twist of willed chance and desired catastrophe, where each man kills the thing he loves because he feels guilty of his inability to love enough. Harry Hope's saloon is Everywhere, and the men in it are drowning a secret guilt they cannot understand. Gorky's outcasts, on the other hand, are boldly, openly immoral; they admit the crimes they have committed and are not ashamed of them, for their crimes, being offenses not against themselves but against something hateful outside themselves, have, in a way, the aspect of righteous vengeance. The depths to which they have sunk are only social depths; what troubles them is a sense not of guilt but of inadequacy, and to find truth is their only salvation. But O'Neill seems to be saying that to live at all man must live on a lie, for the reward of truth is death. Gorky's man can live only by facing himself, O'Neill's cannot live if he faces himself.

The theme of O'Neill's play is not really the difference between illusion and reality, but the difference between two realities: one the reality of belief, the other the reality of the unrecognized and unacknowledgeable forces of existence. Between illusion and reality a man might choose, but O'Neill's two realities are not open to choice; they are related to each other in a fashion so tortuous as to elude consciousness. A man feels and believes the very opposite of what he thinks he feels and believes. And the reason for this is that the understandable necessity to live has imposed on him a habit of unconscious lying; he reiterates a faith in his will to live, in the great capacity and need of love which animates his life, whereas actually his desire is to die and the motivating force of his life is not love but hate. In short, the two realities which inform man's existence are so profoundly contradictory that consciousness must either pass them by, or deal with them in falsehoods, or obliterate itself. Man is, by definition, a deluded being. Thus the poor, harmless souls at Harry Hope's—good-natured, easygoing, and rather appealing with their vague beliefs in love and honor so long as they remain in their drunken stupor—exhibit, as soon as they are forced to consciousness, unsuspected, deep-seated, murderous hatreds. What Hickey's truth brings to light is that everything that seems good covers up basic evil: Hope, whose life of inactivity is postulated on the premise that he is mourning the death of Bessie whom he loved, suddenly finds himself calling her "that nagging bitch"; Jimmy Tomorrow, who thinks he has been drowning his sorrow at Marjorie's defection, admits, to his own surprise, that he never wanted her; Parritt is forced to acknowledge not only that he is guilty of virtual matricide but that this murder was caused by his hatred of his mother; and, as a piece of final irony, Hickey, in the very process of a touching disquisition on his lasting and passionate love of Evelyn, inadvertently blurts out: "You know what you can do with your pipe dream now, you damned bitch!"

In Gorky's view, what men need more than anything is a belief by which to steer their actions, but for O'Neill beliefs are irrelevant to both morality and happiness. Man is born guilty—O'Neill's attempt to rid himself of Puritanism seems to have brought him around to a metaphysical confirmation of its basic tenets—and the more he tries to clear himself of guilt the more entangled he becomes in it. For how shall the kind of truth which consciousness reveals be met except by death? What price life, O'Neill is asking, and is not genial enough to congratulate man on escaping destruction by the skin of his teeth; for, to his severe scrutiny of man, the death wish seems to have moral justification. The last of all illusions is that ideals are something other than Janus-faced inventions, distressing and comforting by turn, without reference to anything beyond themselves other than the reality of man's having to get through his life somehow. In earlier plays there had been a gentler note. "Do not wound me with wisdom," said the wise Kublai of *Marco Millions*, "Speak to my heart!" But now, how shall the heart be spoken to when it has forgotten the only language by which it can be addressed, when all poetic vision has been lost, the great unanalyzable substratum of experience has been given over to dissection, love and hate have become indistinguishable, and the pursuit of happiness has ended not in enjoyment but in oblivion? More unhappy than O'Neill's men, Gorky's are not so lost.

The essential difference in the two situations is perhaps best embodied in the real heroes of the plays: Satin, ruthless in his appraisal of individual failings but with a native respect for humanity and an ardent faith in its grandeur, and Larry, whose cynical philosophy is coupled with an instinctive sympathy of which he is ashamed, and whose sense of justice is based on a hopeless understanding of human beings. With these characters, it seems to me, their authors are identified: Gorky with the man of action, closely involved in the fate of his fellows, but more clear-eyed, farseeing, and confident than they, and able, therefore, to inspire them by a persuasive vision of their strength; O'Neill with the Grandstand Foolosopher, whose function it is to look unsquintingly on man's depravity and, when called upon, to discharge the unwelcome task not of judging men but of letting them pass judgment on themselves. The high point of Satin's act is a stirring speech on man, of Larry's, his waiting by the window to hear the sound of Parritt throwing himself from the fire escape (for Larry's finest deed is to free a man of guilt by driving him to suicide)—just as the purpose of Gorky's life was to stir men to action, and the function of O'Neill's has been to make them aware of the full meaning of the evil that is in them.

This contrast, to my mind, cannot be fully explained by the fact that O'Neill has long been preoccupied with Roman Catholicism, into which he was born, while Gorky was always an agnostic; for these titles of belief may point to tendencies of thinking and perceiving but can neither describe nor account for an artist's original view of life. Some might say that O'Neill's sophisticated, puritanical condemnation of man has proved to be a wise commentary on Gorky's naive Homeric pity, history having shown that it is better for men to mope in harmless inactivity than to follow a leader whose promises fail to take account of the nature of human motives, and that Circe's brutes had better be changed back to men before being urged to action. But to say this would be to disregard both the complexity of historical events and the kinds of plays we are here considering: one of them has as its aim to state a temporary ethical problem affecting men in an unsatisfactory society which might be changed; the other, to scrutinize the eternal dilemma of how conscious man is related to unconscious nature—aims so divergent as to make these two samples of Western art in the twentieth century almost as dissimilar as those produced by the cultures of Byzantium and of ancient Greece.

O'Neill and the Theatre

LOS ANGELES MUST BE KEPT PURE

Conrad Seiler

Lewdness and immorality must not escape punishment in this city of the Angels.

On February 18 at the Orange Grove Theatre seventeen actors in the employ of Mr. Thomas Wilkes, theatrical producer, were presenting Eugene O'Neill's somber tragedy, *Desire Under the Elms*. Little did they know of the awful Nemesis of the Law, lurking within the very portals of the theatre. Members of the City Vice Squad, acting upon the instructions of Sergeant Sidney Sweetnam, were there to see the performance and to ferret out any possible obscenities. As the curtain closed on the last act all the actors were placed under arrest and taken to the Central Police Station. They were accused of having presented a lewd, obscene, and immoral play.

In the Vice Squad Room of the station, where dipsomaniacs, dope addicts, prostitutes, and perverts are sent before their final

From The Nation, *May 19, 1926. Reprinted with permission of the editors.*

consignment either to jail or liberty, as the case may be, these seventeen sons and daughters of Thespis were herded together and their fingerprints taken, like ordinary criminals.

The management of the play made vehement protest. It was absurd to arrest the actors; they could not be held to account. The management itself assumed all responsibility. But all that did not make the slightest impression on the law. The actors were kept under arrest until 4:30 the following morning, when they were set at liberty under $50 bail each—$850 in all. Later, through the solicitation of Attorney Arthur W. Green, the bail was returned, and the actors were released on their own recognizance.

Sergeant Sweetnam, whom one ungracious reporter called "Keyhole Sweetnam," or "the Chemically Pure Cop," asserted that the Parent Teachers' Association and the Board of Education were behind the arrest, and that it was a serious affair. No member, however, of either the Parent Teachers' Association or the Board of Education ever appeared in the court.

After several words in Mr. O'Neill's work were modified to suit the moral sensibilities of the police, particularly Sergeant Sweetnam—that is, after "whore," which was used twice in the play, was changed to "harlot," and "gone a-whoring" to "gone to get himself a woman"—the performances were permitted to continue, pending the final decision of the court.

A jury trial was demanded. On April 8 the case opened in Judge William Fredrickson's court. Twelve men and women—housewives, salesmen, retired farmers—were asked to pass judgment on the morality of a work of art. Such obviously vulgar aphrodisiacs as *Artists and Models*, *Weak Sisters*, *Lady Be Good*, *The Demi-Virgin*, *The Gold Fish*, and scores upon scores of cheap burlesque shows had been produced without interference in Los Angeles. Their intrinsic decency or indecency had never even been questioned.

Le Roy Reams—small in body, large in head, pugnacious, irascible, "the fearless boy prosecutor," as one paper described him—called Officer Taylor to the witness stand. Officer Taylor solemnly testified that he "had went" to the play, *Desire Under the Elms*, on the night of February 18; that he had heard such horrible instances of profanity as "damn," "hell," and "whore" used on innumerable occasions during the evening—he couldn't say how many; that, although as a police officer in pursuance of his onerous duties he had gone to the performance "steeled against" anything obscene, he had really been shocked, yes, shocked. When he left the play he felt "like he couldn't look the world in the face again"; he had to walk up dark alleys to hide his shame. Ephraim Cabot (Mr. Frank McGlynn) at the end of the first act had said: "If I catch ye, I'll break your bones!" Officer Taylor swore that on the night of the 18th he had heard: "If I catch ye, I'll bust your ——!" The dash indicates a word which even the prosecutor pronounced with reluctance. On cross-examination Officer Taylor said that he had not been able to find any good in the play, but he was certain it was very bad, very bad indeed.

Sergeant Sweetnam, City Mother Gilbert, a salesman, and an elevator operator were the principal witnesses for the prosecution. They testified also that they had heard "damns," "hells," and "certain Biblical words galore." The play was unquestionably immoral—a seducing woman in a nightgown, several beds, and so forth. . . . No, the play had not had an immoral effect on them personally, of course not; they had not left the theatre with impure thoughts, or with the intention of committing any abomination, but that was because they had gone "prepared."

The prosecutor stressed the fact that it was not so much the individual lines and expressions—filthy though they were—as the play itself that was in question. Why, the mere idea of a woman seducing her own stepson—think of it, ladies and gentlemen, *her own stepson!*—was lewd and immoral and had no place in any respectable God-fearing community. Would they, the jurors, care to tell that story in their front parlors to their sons and daughters?

Eminent clubwomen, students of the drama, the wife of the dean of the University of Southern California, several producers, all the dramatic critics of the Los Angeles newspapers, and a girl and boy testified in behalf of the defense. To them the play was not immoral—far from it. It was a literary and dramatic *tour de force*. It taught a strong, wholesome, moral lesson; the wages of sin is death. When they came from the theatre they felt cleansed, morally elevated. The chairwoman of the drama committee of the Friday Morning Club said that, after seeing the play, she felt as though she wanted to rise from her seat and say with utmost reverence: "Now let us pray." The repetition of hard, perhaps ugly words, did not embarrass or shock any of the defense's witnesses. Such words impressed each of them as being very natural and necessary expressions in the mouths of O'Neill's crude, pathetic characters.

On the afternoon of April 15, at two o'clock, the entire court, including the judge, jury, prosecutor, attorney for the defense, attachés, and witnesses, and also a few reporters, were given a special performance of *Desire Under the Elms* at the Orange Grove Theatre. No one else was admitted in the audience. The actors were the seventeen persons under indictment.

Before the play began all the players were summoned before the curtain, and the clerk of the court, B. O. Kersey, asked them: "Do each of you solemnly swear that the performance you will give here today is the play *Desire Under the Elms*, word for word, action for action, identically as it was presented in this theatre on the night of February the 18th?" The actors took the oath. And then began the most unusual performance in the annals of the theatre. The actors, with a possible jail sentence staring them in the face, and playing before the most critical audience ever assembled in any theatre, surpassed themselves. Frank McGlynn as Ephraim Cabot gave a magnificent interpretation; Jessie Arnold as Abbie caused even Bailiff Cummings to say: "She's the greatest actress I've ever seen." Women jurors wept copiously; Sergeant Sweetnam and Judge Fredrickson applauded along with the witnesses and reporters. Four curtain calls were demanded at the conclusion of the play.

On Friday morning, April 16, came the final argument. The court allotted one hour to each side. Frank McGlynn—tall, gaunt, dramatic—attorney in his own right as well as leading actor in the play, was granted half of the defense's time. McGlynn appealed to the jury as liberal-minded men and women. He hoped they were not prudes. Surely they were not shocked when life was stripped of its veneer. Surely they felt no embarrassment when he told the story of *Desire Under the Elms*. Sex had its place in life; everyone knew that. There was nothing essentially obscene about it. If persons came to see O'Neill's play and smirked and giggled over the poignant lives of Eben and Ephraim Cabot and Abbie—as the prosecutor said they had—it was a reflection upon *their* morality, not the actors' or the play's. The jury was not called upon to decide whether *Desire Under the Elms* contained a moral lesson. It didn't have to have one. The question was whether the defendants were guilty of presenting an obscene play.

Attorney Green, of the defense, mentioned the classics of literature, the plays of Sophocles, Euripides, Aeschylus, Racine, Schiller (particularly Schiller's *Don Carlos*, Racine's *Phèdre*, and Sophocles' *Phaedra*, in which women are enamored of their stepsons) and the tragedies of a certain well-known playwright, William Shakespeare. Most of them are not only read and studied in the classrooms of our high schools and colleges, but are actually performed by thousands of students every year. . . . Eugene O'Neill is one of the few significant figures in the American drama. He is a famous author; his works are read, played, and admired throughout the civilized world. . . . Many of the words which Officer Taylor and Sergeant Sweetnam testified that they had heard on that memorable night of the 18th, were never in the play. The prosecution had not proved its case; there was absolutely nothing obscene in the play and consequently the defendants must be pronounced innocent.

The prosecutor, in his rebuttal, took occasion to castigate "those Greek and French degenerates" who are sullying the minds of our children. *Desire Under the Elms*, was mere "smut and filth." There was no justification for such a play. O'Neill a famous author! He was infamous—morbid, lewd, obscene. . . . The play was not true to life. Had any member of the jury ever heard of a mother seducing her own stepson in real life? Of course not. Were the lives of O'Neill's characters similar to the lives of any people in New England or elsewhere that they had ever known or heard about? What a question! But they did know of thousands of clean, patient, hardworking farmer folks, didn't they? O'Neill knew nothing of such people; he only knew about morons, adultresses, infanticides, seducing stepmothers. . . . Suppose it were true to life. So are sewers. But that is no reason for putting them on the stage. . . . *Desire Under the Elms* should be suppressed. The defendants were guilty of presenting a lewd, obscene, and immoral play.

The jury retired at three o'clock that afternoon. It deliberated for almost nine hours. Shortly after midnight the verdict was announced: eight for conviction and four for acquittal.

The jury was dismissed.

At the time of writing Judge Fredrickson has voiced his intention of proceeding immediately with a new trial. In the meantime the play, which, normally, would have had a run of two, or at the most, three weeks, is doing capacity business the tenth week, and will soon go to San Francisco to commence its sinister demoralizing work there. But—

Los Angeles must be purified.

Lewdness and immorality must not escape punishment in this City of the Angels.

Kenneth Macgowan

THE O'NEILL SOLILOQUY

O'Neill is a kind of chain-stitch playwright. I don't mean by this that you have only to yank at the thread of his story in some weak spot to see the whole thing ravel out. I mean that his ideas and materials and technique develop through a long chain of links bound inextricably to one another. They develop slowly, perhaps spasmodically, but they develop inevitably from his first plays to his last.

Some candidate for a Ph. D. could turn out a nice and a laborious thesis on the links in O'Neill's thought. He could dig out of a play of 1917 a hint of an idea that comes just a little more to the surface two years later, and by 1927 makes the theme of a whole play. The examples that occur to me now are only the obvious ones. The contrast of the artist failure and the he-man grows from *Beyond the Horizon* into *The Great God Brown*. The happy laughter of God swells up from *The Great God Brown* to its climax in *Lazarus Laughed*. The Venetian traveling man of *Marco Millions* gets a few lines of comment in the play about Ponce de Leon called *The Fountain*. A hint in *Desire Under the Elms* of how we are driven blindly towards so many of our most violent actions is re-emphasized and elaborated in his newest play *Dynamo*, which is soon to be produced.

Various devices in O'Neill's dramaturgy have developed in the same slow way. Masks, for instance, work their way carefully from *The Hairy Ape* through *All God's Chillun* and his arrangement of *The Ancient Mariner* to *The Great God Brown* and *Lazarus Laughed*. But the most striking example of how cautiously but thoroughly O'Neill works along this way lies in his outstanding contribution to modern dramaturgy—the spoken thoughts of

From the Theatre Guild Magazine, *February, 1929. Reprinted by permission of the author and* Theatre Arts *Magazine.*

Strange Interlude and *Dynamo*. The impulse from which they spring is to be found in his first good playlet, "Bound East for Cardiff," written almost fifteen years ago.

Consider the purpose of the spoken thought and you will see how this has to be O'Neill's chief contribution to the art of playwriting; for it matches the chief purpose of O'Neill's art. This purpose is to get behind the surface of things. Realism has never contented him. He had seen too much of life before he began to write. He knew things about men and women that could come out only haltingly through the medium of pure realism. To drag these things out of their souls and put them freely and clearly on the stage has been the obsessing problem of O'Neill's life as an artist.

O'Neill went to work on the problem before he had mastered the long play and when he had only just begun to recognize his proper material—the things and people he had met and understood—and to write with clear, realistic power. He had written a number of indifferent little playlets when in "Bound East for Cardiff" he first turned to the forecastle in which he had spent many weeks of his roving life. And here in the first of his sea plays and the first of his powerful pieces of realism he began to work on the problem of getting out upon the stage more of a man's inner consciousness than a man would ordinarily bare to his fellows. O'Neill did the trick by throwing his chief character into the fever of death. As Yank lay dying in his bunk, his mind wandered through the life he had led, and, taking fire from the fever in his blood, spoke out hot and unashamed.

After more realism, O'Neill was back on the trail again in *The Emperor Jones*. But again there had to be some natural and realistic excuse for a man to speak his mind. This time it was the craze of fear. Lost in the jungle, with the pursuing tom-tom beating his blood in mad rhythms through his mind, Brutus Jones broke into a monologue that seemed to the spectator natural and inevitable. He talked of his terrors. He told of his past in vivid, terrible visions. Soon we were ready to go back through his mind into the terrors of his black people, back into racial memories of slave ship and Congo voodoo.

Next, *The Hairy Ape* and realism thrown overboard for the expressionism of the German stage. The stokehole sailor talked stokehole talk—so far as words went—but in ideas he crashed through to a philosophy of brute labor and brute machines. Mostly he talked to his fellow sailors, not to the audience about, but by grace of the convention of expressionism—and a little booze—he talked about things not ordinarily expressed. Sometimes the abysmal brute talked to himself and let us know that he "didn't belong." But there was never the contrast and conflict of the speech of one man against his thought, and the thought of one man against the thought of another.

For two moments in *Welded* O'Neill came close to spoken thought expressed by well bred and outwardly realistic people in an outwardly realistic play. Twice his man and his woman sat down upon chairs neatly placed side by side facing the audience and talked out their problem in speech that both could hear and yet speech that neither listened to. O'Neill thus describes in his stage directions this germ of the spoken thought which was to ripen into *Strange Interlude*.

"They stare straight ahead and remain motionless. They speak, ostensibly one to the other, but showing by their tone it is a thinking aloud to oneself, and neither appears to hear what the other has said."

The important thing was only that the audience should hear.

With *Welded*, O'Neill was through with realism. After that soliloquy could lead on slowly to spoken thought in alternating dialogue. Prayer and soliloquy filled *Desire Under the Elms* and the very rooms of the New England homestead, stripped of their walls, spoke their most private thoughts. Scenery, too, was working on the problem.

In *The Great God Brown* O'Neill struck boldly towards a solution. To bring upon the stage the two sides of the human mind —the side we speak out in carefully censored form and the inner truths or the inner deceptions that we keep to ourselves—he gave his people masks as well as naked faces. By means of masks and soliloquy and curiously oblique comments in the third person, these people spoke their minds.

From this the step to *Strange Interlude* was direct and easy— for O'Neill. Here he gave us the outward, realistic aspects of his people and the outward realistic talk that they would use. Then, between almost every pair of speeches, he dug down into the minds of his characters and brought out their thoughts in speech that the audience, but not the other characters, could hear. This device was more than soliloquy and it did more than expose the thoughts of people. It was a living and exciting dialogue of a new kind. To the dramatic contrasts and conflicts of ordinary spoken dialogue O'Neill added the contrasts and conflicts of thought. There was the speech of Nina against the speech of Charlie, the thought of Nina against the speech of Nina, the thought of Nina against the thought of Charlie, and sometimes the speech of one against the thought of the other.

It is this new dramatic contrast that sets off O'Neill's method from the free soliloquy and asides of the older romantic stage. And it is the consistent use of this contrast through a complete evening that takes O'Neill's device out of the class of any of its recent forerunners. In "Overtones"—a playlet produced by the Washington Square Players—Alice Gerstenberg bared the minds of two women by setting behind each a veiled figure representing her real ego that spoke out devastating comment. In "The Artist," another playlet, H. L. Mencken made a pianist on the concert platform and his critics in the audience speak their thoughts aloud. In *The Adding Machine* Elmer Rice had a short scene in which bookkeepers, adding up figures aloud, interspersed their sums with caustic reflections on the life they led. Zoe Akins in *The Furies*—which was written, she explains, before *Strange Interlude* was produced—let her characters speak out their secret minds after they had answered more discreetly the questions of a prosecuting attorney investigating a murder.

More recently, Arthur Hopkins, as producer of Sophie Treadwell's *Machinal*, aimed at a similar effect by means of the expressionistic technique. In this play the characters did not so much express their inner thoughts in direct speech, or in "asides," as emphasize their characteristic traits by insistent repetition. The clerk intones his "Hot Dog!" far oftener than any clerk would possibly repeat the words in five minutes. The husband recounts twice too often that he "put over" a business deal. But the effect is (as was intended) to make these characters reveal to the audience precisely that inner preoccupation which they would not for anything reveal to their friends.

None of these attempts comes so close as O'Neill's to the consistent and illusive illumination of realism by the light of the inner mind. O'Neill's device is his own because he has worked long and painfully over it and brought it to a complete development. It is far from perfected, but it seems obviously a means that others besides O'Neill may well use if they care to broaden and deepen the channels of expression in the present day theatre.

Lee Simonson

A MEMO FROM O'NEILL ON THE SOUND EFFECTS FOR *DYNAMO*

Shortly before Dynamo *went into rehearsal, the following memorandum was received from O'Neill:*

The stage effects in Part One and Part Three (the thunder and lightning in Part One, and the sound of the water flowing over the near-by dam and the hum of the generator in Part Two):

I cannot stress too emphatically the importance of starting early in rehearsals to get these effects exactly right. It must be realized that these are not incidental noises but significant dramatic overtones that are an integral part of that composition in the theatre which is the whole play. If they are dismissed until the last dress rehearsals (the usual procedure in my experience), then the result must inevitably be an old melodrama thunderstorm, and a generator sounding obviously like a vaccum cleaner; not only will the true values of these effects be lost but they will make the play look foolish.

I may seem to be a bug on the subject of sound in the theatre—but I have reason. J——— once said that the difference between my plays and other contemporary work was that I always wrote primarily by ear for the ear, that most of my plays, even down to the rhythm of the dialogue, had the definite structural quality of a musical composition. This hits the nail on the head. It is not that I consciously strive after this but that, willy nilly, my stuff takes that form. (Whether this is a transgression or not is a matter of opinion. Certainly I believe it to be a great virtue, although it is the principal

From The Stage Is Set *by Lee Simonson, copyright 1932 by Harcourt, Brace and Company, Inc. Reprinted by permission of the author.*

reason why I have been blamed for useless repetitions, which to me were significant recurrences of theme.) But the point here is that I have always used sound in plays as a structural part of them. Tried to use, I mean—for I've never got what the script called for (even in *Jones*), not because what I specified couldn't be done but because I was never able to overcome the slip-shod, old-fashioned disregard of our modern theatre for what ought to be one of its superior opportunities (contrasted with the medium of the novel, for example) in expressing the essential rhythm of our lives today. This sounds complicated but to illustrate: This is a machine age which one would like to express as a background for lives in plays in overtones of characteristic, impelling and governing mechanical sound and rhythm—but how can one, unless a corresponding mechanical perfection in the theatre is a reliable string of the instrument (the theatre as a whole) on which one composes? The only answer is, it cannot be done. Looking back on my plays in which significant mechanical sound and not music is called for (nearly all of the best ones) I can say that none of them has ever really been thoroughly done in the *modern theatre* although they were written for it. Some day I hope they will be—and people are due to be surprised by the added dramatic value—*modern* values—they will take on.

After which dissertation (which has little or nothing to do with *Interlude* or *Marco* but a hell of a lot to do with *Dynamo*), I would suggest that some special person with the right mechanical flair be sicced on this aspect of *Dynamo* to get perfect results. It can't be done in two or three days. What is needed is lightning that will suddenly light up people's faces in different parts of the set, keep them in the general picture—not literal lightning, but a reproduction of the dramatic effect of lightning on people's faces. And thunder with a menacing, brooding quality as if some Electrical God were on the hills impelling all these people, affecting their thoughts and actions. The queer noise of a generator, which is unlike any other mechanical noise (it is described in the script), its merging with, and contrast with, the peaceful, soft Nature sound of the falls, also needs some doing. The startling, strained, unnatural effect of the human voice raised to try and dominate the generator's hum (in the scenes in the generator room), is also important and part of my conception. All this can be done—and easily—if the person on this job will get a little expert information from the General Electric and go out to the plant at Stevenson, Conn., I visited, and look around and listen in. My scenic scheme is a concentration of the features of this plant.

A designer is more truly creative when he fails with the poet, as I did with O'Neill in *Dynamo*, than when he succeeds with the playwright who is nothing more than an observer. I have never shared more directly the excitement, the adventure, and the power of the modern theatre than in following the trail of O'Neill's mind from a power-house on a Connecticut river to the play that it inspired. When I first read the script, how incredible the singing, crooning dynamo seemed, how strained the effort to apostrophize it as a god whose commands could be interpreted! I visited the power-house. I heard the swish of water in the sluice below, a rushing accompaniment to the one dynamo that happened to be running at so many hundred revolutions per minute. It had a distinct musical note. I noticed that the recording dial was not working. "How can you keep track of it?" I asked the superintendent. "Oh, I know by the sound," he replied. Here was a technician, like a violinist tuning his instrument, relying on his sense of musical pitch to control a machine whose fluctuations had to be mathematically exact. I passed the transformers where the lazy current of a river had been transmuted into an electric current of thirty thousand volts. The heat generated by the change was so great that water could no longer cool the transformer; it had to be jacketed in cylinders of the heaviest oil. I passed a switch-board where tiny red and green lights blinked and winked, signalling changes of load that released enough energy to turn the wheels of entire factories or to light a small city. I stood in front of the condensers on an upper story where the thirty thousand volts of current were fed to the main transmission-line. I was warned to keep ten feet back of a protecting rail. The electric energy streaming through a copper wire at this point was so great that a static spark might jump across the gap and burn me severely. No insulation invented could protect me from those copper wires. If I touched one I would flame like a match and be consumed in an instant to my very bones. I noticed that the porcelain insulators had much the same form as certain ceremonial vases in Chinese temples. I listened to accounts of the terror of one thunderstorm when lightning struck a power line miles away and the immense flow of current, short-circuited, shot back, and burned out one dynamo as if its windings had been so much paper.

Here was water that became fire, energy that sang a monotonous tune, that did croon like a lullaby and then became incandescent light. Here was power that could give man the strength of a god able to move mountains, the source of blind energy that could execute his commands over a network of metallic nerves beyond the reach of his eyes, that could light his way through darkness, reclaim him from toil, and, if not propitiated, consume him with flame. As I left a commonplace bare brick and steel powerhouse, I was touched with a terror and a veneration for the invisible forces controlling modern life that are potentially its salvation and its destruction, its heaven and its hell. I have left many cathedrals less awed and humbled. I had been at a shrine where an invisible miracle was daily performed, a transubstantiation no less miraculous than that of the Mass. And the purely mathematical calculation of engineers had given porcelain insulators the same beauty of form that ancient artists had given to temple vessels.

Rereading O'Neill's script, I seemed to understand for the first time the myth of Prometheus the fire-bringer. I understood why primitive peoples had cringed in terror before thunderbolts and erected altars to invisible gods. I had experienced, through a poet's insight, the wonder, the humility and pride, the hunger for power, the ecstasy of calling it forth, in which religions are born.

I do not for a moment pretend that I succeeded in putting any of this into my setting. The play itself failed at its climax when O'Neill's dynamo became an archaic god that could exact nothing more than an almost pathological desire for sexual purity. The theme of the play was short-circuited before it reached expression. Nevertheless I continue to hope that the play will be rewritten and that the projected trilogy of which it was to be a part will be completed. I continue to feel that in *Dynamo* O'Neill touched the sources of modern faith and despair more nearly than in exploring so much more successfully the insatiable desires of one modern woman for satisfaction in sex or in tracing the meaning of fate and retribution through the forbidden passions of one New England family. For *Dynamo*, despite its failure in performance, was more nearly the kind of success that the theatre needs today than hundreds of its present successes. In setting *Dynamo*, in sharing a poet's intuition, in accepting his symbols, in attempting to make the commonplace mechanical shapes of our industrial environment significant of the forces for good and evil that they released, in building them into a rostrum on which the hope and despair of our effort today to dominate ourselves and the world about us could be voiced—I understood how the designing of a stage setting could be made a creative act, whether or not I myself could make it one.

Croswell Bowen

REHEARSING *THE ICEMAN COMETH*

Readings of *The Iceman Cometh* began in May. James Barton was cast in the role of Harry Hope. O'Neill was impressed with Barton's sensitive reading of the part. It was now a new play to O'Neill; it was always this way when he heard one of his plays read for the first time. Throughout the summer of 1946, the Theatre Guild, the cast and the playwright worked on the rehearsals. Everyone knew that in a sense the play would constitute a kind of reopening of the Broadway theatre after the war. It would be like old times—another O'Neill play on Broadway.

There was more pressure exerted on O'Neill than ever before to get him to cut the play. Langner gave him a copy of the play with passages marked where, in the producer's opinion, cuts were very much indicated. In a blue pencil O'Neill wrote boldly the word "no" opposite most of them. When he wrote "yes" it was in a tiny, faltering script. On the cover of the manuscript he handed back to Langner, he wrote: "The hell with your cuts! E.O'N."

In September, as the rehearsals came closer to being finished performances, Paul Crabtree, one of the actors, studied the script and figured out that O'Neill had made the same point eighteen times. He showed the fruits of his research to Langner who, he reckoned, would have the nerve to raise the point—or rather, the eighteen repeated points—with O'Neill. Langner has set down O'Neill's exact reaction: Gene looked at me and replied in a particularly quiet voice, "I intended to be repeated eighteen times!" Langner then observed that *The Iceman Cometh*, like Shaw's *Saint Joan*, would never be properly produced until the copyright

---

From The Curse of the Misbegotten *by Croswell Bowen. Reprinted by permission of McGraw-Hill Book Co., Inc. and Rupert Hart-Davis, Limited. Title supplied by the editors.*

had expired. Again O'Neill smiled. "It will have to wait," he said, "for just that."

Often the rehearsals of an O'Neill play would degenerate into a series of running battles between the playwright and the producer, the director, and the actors. Invariably, O'Neill was able to stand his ground against them all.

A typical dispute during the rehearsals of *The Iceman Cometh* concerned the play's length, which seemed inordinate to several members of the company. When all other arguments failed, someone came to O'Neill and told him that the play was running at least twenty minutes too long and that a cut would have to be made. Why? O'Neill asked. It was then patiently explained to the author that the last commuting trains would have left Grand Central Station before the audience even got out of the theatre.

O'Neill indicated succinctly that he was interested only in the play, not in whether the audience caught their trains. It was his play, and it would be done his way.

But as the rehearsals proceeded, the cast's affection and respect for O'Neill mounted. He knew the theatre and he knew his play, and the actors were aware that he was part of America's theatrical heritage. Most of the time, O'Neill sat next to Eddie Dowling, the director. Dowling, O'Neill felt, tended to encourage the players to overplay their parts. The cast wanted to get the full implications of the play, its shadings and meanings, and O'Neill was always ready to explain his characters for the actors.

"Raw emotion," O'Neill said, "produces the worst in people. Remember, goodness can surmount anything. The people in that saloon were the best friends I've ever known . . . Their weakness was not an evil. It is a weakness found in all men."

O'Neill tried to explain to the cast the meaning behind the extraordinary behavior of the habitués of the saloon—the meaning behind their deeply troubled words.

"Revenge," he said "is the subconscious motive for the individual's behavior with the rest of society. Revulsion drives a man to tell others of his sins . . . It is the Furies within us that seek to destroy us.

"In all my plays sin is punished and redemption takes place.

"Vice and virtue cannot live side by side. It's the humiliation of a loving kiss that destroys evil."

An eager, aggressive actor asked O'Neill where he stood on "the labor movement." (Two of the characters in the play are disillusioned radicals.)

"I am a philosophical anarchist," O'Neill said, smiling faintly, "which means, 'Go to it, but leave me out of it.' "

The Question of Language

Eugene O'Neill

LANGUAGE IN A FAITHLESS AGE

A Letter to Arthur Hobson Quinn

Much gratitude for your flattering appreciation of *Mourning Becomes Electra!* I only hope it is as worthy as you think it. I am very satisfied with it—(taken all around it *is* my best, I think) —but at the same time, deeply dissatisfied. It needed great language to lift it beyond itself. I haven't got that. And, by way of self-consolation, I don't think, from the evidence of all that is being written today, that great language is possible for anyone living in the discordant, broken, faithless rhythm of our time. The best one can do is to be pathetically eloquent by one's moving, dramatic inarticulations!

From A History of the American Drama, *vol. II, by Arthur Hobson Quinn. Published by F. S. Crofts & Co., 1945.*

Edmund Wilson

EUGENE O'NEILL AS A PROSE WRITER

The new volume of Eugene O'Neill's plays contains *The Hairy Ape*, *Anna Christie* and *The First Man*. The first of these seems to me almost the only thing that Mr. O'Neill has yet written that has very much value as literature apart from its effectiveness as drama. As a rule, the plays of O'Neill are singularly uninviting on the printed page. The dialogue is raw and prosaic, in texture quite undistinguished, and the author has made no attempt to appeal to the imagination by way of the stage directions, which are not lifted above the baldness of the prompt-book. These plays appear too often, in short, as rather second-rate naturalistic pieces that owe their eminence, not to their intrinsic greatness, but, as Marx said of John Stuart Mill, "to the flatness of the surrounding country." The dialogue of *The First Man*, which I have not seen on stage, proves in the reading so tasteless and dreary that one does not see how one could sit through it.

But Eugene O'Neill has another vein in which he is a literary artist of genius. When he is writing the more or less grammatical dialogue of the middle-class characters of his plays, his prose is heavy and indigestible even beyond the needs of naturalism. People say the same things to one another over and over again and never succeed in saying them any more effectively than the first time; long speeches shuffle dragging feet, marking time without progressing, for pages. But as soon as Mr. O'Neill gets a character who can only talk some kind of vernacular, he begins to write like a poet. We had already had evidence of this in the Negro hero of

---

From The Shores of Light, *Farrar, Straus and Young, 1952. Reprinted by permission of the author. Originally appeared as the following articles: "Eugene O'Neill as Prose Writer,"* Vanity Fair, *Nov. 1922;* "All God's Chillun Got Wings and Others," New Republic, *May 28, 1924; "The All-Star Literary Vaudeville,"* American Criticism, *Harcourt, Brace, 1926.*

The Emperor Jones and in the first act of *Anna Christie*, but when one saw *The Hairy Ape* produced by the Provincetown Players, one had the feeling that Mr. O'Neill had for the first time become fully articulate. As Walter Pritchard Eaton said, he wrote slang like "a sort of wild organ music." The scenes in which the non-illiterate characters talk are as clumsy and dead as ever, but the greater part of the play, in which Yank, the stoker, discourses, has a mouth-filling rhythmical eloquence very rare in naturalistic drama.

When the speeches came to life in this way, the drama was always more moving. One felt that Mr. O'Neill, in his gift for drawing music from humble people, had a kinship with Sherwood Anderson. For *The Hairy Ape* is the tragedy not, as in the common formula, of the American pitted against his environment nor even of the proletarian pitted against capitalism, but of the universal human being pitted against himself. It is, as Mr. O'Neill has labelled it, a play "of ancient and modern life." I have heard this disputed by people who had got the impression from seeing the play that the hero of *The Hairy Ape* is thwarted by the forces of society instead of by his own limitations. But I believe that if anyone will read the last scenes in the printed text, he will see that though it is a consciousness of social inferiority that gives the first impetus to Yank's debacle and though he himself at first supposes that it is society he has to fight, the Hairy Ape's ultimate struggle for freedom takes place within the man himself. I am not sure that Mr. O'Neill always gives enough dramatic emphasis to his most important ideas. The significance of these last scenes of *The Hairy Ape* was not thrown into relief on the stage. People seemed to understand the play better when they saw it a second time. This is a reason—aside from the fact that the *Ape* is good literature—that it is useful to have it in a book. . . .

All God's Chillun Got Wings by Eugene O'Neill . . . shows signs of an effort to impose subjective fancies upon an idea objectively conceived. The Provincetown Players, in producing the play, have not tried to carry out the idea that appears in the author's text, of having the walls and ceiling of the interior set contract as the situation becomes more oppressive, but they have made him a present of a curious church with a waist like a human being's and flying buttresses of brick that seem to be streaming away in the wind. The devices, both author's and producer's, strike one as a little mechanical, as not quite belonging with the rest of the play; but, in any case, they are unimportant and not typical of the treatment of the whole. Mr. O'Neill has made a much more effective departure from the cumbersome naturalism of the "transcript from life" of the type of *Catskill Dutch*, by simply throwing overboard most of its detail. He has sheared away, in *All God's Chillun*, almost everything except the relation between his two central characters, and, in doing so, has gained intensity, one of the qualities our realism most needs.

For the rest, *All God's Chillun Got Wings* is one of the best things yet written about the race problem of Negro and white and one of the best of O'Neill's plays. Two of Mr. O'Neill's chief assets are, first, a nervous driving force that carries the audience inescapably along; and, second, a gift for the eloquent use of the various forms of the American vernacular. Both of these *All God's Chillun* has. It is not quite so consistently compelling or well-written as *The Emperor Jones* or *The Hairy Ape;* it has its harsh notes and its raw expanses. But then, it has a certain advantage over either of these other plays in presenting two characters equally strong, in collision with one another, instead of one central character who only contends with himself.

Mr. O'Neill has another qualification which sets him completely apart from the other American dramatists, who have so far done very little more than modify the conventional American comedy in the direction of Shaw or Sinclair Lewis: he nearly always, with whatever crudeness, is expressing some real experience, some impact directly from life. The characters and the scene in O'Neill are sometimes forbiddingly bleak—as in the latter part of *All God's Chillun*—but they are likely at any moment, by taking on the power and the awfulness of naked natural forces, to establish a violent contact between themselves and us. This was true of even *Welded* (on the stage), a monotonous drama of marriage—which failed principally, it seems to me, through not having been well enough written. Mr. O'Neill, with this sort of subject from ordinary middle-class life, does not pay enough attention to style. A play, like anything else that is built of words, is primarily a work of literature, and even the most vigorous dramatic idea cannot be trusted to make its effect without the right words to convey it. All but the greatest of actors are liable to betray a careless text, but an accurate and brilliant text will manage to speak for itself in spite of the very worst. The expressiveness of Mr. O'Neill seems to diminish in direct proportion to his distance from the language of the people. At one pole, you have *The Hairy Ape*, certainly his best-written play; at the other *Welded*, perhaps his worst. In *All God's Chillun Got Wings*, you see his quality rising and falling—between the stale language of stock-company melodrama and the vivid, the racy, the real. . . .

As for the dramatists, there is still only O'Neill, who, for all his efforts to break away from naturalism, remains a typical naturalistic dramatist of something under the very first rank. He is a writer of the same school as Hauptmann, with much the same kind of merits; but, where Hauptmann is as steady as Shakespeare, O'Neill is hysterically embittered. He forces his tragic catastrophes and, at the same time, fails to prepare them; and, despite the magnificent eloquence of which he is sometimes capable, especially when handling some form of the vernacular, he has grave deficiencies of literary taste which allow him to leave great areas of his dialogue either banal or bald.

Alan S. Downer

EUGENE O'NEILL AS POET OF THE THEATRE

The common cry of the higher critics of the theatre in the past century, and particularly in the past twenty-five years, has been a lament over the dearth of dramatic poetry. Brightly they look back upon all the great ages of theatrical man, the classical Greeks, the Elizabethans, the neo-classic French, and discover them to be ages of poetic dialogue; gloomily they look upon the present and see only unabashed prose. They conclude therefore that as long as the modern drama submits to the tyranny of prose, it must remain a third-rate power.

Unfortunately for the Ultimate Truth, few of these gentlemen have bothered to look beyond the printed page to discover the relation of the medium of dramatic dialogue to the forms of expression normal to a given period. Shakespeare after all did not find his theatre prose and leave it poetry; he simply accepted the Elizabethan convention and wrote in blank verse. The convention of our day is prose, and the few men who have gone against it have not achieved very much. The tinsel diction of Christopher Fry has its charms, but their effect is hardly to be distinguished from the epigrammatic glitter of Oscar Wilde. T. S. Eliot has been the most determined experimenter with the possibilities of metrics and other poetic devices; his conclusion, if one may judge from *The Cocktail Party*, seems to be, the closer to prose the greater the effectiveness.

Perhaps this is surrender, an admission that our theatre is doomed to inferiority. Perhaps this is recognition that what Cocteau has called "poetry of the theatre" differs in kind from the poetry of the literary *salon*, the quarterlies, and the proverbial

From Theatre Arts, *February 1951. Reprinted by permission of the author and* Theatre Arts *magazine.*

slender volumes. If to judge an artist is to evaluate his use of his medium, we must observe not so much the dramatist's words as his characters-in-action and, in the modern theatre, his handling of the more mechanical resources of the stage.

For instance, the recurrent critical complaint about Eugene O'Neill is the failure of his language to equal the intensity or excitement of his action or situations. Even Professor Krutch, in a friendly comment, calls *Mourning Becomes Electra* a "scenario" and declares that no modern writer is "capable of language really worthy of O'Neill's play." Yet, are there not compensations? Was not a 1931 audience enwrapped in the five-hours' traffic of the trilogy, sharing the experience of the contemporary audiences of *Othello* or *Antigone?*

Other men have conceived tragic situations, and other men have made full use of the resources of the modern stage. Few, however, have achieved a balanced combination of the two with the consistency of Eugene O'Neill. O'Neill has a unique combination of skill and vision: born and raised in the theatre he was well-versed in the secrets of stage effect; years of travel and experience gave him a sense of the mystery of life which prevented him from using his skill for effect alone.

His earliest vignettes of the sailor's life suggest how his skill is to serve the purposes of his vision. His father, James O'Neill, who destroyed his own artistic career by yielding to his audience's thirst for sensation, would have been baffled by such a play as "Bound East for Cardiff," although the violent action of "Ile" would have comforted him. "Cardiff," however, is a more direct statement of O'Neill's vision; the sailor, dying against a background of his quarreling, disinterested mates, is an image of the loneliness and frustration of man. The playwright's early choice of the sea or the farm as his setting is a recognition of their symbolic, as well as their realistic, value: life on shipboard as the world in miniature, the farm juxtaposing the order of nature and the disorder of man.

In his non-realistic as well as his realistic plays, O'Neill demonstrates the acute sense of organic form which was to make him a leader of American expressionism. The structure of the play, the pattern of the action, even the shaping of the dialogue always follow a strict design, usually one devised for that particular play. The alternating settings of *Beyond the Horizon*, shifting from the open road to the farmhouse interior, parallel the choices which confront the two brothers in the action. The fixed non-realistic nature of the setting in *All God's Chillun Got Wings* creates a dramatic symbol of the forces opposed to the self-realization of the hero and the heroine. In *Mourning Becomes Electra* the completely realistic setting is also completely symbolic. A part of the action takes place before the front of a carefully reproduced New England mansion of the "Greek Revival" period. Since the plot revives a Greek myth, and since Greek tragedies were generally performed in the open area before a pillared temple-like structure, this setting aids in developing more than the literal meaning of the action.

In characterization, too, O'Neill prefers to follow a pattern. His characters are not necessarily stereotypes, but he is at some pains from early in his career to make it apparent that each is but an instrument in the revelation of his theme. At first he frequently describes the "humor" or manner of a character by the figurative suggestion of a mask: "Mrs. Mayo's face has . . . become a weak mask wearing a helpless, doleful expression of being constantly on the verge of comfortless tears." Later, in *The Great God Brown*, each character is equipped with an actual mask which he dons or doffs to indicate his inner nature, his attitude and his emotion. Aware that this restoration of a classical stage property called attention to itself and away from the play as a whole, O'Neill made a further modification. In *Mourning Becomes Electra* where the Greek myth suggested the employment of actual masks, the realism of the setting forced a compromise. The Mannons, in repose, all have mask-like faces, resembling the mask-like portraits on the walls of their library. Since the Mannons are seldom in repose, the effect is more potential than actual, but it underlies the action as a symbol of the chain of evil that binds them together.

The use of the matériel of the theatre, settings and make-up and action, on several levels achieves an effect similar to the effect of poetic language in the older drama, and accounts for the impact of much of O'Neill's work, in spite of the lack of poetic language in his dialogue.

Desire Under the Elms is a singularly effective example of the use of the "poetry of the theatre." Its theme is variations on the first word of the title. Abbie Putnam, the young wife, desires a home, security; Simeon and Peter, the older sons, desire freedom from the hard labor of a New England rock-bound farm; Eben, the youngest son, desires to possess what was his mother's (with the obvious Freudian implication); and Old Ephraim, the father, desires to escape from his tragic sense of aloneness by possessing the farm he has made out of impossible land, since human love fails him in each of his wives and each of his sons.

Life on the farm has been a theatrical cliché for a hundred years exploited by playwrights for sentimentality, low humor, and melodrama. What O'Neill has done is to examine the motive behind the affection for the Old Homestead—the desire to possess—and he equates this desire with the animal desire to possess other things. The romance is gone when the motive is revealed. But O'Neill is making a general, or universal, statement about life. The desire to possess grows out of a feeling of instability or insecurity. Thus his vision is of a life without foundation, without creeds or beliefs, struggling for a symbol of security, a few rocky acres of a New England farmstead.

The abstract idea of desire is of course made concrete by the action, but the poetical use of the elements of the theatre intensifies the concept. Over the farmhouse stand two elms bending heavily upon the roof. "They are like exhausted women resting their sagging breasts and hands and hair on its roof, and when it rains their tears trickle down monotonously and rot the shingles." In the opening scene of the second act, the manner of the characters as they move heavily through the oppressive heat, their actions, carefully guided by the author, even their voices, give the thematic word an almost physical presence. The disappearing wall of the farmhouse, revealing several rooms at once, is a common device of nineteenth-century melodrama. Here, however, it is not merely spectacular or sensational. The multiple playing areas permit O'Neill to create visual ironies and reveal psychological relationships within the conventions of the realistic theatre. The play in performance, taking account of all the elements that have gone into its conception, thus achieves an intensity and concentrated force common enough in poetic drama but rare in the modern prose theatre. Only the wider range of *Mourning Becomes Electra* surpasses *Desire Under the Elms* in tragic vision. The two plays together represent the highest moments of the American drama.

Joseph Wood Krutch

EUGENE O'NEILL'S CLAIM TO GREATNESS

Bernard Shaw once called O'Neill "a banshee Shakespeare." And "banshee," as the historically minded will remember, is what Voltaire called Shakespeare. Shaw's remark was not intended to be entirely uncomplimentary and neither, for that matter, was Voltaire's. A banshee Shakespeare is still some kind of Shakespeare, and "a barbarian genius" (Voltaire's phrase) is still some kind of genius.[1]

Certain American critics, on the other hand, have hurled the insult without the qualifying compliment. Eric Bentley, after calling O'Neill "the Broadway intelligentsia's patron saint" and after explaining how hard he has tried to think well of him winds up by saying that O'Neill cannot write and cannot think. To Mary McCarthy his "lack of verbal gift has a personal affliction that became a curse to the American stage" and the most important conclusion to be drawn from *The Iceman Cometh* is that "you cannot write a Platonic dialogue in the style of *Casey at the Bat*." O'Neill, if not witty himself is, then, like Falstaff, the occasion of wit in others. And Edwin Engel, whose *The Haunted Heroes of Eugene O'Neill* is the only recent book-length study concludes: "O'Neill's style remained not only strained and turgid, but awkward, inarticulate, banal."

From a book review of A Touch of the Poet, New York Times Book Review, *September 22, 1957, p. 1. Used by permission of the author.*

1. Editors' note: Shaw's remark about O'Neill is frequently quoted. In the earliest form of it that we can find, St. John Ervine quotes a conversation between Shaw and Archibald Henderson in which G. B. S. called O'Neill "a Fantee Shakespeare who peoples his isle with Calibans." (St. John Irvine, "Is O'Neill's Power in Decline?" *Theatre Magazine*, vol. 43, May 1926, pp. 12, 58; also "An Appraisal of Mr. O'Neill," London *Observer*, October 29, 1933). *Fantee* apparently refers to the natives of the Gold Coast and perhaps by implication to *The Emperor Jones.*

Of Theodore Dreiser's "style" much the same sort of things have been said. But among critics of general literature there has been, for some reason, more readiness to forgive in him what only those specifically concerned with the theatre have excused in O'Neill. And the reply to his defenders has usually been that they were, in Miss McCarthy's phrase, "Propagating the theory that a playwright was not subject to the same standards as other writers, the theory, in other words, that the theatre is an inferior art."

Mr. Bentley, it is true, goes so far as to admit that an O'Neill play "comes out of a bigger head" than that of certain other contemporary playwrights and Miss McCarthy speaks grudgingly of "the element of transcendence jutting up woodenly—like a great home-made Trojan horse." But the conclusion of both can be summed up in Miss McCarthy's words: "O'Neill belongs to that group of American authors, which includes Farrell and Dreiser, whose choice of vocation was a kind of triumphant catastrophe; none of these men possessed the slightest ear for the word, the sentence, the speech, the paragraphs. . . . How is one to judge the great logical symphony of a tone-deaf musician?"

In the case of Shakespeare the final answer to Voltaire was given by that consensus which alone is capable of giving a final answer in artistic matters. Audiences are often wrong for a time. They often fail to appreciate novel excellences and they are often misled by mere fashion. But in the long run they are right, if only because, as some say, there is no other definition of what right means. And it may be that the astonishingly vigorous O'Neill revival now in progress is posterity giving its decision. Or, if this seems a premature conclusion, the revival is at least a demonstration of O'Neill's power to interest a new audience that is far more significant than his first success—for the simple reason that a second hearing in the contemporary theatre is extremely rare. Has any other American playwright ever enjoyed anything comparable to the O'Neill revival?

To suggest that posterity may even now be proving certain critics wrong is not to say that posterity will call O'Neill a great stylist or list verbal felicity among his virtues. It is to say only that it may well recognize his continued triumph over the defects his recent critics have exaggerated into intolerability.

As a matter of fact his most ardent admirers have, from the

beginning, not only recognized but stressed them. Reviewing the first production of *Mourning Becomes Electra* the present writer made this comment: "The only thing missing is language . . . Take, for example, the scene in which Orin stands beside the bier of his father . . . What one longs for with an almost agonizing longing is something not merely good but magnificent, something like 'Tomorrow, and tomorrow and tomorrow' or 'I could a tale unfold whose lightest word . . .' But no such language does come and *Mourning Becomes Electra* remains, therefore, only the best tragedy in English which the present century has produced. This is the penalty we pay for living in an age whose most powerful dramatist cannot rise above prose."

Or consider the parody written by Lee Simonson who designed some of the sets for O'Neill's plays, was one of the directors of the Theatre Guild and, what is more important, an admirer and personal friend. In his book *The Stage Is Set* he published this version of a Hamlet soliloquy as he imagined that O'Neill might write it: "God! if I could only kill myself—get away from it all. There's nothing to live for. I'm afraid! Afraid to do anything. Afraid of death. Spooks. What they told me when I was a kid. (*Looking at the snowman*) I'm just so much mush—mush like you . . . If I could only thaw with you tomorrow—thaw, just dissolve, trickle into the earth—run off into the sewer."

This is the kind of parody that one conventionally calls "deadly," and it is no more unjust than parody has a right to be. But Mr. Simonson did not think that it was deadly, and he certainly did not want it to be. "Parody," as Oscar Wilde replied to Gilbert's *Patience*, "is the tribute which mediocrity pays to genius." It takes no great gifts to see what is wrong with O'Neill. But not all of the witty are clever enough to recognize sufficiently, as Simonson also did, what is right with him. In the classroom I used always to read this parody, and it never failed to get its laugh. But I never knew any student to dismiss O'Neill because of it.

On occasion he can write almost as badly as his detractors say. Not always, of course, and he has passages powerful simply as writing, though even in them it is not "writing" in the technical sense that one thinks of. And the case is best made for him by admitting his defects. He used dialect a great deal, and he had so little ear for it that good actors always made it better than he had written it. There are seldom any subtle overtones, never that kind of "ambiguity" now so much admired.

And it is, I think, worth remarking that with the exception of the not especially notable "That ol' debble sea" he invented no phrase which passed into current speech, even temporarily or even derisively. Though I think he is likely to be longer remembered than, say, Tennessee Williams, he had nothing comparable to the Williams' gift (shared by Erskine Caldwell) for the vocabulary, the syntax and the rhythm of Southern speech.

Why then does a new generation brought up in the theatre on the neurotic subtlety of Williams turn appreciatively again to O'Neill? What quality has he that is lacking in, to take another example, the whole contemporary French school of which Jean Anouilh is the best-known representative?

Like Williams and like O'Neill, the members of that school are, in a sense, tragic writers, and they are certainly more sophisticated. Perhaps this is, in itself, one of the answers. In Anouilh, the subtlety, the wit and the gift for words are astonishing. So, too, are the endless involutions of a mind always turning back upon itself and, as it were, dying in convulsions. The subtlety is self-destructive, leaving nothing except emptiness when the last ingenious twist has been performed. His plays seem to hope for nothing more than a display of the author's skill at playing an intellectual game.

Perhaps Americans are essentially too serious (too unsophisticated, if you insist) to accept the conclusion that the Pursuit of Truth is no more than a game. They are unwilling to look for the black hat in the dark cellar unless they believe that it may just possibly be there. O'Neill can be deeply involved in genuine passion because he is not merely playing a game to exhibit his skill. He can be black enough at times and on occasion fall a victim to the nihilism against which he perpetually struggled. But there may be "more faith in honest doubt" if "honest doubt" is not "complacent doubt." And O'Neill is never complacent, never other than deeply involved.

Man emerges from the bludgeoning he receives in O'Neill's plays with his essential dignity intact. He is still a creative being worthy of respect. That can hardly be said of either Williams or

Anouilh. And it may be that the present generation has found O'Neill stimulating for precisely that reason.

Mere sincerity of intention is, of course, not enough. As one of Shaw's characters remarks: "Behind every bad poem lies a perfectly genuine emotion." Bentley has the same thing in mind when he gibes at the "recent rehabilitator," of O'Neill for "taking the will for the deed" and "applauding O'Neill for strengthening the pavement of hell." But there is a fallacy in the argument, or at least in its application. It is not merely a question of high intention versus lesser achievement. The crucial question is "To what extent and in what way is one aware of good intentions, of that genuine emotion behind a-less-than-perfect poem?" Is it merely that the author says he has high intentions, that he tells you about them? Or is it that you actually perceive them in the work itself? If the second is true then more than merely the intention is present.

I have read no detraction of O'Neill whose author did not seem slightly uneasy, who did not somewhere concede more than he safely could. O'Neill's first audience did a great deal more than concede and so do the new audiences to many of whom he is a discovery. Whatever his other limitations as a writer, he had the writer's one indispensable gift. He "communicated"—the situation, the characters, and above all the depth of his concern with them. That is not everything; but it is enough.

Somerset Maugham once declared that all the great novelists—Balzac, Dickens and Dostoevsky, for example, "wrote badly." He did not say that the novels were great because they were badly written or that no writer is both a great stylist and great in other ways besides. But he did suggest that, as novelists, his favorites were superior to the Flauberts and the Jameses whom another school admires so much more. He felt that they were superior because Balzac and Dickens and Dostoevsky had virtues more important than those they lacked and because, instead of torturing themselves in the vain attempt to "get a style," they wrote what they had it in them to write. An O'Neill who wrote better would have been a better O'Neill. But he will last longer and mean more than many who can, in the ordinary sense, write rings around him.

APPENDICES

I. ALPHABETICAL CHECK LIST OF PLAYS

TITLES: One-act plays appear in quotation marks, long plays in italics. Identification of plays in the elaborate "Cycle" of plays which O'Neill worked on in the 1930's and 1940's was made possible by Karl-Ragnar Gierow's article "Eugene O'Neill's Posthumous Plays," *World Theatre*, Spring 1958, which is reprinted in this book, and by the plan prepared by Donald C. Gallup of the Yale University Library, recorded in Doris Falk's *Eugene O'Neill and the Tragic Tension* (1959), pp. 205–206.

DATES: It is impossible to name a precise date of composition for every play. As O'Neill wrote to Richard Dana Skinner (in a letter quoted in Skinner's *Eugene O'Neill*, 1935, p. vii), "Some plays were written in one year, and rewritten into their publication and stage-produced forms in a later year—usually this meant only a condensation without any change in essentials." In other instances (such as *The Hairy Ape*, which began as a short story in 1917 and was written as a play—"in three weeks"—in 1921), O'Neill said that the rewriting was much more than a slight revision. In such cases, the earlier and later dates are both listed. Principal authority for dating plays to 1933 is the chronology contained in O'Neill's letter to Skinner (pp. vii–x). Other sources used for establishing dates were O'Neill's notes to the Wilderness Edition of *The Plays* (1935), the letters and other firsthand evidence in Barrett Clark's *Eugene O'Neill: The Man and His Plays* (rev. ed., 1947), and Doris Falk's citations of the mss. in the Yale Collection.

PRODUCTION: For further information about the productions, see Appendix II, O'Neill's Plays in Production.

PUBLICATION: For plays in copyright but never published, the date when the typescript was registered at the Library of Congress ("Lib of Cong") is listed. For further information about publication, see the Bibliography of Works by O'Neill: Plays.

TITLE	APPROXIMATE DATE OF COMPOSITION	DATE OF FIRST PRODUCTION	DATE OF FIRST PUBLICATION
"Abortion"	1913–1914	1959	1950
Ah, Wilderness!	1932	1933	1933
All God's Chillun Got Wings	1923	1924	1924
"The Ancient Mariner"	1923	1924	1960
And Give Me Death	One of the "Cycle" plays, written, destroyed		
Anna Christie	1919–1920	1921	1922
"Atrocity"	1916	Destroyed	
"Before Breakfast"	1916	1916	1916
Belshazzar	1915	Destroyed	
Beyond the Horizon	1917–1918	1920	1920
"Bound East for Cardiff"	1914	1916	1916
Bread and Butter	1914	———	(Lib of Cong, 1914)
By Way of Obit	A planned series of one-act plays of which only one—"Hughie"—was ever completed. (Gierow)		
The Calm(s) of Capricorn	One of the "Cycle" plays, written, destroyed		
The Career of Bessie Bolan	(?) Draft written and destroyed (See *The Life of Bessie Bowen*)		
"Children of the Sea"	1914 (Early title of "Bound East for Cardiff")	———	(Lib of Cong, 1914)
Chris Christophersen	1919	1920 (as Chris)	(Lib of Cong, 1919)
The "Cycle"	See *Tale of Possessors. . . .*		
Days Without End	1931–1934 (See chapter from Falk in this book)	1934	1934
"The Dear Doctor"	1914	Destroyed	
Desire Under the Elms	1924	1924	1924
Diff'rent	1920	1920	1921
"The Dreamy Kid"	1918	1919	1920
Dynamo	1928	1929	1929
The Earth's the Limit	One of the "Cycle" plays, written, destroyed		
The Emperor Jones	1920	1920	1921
"Exorcism"	1919	1920	(Lib of Cong, 1920)
The First Man	1921	1922	1922
"Fog"	1913–1914	1916	1914
The Fountain	1921–1922	1925	1926
"The G.A.N."	1916–1917	Destroyed	
Gold	1920	1921	1921

TITLE	APPROXIMATE DATE OF COMPOSITION	DATE OF FIRST PRODUCTION	DATE OF FIRST PUBLICATION
The Great God Brown	1925	1926	1926
The Greed of the Meek One of the "Cycle" plays, written, destroyed			
Hair of the Dog One of the planned "Cycle" plays, apparently never written			
The Hairy Ape	1917, 1921	1922	1922
(As a short story, written in 1917, never published. As a play, written "in three weeks" in 1921.)			
"Honor Among the Bradleys"	1919	Destroyed	
"Hughie"	1941	1958	1959
The Iceman Cometh	1939	1946	1946
"Ile"	1916–1917	1917	1918
"In the Zone"	1916–1917	1917	1919
The Last Conquest (or *The Thirteenth Apostle*) Draft written, destroyed			
Lazarus Laughed	1925–1926	1928	1927
The Life of Bessie Bowen Reported in preparation, 1934 (*NY Times*, Feb 11, 1934, etc.) (See *The Career of Bessie Bolan*)			
A Long Day's Journey Into Night	1940–1941	1956	1956
"The Long Voyage Home"	1916–1917	1917	1917
The Man on Iron Horseback One of the planned "Cycle" plays, apparently never written			
Marco Millions	1923–1925	1928	1927
"The Moon of the Caribbees"	1916–1917	1918	1918
A Moon for the Misbegotten	1943	1947	1952
More Stately Mansions	1938 (Date on ms found by Gierow in 1957. One of the "Cycle" plays thought destroyed until 1957. Ms now at Royal Dramatic Theatre, Stockholm)		
Mourning Becomes Electra	1929–1931	1931	1931
"The Movie Man"	1914	1959	1950
Nothing Lost but Honor One of the planned "Cycle" plays, apparently never written			
Now I Ask You	1917	——	Lib of Cong, 1917
The Oldest Man (Original title of *The First Man*)	1921	——	Lib of Cong, 1921

TITLE	APPROXIMATE DATE OF COMPOSITION	DATE OF FIRST PRODUCTION	DATE OF FIRST PUBLICATION
"The Ole Devil"	1920	——	Lib of Cong, 1921
(Apparently one stage in the composition of *Anna Christie*. See *Chris*)			
Or Give Us Death (See *And Give Me Death*)			
The Personal Equation	1915	Begun in Professor Baker's class as *The Second Engineer*, destroyed	
"Recklessness"	1914	——	1914
"The Rope"	1918	1918	1919
The Second Engineer	1914	Later called *The Personal Equation*, destroyed	
Servitude	1913–1914	——	1950
"Shell Shock"	1918	——	(Lib of Cong, 1918)
"The Sniper"	1914–1915	1917	1950
S. S. Glencairn	——	1924	——
("Moon of the Caribbees," "Long Voyage Home," "In the Zone," "Bound East for Cardiff")			
Strange Interlude	1926–1927	1928	1928
The Straw	1918–1919	1921	1921
*A Tale of Possessors Self-Dispossessed**	1934–1943	A vast and shifting "Cycle" of seven—or nine or eleven—plays on which O'Neill worked and planned for at least ten years.	
"Thirst"	1913–1914	1916	1914
"Till We Meet"	1918	Destroyed	
A Touch of the Poet	c1940	1957	1957
(Original title of the entire "Cycle"; only "Cycle" play so far produced or published)			
"The Trumpets"	1919	Destroyed	
"Warnings"	1913–1914	——	1914
"The Web"	1913	——	1914
(The first play he wrote, said O'Neill)			
Welded	1922–1923	1924	1924
"Where the Cross Is Made"	1918	1918	1919
"A Wife for a Life"	1913	——	1950

* *A Tale of Possessors Self-Dispossessed: A Cycle of Eleven Plays*, as identified by Gierow, originally included the following, of which only the first six were ever written—in fairly full though probably incomplete form, with the exception of *A Touch of the Poet*, which has been produced and published. *More Stately Mansions* is the only other one extant. I. *The Greed of the Meek*. II. *Or Give Us Death*. III. *A Touch of the Poet*. IV. *More Stately Mansions*. V. *The Calm of Capricorn*. VI. *The Earth's the Limit*. VII. *Nothing Lost but Honor*. VIII. *The Man on Iron Horseback*. IX. *Hair of the Dog*. The Cycle was intended to relate through the tale of an Irish-American family the development of the United States over a century and a half, with stress on the destructive effect of "possessions."

II. O'NEILL'S PLAYS IN PRODUCTION:

A Chronological Record

This is a list of principal American productions, with foreign productions included when they preceded Broadway openings. For other information on O'Neill's plays abroad, see the items listed in the Bibliography of works about O'Neill and his plays, under the following entries: Anon. ("Emperor Jones in Paris"), Barbetti, Boyd, (Ivor) Brown, Dukes, Frenz, Kommer, M.A.B., Martenson, Vetluguin, Zeraffa.

* The asterisk indicates first production of the play anywhere.

Information is presented in this order: Date of opening night, title of play, producer or producing group, theatre—New York City unless otherwise stated, and number of performances (when this information is available).

1916 Summer *"Bound East for Cardiff." Provincetown Players, Wharf Theatre, Provincetown, Mass., 2nd bill of the Summer.

1916 Summer *"Thirst." Provincetown Players, Wharf Theatre, Provincetown, Mass., 4th bill of the Summer.

1916 Nov 3 "Bound East for Cardiff." Provincetown Players, Playwrights' Theatre, MacDougal St., Greenwich Village, opening bill of first season in NY City.

1916 Dec 1 *"Before Breakfast." Provincetown Players, Playwrights' Theatre.

1917 Jan *"Fog." Provincetown Players, Playwrights' Theatre.

1917 Feb 16 *"The Sniper." Provincetown Players, Playwrights' Theatre.

1917 Oct 31 *"In the Zone." Washington Square Players, Comedy Theatre.

1917 Nov 2 *"The Long Voyage Home." Provincetown Players, Playwrights' Theatre.

1917 Nov 30 *"Ile." Provincetown Players, Playwrights' Theatre.

1918 Apr 26 *"The Rope." Provincetown Players, Playwrights' Theatre.

1918 Nov 22 *"Where the Cross Is Made." Provincetown Players, Playwrights' Theatre.

1918 Dec 20 *"The Moon of the Caribbees." Provincetown Players, Playwrights' Theatre.

1919 Oct 31 *"The Dreamy Kid." Provincetown Players, Playwrights' Theatre.

1920 Feb 2 **Beyond the Horizon*. John D. Williams, Morosco Theatre (later the Criterion, then the Little Theatre). First play on Broadway. 111 perfs. Begun on an experimental basis at special matinees, became a regular run and won O'Neill his first Pulitzer Prize.

1920 March 8 **Chris*. George C. Tyler, Atlantic City. This early version of Anna Christie did not survive road tryouts, died in Philadelphia.

1920 March 26 *"Exorcism." Provincetown Players, Playwrights' Theatre.

1920 Nov 3 **The Emperor Jones*. Provincetown Players, Playwrights' Theatre. Moved uptown to the Selwyn, Dec. 27. 204 perfs.

1920 Dec 27 **Diff'rent*. Provincetown Players, Playwrights' Theatre. Moved uptown to the Selwyn, Jan. 21, 1921, then to the Times Square and Princess Theatres. 100 perfs.

1921 June 1 **Gold*. John D. Williams, Frazee Theatre. 13 perfs.

1921 Nov 2 **Anna Christie*. Arthur Hopkins, Vanderbilt Theatre. 177 perfs.

1921 Nov 10 **The Straw*. George C. Tyler, Greenwich Village Theatre. 20 perfs.

1922 March 4 **The First Man*. Augustin Duncan, Neighborhood Theatre. 27 perfs.

1922 March 9 **The Hairy Ape*. Provincetown Players, Playwrights' Theatre. Moved uptown to the Plymouth, April 17. 127 perfs.

1924 March 17 **Welded*. Kenneth MacGowan-Robert Edmond Jones-Eugene O'Neill in association with the Selwyns, 39th Street Theatre. 24 perfs.

1924 Apr 6 **The Ancient Mariner*. Provincetown Players, Provincetown Playhouse. 33 perfs.

1924 May 15 **All God's Chillun Got Wings*. Provincetown Players, Provincetown Playhouse.

1924 Aug 14 **S. S. Glencairn*. The Barnstormers, Barnstormers' Barn, Provincetown, Mass., then at the Provincetown Playhouse, NY (Nov. 3), the Punch and Judy (Dec. 16), the Princess (Jan. 12, 1925). First time the four Glencairn plays performed together.

1924 Nov 11 **Desire Under the Elms*. Provincetown Players, Greenwich Village Theatre. Moved uptown to the Earl Carroll Theatre, Jan. 12. 208 perfs.

1925 Dec 10	*	*The Fountain.* Macgowan-Jones-O'Neill in association with A. L. Jones and Morris Green, Greenwich Village Theatre. 24 perfs.
1926 Jan 23	*	*The Great God Brown.* Macgowan-Jones-O'Neill, Greenwich Village Theatre. Moved uptown to the Garrick, March 1. 283 perfs.
1926 Feb 16		*The Emperor Jones.* Revival staged by James Light, Provincetown Theatre.
1926 Nov 10		*The Emperor Jones.* Revival, Mayfair Productions, Mayfair Theatre. 61 perfs.
1926 Nov 30		*Beyond the Horizon.* Revival by the Actors' Theatre, Mansfield Theatre, 79 perfs.
1928 Jan 9	*	*Marco Millions.* Theatre Guild, Guild Theatre. 92 perfs.
1928 Jan 30	*	*Strange Interlude.* Theatre Guild, John Golden Theatre. 426 perfs.
1928 Apr 9	*	*Lazarus Laughed.* The Pasadena Community Playhouse, Pasadena, California. 28 perfs.
1929 Jan 9		*S. S. Glencairn.* Revival, Provincetown Theatre. 90 performances.
1929 Feb 11	*	*Dynamo.* Theatre Guild, Martin Beck Theatre. 50 perfs.
1929 March 5		"Before Breakfast." Revival, Provincetown Theatre. 27 perfs.
1930 March 3		*Marco Millions.* Revival, Theatre Guild, Liberty Theatre. 8 perfs.
1931 Oct 26	*	*Mourning Becomes Electra.* Theatre Guild, Guild Theatre. 150 perfs.
1932 May 9		*Mourning Becomes Electra.* Revival, Theatre Guild, Alvin Theatre, 16 perfs.
1933 Oct 2	*	*Ah, Wilderness!* Theatre Guild, Guild Theatre. 289 perfs.
1934 Jan 8	*	*Days Without End.* Theatre Guild, Guild Theatre. 57 perfs.
1937 Oct 29		*S. S. Glencairn.* Revival by the WPA Federal Theatre Project, Lafayette Theatre. 68 perfs.
1938 Jan 25		*Diff'rent.* Revival by Charles Hopkins for the WPA NY State Federal Theatre Project, Maxine Elliott Theatre.
1941 Oct 2		*Ah, Wilderness!* Revival, Theatre Guild, Guild Theatre. 29 perfs.
1946 Oct 9	*	*The Iceman Cometh.* Theatre Guild, Martin Beck Theatre. 136 perfs.
1947 Feb 20	*	*A Moon for the Misbegotten.* Theatre Guild, Hartman Theatre, Columbus, Ohio. Closed on tryout tour, St. Louis, Mo., March 29.

1948 May 20	*S. S. Glencairn.* Revival, NY City Theatre Co, NY City Center. 14 perfs.
1951 Jan 9	*Anna Christie.* Revival, NY City Theatre Co, City Center. 29 perfs.
1951 Fall	*Desire Under the Elms.* Revival by the Craftsmen, Barbizon-Plaza Theatre.
1952 Jan 16	*Desire Under the Elms.* Revival by the American National Theatre and Academy, ANTA Playhouse. 46 perfs.
1953 Apr 24	*A Moon for the Misbegotten.* Royal Dramatic Theatre, Stockholm.
1956 Feb 10	**A Long Day's Journey Into Night.* Royal Dramatic Theatre, Stockholm.
1956 May 8	*The Iceman Cometh.* Staged by José Quintero, Circle-in-the-Square. 565 perfs.
1956 Nov 7	*A Long Day's Journey Into Night.* Leigh Connell-Theodore Mann-José Quintero, Helen Hayes Theatre. 390 perfs. (1st appearance on Broadway.)
1957 May 2	*A Moon for the Misbegotten.* Carmen Capalbo and Stanley Chase, Bijou Theatre. 68 perfs. (1st appearance on Broadway.)
1957 March 29	**A Touch of the Poet.* Royal Dramatic Theatre, Stockholm.
1958 Sept 18	*"Hughie." Royal Dramatic Theatre, Stockholm.
1958 Oct 12	*A Touch of the Poet.* Producers Theatre (Robert Whitehead Productions), Helen Hayes Theatre. 248 perfs. (1st appearance on Broadway.)
1959 Oct 6	*The Great God Brown.* Theatre, Inc. (T. Edward Hambleton and Norris Houghton), Coronet Theatre: Renamed The Eugene O'Neill Theatre. 32 perfs.
1959 Oct 27	*"The Movie Man," *"Abortion," and "The Sniper." Key Theatre, St. Marks Place, N.Y.

III. SELECTED BIBLIOGRAPHY

A. *Bibliographies of Works by and about O'Neill*

There have been two book-length bibliographies, one of them (Sanborn and Clark) compiled back in 1931 and moreover rare, the other (Miller) compiled recently but unpublished:

Sanborn, Ralph and Clark, Barrett H., *A Bibliography of the Works of Eugene O'Neill.* N. Y., Random House, 1931. Edition limited to 500 copies. Principally a collation of the texts of works by O'Neill; also a bibliography of books and articles about O'Neill and his plays (through *Dynamo*), lists of unpublished plays and plays in anthologies (and a section of poems by O'Neill).

Miller, Jordan Y., *A Critical Bibliography of Eugene O'Neill*, an unpublished doctoral dissertation, Columbia University, 1957, 2 vols. Detailed and annotated records through 1956 of works by and about O'Neill, full production data, etc., with an analytical introductory essay.

Also useful are the following:

Frenz, Horst, "A List of Foreign Editions and Translations of Eugene O'Neill's Dramas," *Bulletin of Bibliography*, 18 (1943) 33–34.

———, "Eugene O'Neill's Plays Printed Abroad," *College English*, March 1944), 340–41. A further note on foreign editions.

Herndon, Genevra, *American Criticism of Eugene O'Neill, 1917–1948*, an unpublished doctoral dissertation, Northwestern University, 1948. Includes an extensive bibliography of O'Neill criticism.

Quinn, Arthur Hobson, *A History of the American Drama from the Civil War to the Present Day*, N. Y., Crofts, rev. ed., 1936, vol. 2, pp. 384–87. Publication and production data.

Spiller, Robert E., and others, eds., *The Literary History of the United States*, Macmillan, 1948, vol. 3: *Bibliography*, and *Bibliographical Supplement*, Macmillan, 1959. Selected bibliography.

B. *Primary Sources*

DARTMOUTH: The Landauer Collection consists principally of first-night theatre programs of productions of O'Neill plays abroad. There are also some galley proofs, books, and letters. See Landauer, Bella C., "The International O'Neill," *American Book Collector*, 2 (July 1932), 55–56, an article on the collection, which was donated to Dartmouth in 1951.

PRINCETON: The O'Neill Collection consists of some O'Neill manuscripts and some letters. See McAneny, Marguerite L., "Eleven Manuscripts of Eugene O'Neill," *The Princeton University Library Chronicle*, 4 (April 1943), 86–89.

YALE: The O'Neill Collection at the Yale University Library is the outstanding single depository of material. It has O'Neill's personal scrapbooks, with newspaper clippings from all over the world; a large collection of letters, papers, manuscripts, notes, etc. See Eaton, Walter Prichard, "The Eugene O'Neill Collection," *Yale University Library Gazette*, 18 (July 1943), 5–8.

NEW YORK PUBLIC LIBRARY: The Theatre Collection has scrapbooks of the Provincetown Players and clipping collections of all sorts that are crumbling rapidly but still afford valuable and frequently unexpected information. The Collection also has in good condition play reviews and other clippings, playbills, and miscellaneous material.

See Frenz, Horst, "O'Neill Collections I Have Seen," *Indiana Quarterly for Bookmen*, January 1945, pp. 27–34.

C. *Works by O'Neill: Plays*

This does not pretend to be a comprehensive chronological listing. It is an effort to list first and other principal American editions of the individual plays and of collections of the plays. For the location of plays reprinted in anthologies, consult John H. Ottemiller's *Index to Plays in Collections* (N. Y., Scarecrow Press, 3rd ed., 1957)—which lists all full-length plays. For one-acters, consult *An Index to One-Act Plays*, by Hanna Logosa and Winifred Ver Nooy, (Faxon, 1924), which covers 1900 to 1924, and its Supplements, which cover 1924 to 1950.

* The asterisk indicates first publication of the full play.

Titles of individual plays follow the style of appendices I and II; titles of books are italicized.

***Thirst, and Other One-Act Plays*. Boston, The Gorham Press, 1914. Limited to 1,000 copies (published at the expense of James O'Neill); rare now. Contents: *"Thirst," *"The Web," *"Warnings," *"Fog," and *"Recklessness."

*"Bound East for Cardiff." In *The Provincetown Plays, First Series.* N. Y., Frank Shay, 1916, pp. 5–25.

*"Before Breakfast." In *The Provincetown Plays, Third Series.* N. Y., Frank Shay, 1916, pp. 193–207.

"Before Breakfast." N. Y., Frank Shay, 1916. First separate edition.

*"The Long Voyage Home." In *The Smart Set* (a magazine edited by H. L. Mencken and George Jean Nathan), 53 (Oct. 1917), 83–94.

*" 'Ile." In *The Smart Set*, 55 (May 1918), 89–100.

*"The Moon of the Caribbees." In *The Smart Set*, 55 (Aug. 1918), 73–86.

The Moon of the Caribbees, and Six Other Plays of the Sea. N. Y., Boni and Liveright, 1919. First publication of *"In the Zone," *"Where the Cross Is Made," and *"The Rope." Revised texts of "Moon of the Caribbees," "Long Voyage Home," and " 'Ile." Also contains "Bound East for Cardiff."

Reissued by Boni and Liveright as a "Modern Library" book in 1923, with an introduction by George Jean Nathan.

Reissued as *The Long Voyage Home: Seven Plays of the Sea*, N. Y., Modern Library, 1940.

*"The Dreamy Kid." In *Theatre Arts Magazine*, 4 (Jan. 1920), 41–56.

**Beyond the Horizon.* N. Y., Boni and Liveright, 1920. First long play to be published.

**The Emperor Jones.* In *Theatre Arts Magazine*, 5 (Jan. 1921), 29–59.

The Emperor Jones, **Diff'rent*, **The Straw.* N. Y., Boni and Liveright, 1921.

The Emperor Jones. Cincinnati, Stewart Kidd, 1921. First separate edition.

**Gold.* N. Y., Boni and Liveright, 1921.

**The Hairy Ape*, **Anna Christie*, **The First Man.* N. Y., Boni and Liveright, 1922.

"The Dreamy Kid." In *Contemporary One-Act Plays of 1921*, ed. Frank Shay, Cincinnati, Stewart Kidd, 1922, pp. 487–517. In later editions, the title of the volume became *Twenty Contemporary One-Act Plays.*

**All God's Chillun Got Wings.* In the *American Mercury* (edited by Mencken and Nathan), 1 (Feb. 1924), 129–48.

*All God's Chillun Got Wings, and *Welded.* N. Y., Boni and Liveright, 1924.

(*The Ancient Mariner*—excerpts. In *The New York Times*, April 13, 1924, VIII, 1.)

The Complete Works of Eugene O'Neill. N. Y., Boni and Liveright, 1924–25, 2 vols. First publication of **Desire Under the Elms*, vol. 2. Edition limited to 1,200 autographed sets.

Contents: Vol. 1: *Anna Christie*, *Beyond the Horizon*, *The First Man*, *Diff'rent*, *Gold*, "Moon of the Caribbees," "Bound East for Cardiff," "Long Voyage Home," "In the Zone," "Ile." Vol. 2: *Emperor Jones*, *The Hairy Ape*, *All God's Chillun Got Wings*, *Desire Under the Elms*, *Welded*, *The Straw*, "The Rope," "The Dreamy Kid," "Where the Cross Is Made," "Before Breakfast."

Desire Under the Elms. N. Y., Boni and Liveright, 1925. First separate edition.

Reissued as a New American Library paperback edition (Signet), 1958.

The Works of Eugene O'Neill. N. Y., Boni and Liveright, 1925, 4 vols. Differs from the *Complete Works*, 1924–1925, in omitting the sea plays. Contents:

(VOL. 1) *Anna Christie*, *All God's Chillun Got Wings*, *Diff'rent.*
(VOL. 2) *Beyond the Horizon*, *The Straw*, "Before Breakfast."
(VOL. 3) *Desire Under the Elms*, *The Hairy Ape*, *Welded.*
(VOL. 4) *The Emperor Jones*, *Gold*, *The First Man*, "The Dreamy Kid."

**The Great God Brown*, **The Fountain*, *The Moon of the Caribbees, and Other Plays*, N. Y., Boni and Liveright, 1926. Uniform with the 4-volume Works, 1925. The "Other Plays" are the five one-acters which round out *The Moon of the Caribbees* volume (1919, 1923).

**Marco Millions.* N. Y., Boni and Liveright, 1927.

Lazarus Laughed, Act One. In *A Yearbook of American Literature*, edited by Van Wyck Brooks, Lewis Mumford, Alfred Kreymborg, and Paul Rosenfeld. N. Y., The Macaulay Co., 1927, pp. 807–33. The "Act One" published here differs substantially from the first act of the full play as published later in the year.

**Lazarus Laughed.* N. Y., Boni and Liveright, 1927. First publication of full play.

**Strange Interlude.* N. Y., Boni and Liveright, 1928.

The Emperor Jones and The Straw. Introduction by Dudley Nichols. N. Y., Modern Library, 1928.

**Dynamo.* N. Y., H. Liveright, 1929.

**Mourning Becomes Electra.* N. Y., H. Liveright, 1931. (Regular edition)

Mourning Becomes Electra. N. Y., H. Liveright, 1931. Special limited edition containing O'Neill's "Working Notes and Extracts from a Fragmentary Work Diary." These "Notes and Extracts" were later reprinted in *European Theories of the Drama*, ed. Barrett H. Clark, N. Y., Crown, rev. ed., 1947.

Representative Plays. . . N. Y., Liveright, (1932). Contents: *Marco Millions*, *The Emperor Jones*, *Anna Christie*, "Where the Cross Is Made," "The Moon of the Caribbees."

Nine Plays, selected by the author. Introduction by Joseph Wood Krutch. N. Y., Liveright, 1932. Contents: *Emperor Jones*, *The Hairy Ape*, *All God's Chillun Got Wings*, *Desire Under the Elms*, *Marco Millions*, *The Great God Brown*, *Lazarus Laughed*, *Strange Interlude*, *Mourning Becomes Electra*.

Reissued by Random House (© 1932), 1936, and became a standard Modern Library edition (© 1932), 1941 (© 1954).

**Ah, Wilderness!* N. Y., Random House, 1933.

**Days Without End*. N. Y., Random House, 1934.

The Plays of Eugene O'Neill. Wilderness Edition, N. Y., Scribner's, 1934–35, 12 vols., with illustrative plates and with introductory notes by O'Neill in each volume explaining when and where the plays were written. Edition limited to 770 autographed sets. Contents: I. *Strange Interlude*. II. *Mourning Becomes Electra*. III. *The Emperor Jones*, *Ah, Wilderness!* IV. *All God's Chillun Got Wings*, *Lazarus Laughed*. V. *Marco Millions*, *The Hairy Ape*. VI. *Beyond the Horizon*, *Welded* VII. *Dynamo*, *Diff'rent*. VIII. *The Straw*, *The First Man*. IX. *Days Without End*, *Gold*. X. *The Great God Brown*, *Anna Christie*. XI. *Desire Under the Elms*, *The Fountain*. XII. *Nine One-Act Plays*.

The Emperor Jones, *Anna Christie*, *The Hairy Ape*. Introduction by Lionel Trilling. N. Y., Modern Library, 1937. Reissued 1949.

The Long Voyage Home: Seven Plays of the Sea. N. Y., Modern Library, 1940. A reissue of *The Moon of the Caribbees* volume (1919, 1923) retitled after the motion picture based on the sea plays.

The Plays of Eugene O'Neill. N. Y., Random House, 1941, 3 vols. All the published plays up to the date except the plays in the *Thirst* volume (1914).

Contents. I. *Strange Interlude*, *Desire Under the Elms*, *Lazarus Laughed*, *The Fountain*, *The Glencairn Series*, "Ile," "Where the Cross Is Made," "The Rope," "The Dreamy Kid," "Before Breakfast."

II. *Mourning Becomes Electra*, *Ah, Wilderness!*, *All God's Chillun Got Wings*, *Marco Millions*, *Welded*, *Diff'rent*, *The First Man*, *Gold*.

III. *Anna Christie*, *Beyond the Horizon*, *The Emperor Jones*, *The Hairy Ape*, *The Great God Brown*, *The Straw*, *Dynamo*, *Days Without End*.

**The Iceman Cometh*. N. Y., Random House, 1946. Reissued as a Modern Library Paperback ed.

The Lost Plays. N. Y., New Fathoms, 1950. Contents: *"Abortion," *"The Movie Man," *"The Sniper," **Servitude*, *"A Wife for a Life." These were plays not "lost" but forgotten by O'Neill—the copyright had not been renewed, and they were published without the author's consent. Reissued by Citadel Press, (1958).

The Plays of Eugene O'Neill. N. Y., Random House, 1951, 3 vols. Contents the same as The Plays, 1941, with the addition of *The Iceman Cometh* to vol. 3.

**A Moon for the Misbegotten*. N. Y., Random House, 1952.

**A Long Day's Journey into Night*. New Haven, Yale University Press, 1956.

**A Touch of the Poet*. New Haven, Yale University Press, 1957. Issued as a Yale paperbound.

*"Hughie." New Haven, Yale University Press, 1959.

**The Ancient Mariner*. ed. Donald Gallup. In the *Yale University Library Gazette*, 35 (Oct. 1960), 61–86.

D. *Nondramatic Works by O'Neill*

POEMS

"Collected Poems by O'Neill," in *A Bibliography of the Works of Eugene O'Neill*, by Ralph Sanborn and Barrett H. Clark, N. Y., Random House, 1931, Part III, pp. 109–61. The following poems are here reprinted:

"Free," a poem originally published in the *Pleiades Club Year Book*, N. Y., April, 1912, which O'Neill is said to have called his first published work.

Poems contributed by O'Neill to a column titled "Laconics" on the editorial page of the New London *Telegraph*, from August 26 to December 9, 1912.

"Fratricide," New York *Call*, May 17, 1914.

"Speaking, to the Shade of Dante, of Beatrices," in F. P. A.'s column "The Conning Tower," New York *Tribune*, July 5, 1915, p. 7. (Reprinted in F.P.A.'s column in the N. Y. *Herald Tribune*, March 9, 1935.)

"Submarine" (unsigned), *The Masses*, February, 1917, p. 43.

SHORT STORY

"Tomorrow," *The Seven Arts [Magazine]*, 2 (June 1917) 147–70. O'Neill's only published story. He forbade the reprinting of it "because of its very personal nature." (Sanborn and Clark, p. 15) O'Neill said that he had also written a story (unpublished) containing the germ of *The Hairy Ape*.

ARTICLES, LETTERS, ETC.

*Items in this section marked with an asterisk are reprinted, in whole or in part, in this book.

Unpublished letters can be found in the Dartmouth (Landauer Collection), Princeton, and Yale Collections of O'Neill material described above ("Primary Sources"). The following list by no means includes a complete record of the O'Neill letters that have found their way into print. The material is listed chronologically.

Letter to *The New York Times*, April 11, 1920, VI, 2, explaining origins of *Beyond the Horizon*.

*"Eugene O'Neill's Credo and His Reasons for His Faith," *New York Tribune*, Feb. 13, 1921, pp. 1, 6. Anonymous, but known to have been written by O'Neill.

Letter to Pierre Loving, in Loving's "Eugene O'Neill," *The Bookman*, 53 (Aug. 1921) 511–20.

Letter to *The New York Times*, Dec. 18, 1921, VI, 1, on the question of *Anna Christie*'s "happy ending."

*"Strindberg and Our Theatre," Provincetown Playbill No. 1, Season 1923–24 (Jan. 1924), reprinted in *The New York Times*, Jan. 6, 1924, VII, 1; in Deutsch and Hanau, *The Provincetown*, pp. 191–93; and in this book.

*"Are the Actors To Blame?," Provincetown Playbill No. 1, Season 1925–26 (Nov. 1925). Reprinted in *The New York Times*, Nov. 8, 1925, VIII, 2; in Deutsch and Hanau, *The Provincetown*, pp. 197–98; and in this book.

A statement about the intent of *The Fountain*, in the Greenwich Village Theatre Program No. 3, Season 1925–26.

Letter to the press explaining *The Great God Brown*, appeared in several New York City newspapers Feb. 13 and 14, 1926—in *The New York Times*, Feb. 14, 1926, VIII, 2. Reprinted in its entirety in Arthur Hobson Quinn's *History of the American Drama . . .*, vol. 2, pp. 192–94.

*"Eugene O'Neill to George Jean Nathan (1919–1926)," in *The Theatre of George Jean Nathan*, by Isaac Goldberg, N. Y., Simon and Schuster, 1927, pp. 140–65. An excellent collection of letters most of which originally appeared in the *Boston Evening Tran-*

script, Oct. 31, 1925, in an article by Goldberg called "Playwright and Critic: The Record of a Stimulating Correspondence." Three additional letters were published in the book for the first time.

Foreword, in Benjamin DeCasseres, *Anathema! Litanies of Negation*, N. Y., Gotham Book Mart, 1928 (a limited edition of a volume of poems by a friend of O'Neill), pp. vii–xi.

Letter to George Jean Nathan, in Nathan's "The Theatre," *American Mercury*, 16 (Jan. 1929), 119.

*Letters to George Jean Nathan, in *The Intimate Notebooks of George Jean Nathan*, N. Y., Knopf, 1932. "Eugene O'Neill," pp. 21–38.

Letter to Martha Carolyn Sparrow, in Arthur H. Nethercot's "O'Neill on Freudianism," *Saturday Review of Literature*, 8 (May 28, 1932), 759.

*Letter to the Kamerny Theatre, New York *Herald-Tribune*, June 19, 1932.

*"Memoranda on Masks," *American Spectator*, 1 (Nov. 1932), 3.

*"Second Thoughts," *American Spectator*, 1 (Dec. 1932), 2.

*"A Dramatist's Notebook," *American Spectator*, 2 (Jan. 1933).

"Editorial Conference," among O'Neill, George Jean Nathan, Ernest Boyd, Theodore Dreiser, and James Branch Cabell, in *The American Spectator Year Book*, edited by the above-named, plus Sherwood Anderson, N. Y., Frederick A. Stokes, 1934, pp. 346–59. A conversation on the Jewish question, on Catholicism, on nationalism in general.

The three preceding items in this list were reprinted in *The American Spectator Year Book*, pp. 159–67.

Introductory notes to each volume of the Wilderness Edition of *The Plays of Eugene O'Neill*, 1934–35, 12 vols., a limited edition. The notes give data and some of the circumstances about the composition and first production of the plays.

"Professor George Pierce Baker," *The New York Times*, Jan. 13, 1935, IX, 1. Brief tribute on the occasion of Baker's death.

Letter to Richard Dana Skinner, in Skinner's *Eugene O'Neill*, N. Y., Longmans, Green, 1935, pp. vii–x. The letter includes a chronology of composition of the plays.

*Letter to Arthur Hobson Quinn, in his *History of the American Drama . . .*, N. Y., Crofts, 1936, vol. 2, p. 199. Other letters reprinted on pp. 177, 192–94, 258.

"Professor George Pierce Baker: A Note and Some Communications," in *George Pierce Baker: A Memorial*, N. Y., Dramatists' Play Service, 1939, pp. 20–23.

Suggestions for a National Theatre Reportory, in "What Shall We Play?", *Theatre Arts Monthly*, 25 (Feb. 1941), 147. Lists 12 plays from *Agamemnon* through *Macbeth* and the *Tempest*, to *Peer Gynt*, *Dance of Death*, and *Cherry Orchard*.

*Letters to Barrett Clark, in his book *Eugene O'Neill: The Man and His Plays*, N. Y., Dover, rev. ed., 1947. Publishes several letters in full, and excerpts from others. The revised edition has correspondence not included in the original edition.

Letters to Lawrence Langner, in his book *The Magic Curtain*, New York, Dutton, 1951, pp. 275–87, 397–401.

Letter to Brooks Atkinson, in his article "Eugene O'Neill," *The New York Times*, Dec. 13, 1953, VI, 1. On love of driving fast cars.

*Letters to George Pierce Baker, in Wisner Payne Kinne's *George Pierce Baker and the American Theatre*, Cambridge, Mass., Harvard University Press, 1954, pp. 191–98.

The Last Will and Testament of Silverdene Emblem O'Neill. New Haven, privately printed "for Carlotta" by the Yale University Press, 1956, on the occasion of the publication of *A Long Day's Journey Into Night*. Tribute to the family dog.

Inscriptions: Eugene O'Neill to Carlotta Monterey O'Neill. New Haven, Yale University Press, 1960. Edition limited to 500 copies.

Letters to John S. Mayfield, in his article "Eugene O'Neill and the Senator from Texas," *Yale University Library Gazette*, 35 (1960), 87–93.

E. *Works about O'Neill and His Plays*

A Note about the Criticism: This part of the bibliography is an attempt to list, with comments wherever necessary and possible, the most important books and articles about O'Neill and his plays through 1960. Reviews of individual plays have been listed when they are of particular interest or value. Attention is called to the few book-length studies of the plays in English—by Barrett H. Clark, a critical biography first written in 1926 and revised through 1947; by Sophus K. Winther and Richard Dana Skinner, in the mid-thirties; and by Edwin Engel and Doris Falk in the late 1950's.

A Note on Biography: The semi-official biography, with critical comments, by Barrett H. Clark was the only account of the life from its first edition in 1926 through its last rewriting in 1947. After O'Neill's death, a growing number of old friends, scholars, and newspapermen have declared their intention of writing the O'Neill story. So far, we have had a very personal memoir by Agnes Boulton, O'Neill's second wife, covering the period from 1917 to 1919; and a journalistic account of the whole life by Croswell Bowen, with the assistance of O'Neill's son Shane. A study by Doris Alexander, one of the leading O'Neill scholars, of the parental and theatrical background and early years is promised by Harcourt, Brace & World for February 1962. Also heralded as forthcoming by Harper's is a biography by Arthur and Barbara Gelb, a section of which has been published in *Horizon* (see below).

* Items marked with an asterisk are reprinted, in whole or in part, in this book.

Abel, Lionel, "O'Neill and His Critics," *The New Leader*, 41 (Jan. 6, 1958), 25–26. In a controversy about O'Neill's language, sides with Krutch versus Bentley and Mary McCarthy: His "characters speak authentically at the critical points of their life experience."

Adler, Jacob H., "The Worth of *Ah, Wilderness!*," *Modern Drama*, 3 (Dec. 1960), 280–88. "Of its kind . . . a distinguished play."

Ahlgren, Stig, "Eugene O'Neills författarskap," *Ord och Bild* (Stockholm), 46 (no. 3, 1937), 175–82.

Alexander, Doris M., "Captain Brant and Captain Brassbound: The Origin of an O'Neill Character," *Modern Language Notes*, 74 (April 1959), 306–10.

———, "Eugene O'Neill and *Light on the Path*," *Modern Drama*, 3 (Dec. 1960), 260–67. The Theosophical Society book that made O'Neill "an active mystic."

*———, "Eugene O'Neill as Social Critic," *American Quarterly*, 6 (Winter 1954), 349–63.

———, "Eugene O'Neill, 'The Hound of Heaven,' and the 'Hell Hole,'" *Modern Language Quarterly*, 20 (Dec. 1959), 307–14. "Married love" in *Servitude*, *Welded*, and *Days Without End.*

———, "Hugo of *The Iceman Cometh:* Realism and O'Neill," *American Quarterly*, 5 (1953), 357–66. O'Neill created Hugo in the image of a personal acquaintance.

———, "*Lazarus Laughed* and Buddha," *Modern Language Quarterly*, 17 (Dec. 1956), 357–65. Lazarus as "a composite of saviours."

———, "Psychological Fate in *Mourning Becomes Electra*," *PMLA*, 68 (1953), 923–24. O'Neill's indebtedness to G. V. Hamilton and K. Macgowan, co-authors of *What Is Wrong with Marriage.*

———, "*Strange Interlude* and Schopenhauer," *American Literature*, 25 (1953), 213–28. Finds influence of Schopenhauer, not Freud.

Anderson, John, "Eugene O'Neill, *Theatre Arts Monthly*, 15 (Nov. 1931), 938–42. Sees O'Neill at peak of maturity, master of the theatre's tricks and "poet enough to disdain them" in his uncompromising integrity. (See Geddes, in same issue.)

*Anonymous, "Counsels of Despair," *Times Literary Supplement*, no. 2410 (April 10, 1948), 197–99.

———, "*Emperor Jones* in Paris," *The Literary Digest*, 79 (Dec. 29, 1923), 24–25. Brief selections from reviews of the French production.

———, " 'Moon' in Columbus," *Time*, 49 (March 3, 1947), 47–48. Account of world premiere of *A Moon For the Misbegotten* in Columbus, Ohio.

*———, "Mr. Eugene O'Neill: An Iconoclast in the Theatre," *Times Literary Supplement*, no. 1840 (May 8, 1937), 353–54.

———, "The Ordeal of Eugene O'Neill," *Time*, 48 (Oct. 21, 1946), 71–72, 74–78. Account of world premiere of *The Iceman Cometh* in New York, of the mass press interview that preceded it, and of some events in O'Neill's life.

———, "Pasadena Community Playhouse Produces *Lazarus Laughed*," *Theatre*, 48 (July 1928), 42–44. One of the few reports on this event.

Anschutz, Grace, "Masks: Their Use by O'Neill and Pirandello," *The Drama*, 17 (April 1927), 201–202, 224. The multiplicity of personalities in Pirandello's characters allows for more subtle analysis than the "actual masks" of O'Neill's.

Arested, Sverre, "*The Iceman Cometh* and *The Wild Duck*," *Scandinavian Studies*, 20 (Feb. 1948), 1–11. Sixty years later, O'Neill found man still cannot face truth. Offers evidence of direct influence.

Arndt, Horst, *Eugene O'Neills antitradionalistische Gesellschaftskritik.* (Munich), 1956.

Aronstein, Philipp, "Eugene O'Neill," *Neuphilologische Monatsschrift*, 1 (June 1930), 311–25; (July–Aug. 1930), 376–82.

Asselineau, Roger, "*Mourning Becomes Electra* as a Tragedy," *Modern Drama*, 1 (Dec. 1958), 143–150. More profound than Aeschylus' *Oresteia;* a modern realization of Aristotelian tragedy.

Atkinson, Brooks, "*The Emperor Jones* to Music," *The New York Times*, Jan. 15, 1933, IX, 1. Prefers the play to the opera.

———, "*The Iceman Cometh*," *The New York Times*, October 20, 1946. Reprinted in Atkinson's *Broadway Scrapbook*, N. Y., Theatre Arts Inc., 1947, pp. 241–46.

———, "Theatre: O'Neill Tragedy Revived," *The New York Times*, May 9, 1956, p. 38. *The Iceman* ten years later.

*Bab, Julius, "Eugene O'Neill: As Europe Sees America's Foremost Playwright," *The Theatre Guild Magazine*, 9 (Nov. 1931), 11–15.

*Baker, George P., "O'Neill's First Decade," *Yale Review*, 15 (July 1926), 789–92.

Baldensperger, Fernand, "Eugène O'Neill, Prix Nobel de Littérature," *Revue Bleue Politique et Littéraire*, 75 (Feb. 6, 1937), 73–78.

Barbetti, Emilio, "O'Neill sulla scena Italiana," *Anglica* (Florence), 1 (Dec. 1946), 270–76.

Barron, Samuel, "The Dying Theatre," *Harper's*, 172 (Dec. 1935), 108–17. By its nature the theatre cannot embody the complex insights of modern times—as evidenced by O'Neill's failure.

Basso, Hamilton, "The Tragic Sense," *New Yorker*, 24 (Feb. 28, 1948), 34–38 ff.; (March 6), 34–38 ff.; (March 13), 37–40 ff. A detailed profile, in three installments.

Battenhouse, Roy W., "*Mourning Becomes Electra*," *Christendom*, 7 (Summer 1942), 332–35. The Christian concept of Original Sin is at the root of the play.

———, "*Strange Interlude* Restudied," *Religion in Life*, 15 (Spring 1946), 202–13.

Baughan, E. A., "Plays of Eugene O'Neill," *The Fortnightly Review* (London), 119 (May 1923), 852–60. Very favorable, early British evaluation.

Baum, Bernard, "*The Tempest* and *The Hairy Ape*," *Modern Language Quarterly*, 14 (Sept. 1953), 258–73. The naturalism of *The Hairy Ape* is "a travesty of man's quest for his lost selfhood as dramatized in *The Tempest*." (Yank and Caliban.)

*Benchley, Robert C., "*Dynamo*," *Life*, 93 (March 8, 1929), 24, 37.

———, "*Mourning Becomes Electra*," *New Yorker*, 7 (Nov. 7, 1931), 28, 30. Praises as sheer theatre—the deuce with the highfalutin talk about Greek tragedy.

Bentley, Eric, "*A Moon For The Misbegotten*," *New Republic*, 127 (Aug. 4, 1952), 17. Reprinted as "Eugene O'Neill's Pietà," *The Dramatic Event*, N. Y., Horizon Press, 1954, pp. 30–33. "Its central image—that of a giant virgin holding in her arms a dipsomaniacal lecher with a heart of gold—may stand in all minds as O'Neill's monument": to his grandeur, or to his inadequacies.

———, *The Playwright as Thinker*, N. Y., Harcourt, Brace, 1946. "Tragedy in Modern Dress" includes a section, and notes, on Wedekind and O'Neill as followers of Ibsen's Bourgeois Tragedy, pp. 67–69, 318–22.

———, "The Return of Eugene O'Neill," *Atlantic Monthly*, 178 (Nov. 1946), 64–66. Having read advance proofs of *Iceman*, predicts it will be effective theatre.

*———, "Trying To Like O'Neill," *Kenyon Review*, 14 (Summer 1952), 476–92. Reprinted in *In Search of Theater*, N. Y., Knopf, 1953, pp. 233–47. Reverses opinion of preceding item.

Berkelman, Robert, "O'Neill's Everyman," *South Atlantic Quarterly*, 58 (Autumn 1959), 609–16. *The Great God Brown* as "a modern morality play."

Blackburn, Clara, "Continental Influences on Eugene O'Neill's Expressionistic Dramas," *American Literature*, 13 (May 1941), 109–33.

Block, Anita, *The Changing World in Plays and Theatre*, Boston, Little, Brown, 1939, pp. 137–93, and passim. Detailed study of the plays—especially as "revelation of the inner conflicts of the individual."

*Bodenheim, Maxwell, "Roughneck and Romancer," *New Yorker*, 1 (Feb. 6, 1926), 17–18.

Boulton, Agnes, *Part of a Long Story*, N. Y., Doubleday, 1958. O'Neill's second wife, mother of Shane and Oona, reminisces via forty-year recall about their first two years together, 1917 to 1919.

*Bowen, Croswell, "The Black Irishman," *PM*, Nov. 3, 1946.

*———, *The Curse of the Misbegotten: A Tale of the House of O'Neill*, written "with the assistance of Shane O'Neill," N. Y., McGraw-Hill, 1959. The first full-scale biography since Clark's pioneer work. Often uses the authority of Agnes Boulton uncritically. Rich in journalistic data and family gossip (none *from* Carlotta Monterey O'Neill), but undocumented.

Boyd, Alice K., *The Interchange of Plays between London and New York, 1910–1939*, N. Y., King's Crown Press, 1948. Includes statistical data on O'Neill plays produced in England, and analysis of audience response.

Breese, Jessie Martin, "A Home on the Dunes," *Country Life in America*, 45 (Nov. 1923), 72–76. Detailed description, with photographs, of the old Peaked Hill Bars Coast Guard Station, O'Neill's home on Cape Cod.

Brie, Friedrich, "Eugene O'Neill als Nachfolger der Griechen (*Mourning Becomes Electra*)," *Germanisch-Romanische Monatsschrift*, 21 (Jan.–Feb. 1933), 46–59.

Brodin, Pierre, *Ecrivains Américains du vingtieme siécle*, Paris, Horizons de France, 1947, pp. 73–102. Discusses individual plays, influences, ideas, place in American literature.

Brown, Ivor, "American Plays in England," *American Mercury*, 33 (Nov. 1934), 315–22. The English cannot tolerate O'Neill's intensity.

Brown, John Mason, "American Tragedy," *Saturday Review of Literature*, 32 (Aug. 6, 1949), 124–27. Reprinted in *Still Seeing Things*, N. Y., McGraw-Hill, 1950, pp. 185–90. O'Neill has the "tragic vision," but he cannot claim "the tragic tongue"—in rebuttal to Krutch.

Brown, John Mason, "Christopher Marlowe to Eugene O'Neill," *Letters from Greenroom Ghosts*, N. Y., Viking, 1934, pp. 69–116. Critical remarks on tragedy and O'Neill's plays, in the form of imaginary letter.

———, "Finders Keepers, Losers Weepers," *Saturday Review of Literature*, 33 (June 17, 1950), 28, 30–31. Informed indignation at the "reprehensible" publication of the so-called *Lost Plays.*

———, *Upstage: The American Theatre in Performance*, N. Y., W. W. Norton, [c 1930], pp. 60–77.

Brugger, Ilse, "Verswendung und Bedeutung der Maske bei O'Neill," *Die Neueren Sprechen* (1957), 153–67.

Bruns, Friedrich, "Eugene O'Neill," *Die Amerikanische Dichtung der Gegenwart*, Leipzig, 1930, pp. 111–24.

Cambon, Glauco, "O'Neill e il dramma dell' anima americana," *Studi Americani*, no. 3 (1957), 293–313.

Canby, Henry Seidel, "Scarlet Becomes Crimson," *Saturday Review of Literature*, 8 (Nov. 7, 1931), 257–58. Reprinted in Canby's *Seven Years' Harvest: Notes on Contemporary Literature*, N. Y., Farrar and Rinehart, 1936, pp. 139–46. Attacks O'Neill (*Mourning Becomes Electra*) as a decadent sensationalist who employs special situation and abnormality, which can never be basis of tragedy.

Canfield, Mary Cass, "The Provincetown Playhouse Takes a Chance," *The Independent*, 112 (May 10, 1924), 259. Describes staging of *Ancient Mariner.*

Carb, David, "Seen on the Stage," *Vogue*, 68 (Sept. 15, 1926), 100–101, 154. Praises O'Neill as "the only American dramatist who has dared to be himself."

*Cargill, Oscar, *Intellectual America*, N. Y., Macmillan, 1941, pp. 332–40, 685–720. The early O'Neill studied among "The Primitivists," the later among "The Freudians."

Carpenter, Frederic I., "The Romantic Tragedy of Eugene O'Neill," *College English*, 6 (Feb. 1945), 250–58. Traces a sequence through the plays of O'Neill's extreme idealism.

Cestre, Charles, "La Dernière Œuvre dramatique d'Eugène O'Neill," *Revue Anglo-Américaine*, 4 (Dec. 1926), 118–21. Reviewing *Great God Brown*, sees O'Neill joining the "insurgents" who have set out to liberate American society from Puritan constraints.

———, "Eugène O'Neill et les Surgissements du Tréfond," *Revue Anglo-Américaine*, 6 (Dec. 1928), 131–44.

Catel, Jean, "Eugene O'Neill, prix Nobel de littérature 1936," *Mercure de France*, 274 (March 1, 1937), 422–26.

Chaitin, Norman, "O'Neill: The Power of Daring," *Modern Drama*, 3 (Dec. 1960), 231–41.

Chiaromonte, Nicola, "Eugene O'Neill (1958)," translated by M. Arnett, *Sewanee Review*, 68 (Summer 1960), 494–501.

Chiesura, Giorgio, "Intorno a una commedia di O'Neill," *Letteratura* (Florence), 9 (May–June 1947), 126–33. Critical study of *Welded*.

Clark, Barrett H., "Aeschylus and O'Neill," *English Journal*, 21 (Nov. 1932), 699–710.

———, *Eugene O'Neill*, N. Y., Robert M. McBride, 1926. Revised editions called *Eugene O'Neill: The Man and His Plays*, McBride, 1929, 1933, 1936; N. Y., Dover, 1947. Approved and even edited by O'Neill in the original edition, the book is rich in source material, containing many letters from O'Neill to Clark and frequent conversations from 1926 to 1946, especially in the earlier years when O'Neill was responding to Clark's appreciation. Valuable as the first biography, as an account of the facts about the life and work checked by O'Neill. The critical comments are uneven.

*Clurman, Harold, *Lies Like Truth*, Macmillan, 1958, pp. 24–33.

Cohen, Helen L., ed., *More One-Act Plays by Modern Authors*, N. Y., 1927. An introduction to "Where the Cross Is Made," pp. 311–28, compares its plot in detail with that of *Gold*. A bibliography, pp. 349–50, lists the 47 plays O'Neill wrote from 1913–25, and identifies them as published, produced, destroyed—based on the list in the *Fountain* playbill, Greenwich Village Theatre, 1925.

Cole, Lester, and Lawson, John Howard "Two Views on O'Neill," *Masses and Mainstream*, 7 (June 1954), 56–63. Cole finds O'Neill so limited by "Mysticism, Freudianism, Godism," that no merit remains. The other Marxist critic, Lawson, praises the art and integrity, though condemning the sterility and hopelessness. (See Lawson.)

Colin, Saul, "Without O'Neill's Imprimatur," *New York Times Book Review*, June 18, 1950. On the legal facts surrounding the publishing of the *Lost Plays*.

Colum, Mary M., "The Drama of the Disintegrated," *The Forum*, 94 (Dec. 1935), 358–59. O'Neill portrays with vitality "that common character in American life, the disintegrated person." Compares Shaw's characters unfavorably, as abstractions.

Colum, Padraic, "The Theatre," *Dial*, 86 (April 1929), 349–50. O'Neill "is a child when he thinks"—a denunciation of *Dynamo*.

Comarnesco, Pierre, "Le drame de la vie et de la connaissance dans l'œuvre du dramaturge américain Eugène O'Neill," *Revue Hebdomadaire* (Paris), 47 (Jan. 15, 1938), 311–29.

Conlin, Matthew T., O.F.M., "The Tragic Effect in *Autumn Fire* [by T. C. Murray] and *Desire Under The Elms*," *Modern Drama*, 1

(Feb. 1959), 228–35. Finds Murray superior in handling essentially the same plot, O'Neill suffering from Strindbergian nihilism.

Corbin, John, "O'Neill and Aeschylus," *Saturday Review of Literature*, 8 (April 30, 1932), 693–95. Reprinted in *Essay Annual*, ed. Erich A. Walter, N. Y., Scott, Foresman. Possible decline of creative powers evidenced in increasing interest in technical stunts and morbid psychology.

Cowley, Malcolm, "Eugene O'Neill: Writer of Synthetic Drama," *Brentano's Book Chat*, July–Aug. 1926. Objects to stylization on stage.

*———, "A Weekend with Eugene O'Neill," *The Reporter*, 17 (Sept. 5, 1957), 33–36.

Crichton, Kyle, "Mr. O'Neill and the Iceman," *Collier's*, 118 (Oct. 26, 1946), 18–19, 39, 40, 42. Reports O'Neill's comments on post-1920 affairs, on his return to New York for *The Iceman Cometh* opening.

Dahlström, Carl E. W. L., "*Dynamo* and *Lazarus Laughed:* Some Limitations," *Modern Drama*, 3 (Dec. 1960), 224–30.

Dansereau, Pierre MacKay, "Notes sur O'Neill," *Les Idées* (Montreal), 1 (April 1935) 211–20.

Day, Cyrus, "*Amor Fati:* O'Neill's Lazarus as Superman and Savior," *Modern Drama*, 3 (Dec. 1960), 297–305.

———, "The Iceman and the Bridegroom," *Modern Drama*, 1 (May 1958), 3–9. *The Iceman Cometh* is "a parable of the destiny of man" who waits for Christian fulfillment and finds only death: A repudiation of Christianity.

DeCasseres, Benjamin, "Eugene O'Neill: From Cardiff to Xanadu," *Theatre Magazine*, 46 (Aug. 1927), 10, 58. Eulogy by a friend.

———, "The Triumphant Genius of Eugene O'Neill," *Theatre Magazine*, 47 (Feb. 1928), 12–13, 62.

De Onis, Harriet, "Eugene O'Neill," *Asomante* (Puerto Rico), 15 (Jan.–March 1959), 14–26.

———, "Eugene O'Neill," *Sur*, no. 248 (1957), 53–70.

De Pue, Elva, "The Tragedy of O'Neill," *The Figure in the Carpet* (New School, N. Y.—title subsequently changed to *Salient*), [vol. 1] no. 4 (May 1928), 18–25. Despite all the pertinacious effort, O'Neill "very often fails to convey anything but the intimation of his precious, his tragic sincerity."

*Deutsch, Helen, and Hanau, Stella *The Provincetown, A Story of the Theatre, 1915–1929*, N. Y., Farrar and Rinehart, 1931. Programs and lists of plays and casts, as well as descriptive comment.

Reprints two articles by O'Neill, pp. 191–93, 197–98. (See Bibliography: Nondramatic Works by O'Neill.)

*De Voto, Bernard, "Minority Report," *Saturday Review of Literature*, 15 (Nov. 21, 1936), 3–4, 16. Reprinted in De Voto's *Minority Report*, Boston, Little-Brown, 1943, as "Monte Cristo in Modern Dress," pp. 190–97. O'Neill has only tricks and theatrical devices, doesn't deserve Nobel Prize. (Many letters came to the magazine in support of De Voto's position, though of course some disagreed.)

Dickinson, Thomas H., "The Playwright Unbound: Eugene O'Neill," *Playwrights of the New American Theatre*, N. Y., Macmillan, 1925, pp. 56–123. Surveys the plays to 1925, finds O'Neill "unbound" by convention—not stage struck, but "world struck."

Dirvana, Nesterim, "Théatre Pur et Rythme Biologique," *Dialogues* (Istanbul), 1: no. 1 (June 1949), 87–105. Analysis of *Strange Interlude.*

Dobree, Bonamy, "Mr. O'Neill's Latest Play," *Sewanee Review*, 56 (Winter 1948), 118–26. On basis of *Iceman Cometh*, reiterates earlier opinion (next item) that O'Neill writes plays that are like novels.

———, "The Plays of Eugene O'Neill," *Southern Review*, 2 (Winter 1937), 435–46. Fails in effort to combine modern naturalism with medieval morality play.

Dony, Françoise, "La tragédie d'Eugène O'Neill et l'idée de fatalité," *Revue de l'Univérsitaire de Bruxelles*, 41 (Dec. 1935), 170–88.

———, "Vices et vertus du personnage O'Neillien," *Renaissance*, N. Y., 1 (Oct.–Dec. 1943), 589–98. On the weakness of O'Neill's aesthetique, the rigidity of his "type"-characters.

*Downer, Alan S., "Eugene O'Neill as Poet of the Theatre," *Theatre Arts*, 35 (Feb. 1951), 22–23.

———, *Fifty Years of American Drama: 1900–1950*, Chicago, Regnery, 1951, pp. 64–70, 92–97, and passim.

Driver, Tom F., "On the Late Plays of Eugene O'Neill," *Tulane Drama Review*, 3 (Dec. 1958), 8–20.

Dukes, Ashley, "The English Scene: O'Neill Succeeds," *Theatre Arts*, 22 (Feb. 1938), 101–107. *Mourning Becomes Electra* in London, with critical comments.

Eaton, Walter Prichard, "Eugene O'Neill," *Theatre Arts*, 4 (Oct. 1920), 286–89. Typical early praise for realism, "rough, tough talk," the "tense, driving emotional sincerity" of the early plays.

———, "O'Neill—'New Risen Attic Stream'?" *American Scholar*, 6 (Summer 1937), 304–12. Ironically, *Mourning Becomes Electra* is less Greek than others, e.g., *Desire Under the Elms.*

Eaton, Walter Prichard, *The Theatre Guild: The First Ten Years . . .*, N. Y., Brentano's, 1929. Chapter 11 is on the productions of *Marco Millions* and *Strange Interlude.*

Edel, Leon, "Eugene O'Neill: The Face and the Mask," *University of Toronto Quarterly*, 7 (Oct. 1937), 18–34. The earlier "face" plays were about adventure; the next group were inner "mask" plays.

*Eliot, T. S., "Books of the Quarter": A review of *All God's Chillun*, *The New Criterion*, 4 (April 1926), 395–96.

Emmel, Felix, "O'Neill: Kaiser Jones," *Das ekstatische Theatre*, Prien, Kampmann and Schnabel, 1924, 318–22. An early German study.

Engel, Edwin A., *The Haunted Heroes of Eugene O'Neill*, Cambridge, Mass., Harvard, 1953. Traces recurrent themes in O'Neill's plays, his "ideological" development: Thus, the phase of Peace-Love-Harmony (*Desire Under the Elms*) yields to the skeptical phase of Death-Chaos-Futility (*Mourning Becomes Electra*, *Iceman Cometh*).

———, "O'Neill, 1960," *Modern Drama*, 3 (Dec. 1960), 219–23.

Ervine, St. John, "An Appraisal of Mr. O'Neill," London *Observer*, Oct. 29, 1933. "Mr. O'Neill does not grow; he merely enlarges"; he "swells," says this former admirer.

———, Introduction, *The Moon of the Caribbees . . .*, London, Cape, 1923, pp. 7–17. "The most interesting man of letters that America has produced since the death of Walt Whitman."

———, "Is O'Neill's Power in Decline?" *Theatre Magazine*, 43 (May 1926), 12, 58. Yes, on the basis of *Desire Under the Elms*, *All God's Chillun*, and *Welded.* See Freed for rebuttal.

Fagin, N. Bryllion, "Eugene O'Neill," *Antioch Review*, 14 (Spring 1954), 14–26. Responsible for the American theatre's growing up.

*———, "Eugene O'Neill Contemplates Mortality," *The Open Court*, 45 (April 1931), 208–31.

———, " 'Freud' on the American Stage," *Educational Theatre Journal*, 2 (Dec. 1950), 296–305. Including Freudian elements in O'Neill's plays.

*Falk, Doris, *Eugene O'Neill and the Tragic Vision: An Interpretative Study of the Plays*, New Brunswick: Rutgers, 1958. Best critical volume in English to date. Chronological analysis of the plays as reflecting clash between aspects of the self, a source of strength and weakness. Views of Jung, Fromm, and especially Karen Horney brought to bear illuminatingly.

Falk, Signi, "Dialogue in thc Plays of Eugene O'Neill," *Modern Drama*, 3 (Dec. 1960), 314–25.

*Fergusson, Francis, "Eugene O'Neill," *Hound and Horn*, 3 (Jan.–March 1930), 145–60.

Fergusson, Francis, "Mr. O'Neill's New Play," *American Review*, 2 (Feb. 1934), 491–95. *Days Without End* is no worse than the others, after all; has "that lifelessness and *ennui* . . . , that triteness," which make up the unique O'Neill quality and inform us that he is toying with an Idea.

Firkins, Oscar W., "Eugene O'Neill in *Gold*—The Provincetown Players," *The Weekly Review*, 4 (June 18, 1921), 584–85. "A play that begins in plot should hardly end in psychology": Thus, this one deteriorates from Stevenson to Conrad. An interesting and not unrepresentative early comment.

Fiskin, A. M. I., "The Basic Unity of Eugene O'Neill," in *Writers of Our Years*, ed. Fiskin, Denver, University of Denver Press, 1950, pp. 101–17. An ideological systematization of the plays.

Flèche-Salgues, Suzanne, "Trois Pièces récentes d' Eugène O'Neill," *Études Anglaises*, 10 (Oct.–Dec. 1957), 410–20. (This is a special issue, called *Le Théâtre contemporain en Grande-Bretagne et aux États-Unis*, ed. by L. Bonnerot, M. Le Breton, and P. Legouis.)

Fleisher, Frederic, "Strindberg and O'Neill," *Symposium* (Syracuse University), 10 (Spring 1956), 84–94. O'Neill overemphasized debt to Strindberg in Nobel acceptance speech.

———, "Swedes in the Published Plays of O'Neill," *Orbis litteratum*, 12 (1957), 99–103.

Flexner, Eleanor, *American Playwrights: 1918–1938: The Theatre Retreats from Reality*, N. Y., Simon and Schuster, 1938, pp. 130–97. Detailed criticism of O'Neill's inadequate social consciousness: He has never outgrown his overriding concern for "the condition of the individual soul"—a disappointment to his early socialist champions.

Freed, Frank H., "Eugene O'Neill in the Ascendant," *Theatre Magazine*, 44 (Oct. 1926), 30, 64. Reply to Ervine's 1926 article (above): Rejects Aristotle's criteria for judging, defends "unpleasantness" in *Desire Under the Elms*, etc.

Frenz, Horst, "Eugene O'Neill in Deutschland," *Euphorion* (Heidelberg) 50 (1956), 307–27. One of many studies by Frenz of O'Neill's plays abroad.

———, "Eugene O'Neill in France," *Books Abroad*, 18 (Spring 1944), 140–41.

———, "Eugene O'Neill in Russia," *Poet Lore*, 49 (Autumn 1943), 241–47.

———, "Eugene O'Neill on the German Stage," *Theatre Annual*, 11 (1953), 24–34.

Frenz, Horst, "Eugene O'Neill on the London Stage," *Queens Quarterly*, 54 (Summer 1957), 223–30.

———, "Notes on Eugene O'Neill in Japan," *Modern Drama*, 3 (Dec. 1960), 306–13.

Furst, Henry, "L'Opera di Eugene O'Neill," *Scenario*, 2 (March 1933), 119–28.

Gagey, Edmond McAdoo, *Revolution in American Drama*, N. Y., Columbia, 1947, pp. 39–70. O'Neill's contributions to the stage summarized, in survey of plays.

Galinsky, Hans, "Eugene O'Neill: Die Wendung des modernen amerikanischen Theaters zur Tragödie," *Die Neueren Sprachen*, 6 (1953), 233–46.

Gallup, Donald, "Eugene O'Neill's *The Ancient Mariner*," *Yale University Library Gazette*, 35 (1960), 61–86.

Gassner, John, "Eugene O'Neill: The Course of a Modern Dramatist," *Critique*, 1 (1958), 5–14.

———, "The Electras of Giraudoux and O'Neill," *The Theatre in Our Times*, N. Y., Crown, 1954, pp. 257–66.

*———, "Homage to O'Neill," *Theatre Time*, 3 (Summer 1951), 17–21. Reprinted in *The Theatre in Our Times*, pp. 249–56.

———, *Masters of the Drama*, N. Y., Dober, 3rd revised ed., 1954, pp. 629–61 and passim. O'Neill in the perspective of a history of world drama.

Geddes, Virgil, "Eugene O'Neill," *Theatre Arts*, 15 (Nov. 1931), 943–46. A self-conscious romanticist who, lacking the artistic power of his good intentions, uses theatrical tricks. (See Anderson, above, in same issue.)

———, *The Melodramadness of Eugene O'Neill*, Brookfield, Conn., The Brookfield Players, 1934. A fellow playwright's severe attack, in a 48-page pamphlet.

Geier, Woodrow, "O'Neill's Miracle Play," *Religion in Life*, 16 (Autumn 1947), 515–26. *Days Without End* has the Christian solution for modern times.

Gelb, Arthur and Barbara, "The New London Youth of Eugene O'Neill," *Horizon*, 2 (March 1960), 25–40. "Sections from two chapters" of the Gelbs' promised book.

*Gierow, Karl-Ragnar, "Eugene O'Neill's Posthumous Plays," *World Theatre*, 7 (Spring 1958), 46–52.

———, *Introduktioner till Eugene O'Neills dramatik*, Stockholm, Sveriges radio, 1958.

*Gilder, Rosamond, "Each in His Own Way . . . *The Iceman Cometh*," *Theatre Arts*, 30 (Dec. 1946), 684–90.

Gillet, Louis, "La Clef des songes," *Revue des deux Mondes*, 49 (Jan. 15, 1929), 453–64. *Strange Interlude* is adolescent, O'Neill overrated.

*Gilman, Lawrence, "*Emperor Jones* as Opera Fills the Metropolitan," N. Y. *Herald Tribune*, Jan. 8, 1933.

*Glaspell, Susan, *The Road to the Temple*, N. Y., Frederick A. Stokes, 1927. Biography of George Cram Cook by his wife, and account of development of Provincetown Players.

*Goldberg, Isaac, *The Drama of Transition*, Cincinnati, Stewart Kidd, 1922, pp. 457–71.

*———, *The Theatre of George Jean Nathan*, N. Y., Simon and Schuster, 1926, pp. 140–65. Includes excellent collection of letters from O'Neill to Nathan.

Granger, Bruce Ingham, "Illusion and Reality in Eugene O'Neill," *Modern Language Notes*, 73 (March 1958), 179–86.

Gregory, Horace, "Suicide in the Jungle," *New Masses*, 10 (Feb. 13, 1934), 18–19. The waste of talent as O'Neill goes on unconsciously expressing the spirit of the American middle class and its lost soul.

Gump, Margaret, "From Ape to Man and from Man to Ape," *Kentucky Foreign Language Quarterly*, 4 (1957), 177–85.

Hamilton, Clayton M., *Conversations on Contemporary Drama*, N. Y., Macmillan, 1924, pp. 198–218 (ninth lecture: "Eugene G. O'Neill," April 7, 1924). Includes personal reminiscences.

———, *Seen on the Stage*, N. Y., Henry Holt, 1920, pp. 184–91. Tells of early advice given the playwright; reports production history of *Beyond the Horizon*.

*———, "A Shelf of Printed Plays," *The Bookman*, 41 (April 1915). Includes the only review of the *Thirst* volume, p. 182.

*Hamilton, Gladys, "Untold Tales of Eugene O'Neill," *Theatre Arts*, 40 (Aug. 1956), 31–32, 88.

Hayward, Ira N., "Strindberg's Influence on Eugene O'Neill," *Poet Lore*, 39 (Winter 1928), 596–604. Credits Strindberg with keeping O'Neill from being a mere pamphleteer, a photographic realist.

Helburn, Theresa, "O'Neill: An Impression," *Saturday Review of Literature*, 15 (Nov. 21, 1936), 10. Personal sketch by a member of the Theatre Guild Board, written in the joy of his friends at the Nobel Prize award.

Hersey, F. W., "*Lazarus Laughed:* A World Premiere at Pasadena," *Drama*, 18 (May 1928), 244–46.

*Hewes, Henry, "O'Neill: 100 Proof,—Not a Blend," *Saturday Review*, 39 (Nov. 24, 1956), 30–31. On *Long Day's Journey Into Night*—one of the best of the O'Neill reviews.

*Hewes, Henry, "Self-Delusion in Stockholm," *Saturday Review*, 40 (April 13, 1957) 24. *A Touch of the Poet* in world premiere, reviewed.

*———, "Short Night's Journey Into Day," *Saturday Review*, 41 (Oct. 4, 1958), 27. Premiere of "Hughie," in Stockholm, reviewed.

Hilton, James, "The Short Plays of Eugene O'Neill," *The Bookman* (London), 84 (Sept. 1933), 288–89. Comparison with Conrad's sea plays.

Hohoff, Curt, "Uber Eugene O'Neill," *Hochland*, 1 (Oct. 1938), 40–50.

Hopkins, Vivian C., "*The Iceman* Seen through *The Lower Depths*," *College English*, 11 (Nov. 1949), 81–87. While "O'Neill's philosophic searching goes deeper, his negative solution" makes for less powerful *drama.*

Isaacs, Edith J. R., "Meet Eugene O'Neill," *Theatre Arts*, 30 (Oct. 1946), 576–87. Reprinted in *Theatre Arts Anthology*, N. Y., Theatre Arts Books, 1950, pp. 168–76. Balanced and perceptive summary-estimate, for a new generation, "a new public," of O'Neill's personal and literary quest.

Kalonyme, Louis, "O'Neill Lifts Curtain on His Early Days," *The New York Times*, Dec. 21, 1924, IV, 7.

Karsner, David, *Sixteen Authors to One: Intimate Sketches of Leading American Story Tellers*, N. Y., Lewis Copeland, 1928, pp. 101–22. Portrait by Karsner, who spent time with O'Neill in Maine woods.

Katzin, Winifred, "The Great God O'Neill," (American) *Bookman*, 68 (Sept. 1928), 61–66. An imaginary conversation between an American critic, who idolizes O'Neill, and a French journalist, who finds no masterworks there.

Kaucher, Dorothy, *Modern Dramatic Structure*, Columbia, Mo., University of Missouri Studies, 3 (Oct. 1928), 125–58 ("Eugene O'Neill"). Dialogue, stage directions, structure, studied in all major plays.

Kemelman, H. G., "Eugene O'Neill and the Highbrow Melodrama," *Bookman*, 75 (Sept. 1932), 482–91. Probably the most extreme of the extremist attacks: Exaggerated and unreal events, stereotyped characters, etc., etc.

Kemp, Harry, "Out of Provincetown: A Memoir of Eugene O'Neill," *Theatre Magazine*, 51 (April 1930), 22–23, 66.

*Kenton, Edna, "Provincetown and MacDougal Street," preface to George C. Cook's *Greek Coins, Poems*, N. Y., Doran, (© 1925), pp. 17–30.

*Kinne, Wisner Payne, *George Pierce Baker and the American Theatre*, Cambridge, Mass., Harvard, 1954, pp. 191–98 and passim. On relationship between O'Neill and his teacher at Harvard; includes letters from O'Neill.

Kirchner, Gustav, "Eugene Gladstone O'Neill (1888–1953). Ein Ruckblick," *Zeitschrift fur Anglistik und Amerikanistik*, 2 (1954), 137–89.

Klavsons, Janis, "O'Neill's Dreamer: Success and Failure," *Modern Drama*, 3 (Dec. 1960), 268–72.

Knickerbocker, Frances Wentworth, "A New England House of Atreus," *Sewanee Review*, 40 (April–June 1932), 249–54.

Koischwitz, Otto, *O'Neill*, Berlin, Junker and Dünnhaupt, 1938. Book-length study of the plays.

*Kommer, Rudolf, "O'Neill in Europe," *New York Times*, Nov. 9, 1924, VIII, 2.

Kramer, Edgar, *Freiheit und Notwendigkeit als tragisches Problem bei O'Neill*, Kiel, 1953.

Krutch, Joseph Wood, *American Drama Since 1918*, N. Y., Random House, 1939 (revised ed., Braziller, 1957), pp. 77–133. O'Neill's works occupy a large portion of this critical survey of the American drama since it became literature.

———, "Eugene O'Neill," *Literary History of the United States*, N. Y., Macmillan, 1948, vol. 2, pp. 1237–50 (Chapter 73).

*———, "Eugene O'Neill's Claim to Greatness," *New York Times Book Review*, Sept. 22, 1957, IV, 1.

———, "Eugene O'Neill, the Lonely Revolutionary," *Theatre Arts*, 36 (April 1952), 29–30 ff. Like Poe, Hawthorne, Thoreau, etc., O'Neill was isolated from the spirit of his age, tried to relate man to a "universe."

———, "Introduction," *Nine Plays* by Eugene O'Neill, N. Y., Horace Liveright, 1932. (Reissued by Random House and Modern Library, 1936, 1939, 1941.) Marked Krutch's growing admiration for O'Neill's power, after his pessimistic report on modern drama in "The Tragic Fallacy" (*The Modern Temper*, N. Y., Harcourt-Brace, 1929), where O'Neill was not even mentioned.

———, "O'Neill's Tragic Sense," *American Scholar*, 16 (Summer 1947), 283–90. Vast conflict between those who think O'Neill top dramatist and those who place him very low rests on whether they accept his intention to show man's relation to God. O'Neill has genius, lacks talent.

Kuhnemund, Richard, "Das Drama Eugene O'Neills: Eine kritische Interpretation," *Anglia*, 52 (Sept. 1928), 242–87.

Lamm, Martin, *Modern Drama*, N. Y., Philosophical Library, 1953, pp. 315–33, translated from the Swedish by Karin Elliott. Review of O'Neill's life and plays, with interesting references to O'Neill's relationship to European dramatists.

Lanoire, Maurice, "Eugene O'Neill," *Revue de Paris*, 44 (Feb. 1937), 595–611. Looking over the plays, finds work uneven but rich, vital, provocative.

Lawson, John Howard, *Theory and Technique of Playwriting*, N. Y., Putnam's, 1936, pp. 129–41. On O'Neill's attempt "to sever contact with the world by setting up an inner kingdom which is emotionally and spiritually independent."

———, "The Tragedy of Eugene O'Neill," *Masses and Mainstream*, 7 (March 1954), 7–18. Though potentially great artist, fatally limited by class ties. Lawson's failure to condemn outright provoked attack and rejoinder in June 1954 issue. (See Cole, Lester.)

Le Bréton, Maurice, "Eugene O'Neill and le théâtre américain," *Revue d'Histoire de la philosophie et d'histoire general de la civilisation*, n.s. 7 (April–June 1939), 168–92. Neo-Classical traditions and habits of thought predispose the French against plays like O'Neill's. Calls for special effort to understand the neo-Romantic spirit of American theatre, the psychoanalytic mode of modern American literature—as found in O'Neill.

Lecky, Eleazer, "*Ghosts* and *Mourning Becomes Electra:* Two Versions of Fate," *Arizona Quarterly*, 13 (Winter 1957), 320–38. Finds many parallels, but where Ibsen was optimistic, leaving room for change, O'Neill pessimistic because hopeless.

Levinson, Andrei Y., *Figures Americaines*, Paris, Attinger, 1929, pp. 64–73 ("Eugene O'Neill et le gênie primitif"), 74–85 ("Marco Le Nebab").

Lewisohn, Ludwig, "An American Tragedy," *Nation*, 110 (Feb. 21, 1920), 241–42. *Beyond the Horizon* "establishes America's kinship with the stage of the modern world."

———, "Eugene O'Neill," *Nation*, 113 (Nov. 30, 1921), 626. Remarkable early analysis, based especially on *Anna Christie* and *The Straw*, of O'Neill's use of "gross and palpable devices of the theatre," which he of all dramatists can afford to forego.

———, *Expression in America*, N. Y., Harper's, 1932, revised edition titled *The Story of American Literature*, Modern Library, 1939, pp. 543–53. On the element fatally lacking in the otherwise enormously talented work of O'Neill: "Creative love" toward his characters.

Lovell, John, Jr., "Eugene O'Neill's Darker Brother," *Theatre Arts*, 32 (Feb. 1948), 45–48. From "The Dreamy Kid" and *The Emperor Jones* through *All God's Chillun* and *The Iceman Cometh* (Joe Mott), handling of Negro characters is democratic, but "some of the cruelly belittling elements of the plantation tradition" remain.

Loving, Pierre, "Eugene O'Neill," *Bookman*, 53 (Aug. 1921), 511–20. Reminiscences about the young O'Neill of Buenos Aires and Sixth Avenue taverns, with a fine piece of a letter about aloneness and integrity and purity at Cape Cod.

M. A. B., "O'Neill in Paris," *New York Times*, Nov. 18, 1923, VIII, 2. Reception of the plays.

*McCarthy, Mary, "A Moon for the Misbegotten," *The New York Times*, Aug. 31, 1952. Reprinted in *Sights and Spectacles*, N. Y., Meridian Books, 1957, 86–88.

Macgowan, Kenneth, "O'Neill in His Own Plays?" *The New York Times*, Jan. 9, 1927, VII, 2. Revival of *Beyond the Horizon* while *The Great God Brown* still running suggests that these plays have "the same two protagonists—the baffled artist and the baffled 'he-man' acting out their tragedies."

*———, "The O'Neill Soliloquy: Notes on the Evolution of a Modern Technique," *Theatre Guild Magazine*, 6 (Feb. 1929), 23–25.

Mainsard, Joseph, "Le Theatre d'Eugene O'Neill," *Etudes*, 205 (Oct. 5, 1930), 57–78.

*Malone, Andrew E., "The Plays of Eugene O'Neill," *The Dublin Magazine*, 1 (Dec. 1923), 401–409.

Martenson, Sigvard, *Eugene O'Neills dramatik*, Stockholm, Radiotjanst, 1957. Full-length study in Swedish, with index and bibliographies, production history in Sweden, excellent photographs of O'Neill from childhood to last years and of productions in New York and Sweden.

Mickle, Alan D., *Six Plays of Eugene O'Neill*, N. Y., Liveright, 1929. Highest praise (equal to Shakespeare, Ibsen, Goethe, etc.) by an Australian who had never seen an O'Neill play, but had read six of the major works.

Miller, Jordan Y., "The Georgia Plays of Eugene O'Neill," *The Georgia Review*, 12 (Fall 1958), 278–90. *Days Without End* and *Ah, Wilderness!* are uncharacteristic, "marked the sharp turn downward" into the twelve-year silence.

Moses, Montrose, J., "Eugene O'Neill and the 'New Drama,'" *The American Dramatist*, Boston, Little-Brown, 1925, 415–39. The only non-show-shop dramatist in America—excellent analysis of qualities and potential development.

Motherwell, Hiram, "O'Neill: What Next?" *Stage*, 12 (Aug. 1935), 28–30. Reprinted in *Essay Annual*, ed. Erich A. Walter, N. Y., Scott, Foresman, 1936, p. 202. O'Neill as "ruthless pathologist of individualism." Traces theme of revolt versus father.

*Muchnic, Helen, "Circe's Swine: Plays by Gorky and O'Neill," *Comparative Literature*, 3 (Spring 1951), 119–28.

Muller, Herbert J., "Tragedy in America: O'Neill," *The Spirit of Tragedy*, N. Y., Knopf, 1956, pp. 311–19. Finds it "melancholy" to reread the works of O'Neill in perspective of best world drama.

Mullett, Mary B., "The Extraordinary Story of Eugene O'Neill," *American Magazine*, 94 (Nov. 1922), 34, 112–20. Interview elicits statements about esthetic creed, general philosophy, etc.

Myers, Henry Alonzo, "*Macbeth* and *The Iceman Cometh:* Equivalence and Ambivalence in Tragedy," *Tragedy: A View of Life*, Ithaca, N. Y., Cornell, 1956, pp. 98–109. (See also passim.)

*Nathan, George Jean, "Eugene O'Neill," *The Intimate Notebooks of George Jean Nathan*, N. Y., Knopf, 1932, pp. 21–38.

———, "Eugene O'Neill after Twelve Years," *American Mercury*, 63 (Oct. 1946), 462–66. Offers information about what O'Neill has accomplished during the twelve-year absence.

———, "O'Neill: A Critical Summation," *American Mercury*, 63 (Dec. 1946), 713–19.

———, "O'Neill's Latest," *American Mercury*, 7 (Feb. 1926), 247–49. On fatal changes which turned the original script of *The Fountain* into a disappointing production.

*———, "Our Premier Dramatist," *Intimate Notebooks of George Jean Nathan*, N. Y., Knopf, 1932, pp. 188–98.

———, "The Recluse of Sea Island," *The Theatre of the Moment*, N. Y., Knopf, 1936, pp. 196–207.

Nethercot, Arthur A., "The Psychoanalyzing of Eugene O'Neill," *Modern Drama*, 3 (Dec. 1960), 242–56; (Feb. 1961), 357–72. A two-part survey of the criticism on psychological elements in the plays.

Norwood, Gilbert, "The Art of Eugene O'Neill," *Dalhousie Review*, 21 (July 1941), 143–57. Though not a poet, "of realists he is perhaps the very greatest" of the world's playwrights—of all time.

Pallette, Drew B., "O'Neill and the Comic Spirit," *Modern Drama*, 3 (Dec. 1960), 273–79.

Parajon, Mario, *El Teatro de O'Neill*, Havana, Origenes, 1952.

Parks, Edd Winfield, "Eugene O'Neill's Quest," *Tulane Drama Review*, 4 (March 1960), 99–107. Stresses the need of man, in O'Neill's plays, for "something beyond rationalism."

———, "Eugene O'Neill's Symbolism: Old Gods for New," *Sewanee Review*, 43 (Oct.–Dec. 1935), 436–50. Symbols overused. See also "Eugene O'Neill's Symbolism," in Parks's *Segments of Southern Thought*, Athens, University of Georgia Press, 1938, pp. 293–313.

*Peck, Seymour, "Talk with Mrs. O'Neill," *New York Times*, Nov. 4, 1956, II, 1, 3.

Peery, William, "Does the Buskin Fit O'Neill?," *University of Kansas City Review*, 15 (Summer 1949), 281–87. Characters lack nobility of character; fails to match ambitious aims.

*Pellizzi, Camillo, *English Drama: The Last Great Phase*, translated from the Italian by Rowan Williams, N. Y., Macmillan, 1935, pp. 253–62.

Poupeye, Camille, "Eugene O'Neill," *Renaissance d'Occident* (Belgium), Feb. 1923, pp. 262–73.

———, "Le théâtre américain: Eugene O'Neill," *Les Dramaturges Exotiques*, Brussels, 3rd ed., 1924, pp. 75–101.

Pratt, Norman T., Jr., "Aeschylus and O'Neill: Two Worlds," *Classical Journal*, 51 (Jan. 1956), 163–67.

Quinn, Arthur Hobson, "Eugene O'Neill, Poet and Mystic," *Scribner's Magazine*, 80 (Oct. 1926), 368–72. Reprinted and considerably expanded in Quinn's *History of American Drama . . .*, vol. 2, N. Y., Crofts, rev. ed., 1936, pp. 165–206.

———, "The Significance of Recent American Drama," *Scribner's Magazine*, 72 (July 1922), 97–108. O'Neill's plays, coming in the three seasons from 1919 to 1922, provide reason for hope for the American drama.

Raleigh, John Henry, "O'Neill's *Long Day's Journey Into Night* and New England Irish-Catholicism," *Partisan Review*, 26 (Fall 1959), 573–92.

Rubinstein, Annette, "The Dark Journey of Eugene O'Neill," *Mainstream*, 10 (April 1957), 29–33.

Sayler, Oliver M., "The Artist of the Theatre," *Shadowland* (N. Y.), 6 (April 1922), 49, 66, 77. A fruitful "colloquy" at O'Neill's Provincetown home.

*———, "The Real Eugene O'Neill," *The Century Magazine*, 103 (Jan. 1922), 351–59. Reprinted as Chapter 3, "Eugene O'Neill, the American Playwright," in Sayler's *Our American Theatre*, N. Y., Brentano's, 1923, pp. 27–43. Includes some fascinating comments by O'Neill and vivid description of the O'Neill way of life, with Shane and Agnes at Provincetown.

Sergeant, Elizabeth S., "Eugene O'Neill: The Man with a Mask," *New Republic*, 50 (March 16, 1927), 91–95. (See also "Eugene O'Neill," in Sergeant's *Fire under the Andes*, N. Y., Knopf, 1927, pp. 81–104.) Observations, reminiscences, comments on O'Neill's reading habits, ideals, etc.

Shawcross, John T., "The Road to Ruin: The Beginning of O'Neill's Long Day's Journey," *Modern Drama*, 3 (Dec. 1960), 289–96. *Ah, Wilderness!* and *Long Day's Journey Into Night* compared for autobiographical revelations.

Shipley, Joseph T., *The Art of Eugene O'Neill*, Seattle, University of Washington Chapbooks, 1928. Brief critical estimates of several plays in a 34-page pamphlet. Stresses the bitterness, lack of joy.

Sievers, W. David, *Freud on Broadway*, N. Y., Hermitage House, 1955, pp. 97–133 ("Freud, Jung, and O'Neill") and passim. "It is only after O'Neill underwent psychoanalysis in 1927 that his most mature and most Freudian plays were written, *Strange Interlude* and *Mourning Becomes Electra.*" But Jungian influence was strong too. Not very well organized discussion.

*Simonson, Lee, *The Stage Is Set*, N. Y., Harcourt, Brace, 1932, pp. 116–20, 459–61, and passim.

Skinner, Richard Dana, *Eugene O'Neill: A Poet's Quest*, N. Y., Longmans, Green, 1935. Quest for faith, as seen in Catholic perspective, leads through despair to goal: *Days Without End*, in a "continuous poetic progress."

———, *Our Changing Theatre*, N. Y., Dial Press, 1931, pp. 76–96, and passim. Plays discussed from purely dramatic view, as distinct from treatment in preceding item.

Slater, Montagu, "Eugene O'Neill," *Nation*, 178 (Feb. 27, 1954), 174–75. British poet-novelist finds O'Neill possibly the creator of the "tough guy" in literature—the "atomic man"—lonely, self-searching, self-destroying.

*Slochower, Harry, "Eugene O'Neill's Lost Moderns," *The University [of Kansas City] Review*, 10 (Autumn 1943), 32–36. Reprinted as part of chapter "In Quest of Everyman: Eugene O'Neill and James Joyce," in Slochower's *No Voice Is Wholly Lost*, N. Y., Creative Age Press, 1945, pp. 248–54.

Stamm, Rudolf, "The Dramatic Experiments of Eugene O'Neill," *English Studies* (Amsterdam), 28 (Feb. 1947), 1–15. The philosophy of the plays can be defined as "determinism experienced as something that is not enough, that provokes an insatiable metaphysical thirst." Studies also the methods by which O'Neill "turned his philosophy into drama."

———, " 'Faithful Realism,': Eugene O'Neill and the Problem of Style," *English Studies*, 40 (Aug. 1959), 242–50.

———, "A New Play by Eugene O'Neill," *English Studies*, 29 (Oct. 1948), 138–45. A detailed analysis of *Iceman Cometh*, "among his few impeccable artistic creations."

———, "The Orestes Theme in Three Plays by Eugene O'Neill, T. S. Eliot, and Jean-Paul Sartre," *English Studies*, 30 (Oct. 1949), 244–55.

———, "Das Spatwerk Eugene O'Neills," *Deutsche Vierteljahrsschrift fur Literaturwissenschraft und Geistergeschichte*, 34 (1960), 66–83.

Steinhauer, H., "Eros and Psyche: A Nietzschean Motif in Anglo-American Literature," *Modern Language Notes*, 64 (April 1949), 217–28. An investigation of the pagan-Christian conflict in the works of D. H. Lawrence and O'Neill.

Stevens, Thomas Wood, "How Good is Eugene O'Neill?," *English Journal*, 26 (March 1937), 179–87. An evaluation in the midst of the Nobel-award controversy: He holds his own on foreign stages.

Straumann, Heinrich, "The Philosophical Background of the Modern American Drama," *English Studies*, 26 (June 1944), 65–78. O'Neill at best when tossed between poles of determinism-pragmatism and the ethico-religious tradition. (See also the chapter on O'Neill in this Swiss critic's *American Literature in the Twentieth Century*, London, Hutchinson's, 1951, pp. 163–69, and passim.)

Sullivan, Frank, "Life Is a Bowl of Eugene O'Neills," *New Yorker*, 71 (Nov. 21, 1931), 17–18. Parody (a "Sextilogy") of *Mourning Becomes Electra.*

Thompson, Alan Reynolds, "The Dilemma of Modern Tragedy: Eugene O'Neill," in *The Anatomy of Drama*, Beverly, University of California Press, 2nd ed., 1946, pp. 303–12. Based on an essay in *Humanism in America*, ed. Norman Foerster, N. Y., Farrar and Rinehart, 1930, pp. 127–48. O'Neill's genius for the theatre, and his "powerful emotional force" are unable to find a way to tragedy.

*Trilling, Lionel, "Eugene O'Neill," *New Republic*, 88 (Sept. 23, 1936), 176–79.

———, "Introduction" to *The Emperor Jones, Anna Christie, The Hairy Ape*, N. Y., Modern Library, 1937, pp. vi–xix.

Tynan, Kenneth, "O'Neill in Embryo," *New Yorker*, Oct. 17, 1959, pp. 131–32. Reviewing a revival of *Great God Brown*, finds the play illuminated as the author's personal outcry, in the light of the subsequently written *Long Day's Journey Into Night.*

Vetluguin, Voldeman, "*Anna Christie* in Russia," *Nation*, 120 (March 4, 1925), 242.

*von Hofmannsthal, Hugo, "Eugene O'Neill," *Freeman*, 7 (March 21, 1923), 39–41.

Vorse, Mary Heaton, "The Provincetown Players," *Time and the Town*, N. Y., Dial Press, 1942, pp. 116–26. By the woman who owned the Wharf Theatre.

Walker, Roy, "The Right Kind of Pity," *Twentieth Century*, 155 (Jan. 1954), 79–86. Defense of O'Neill, acknowledging weaknesses of *Welded* and *Days Without End;* but though *Iceman Cometh* declares the human condition "incurable" its theme is the search for "the right kind of pity" in each human situation.

Walton, Ivan H., "Eugene O'Neill and the Folklore of the Sea," *Western Folklore*, 14 (July 1955), 153–69.

Weissman, Dr. Philip, "Conscious and Unconscious Autobiographical Dramas of Eugene O'Neill," *Journal of the American Psychoanalytic Association*, 5 (July 1957), 432–60. O'Neill's works viewed as a sublimation of his own Oedipal drives, examined in the "unconscious autobiography" *Desire Under the Elms*, and in the "conscious autobiography" *Long Day's Journey Into Night.*

*Welch, Mary, "Softer Tones for Mr. O'Neill's Portrait," *Theatre Arts*, 41 (May 1957), 67–68, 82–83.

Whicher, Stephen, "O'Neill's Long Journey," *Commonweal*, 63 (March 16, 1956), 614–15. Excellent review of the Stockholm premiere.

Whipple, Thomas K., "Eugene O'Neill," *Spokesmen, Modern Writers, and American Life*, N. Y., Appleton, 1928, pp. 230–53—an expansion of an article in the *New Republic*, 41 (Jan. 21, 1925), 222–25. Limited to tragedy of frustration, disinherited characters without dimension or subtlety—though *Great God Brown* penetrates the human mystery.

White, Arthur Franklin, "The Plays of Eugene O'Neill," *Western Reserve University Bulletin*, no. 25, Cleveland, Western Reserve University, 1923, pp. 20–36. Early scholarly study.

Whitman, Robert F., "O'Neill's Search for 'A Language of the Theatre'," *Quarterly Journal of Speech*, 46 (1960), 153–70.

*Wilson, Edmund, *The Shores of Light*, N. Y., Farrar, Straus and Young, 1952, pp. 99–104 ("Eugene O'Neill and the Naturalists"), reprinting articles from *Vanity Fair* (Nov. 1922), the *New Republic* (May 20, 1924), and *American Criticism*, Harcourt, Brace, 1926.

Winther, Sophus Keith, "*Desire Under the Elms:* A Modern Tragedy," *Modern Drama*, 3 (Dec. 1960), 326–32.

———, *Eugene O'Neill: A Critical Study*, N. Y., Random House, 1934. Systematic classification and study of O'Neill's "dominant ideas" in relation to modern industry and modern thought.

———, "O'Neill's Posthumous Plays," *Prairie Schooner*, 32 (Spring 1958), 7–12.

———, "O'Neill's Tragic Themes: *Long Day's Journey Into Night*," *Arizona Quarterly*, 13 (Winter 1957), 295–307. Play "revolves around four dominant themes: the father, the mother, the home, and the poet"—O'Neill's "basic philosophy."

———, "Strindberg and O'Neill: A Study of Influence," *Scandinavian Studies*, 31 (Aug. 1959), 103–20.

*Woodbridge, Homer E., "Eugene O'Neill," *South Atlantic Quarterly*, 37 (Jan. 1938), 22–35.

*Woollcott, Alexander, *Shouts and Murmurs*, N. Y., Century, 1922, pp. 144–70. Reprints some of Woollcott's best and most important O'Neill reviews—comments on *Beyond the Horizon*, *The Emperor Jones*, *The Hairy Ape*.

———, "Giving O'Neill Till It Hurts: Being Some Highly Unofficial Program Notes for the Most Punishing of His Plays," *Vanity Fair*, 29 (Feb. 1928), 48, 114. On *Marco Millions* and *Strange Interlude*, in a less favorable vein.

Wylie, Max, *Trouble in the Flesh*, N. Y., Doubleday, 1959. A novel, based roughly, as the publishers hinted and reviewers inferred, on the career of O'Neill.

Young, Stark, "Eugene O'Neill: Notes from a Critic's Diary," *Harper's*, 214 (June 1957), 66–74. An interesting miscellany, from 1923 to 1956, based on personal associations.

———, *Immortal Shadows*, N. Y., Scribner's, 1948. Reprints reviews of *Great God Brown*, *Dynamo*, *Mourning Becomes Electra*, *The Iceman Cometh*.

Zeraffa, Michael, *Eugene O'Neill: Dramaturge*, Paris, L'Arche, 1956. Book-length survey leads to final chapter on "La Tragedie Impossible": "The malaise Américain" is the bad conscience of an American torn between religious spirit and material power, which results in confusion and frustration.

INDEX